The Rich, the Poor, and
the Taxes they Pay

The Rich, the Poor, and the Taxes they Pay

Joseph A. Pechman
The Brookings Institution

WESTVIEW PRESS
Boulder, Colorado

Copyright © in England by Joseph A. Pechman, 1986
Published in 1986 by Wheatsheaf Books

Published in 1986 in the United States by
  WESTVIEW PRESS
  Frederick A. Praeger, Publisher
  5500 Central Avenue
  Boulder, Colorado 80301

ISBN 0-8133-0376-1
LCN 85-52292

HJ
2381
.P42
1986

To Jonathan, Rebekah and Alexander

Contents

Part Seven. Foreign Tax Systems

List of Tables

List of Figures

Foreword

I am pleased to have this opportunity to present a selection of my essays on public finance. The selection is limited to matters of taxation, income maintenance, and social security, with emphasis on the analysis of policy alternatives to improve tax and transfer systems. I have omitted a number of articles which might have been included had there been no space limitation; the most important omissions are those concerning the measurement of built-in flexibility of the income tax and current budget and fiscal policies. Some of the essays have been updated and others have been shortened, but I have not attempted to rewrite them or to redo the complicated statistical analyses on the basis of more recent data.

My particular contribution to the public finance literature has been, I believe, to provide an empirical basis for the analysis of tax and transfer policy issues. So, for example, I have prepared estimates of the actual degree of progressivity of the US income tax and of the reduction in tax rates that might be possible if a comprehensive income tax base were adopted. I am persuaded that these calculations helped to dramatise the advantages of comprehensive income taxation, which is now being seriously considered in the United States. I have also prepared estimates of the distribution of federal, state, and local tax burdens in the United States on the basis of the most widely accepted incidence theories held by economists. Such estimates have provided an empirical basis for the discussion of various methods of reforming the tax-transfer system.

I have included a section on fiscal federalism both because of the importance of the subject and the particular role I played in the development of US inter-governmental fiscal policy. In 1964, I chaired a presidential task force which proposed the enactment of a plan by the federal government to share its revenues with the states and local governments. This plan, which was soon called the Heller-Pechman plan (the senior member of the combination being Walter W. Heller, who was then Chairman of the president's Council of Economic Advisers and a major contributor to the idea of revenue sharing) was rejected by President Lyndon B. Johnson, but enacted almost intact in Present Richard M. Nixon's administration. The text of the task force report is reproduced for the first time in chapter 14 of this volume.

Although most of the essays in this volume are directed at the US scene, I believe that the analysis is generally relevant to the situation in other countries as well. I have included a section on foreign tax systems to illustrate how the ideas and techniques I have developed can be applied to other countries. The chapters on the Japanese and British tax systems illustrate the pervasiveness of policies that erode the income tax base, without really achieving the economic or social results that were sought. Regretfully, income tax erosion and the adoption of regressive payroll and value added taxes to raise necessary revenues have greatly reduced or eliminated tax progressivity in many countries. The book concludes with a chapter arguing that the trend toward regressive taxation almost everywhere has been carried too far and that there is room to improve tax progressivity without running the risk of raising tax rates to punitive levels.

I have accumulated many debts during my career to teachers, friends, and colleagues who have contributed to my intellectual development and research. Foremost among them are Harold M. Groves, my teacher at the University of Wisconsin, and Walter Heller, a classmate at Wisconsin and life-long friend and collaborator. It was Harold Groves who instilled in me the idea that rich people often pay less taxes than the nominal tax rates would suggest and encouraged me to develop estimates of the distribution of tax burdens by income classes. Walter Heller has been a continual source of ideas, inspiration, and encouragement. He and I collaborated on many projects, revenue sharing and tax reform being the most notable examples, and we have continued our close association to this day.

I have also been closely associated with Stanley S. Surrey of the Harvard Law School and Richard A. Musgrave of Harvard University in the battles for tax reform. Stanley Surrey kept my research relevant to the major policy issues in taxation and insisted that only the highest standards of economic and statistical analysis would promote serious tax reform. Richard Musgrave's work helped me understand the major problems of measuring the distribution of tax burdens and to develop the techniques I have since used to make my own estimates. Arnold C. Harberger of the University of Chicago and Lord Nicholas Kaldor of Cambridge University also greatly influenced my work on taxation, the former on tax incidence and the latter on tax reform.

I was fortunate to be a member of four outstanding research organisation which had major influences over my ideas in tax policy and provided the resources I needed to pursue my rather expensive tastes in research. They were the Wisconsin Income Tax Study, the Division of Tax Research (now the Office of Tax Analysis) of the Treasury Department, the Committee for Economic Development, and the Brookings Institution.

The Wisconsin Income Tax Study gave me my first opportunity to develop distributions of income on the basis of tax data. I am indebted to my colleagues Frank A. Hanna and Sidney M. Lerner for their assistance and cooperation in these early stages of my career and to Milton Friedman and Herbert E. Klarman for their technical and editorial advice on my doctoral dissertation on patterns of income in Wisconsin, which was based on data developed by the Wisconsin Income Tax Study.

At the Treasury I had the benefit of an education in tax research by such notable tax economists as E. Cary Brown, Roy Blough, L. Laszlo Ecker-Racz, Marius Farioletti, Richard Goode, Walter Heller, Louis Shere, Richard Slitor, and William Vickrey, who were members of the staff, and Richard Musgrave, Paul Samuelson, Lawrence H. Seltzer, and Carl S. Shoup, who were consultants. I also learned a great deal from the outstanding staff of tax lawyers at the Treasury, particularly Charles W. Davis, Adrian W. A. DeWind, Louis Eisenstein, James B. Lewis, Randolph Paul, and Stanley Surrey.

The Committee for Economic Development is the first (and perhaps the only) business organisation which has endorsed the idea of comprehensive income taxation. At CED, I had the opportunity to learn first-hand the businessman's views on taxation and benefited from the wisdom and experience of my distinguished colleagues on the research staff, Edward F. Denison and Herbert Stein.

I have spent the last twenty-five years in the unusually stimulating and congenial intellectual environment at the Brookings Institution. I am especially grateful to the three presidents of the Brookings Institution with whom I served, Robert D. Calkins, Kermit Gordon, and Bruce K. MacLaury for their support and encouragement, to Marshall A. Robinson who first suggested the idea of my joining the Brookings staff and later helped finance much of my tax research as an official of the Ford Foundation, and to my colleagues Henry J. Aaron, Barry Bosworth, Gary Burtless, Harvey Galper, Richard Goode, Robert W. Hartman, Arthur M. Okun, George Perry, Alice M. Rivlin, Charles L. Schultze, and Emil M. Sunley for the opportunity to collaborate on numerous projects on budget and tax policy, I also profited from my association with George F. Break, Otto Eckstein, Charles E. McClure, Jr., Alicia H. Munnell, and Michael K. Taussig who contributed to the lively conferences and research projects at Brookings.

The pioneering study by Gerhard Colm and Helen Tarasov, *Who Pays the Taxes?* (1940), inspired me to devote so much attention to the distribution of income and tax burdens. After my work on the Wisconsin data, I turned to estimates for the nation as a whole in collaboration with Hildegarde Kneeland, Selma Goldsmith, and Maurice Liebenberg, when we were all working for the federal government of the United States. Later, the Brookings Institution permitted me to establish a research programme on the distribution of tax burdens, which extended over a period of more than two decades. Many talented and imaginative people were associated with me during this period. I am particularly indebted to Benjamin A.

Okner, Joseph J. Minarik, and John Karl Scholz, who developed the basic
files for making tax burden estimates, to Mark J. Mazur, Andrew Williams,
and John Yinger, who assisted me at crucial stages of the research, to
Evelyn P. Fisher, who enforced an exacting standard for accuracy on
our publications, and to Marcia Appel, who administered the project for us
efficiently and gracefully. The work at Brookings was supported by
generous grants from the Ford Foundation and the National Science
Foundation, but the major financial burden was carried by Brookings.

In 1966-67 I joined Boris Bittker, Peter M. Mieszkowski, and James
Tobin in a stimulating seminar on negative income taxation while I was
Irving Fisher Research Professor at Yale University. Chapter 16 on
methods of implementing a negative income tax was prepared jointly with
Tobin and Mieszkowski on the basis of the seminar discussions. I also spent
productive sabbatical years of research at the Center for Advanced Study
in the Behavioral Sciences and the Hoover Institution of Stanford
University.

Romesh Vaitilingam of Wheatsheaf Books suggested this project to me
and gave me invaluable support and encouragement to complete it. The
volume was prepared during the spring and summer of 1985 at the
Brookings Institution and the Suntory Toyota International Centre for
Research in Economics and Related Disciplines of the London School of
Economics. I wish to express my appreciation to Bruce MacLaury,
President of Brookings, and Anthony B. Atkinson, Chairman of the
Suntory Toyota Centre, for providing the facilities necessary to prepare
such a book.

This volume is intended to be read by people who are interested in
learning about tax policy issues, as well as those who have been working in
the field. My hope is that some will be persuaded to join the growing group
of taxpayers and tax experts in all countries who are actively supporting
major tax reform to promote equity, simplicity, and economic efficiency.

The views expressed in this volume are entirely my own and should not
be ascribed to any of the individuals or organisations here mentioned. I
alone am responsible for any errors of analysis or judgement that may have
been committed.

Joseph A Pechman
Washington, November 1985

Introduction

This introduction summarises the major points made in each section of the book and discusses the policy implications of the data and analysis. The reader will quickly learn that I support progressive, but not punitive, taxation and a system of transfer payments to provide a safety net for the unfortunate who cannot earn their livelihoods through the market system. Much of my work has been devoted to the preparation of estimates of the degree of progressivity achieved in modern tax-transfer systems and to the development of methods of improving the structure of taxation and making transfer systems adequate and efficient.

DISTRIBUTION OF TAX BURDENS

The major sources of information on the distribution of income and tax burdens in the United States are the annual *Statistics of Income* published by the Internal Revenue Service and the annual consumer population surveys conducted by the Census Bureau. The sources are different in major respects: the tax data do not have information for persons who are not required to file tax returns, while the survey data are hopelessly deficient in the top tail of the income distribution. I have used the best features of the two sets of data to obtain comprehensive estimates of the distribution of income before and after taxes (ch. 2).

The methodology used to prepare the estimates is described in detail in chapter 2 of *Who Pays the Taxes, 1966-85?* Briefly, it involves matching through simulation techniques the individuals and families in the consumer files with returns that are 'similar' in the tax files. The data in the resulting MERGE files were adjusted to the official national income totals to be sure that the totals of all the income sources (labour income, property income, and transfer payments) corresponded to national income aggregates. Such files were prepared for the years 1966, 1970, 1975, 1980, and 1985, so that developments over a period of about two decades can be studied.

Tax burdens were estimated by calculating federal, state and local taxes paid by each unit in the MERGE files and these were then weighted to arrive at totals for income classes, percentile groups, and the nation as a whole. Since there are differences of opinion about the incidence of the various taxes, tax burdens were estimated on eight sets of incidence assumptions that span the range of opinion among most economists.

Perhaps the most important conclusion produced by these data is that the US tax system as a whole is mildly progressive if it is assumed that the corporation income and property taxes are borne by owners of capital and the payroll tax is borne by workers. The system is slightly regressive if it is assumed that these taxes are shifted in part to consumers through higher prices. My own view is that the taxes on capital and labour income are borne by owners of capital and labour. Thus, I believe that the US system has been progressive in recent years, but the degree of progression is very mild.

Taxes in the United States have become less progressive in the last two decades. This has occurred because payroll tax rates increased sharply, while corporation income taxes, and to a lesser extent property taxes, declined in importance. Mainly because of the de-emphasis of the corporation income tax, the federal tax system has become less progressive. State and local taxes, which are either proportional or regressive depending on the incidence assumptions used, remained roughly the same.

The distribution of income before taxes has remained remarkably stable throughout the period studied. This appears to be the result of two opposing tendencies: first, the distribution of income from market activity (wages and salaries, entrepreneurial incomes and property incomes) has become more concentrated; but, second, transfer payments (social security and unemployment benefits, welfare payments, medicaid and medicare, housing assistance, and so on) have increased sharply. According to the tax-return data, the increased concentration of market incomes was the result mainly of increased shares received by the 13 per cent of income recipients just below the top 2 per cent and not by those at the very top (see ch.1). Why the rise in transfer payments has just exactly offset the increasing concentration of market incomes is a mystery that cannot be explained by the data.

Since the US distribution of income before taxes (including transfer payments) has remained roughly the same and the tax system has become less progressive, the distribution of income *after* taxes has become less equal. But the increase in inequality was relatively small. Had it not been for the growth in transfer payments, the distribution of income both before and after taxes would have been decidedly more unequal in 1985 than it was in 1966.

The policy implications I draw from these developments concern both the tax and transfer systems. With regard to the tax system, it is clear that US taxes have not been, and are not, excessively progressive. Reforms to make the tax system more progressive would not lead to punitive taxation in the United States. The transfer system, by contrast, is a highly progressive element in the tax-transfer system, and it would be unfortunate if its impact were eroded in the search for reductions in outlays by the federal government.

INDIVIDUAL INCOME TAXATION

Practically all the developed countries, and many underdeveloped countries, rely on the individual income tax for a significant portion of their revenues. This is no accident. Income is widely regarded as the best measure of ability to pay, and there is widespread agreement that the income tax should be progressive (ch.3). Although tax rates are high in many countries, actual tax burdens are much lower than they appear to be merely by examining the statutory rates. The reason is that all income is not taxed and numerous unnecessary deductions are provided for various social and economic reasons.

As a result of the erosion of the tax base, the actual taxes paid by people in all income classes are much lower than the marginal tax rates suggest. For example, the marginal rates in the United States reached a maximum of 50 per cent in 1985, yet the maximum effective rate on total income in the top income classes did not exceed about 25 per cent. The result of this peculiar system is that many people pay different taxes on the same income and huge distortions are introduced into the economy. The tax system has become so complicated that few people understand it and many taxpayers —even those with modest income—seek professional assistance to prepare their tax returns.

Tax experts and political leaders in the United States have responded to this state of affairs with proposals that would move toward a more comprehensive tax base and use the revenues generated to reduce the tax rates. My own plan, which is perhaps the purest of all (see ch.4), would eliminate virtually all the personal deductions, exclusions, and investment incentives in the US income tax. On such a tax base, it would be possible to reduce the individual income tax rates from the 1985 range of 11-50 per cent to 8-28 per cent, raise the personal exemptions to a level that frees those whose incomes are below the official poverty-line incomes from tax, keep the effective tax rates in higher classes close to those in present law, and still raise the same revenues produced by the present tax. Similarly, the corporate tax rate could be reduced from 46 per cent to 28 per cent if corporations were taxed on their full economic income (i.e., net income after allowing for true depreciation). The rationale of this approach is described in chapters 4 and 6 and the details of how a comprehensive tax base is put together are described in chapter 5.

Comprehensive income taxation seems to make so much sense, one wonders why there has been so little progress in reforming tax systems along these lines. The answer seems to be that the groups benefiting from the special provisions resist any inroads into their favoured tax status. Moreover, politicians are more interested in using the tax system to promote their economic and social objectives than in improving equity and economic efficiency. Political leaders will change their views only when the general public understands the issues and demands action to reform and simplify the tax system.

MAJOR TAX ISSUES

From among the numerous difficult issues in tax policy, I have selected seven for discussion in this volume. These issues are pervasive and few countries have resolved any of them satisfactorily.

Tax Treatment of the Family

The unit of taxation varies widely among different countries. Some tax individuals, others tax the family, and still others permit taxpayers to make the selection. The definition of the tax unit is important because it affects the progressivity of the tax system and influences major personal decisions, such as marriage and divorce.

In the United States, the family has been the unit of taxation since the enactment of income splitting for married couples in 1948. But in the search for tax equity, numerous modifications have been made in the rates applying to single persons, unmarried heads of families, and married couples. The result has been a hodge-podge of rates for different types of family units, separate standard deductions for single people and married couples, and a special deduction for two-earner couples. Nevertheless, single people still consider themselves overtaxed, while some people pay a penalty on marriage and others receive large tax cuts.

The solution is *not* to tax on an individual basis, as some have proposed. Some countries have adopted this approach, but it requires arbitrary rules to divide property income and personal deductions among spouses and encourages transfers of property between them to achieve the benefits of income splitting. My solution (see ch.7) is to tax single people and married couples at the same rates, but provide a deduction based on the earnings of the spouse with the lower earnings in two-earner couples and on the earnings of the head in families with single parents. (As already noted, the United States enacted such a deduction in 1981, but only for married couples.) The deduction has the great advantage that it corrects for the omission from the tax base of the imputed income generated by spouses who remain at home while their husbands or wives are working.

Capital Gains

In principle, capital gains should be taxed annually (or periodically) as they accrue. In practice, they are taxed only when realised and at reduced rates. In many countries, all or a major share of capital gains are not subject to tax.

When inflation was moderate, the major rationale for reduced rates or complete exemption was that it would be unfair to tax at regular rates realised capital gains that accrued over many years. More recently, the argument has shifted. It is now argued that capital gains must be treated lightly to avoid taxing illusory gains during inflation. Preferential treatment for capital gains is also justified regardless of the degree of inflation on the ground that something special is needed in the tax system to promote investment and risk-taking.

The proper treatment of capital gains under an income tax would take all these considerations into account. The tax would apply only to real capital gains, accrued gains transferred at gift or death would be taxed as if realised, interest would be charged on the tax deferred until realisation, and averaging would be allowed to avoid the tax penalty resulting from the bunching of gains at realisation (ch. 8). If real capital gains were taxed in full, special investment incentives would be unnecessary because rates could be reduced to modest levels even in the highest tax brackets.

The treatment of capital gains does not even remotely resemble this theoretically correct treatment of capital gains anywhere. Instead, most capital gains escape taxation and a maze of limitations is needed to prevent the conversion of ordinary income into capital gains. It is no exaggeration to say that capital gains taxation is the major source of complication and economic distortion in tax systems everywhere.

Adjusting Taxes for Inflation

During the period of rampant inflation in the 1970s, real tax rates rose where automatic inflation adjustments were not adopted. This occurred for two reasons. First, individuals were being taxed on illusory rather than real incomes. Second, taxpayers crept into higher tax brackets as nominal incomes rose. Where indexation has been tried, adjustments are made for 'bracket creep', but few countries adjust the tax base, which is the more important distortion.

Unfortunately, the problems of adjusting the tax base are enormous. Income taxes on wages and salaries are paid roughly at the same price level as the level when the income was received, so no correction is necessary for earned incomes. Recipients of property income, on the other hand, do not receive any real income until their nominal rate of return exceeds the rate of inflation, and this requires an adjustment to exclude the inflation component of such income

To make the proper correction, creditors should deduct from their interest receipts the erosion of the real value of their claims, and debtors should deduct the same amount from their payments. Thus, for example, if inflation is 6 per cent and the real rate of interest is 6 per cent, half the nominal interest payment would not be taxable to the creditor and half would not be deductible by the debtor. The U.S. Treasury proposed a scheme that would apply the same correction for all assets, and it was criticised because it dealt too leniently with some assets and too harshly with others. To be accurate, the adjustment must be made asset by asset, a monumental undertaking in a modern economy where even people of modest means have financial transactions.

The correction of capital gains for inflation is straightforward. Real gains may be calculated by correcting the purchase price of assets for the inflation from the time of purchase to time of sale and then deducting the corrected amount from the sales price. As already indicated, if this were done, there would be no reason for having preferential rates on capital gains.

Income from operating a business is affected by inflation because depreciation and inventory allowances are usually based on historical costs and no allowance is made for gains resulting from the use of borrowed capital. Real depreciation and inventory costs can be calculated by adjusting actual depreciation and the purchase price of inventories for inflation. The inflation component of interest on borrowed capital can be removed by the method already explained above.

I believe that it is probably impractical to design and implement a tax system that would be applied to real income rather than to nominal income. It would be better to control inflation than to complicate the tax system. It is fortunate that inflation has come down substantially during the 1980s, though it has not come down enough in many countries. Since productivity and growth are related to business investment, I would limit inflation adjustments during periods of moderate inflation to depreciation and inventory costs. At the same time, interest deductions for borrowed money should be adjusted to allow for the reduction in the real value of the loans used to finance the purchase assets. If any inflation adjustment is made for property incomes, the adjustment should be applied both to interest income as well as to capital gains, to avoid discriminating against low- and middle-income taxpayers who have few capital gains.

Since the rise in real effective tax rates during periods of moderate inflation is small, I do not believe that automatic adjustments of tax brackets and personal exemptions are urgent during such periods. The major argument for automatic adjustment is that the increases in effective rates in a nominal tax system, which are unintentional by-products of the rise in nominal incomes, are used to finance higher government expenditures without requiring legislatures to raise taxes. On the other hand, automatic adjustment presupposes that the degree of progression in the income tax is 'correct' in some sense. Moreover, indexation reduces the stabilising effect of the income tax during periods of inflation and might reduce the government's resolve to fight inflation. On balance, I would

leave the timing of the adjustments for bracket creep to the discretion of the
legislature.

The Consumption Expenditure Tax

Economists have lately become enamoured of an old idea, going back to
David Hume and John Stuart Mill, to reform modern tax systems. The idea
is to replace the income tax with a tax that would be levied on consumption
expenditure. Progression is not an issue because, in theory at least it is
possible to approximate the degree of progression in the income tax by
graduating the rates under the expenditure tax.

The major argument in favour of a consumption expenditure tax is that it
would eliminate all the problems of income measurement discussed above,
particularly during periods of inflation. However, there are theoretical and
practical problems with the implementation of a consumption expenditure
tax that would make it a hazardous, and potentially retrogressive step, in
tax policy.

It can be shown that an expenditure tax is equivalent to a tax on earned
incomes (see ch. 10). Thus, taxpayers who save large fractions of their
income would be able to accumulate large fortunes over a lifetime. To
prevent excessive concentrations of wealth, it would be essential to impose
effective estate and gift taxes. Many supporters of the expenditure tax do
not favour estate and gift taxation, and those that do acknowledge that
experience with wealth taxation in virtually every country suggests that in
practice such taxes would not nearly offset such increases in wealth
concentration.

Proponents of an expenditure tax often compare the merits of that tax
with the income tax as it has actually developed. In fact, most of the
unnecessary features of the income tax could be carried over to an
expenditure tax. For example, housing is treated favourably under the
income tax and would almost certainly be treated at least as well under an
expenditure tax. Special deductions for the elderly and disabled, charitable
contributions, child care, and other outlays could also be carried over. The
result would not be a very attractive tax.

The transition from an income tax to an expenditure tax would be
extremely difficult. It would be necessary to avoid taxing asset accumulations that were already taxed under the income tax. Otherwise, the retired
elderly who are drawing down their assets would be double taxed. One
possibility would be to exempt all accumulated assets from the expenditure
tax, but this would leave a big loophole for people who have large amounts
of capital not previously taxed. To trace assets in order to identify those
that had been previously taxed would be an administrative nightmare.

In summary, despite some superficial virtues, replacement of the income
tax with an expenditure tax would be a serious mistake. The expenditure

tax would be subject to the same, or greater, pressures for special treatment that are evident in the income tax. It would also lead to a more unequal distribution of wealth. Income is a better measure of ability to pay than consumption and it would be unwise to depart from this familiar and widely-approved basis of taxation.

Value-added Tax

The value-added tax has been almost universally adopted in Europe and is being seriously proposed in other countries, particularly the United States, Canada, and Japan, which have recently been running large deficits. The value-added tax is similar to a sales tax, except that it is collected as goods move through the production and distribution system rather than only at the retail or final stage of sales. Since it is levied on a substantial part, though not all, of consumption, it can be a large revenue producer.

In Europe, the value-added tax was generally used to replace turnover taxes which are pyramided and impose widely different burdens on different commodities, depending on the degree of integration of the production and distribution processes. Thus, the enactment of the value-added tax eliminated major distortions and could be regarded as a real reform when it was introduced in Europe. In the United States, Canada, and Japan, the value-added tax would be a new tax and must be evaluated on its merits.

The most controversial feature of the value-added tax is its regressivity. Since saving rises as a percentage of income as income rises, the burden of a value-added tax declines as incomes rise. Thus, to justify the enactment of a value-added tax, it would be necessary to argue that the tax system in which it is to be introduced is too progressive or that additional revenues could not be obtained from the income taxes, conditions which do not apply in the countries where it is being considered.

Many countries have tried to moderate the regressivity of the value-added tax by exemptions or tax-rate reductions for particular commodities or services that are regarded as 'essential' and account for a large share of consumption of those in the lower income classes. Such exemptions or rate reductions do moderate the regressivity of the value-added tax and may even make it proportional to income for the lower half or two-thirds of the income distribution. But it would continue to be regressive in the upper end of the distribution.

Some have suggested that the regressivity of the value-added tax can be offset by tax credits at the lower income levels, but as I explain in chapter 11, this is not a complete remedy. Tax credits would make the value-added tax progressive up to the point where the credit begins to phase out; beyond this point, the tax would remain regressive. Needless to say, exemptions, rate reductions, or tax credits complicate administration and compliance and increase the cost of collecting the value-added tax.

The real issue is whether progressivity has been overdone in the countries where it is now being debated. As I have already pointed out, the income tax in most countries is not nearly as progressive as it appears and substantial revenues could be obtained by broadening the tax base. It seems to me that there is no good reason to introduce a regressive tax when the income tax has been eroded by so many unnecessary, and often distortionary, special provisions.

Estate Taxes

Taxes on the privilege of transferring wealth to one's heirs are levied almost everywhere, but the revenues produced are generally insignificant. The estate tax is a desirable revenue source because it can help to reduce the concentration of wealth with less effect on saving and work effort than an income tax. Many people, including some who are wealthy, support estate taxation because they believe that large inheritances greatly reduce the incentives of the recipients to lead productive and useful lives.

Taxes at death could be avoided simply by transferring property by gift. For this reason, estate taxes are usually associated with gift taxes, which are imposed on the donor. There has been a trend in recent years, to integrate the taxes on estates and gifts into one cumulative tax, but the degree of integration is often imperfect.

Estate and gift taxes produce relatively little revenue because they are inherently complicated (ch. 12). Wealth transfers can take various forms and it is difficult to devise a system that would tax all transfers equally. In Anglo-Saxon countries, wealth is often placed in trust for one or more generations, requiring complicated rules to prevent tax avoidance as enjoyment of trust property passes to succeeding generations. Where money is held in large industrial or commercial corporations, it is possible to avoid tax through recapitalisations of stock ownership which siphon off profits to heirs without any property passing through the estate or gift tax net. Finally, the value of property held by small businessmen and farmers is difficult to measure, and in many countries such property is undervalued for estate and gift tax purposes by legislative intent.

One can only speculate why so much avoidance of the estate and gift taxes is condoned almost everywhere. The answer seems to be that taxation for redistributive purposes is not really popular, or at least not popular enough to encourage political leaders to put the estate and gift taxes on the tax reform agenda. Public education to explain the merits of estate and gift taxes for revenue as well as social purposes is urgently needed.

Tax Based Incomes Policies

During the 1960s and 1970s, many economists and policy-makers supported the adoption of policies to restrain the growth of prices and wages as the economy approached full employment. Such policies, often called 'incomes policies', were tried in many countries, with varying degrees of success. On the whole, however, the concensus seems to be that incomes policies were not very effective or were effective only for brief periods. Thus, inflation has been restrained in the 1980s in Europe and the United States largely by restrictive monetary policies which have left a high level of unemployment in their wake.

Economists are still searching for a mechanism to prevent inflation without the need to maintain a high level of unemployment. Some have suggested that the undesirable features of incomes policies could be avoided by using the tax system to encourage non-inflationary price and wage behaviour on the part of business firms and workers. There are numerous possibilities, but the major feature of such tax based-incomes policies would be to impose a penalty, or provide a subsidy, to firms and workers who meet certain prescribed guidelines for wage and price increases. They are called *tax-based* incomes policies because the penalties or subsidies would be administered by the tax collection authorities.

Although I am a strong supporter of incomes policies, I have been urging caution about using the tax system to enforce them. Tax-based incomes policies require the calculation of average increases of wages and prices for *each* firm in the economy. As I explain in chapter 13, this is virtually impossible in a modern industrial economy where companies actually have many different firms, produce large numbers of different products, and have contracts with many different unions. I conclude that tax-based incomes policies are unworkable and that, however messy they are likely to be, voluntary guidelines (or, if necessary, direct controls) for price and wage behaviour of the largest firms in the economy are the only practical solution.

FINANCING A FEDERAL SYSTEM

Government finance in federal systems like those in the United States, Canada, and Australia, must accommodate to the reality of the separation of powers between the central and state (or provincial) and local governments. Most countries have developed grant systems that help to finance local activities, but the problem is more complicated in federal systems.

In the United States, there has been almost continuous tension between the federal and state and local governments. There is considerable overlapping of tax sources and substantial flows of funds from the federal to the lower governmental levels, as well as from state to local governments. In 1964, I headed a task force, appointed by President Lyndon B.

Johnson, to evaluate inter-governmental fiscal arrangements in the United States. The report of the task force, the text of which is reprinted in chapter 14, proposed a major change in the system of grants in order to reduce the disparities in the fiscal capacities of the various states and local governments.

The task force argued that, while the responsibilities for providing governmental services had been increasing at the state and local levels, the fiscal resources of these units of government were not rising at a rapid enough rate to finance these services. The task force also noted that, by contrast, the fiscal resources of the federal government would be growing at a rapid rate if the economy continued to grow at a healthy rate. Thus, the task force proposed that a new system of general purpose grants be added to the federal grant system, so that the state and local governments would be able to share in the growth of federal revenues.

Although the task force was much too optimistic about the fiscal outlook for the federal government, its proposal to establish a new grant to help equalise the fiscal capacities of the states and local governments was enacted in President Richard M. Nixon's administration. The task force envisaged that a share of the federal individual income tax collections would be placed in a national trust fund, to be distributed to the states and local governments on a per capita basis. As finally passed, a fixed amount was allocated to these new grants, but the grants continue to be called 'revenue-sharing'. The final legislation also added a number of additional factors beside population for calculating the amounts to be received by each unit of government (e.g., per capita income and tax effort).

The rationale for having such general purpose grants is that, in a federal system, all states and local governments do not have equal capacity to pay for public services. Even though the poorer states make a relatively larger revenue effort, they cannot match the revenue-raising ability of the richer states and thus cannot provide the range of services offered elsewhere. In actual practice, the revenue sharing programme has helped equalise the fiscal resources of the states (see ch. 15), but the degree of equalisation is rather small. It would be better to confine the grants only to the poorest states (as Australia does), but this is impossible in the United States where each state is equally represented in the Senate.

Since the original legislation was passed, revenue sharing has not achieved the status envisaged for it by the task force, largely because the federal government has mismanaged its own budget. The amounts distributed under these grants have declined and the states have been excluded from the programme. Because of the continued stringency in the federal budget, the future of the entire programme is dim.

I believe that revenue sharing continues to have a place in a federal system of government. Categorical grants to provide particular services of facilities (for example, roads, medical care, and welfare) cannot give the poorer state and local governments the capacity to provide the public services for which they are responsible. Some form of general purpose grant, along the lines envisaged by the task force and perhaps limited to the poorer units of government, is needed to achieve greater geographic equalisation of governmental fiscal capacity.

INCOME MAINTENANCE

Although every civilised country in the world has some system for helping the poor, the particular programmes are almost universally unsatisfactory. What is not fully recognised is that welfare systems and income taxes, which have developed side-by-side without any coordination, are really different sides of the same coin. Assistance to the poor is an extension of progressivity into the lowest income brackets, with negative rather than positive rates. The idea of the negative income tax has been actively discussed for many years, but it has not been adopted anywhere because of the resistance of taxpayer groups to a universal income maintenance plan without any strings attached.

The negative income tax would require the computation of taxable income, just as in the positive income tax. If taxable income turns out to be negative, the government would make a payment to the taxpayer rather than require a tax to be paid. In principle, the payment would provide enough for a family to meet its subsistence needs, but most plans would be much less generous.

Chapter 16 explains how a negative income tax could be made to work. In principle, it would be possible to have exactly the same rules under the negative income tax as the rules that apply in the positive income tax. Such a system would have the maximum degree of coordination between the two. In practice, some variation from the positive income tax rules would be required if, for example, the income definitions under the two are different and assets as well as income are taken into account in determining eligibility for negative income tax payments.

The major doubts about the negative income tax have been whether it would discourage some people from working and disrupt family life, thus increasing the cost of the plan substantially. Politicians were loath to accept the negative income tax idea in the absence of hard data to evaluate its effects. To answer the questions, the federal government of the United States financed a number of experiments in various parts of the country to measure the effects of the negative income tax on the economic and social behaviour of potential recipients.

The first of these experiments was conducted in the state of New Jersey in the late 1960s and early 1970s (see ch.17). The major conclusion of this experiment was that there was only a small reduction (5 or 6 per cent) in the average hours worked by white male family heads who received negative income tax payments, but a much larger reduction (about a third) for white and Spanish-speaking working wives, presumably reflecting their preferences to stay at home when they receive additional financial resources. The response of black men and women was insignificant. Other responses were on the whole ambiguous, but there was some evidence that experimental families increased their investments in housing and durable goods and that educational attainment was improved in these families.

A number of other experiments were conducted along the same lines, the most recent and most comprehensive one being the Seattle and Denver experiment (known as SIME/DIME). This experiment confirmed that the labour supply response of women to a negative income tax is larger than the response of men. For men, the reduction in labour supply was larger than the reduction estimated from the New Jersey results—9–10 per cent compared with 5–6 per cent for the earlier experiment. The SIME/DIME experiment also revealed that the negative income tax increased marital instability, but this result has been challenged by a number of experts on technical grounds.

The negative income tax has remained dormant since the US experiments were completed, largely because of the fiscal stringency in which most governments have found themselves. Some people will regard the labour supply results of the experiments damaging to the cause of negative income taxation. However, it should be recognised that the negative income tax plans that were tested were more generous than any plan that is likely to be enacted initially. My own view is that the labour supply effects of a modest negative income tax would not be serious and that the improvements in welfare systems would be worth the cost.

SOCIAL SECURITY

Social security has become the most important social programme of governments in all the developed countries. The term is usually meant to include benefit payments on retirement or disability and during periods of unemployment, payments to the poor, health services or health insurance, family allowances, and other programmes. In this section, I address only the issues concerning the provision of retirement and disability benefits.

It is widely agreed that government bears the responsibility to provide the aged and disabled with a minimum level of support sufficient to prevent them and their dependants from living in destitution. Much more controversial is the question whether government support should go beyond a minimum subsistence level. This question has been answered affirmatively in most countries, but it is still unresolved—particularly since demographic conditions in the twenty-first century are expected to increase costs per employed worker as populations age.

Chapter 18 argues that an impressive case can be made for providing retirement and disability benefits that exceed minimum subsistence levels and bear some relationship to a worker's lifetime earnings up to some reasonable maximum. The basic reason is that many people will not set aside during their working careers enough saving to prevent their living standards from falling sharply on retirement or disability. In the absence of social security, heavy burdens are imposed on children and others to support the aged and disabled at living standards close to those they had enjoyed earlier. The same objective could conceivably be attained if the government required employers to provide 'adequate' pensions. In practice, however, private pension systems cannot guarantee adjustment of benefits for inflation and cannot insure portability of pension rights when workers move from job to job.

In the United States, two financial crises developed in the mid-1970s and early 1980s that threatened the solvency of the retirement and disability system. In the first case, the crisis was caused by an error in the basic legislation which over-adjusted for inflation; in the second, the crisis occurred because the economy was plagued by recession and slow growth. The first crisis was resolved by correcting the legislation, the second by increasing taxes and raising the retirement age from sixty-five to sixty-seven over a period of twenty years beginning in the year 2000 (see ch. 19).

A major unresolved issue in the United States is whether the retirement and disability system should continue to be financed exclusively by the payroll tax, which is a regressive tax. The case for introducing general revenues (i.e., revenues that are to a large extent obtained from the income taxes) is that benefits for low-wage workers greatly exceed the amounts they would be entitled to on the basis of an earnings-related benefit. This solution is resisted, however, by those who oppose further use of progressive taxation to finance government programmes.

Some economists have argued that the US social security system has reduced national saving and, therefore, should be curtailed. The econometric evidence does not support this view and, in any case, the recent reduction of national saving in the United States is clearly the result of large federal budget deficits which were created by excessive tax cuts and not by the social security system.

Social security is a necessary and even vital government responsibilty. Attempts to convert it to a welfare programme or to rely on private pensions would violate its basic rationale. It is, of course, important to avoid imposing excessive burdens on future generations, but this can be accomplished by establishing a realistic benefit structure and not by destroying the system.

FOREIGN TAX SYSTEMS

The United States is not alone in proliferating unnecessary deductions and exclusions that complicate the tax system, narrow the tax base, and require higher tax rates to meet revenue needs. Two other examples are Japan and Britain, which have very different tax traditions from those in the United States but are similar in their use of income tax preferences to achieve various economic and social objectives. The result is that their nominal tax rates remain high, even though the effective degree of progression of their income taxes is modest.

In Japan (see ch. 20), the tax preferences are actually brought together in a Special Tax Measures Law, which catalogues most, but not all, of the incentive provisions introduced to stimulate saving and investment. These include exclusions for interest and dividends, exemption of capital gains from the sale of securities, accelerated depreciation, tax free reserves and tax credits. The coverage of the special tax measures has been narrowed in recent years, but they are still significant in reducing the taxes paid on income from capital.

A number of other characteristics peculiar to the Japanese system greatly reduce the revenue potential of the income taxes. The standard deduction for low-income wage earners is excessively generous, ostensibly to give wage earners a tax advantage to counterbalance the admittedly serious evasion of taxes by small businessmen. Anonymous accounts are widely used to take advantage of the exclusions for interest on bank deposits, yet the Japanese government has not been able to stop this practice. Expense accounts for businessmen are lavish, and payments for retirement are effectively exempt for all but the highest salaried employees.

In Britain (see ch. 21), marginal tax rates were driven up to a maximum of 98 per cent on investment income and 83 per cent on earned income during the 1970s. These rates have been reduced since then to a maximum of 60 per cent, but the reductions were financed by increasing the value added tax rather than by broadening the income tax base. Like Japan, Britain does not tax interest on designated savings accounts, tolerates large business expense accounts, exempts a substantial amount of capital gains and taxes the rest at a reduced rate, and until recently gave generous allowances for plant and equipment. Tax reform in Britain and Japan along the lines developed in chapter 4 would pay handsome dividends in greater equity, simplicity, and reduced tax rates.

Partly as a result of the high rates of income tax brought about by the narrowing of the income tax base, European countries have placed much heavier emphasis on consumption and payroll taxes than the United States. Although it is not possible to make the same type of tax-burden calculations as I have made for the United States, it is clear that the European tax systems are not very progressive and may well be distinctly regressive in many countries. I suggest in chapter 22 that it is time to move progressive taxation to a higher place in the social and economic agenda of democratic nations.

Part One
Distribution of Tax Burdens

1. The Rich, the Poor, and the Taxes they Pay*

The distribution of income has always been a hotly debated subject. Whatever has happened or is happening to the distribution of income, some people will always assert that the rich are getting a bigger share of the pie than is 'fair', while others will seek to show that this is not the case. Few people, however, bother to find out the facts, and fewer still understand what they mean.

The same applies to the tax system. Everybody knows that there are loopholes in the federal tax laws, but few realise that there are loopholes for persons at all income levels. Even fewer have a clear idea about the effects on the distribution of income of closing the more controversial loopholes. And only the experts know the state-local tax structure is in more urgent need of reform than the federal structure.

This chapter is intended to put these matters in perspective by summarising the available information. What has happened to the distribution of income before taxes in recent years, and how has the tax system modified it? What changes are needed to make it a fairer system? What would be the shape of a tax distribution that most Americans today might agree to be 'fair'?

THE DISTRIBUTION OF INCOME

Despite the proliferation of sophisticated economic data in this country, the United States government does *not* publish official estimates of the distribution of income. Such estimates were prepared by the Office of Business Economics for a period of years in the 1950s and early 1960s, but were discontinued because the sources on which they were based were acknowledged to be inadequate. We have data from annual field surveys of some 60,000 households conducted by the Bureau of the Census, as well as from the annual *Statistics of Income* prepared by the Internal Revenue Service from federal individual income tax returns. But both sources have their weaknesses: the Census Bureau surveys systematically understate

* Adapted from 'The Rich, the Poor, and the Taxes they Pay', *The Public Interest*, No. 17, Fall 1969, pp. 21–43; and 'The Rich, the Poor and the Taxes they Pay: An Update', with Mark Mazur, *The Public Interest*, No. 77, Fall 1984, pp. 28–36.

income particularly in the top brackets; tax returns, on the other hand, understate the share received by low income recipients who are not required to file. Nevertheless, if used with care the two sources provide some interesting insights.

Before turning to the most recent period, it should be pointed out that a significant change in the distribution of pre-tax income occurred during the Great Depression and the Second World War. All experts who have examined the data agree that the distribution became more equal as a result of (a) the tremendous reductions in business and property incomes during the Depression, and (b) the narrowing of earnings differentials between low-paid workers and higher-paid skilled workers and salaried employees when full employment was re-established during the war. The most authoritative estimates, prepared by the late Selma Goldsmith and her associates, suggest that the share of personal income received by the top 5 per cent of the nation's consumer units (including families and unrelated individuals) declined from 30 per cent in 1929 to 26.5 per cent in 1935-36; the share of the top 20 per cent declined from 54.4 per cent to 51.7 per cent in the same period. The movement towards greater equality appears to have continued during the war up to about 1944. By that year, the share of the top 5 per cent had dropped another notch to 20.7 per cent, and of the top 20 per cent to 45.8 per cent.

The income concept used by these researchers did not include undistributed corporate profits, which are a source of future dividends or of capital gains for shareholders; if they had been included, the movement of the income distribution toward equality from 1929 to 1944 would have been substantially moderated, but by no means eliminated.[1]

The movement toward equality seems to have ended during the Second World War, at least on the basis of the available statistics. In 1952, for example, the share of the top 5 per cent was 20.5 per cent and of the top 20 per cent, 44.7 per cent. (The differences from the 1944 figures are well within the margin of error of these data, and can hardly be called significant.)

To trace what happened since 1952, we shift to the census data that provide the longest continuous and comparable income distribution series available to us. The best way to appreciate the trend is to look at the figures for income shares at five-year intervals (table 1.1):

The figures indicate that the share of the top 5 per cent declined slightly between 1952 and 1957, and has remained virtually unchanged since 1957; the share of the top 20 per cent changed very little. Correspondingly, the shares of the groups at the bottom of the income scale (not shown in the table) also changed very little throughout the period.

Tax data are needed to push the analysis further. These data are better than the census data for our purposes, because they show the amount of

Table 1.1: Before-Tax Income Shares, Census Data
(per cent)

Year	Top 5 per cent of families	Top 20 per cent of families
1952	18	42
1957	16	40
1962	16	42
1967	15	41
1972	16	41
1977	16	42
1981	15	42

Source: Bureau of the Census. Income includes transfer payments (e.g. social security benefits, unemployment compensation, welfare payments, etc.), but excludes capital gains, and single persons living alone.

realised capital gains and also permit us to calculate income shares *after* the federal income tax. But the great disadvantage of the tax data is that the bottom part of the income distribution is under-represented because of an unknown number of non-filers. Furthermore, the taxpayer unit is not exactly a family unit, because children and other members of the family file their own income tax returns if they have income, and a few married couples continue to file separate returns despite the privilege of income-splitting, which removed the advantage of separate returns with rare exceptions.

There is really no way to get around these problems, but the tax data are too interesting to be abandoned because of these technicalities. So, we make an assumption that permits us to use at least the upper tail of the income distribution. The assumption is that the top 10 or 15 per cent of the nation's tax units are for the most part similar to the census family units and the cases that differ represent roughly the same percentage of the total number of units each year. Because we have official Department of Commerce estimates of income (as defined in the tax code) for the country as a whole, the assumption enables us to compute income shares before and after tax for the top 1, 2, 5, 10 and 15 per cent of units annually for the entire post-war period.[2]

The tax series confirms much of what we learned from the census series, and adds a few additional bits of information besides. Table 1.2 presents the data for selected years beginning with the Korean War.

According to tax returns, the share of total income, including all realised capital gains, going to the top 1 and 2 per cent of the tax units were about the same for the entire period from 1952 to 1981. But the shares of the top 5, 10 and 15 per cent—which, of course, include the top 1 and 2 per cent—all

Distribution of Tax Burdens

rose somewhat. These trends differ from the census figures which show that the entire income distribution was stable. By contrast, the tax data show that the 13 per cent of income recipients just below the top 2 per cent—this group reported incomes between $37,600 and $70,800 in 1981 *increased* their share of total income from 21 per cent to 26 per cent.

Table 1.2: Before-Tax Income Shares, Tax Data
(per cent)

	Top 1% of tax units	*Top 2% of tax units*	*Top 5% of tax units*	*Top 10% of tax units*	*Top 15% of tax units*
1952	9	12	19	27	33
1963	8	12	19	28	35
1967	9	13	20	29	36
1972	8	12	20	29	37
1977	8	12	20	30	38
1981	8	12	20	30	38

Source: Statistics of Income. Income excludes transfer payments, but includes realised capital gains in full.

If the figures are anywhere near being right, they suggest two significant conclusions: First, in recent years the very rich in our society have not enjoyed larger increased in incomes, as defined in the tax code, than the average income recipient. Although realised capital gains are included in the figures, they do not include non-reported sources such as tax-exempt interest and excess depletion; correction for these omissions would probably not alter the results very much, because the amounts involved are small relative to the total of reported incomes. Even a correction for the undistributed profits of corporations would not change the result very much because undistributed gross corporation profits have remained below 13 per cent of total reported income since 1950.

Second, a change in the income distribution occurred in what are sometimes called the 'middle income' classes. These classes consist of most of the professional people in this country (doctors, lawyers, engineers, accountants, college professors, etc.) as well as the highest paid members of the skilled labour force and white-collar workers. The increase in their share of total income from 21 per cent to 26 per cent represents a not insignificant improvement in their relative income status.

Clearly, this improvement in the income shares of the middle classes coud come only at the expense of the lower 85 per cent of the income distribution. But this is not the whole story. These figures contain only incomes that are generated in the private economy; they do not include transfer payments (e.g. social security benefits, unemployment compensation, welfare payments, etc.) which are, of course, concentrated in the lower income classes. Correction of the figures for transfer payments might be just enough to offset the increased share of the middle income classes. If this is the case, the constancy of the shares of pre-tax income shown by the census data is fully consistent with the growth in shares of the middle incomes shown by the tax data. And, if this is the explanation of the constancy of the income shares in the census distribution, it means that the lower classes have not been able to hold their own in the private economy; large increases in government transfer payments were needed to prevent a gradual erosion of their income shares.

THE EFFECT OF TAXES

Since one of the major objectives of taxation is to moderate income inequality, it is appropriate to ask how the tax system actually affects the distribution of income and whether it has become more or less equalising. We examine first the impact of the federal individual income tax, which is the most progressive element in the nation's tax system and for which data by income classes are readily available annually, and then show the effect of the other taxes in the system[3].

Before looking at the data, it may be helpful to review some of the changes in the federal income tax during the past half century. Tax rates rose to a peak during the Second World War, when top rates exceeded 90 per cent and personal exemptions were sharply reduced to raise the necessary wartime revenue. Those in the lowest income bracket were subject to a tax of 23 per cent (in 1944). Immediately after the war, rates declined, only to be raised again during the Korean War. Starting in 1964, Congress began lowering the income tax rates, pausing only in the late 1960s for a temporary surcharge imposed to finance the Vietnam War. This surcharge lapsed in 1970, and rates remained constant until 1981, when the top rate was reduced from 70 per cent to 69.125 per cent, and the lowest bracket rate was reduced from 14 per cent to 13.825 per cent. When the Reagan tax cuts became fully effective at the beginning of 1984, the top rate had been reduced further to 50 per cent and the bottom rate to 11 per cent. Thus, the recent trend in the nominal tax rates is one of reasonably steady decline.[3]

At the same time, people have rightly complained about being pushed into higher and higher tax brackets by the combination of both real income growth and inflation. In the past, Congress reacted to this 'bracket creep' by periodically reducing statutory rates and increasing personal exemptions; in 1981 it indexed the tax rate brackets and the exemptions automatically for changes in the general level of prices beginning in 1985.

Simple comparisons of statutory tax rates are misleading where nominal rather than inflation-adjusted incomes are taxed during a period of high inflation (such as the past 15 years in the United States).

Table 1.3, which provides a series on the average tax rates paid by various groups of taxpayers, reveals the extent to which bracket creep has increased the effective tax rates of those at the top of the income distribution. Four important points may be noted: first, the effective rates decline as one moves down the income distribution from the highest incomes, showing the effect of progressive rates,[4] second, effective tax rates declined steadily from 1952 to 1972; third, the decline in effective rates was reversed during the past 10 years as bracket creep reached significant proportions; and, finally, the burden imposed on taxpayers by bracket creep was much larger for those in the 11th to 15th percentiles of the income distribution (more than a 20 per cent increase in average effective rates between 1972 and 1981) than for those in, say, the top percentile of the income distribution (approximately a 10 per cent increase in effective rates over the same period). The tax rate reductions made in the Economic Recovery Act 1981 reversed the effect of bracket creep and probably restored the effective tax rates of the taxpayers considered here to the levels of the mid-1970s.

Table 1.3: Effective Federal Tax Rates on Total Income (per cent)

	Top 1% of tax units	Next 1% of tax units	Next 3% of tax units	Next 5% of tax units	Next 5% of tax units
1952	33	20	16	14	12
1963	27	20	16	14	13
1967	26	18	15	13	12
1972	27	19	16	14	13
1977	31	22	18	16	14
1981	30	23	21	18	16

It is a fairly simple matter to deduct the tax paid by each of the income groups from their before-tax incomes to obtain a distribution of disposable income. These results, shown in Table 1.4, modify only slightly the conclusions derived from the before-tax distributions. The shares of after-tax income received by the top 3 per cent remain amazingly stable, but those received by the next 12 per cent, the 'middle income classes', increase substantially (from 20 to 25 per cent), over the period 1952–81. This increase parallels the one noted in the before-tax income shares.

One may conclude, then, that the federal income tax reduces the inequality in the overall distribution to a modest degree (compare the before-tax and after-tax shares). This reduction became less pronounced between 1952 and 1972, but more pronounced during the period of bracket creep thereafter. As effective tax rates declined in the earlier period, the share of the top taxpayers in disposable income either remained the same or increased despite the constancy of the before-tax income shares. Since 1972, their disposable income shares remained the same, even though their before-tax income shares increased. Bracket creep seems to have been the instrument by which the increasing inquality of before-tax income was moderated.

Table 1.4: After-Tax Income Shares
(per cent)

	Top 1% of tax units	Top 2% of tax units	Top 5% of tax units	Top 10% of tax units	Top 15% of tax units
1952	7	10	16	24	30
1963	7	10	17	26	33
1967	7	11	17	26	34
1972	7	10	17	27	35
1977	6	10	17	27	35
1981	7	10	17	27	35

THE EFFECT OF TRANSFER PAYMENTS

The other major element of government policy affecting the distribution of income is the system of transfer payments. This system includes programmes of public assistance that are designed explicitly to help the poor as well as others not designed primarily for this purpose (for example, unemployment and retirement benefits). While the effects of transfer programmes on the distribution of income cannot be measured exactly, the Brookings Institution has run computer simulations of the tax and transfer system in the United States for a number of years. Table 1.5 presents the set generated for the year 1980.

It should be noted that, for several reasons, these data are not directly comparable with those presented earlier. First, the income definition used in Table 1.5 includes several sources of economic income that are not taxable (for example, imputed rent on owner-occupied housing, unrealised appreciation of capital assets and pension fund accumulations). Second, total taxes consist of *all* taxes levied by federal, state and local governments. They include sales and excise taxes, property taxes, corporation income taxes and state and local income taxes, in addition to the federal income tax levies on individuals. Third, percentile groupings of family units are used rather then tax units.

Table 1.5 makes obvious the relatively mild degree of progressivity of the tax system and the highly progressive nature of the transfer system. Taxes go from 23 per cent of income in the second decile to 29 per cent in the top decile.[6] Transfer payments, on the other hand, fall dramatically as incomes rise from the almost 100 per cent of income in the lowest decile to 3 per cent in the highest.[7]

Clearly, redistributing income in this fashion moderates income inequality more by increasing resources available to those at the base of the income pyramid than by taking away more in taxes at the top. The result, however, is that the income moderation achieved by the combined tax-transfer system is quite substantial. The last column of Table 1.5 bears this out. Negative numbers in this column indicate that the families receive more in transfer payments than they pay in taxes of all types; positive figures indicate that they pay more in taxes. On balance, families in the lowest three deciles receive more transfers than they pay in taxes, while those in the top seven deciles pay more taxes then they receive in transfers. The tax-transfer system is, therefore, highly progressive.

Table 1.5: Taxes and Transfers as per cent of Income, 1980

Family income percentiles[a]	*As per cent of income:*		
	Taxes[b]	Transfers	Taxes less transfers
0–10	33	98	−65
10–20	23	58	−36
20–30	24	35	−11
30–40	25	24	1
40–50	26	15	11
50–60	26	11	15
60–70	26	8	19
70–80	27	6	22
80–90	28	4	24
90–100	29	3	26
All families	28	10	18

a. Income includes wages and salaries, fringe benefits, interest, dividends, rents, entrepreneurial incomes and retained corporate earnings, but excludes transfer payments.
b. Assumes that the corporation income and property taxes are borne by owners of capital and pay-roll taxes are borne by workers. The individual income tax is assumed to be paid by the taxpayer and sales and excise taxes are assumed to be paid by the consumers of the taxed items.

WHAT A PROGRESSIVE TAX SYSTEM WOULD LOOK LIKE

The classic objection against an attack on tax regressivity has been that there is simply not enough income in the higher classes to do the job. Would a substantial reduction in regressivity require confiscatory rates? To appreciate one of the significant magnitudes incolved, suppose the tax burden of family units in the bottom 20 per cent (quintile) of the income distribution were somehow reduced by 75 per cent. These reductions would have amounted to $17 billion in 1980, or less than 2.5 per cent of the total taxes collected by federal, state and local governments in that year.

It might be thought that such a proposal—to lift three-quarters of the tax burden of the bottom decile—is too one-sided; after all, it is both inequitable and politically impossible to create a noticeable 'tax divide' between the poor (a fluid concept, in any case) and the rest of society. To make the tax system progressive, it would not be enough drastically to reduce the tax burden of the poor; the burdens of the near poor and others at the lower end of the income scale would have to be cut simultaneously. Indeed—again, on principles of equity and political feasibility—the relief should be diffused upwards until it benefits, say, the lower half of the income distribution (or, more technically, those receiving less than the median income, which was $26,300 in 1980).

There are a number of ways of modifying the tax system to redistribute the tax burden in this way. The most straightforward, and perhaps even the most practical, given the federal system of government in the United States, would be to give taxpayers credits against the federal income tax for a declining percentage of the major taxes they now pay to federal, state and local governments, except for income taxes. Suppose we permit family units of the income distribution to claim credit against their federal income taxes for 75 per cent of the taxes they now pay if they are in the bottom quintile, and 25 per cent if they are in the second quintile. (Obviously, refunds would be paid to those with credits larger than their federal income taxes.)[8]

Let us further assume that the taxes paid by those in the third and fourth quintiles remain the same, and that the revenues needed to pay for the relief provided in the first two quintiles would come entirely from those with incomes in the top quintile. Again, we need not be concerned with the details of how this can be done. It would certainly be more equitable to close the major federal income tax loopholes first, and then raise whatever additional revenue is needed by an increase in the tax rates for families in the sixth decile and higher. Either way, the ratio of total taxes to income for any specific income class could be set at the same figure, although the burden *within* each class would be distributed much more equitably if the loopholes were closed first.

It turns out that, in 1980, the credits (and refunds) would have reduced taxes for those in the two lowest quintiles by $30 billion. This could be recovered by increasing the taxes paid by those in the top quintile by 8 per cent, without altering the tax burdens of those in the third and fourth quintiles. Table1.6 compares the resulting effective rates of tax in this system with the rates as they where in 1980.

A glance at Table 1.6 should convince anyone that this system would by no means eradicate taxes at the lower end of the income scale, nor would it impose excessive burdens at the top. Many people would regard tax burdens of as much as 8 per cent in the bottom quintile (those with incomes below $11,800 and 19 per cent for the second quintile (those between $1,800 and $21,300) as fairly high. Yet the idea of relieving tax burdens for the lower half of the income distribution even in this relatively modest way is probably impractical. Congress would face stiff opposition if it tried to raise taxes in the top quintile (incomes above $60,500) even by as little as 8 per cent on the average.

Table 1.6: Taxes as per cent of Income, 1983

Population quintile [a]	Present tax system [b]	Alternative tax system
First	30	8
Second	25	19
Third	26	26
Fourth	27	27
Fifth	29	31
Total	28	28

a. Family units are arrayed by size of their incomes from market activity, i.e. income excluding transfer payments.
b. See Table 1.5, note b, for incidence assumptions.

The prospects for making the tax system progressive are more discouraging when one notes the way Congress usually behaves when it reduces taxes. On the basis of past performance, one can predict with certainty that Congress will not limit income tax reduction to the lowest income classes. In 1981, federal income taxes were reduced by an average of 23 per cent in all tax brackets, not just for those at the bottom of the income scale. All tax reform proposals now being given serious consideration would increase personal exemptions but they would also reduce the tax rates throughout the income scale, particularly those at the top. Of course, these actions reflect the pressures on Congress. The influence of the groups arrayed against a significant redistribution of the tax burden is enormous, and there is no effective lobby for the poor and the near-poor.

CONCLUSIONS

On the basis of the data presented here we may draw a number of conclusions:

1. The market distribution of income in the United States has become more unequal over the past three decades. Thus, the share of society's product accruing to the top 15 per cent of families has increased steadily over this period.
2. The federal income tax is only mildly progressive and has not moderated income inequality to a significant degree. The income distribution after the payment of federal income taxes is more equal than before, but only slightly.
3. The system of transfer payments, which has grown rapidly over the past 30 years, is highly progressive. Even though many of its components are not means-tested, it does have a big moderating effect on income inequality. While transfers rose rapidly between 1952 and 1980, they reduced the inequality in the distribution of income significantly. This growth in equality was reversed to some degree by the Reagan budget and tax cuts beginning in 1981.
4. The tax system could be made more progressive, but this would involve increases in the taxes paid by those in the high income classes. But there is little evidence from recent experience that Congress is willing to increase taxes for the well-to-do in order to moderate the tax burdens of the lowest income groups.

It may be that, at some distant future date, the rich will have enough income to satisfy not only their own needs, but also to help relieve the tax burdens of those who are less fortunate. In the meantime, the tax system will continue to disgrace the most affluent nation in the world.

NOTES

1. The year 1929 must have been the high point of inequality during the 1920s, so that the distribution of income in the more recent period may not have been very different from what it was in the early 1920s if account is taken of undistributed profits. Unfortunately, the available data for those years are simply not good enough to say much more.

2. People with money always feel poorer than they are, and it might be useful to indicate what kinds of income we are talking about for these various categories. For the year 1981, a taxpayer was in the top 1 per cent if his income (including realised capital gains) was over $91,000, the top 2 per cent if his income was over $70,800, the top 5 per cent if his income was over $49,200, the top 10 per cent if his income was over $39,400, the top 15 per cent if his income was over $34,600.

3. Since the terms are often used loosely, it might be a good idea explicitly to define what *regressive, proportional* and *progressive* taxation mean. A tax is *regressive* when it takes a larger proportion of a poor person's income than of a rich man's, *proportional* when it takes equal proportions of such incomes, and *progressive* when it takes a larger proportion of a rich man's income than of a poor man's.

4. Over this same period, personal exemptions were increased gradually. These went from $500 in 1944 to $600 in 1948, $750 in 1972, and the current $1000 in 1979.

5. Of course, these are aggregate figures and thus conceal wide variations in average tax rates paid by different families in each income class.

6. The decline in the effective tax rate from 33 per cent in the first decile to 23 per cent in the second is an artefact of annual accounting. People who have temporarily low incomes spend more than their incomes and therefore appear to be taxed more heavily. If the figures were available for a longer period, this effect would be reduced or wiped out. The assumptions used (see footnote b, Table 1.5) to distribute taxes by income classes are those generally supported by modern tax economists. Alternative assumptions (e.g. that the corporate tax is passed on to the consumer) would make the tax system less progressive or even regressive.

7. The progressivity of the tax system may be understated in Table 1.5 because the payroll taxes levied to support social security retirement and disability benefits are regressive, but the benefits are progressive. On a lifetime basis, if taxes and transfers were netted out for the same individuals, the tax system would appear to be more progressive. However, the progressivity of the tax-transfer system as a whole (shown in the last column of Table 1.5) is not greatly affected by the separation of taxes and transfers.

8. In practice, the credits for families of different size would be varied, but this is a refinement which need not concern us here.

2. Who Paid the Taxes, 1966–85?*

The taxes paid by the nation's family units to the federal, state and local governments amounted to 25 per cent of total family income in 1980.[1] Strong views are held as to whether the burden of these taxes is distributed fairly by income class or among persons with substantially equal incomes. Some believe that the tax system is regressive; others consider it to be progressive.[3] Still others are concerned not only about the equity of the tax system across income classes (vertical equity), but also about its equity among those with the same income (horizontal equity). To a large extent, the debate has centred on the individual income tax, which is the largest source of government revenue in the United States. Even though the other taxes account for more than twice the revenue produced by the individual income tax, the distribution of these taxes by income classes is not generally known. Nor is it generally known if the tax system as a whole has become more or less progressive in recent years. The purpose of this study is to estimate the effect of all US taxes on the distribution of income, and how this distribution has changed in the last two decades.

MAJOR FEATURES OF THE STUDY

Although others have made similar estimates, this study is unique in three respects. First, the estimates are based on microunit data files for representative samples of families (referred to as the MERGE files);[4] when properly weighted, the samples account for the estimated total income received by family units in the United States. In addition to data on income, the files contain demographic and other economic information about each of the sample units (for example, home-ownership, place of residence, age of family members, and so on). This information is available on computer tape and can be processed quickly and efficiently on an electronic computer, thus permitting estimates to be prepared in more detail than was possible with the previous data-processing techniques.

Second, although progress has been made in recent years in improving the methodology of tax analysis, economists still disagree about the incidence of several of the most important taxes in the tax system. Instead

Reprinted from *Who Paid the Taxes, 1966–85?* (Brookings Institution, 1985), Ch. 1, pp. 1–10.

of limiting the analysis to one or a few views, estimates were prepared on the basis of eight sets of assumptions that span the range of opinions currently held by most economists (see Table 2.1).

Third, MERGE files have been developed for the years 1966, 1970 and 1975, and the 1975 file has been projected to 1980 and 1985. Thus the data provide estimates of the changes in the distribution of tax burdens over a period of about two decades.

Table 2.1: Tax Incidence Assumptions Used in This Study[a]

Tax and basis of allocation	Variant 1			Variant 2		Variant 3		
	a	b	c	a	b	a	b	c
Individual income tax								
To taxpayers	x	x	x	x	x	x	x	x
Sales and excise taxes								
To consumption of taxed commodities	x	x	x	x	x	x	x	x
Corporation income tax								
To dividends				x	x			
To property income in general	x	x						
Half to dividends, half to property income in general			x					x
Half to dividends, one-fourth to consumption, one-fourth to employee compensation						x		
Half to property income in general, half to consumption							x	
Property tax on land								
To landowners	x			x	x	x	x	x
To property income in general		x	x					
Property tax on improvements								
To shelter and consumption				x	x	x	x	
To property income in general	x	x	x					
Half to property income in general								x
Half to shelter and consumption, half to property income in general								
Payroll tax on employees								
To employee compensation	x	x	x	x	x	x	x	x
Payroll tax on employers								
To employee compensation	x	x	x	x		x		x
Half to employee compensation, half to consumption					x		x	

a. See text for a detailed description of the incidence variants.

The income concept used here corresponds closely to an economist's comprehensive definition of income for family units. In addition to the incomes earned in the market system (wages, interest, dividends, rents, business profits), this concept includes transfer payments and capital gains accrued during the year (whether realised or not).[5] To convert income to a before-tax basis, indirect business taxes as well as direct taxes, are included in income.[6]

The incidence of tax—used synonymously with 'tax burden' in this study— is measured by the reduction in real incomes that results from the imposition of that tax. Taxes affect real income in either or both of two ways: they may reduce the incomes of individuals in their role as producers; or they may increase the prices of consumer goods and thus reduce the purchasing power of a given amount of money income. The former effect is the burden of taxation on the 'sources' of income; the latter is the burden on the 'uses' of income. Both of these effects are measured in this study. However, no attempt is made to measure the burden that results from the reallocation of resources or the changes in consumption patterns that may be caused by taxation because such effects cannot be measured with sufficient accuracy.

This study is concerned solely with the distribution of tax burdens, without any reference to the distribution of benefits from the governmental activities that are supported by taxes. It attempts to show how the distribution of disposable income in the past two decades differed from what the distribution would have been if all tax revenues had come from a proportional income tax with the same yields.[6] This differential incidence approach was adopted because the benefits of many, if not most, government activities cannot be allocated even in principle.[7] However, transfers by government to individuals (social security and unemployment benefits, welfare payments, workmen's compensation, food stamps, Medicare and Medicaid) can be allocated to family units, and this allocation is made here.

DISTRIBUTION OF TAX BURDENS, 1980

The major conclusions of this study may be seen in Figure 2.1, which shows the 1980 effective rates of tax by population percentiles ranked according to income for the most progressive and the least progressive sets of incidence assumptions used.[8] Under the most progressive assumptions (variant 1c) effective tax rates in 1980 ran from about 20 per cent at the lowest end of the income scale to 27 per cent at the top. Under the least progressive assumptions (variant 3b) effective tax rates declined from over 30 per cent at the lowest end of the distribution to about 25 per cent in the second decile and remained at that level until they declined to 22 per cent in

Effective tax rate (per cent)

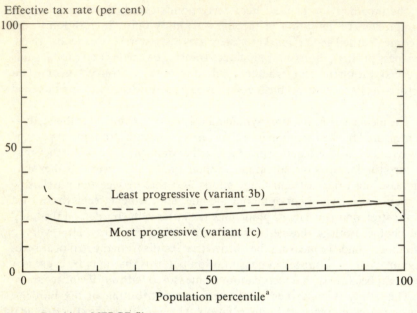

Source: Brookings MERGE file.
a. Arrayed by size of adjusted family income.

Figure 2.1: Effective Rates of Federal, State and Local Taxes under the Most and Least Progressive Incidence Variants, by Population Percentile, 1980

the top percentile. For the distribution as a whole, the tax system was either moderately progressive (variant 1c) or slightly regressive (variant 3b). The differences in effective rates between the two variants were relatively small except at the bottom of the income scale, where the tax burden was much higher under variant 3b than it was under 1c, and at the top, where the tax burden was higher under variant 1c.

Because the degree of progressivity or regressivity is relatively small under any of the incidence assumptions, it is clear that the tax system has very little effect on the distribution of income. However, the system of transfer payments is highly progressive and has a major effect on the income distribution. This is illustrated in Figure 2.2, which shows the Lorenz curves for the 1980 distributions of income before and after transfers and taxes when taxes are allocated under variant 1c assumptions.[9] As might be expected in the case of a progressive tax and transfer system, the Lorenz curve for the distribution of after-tax and after-transfer income under variant 1c lies 10 per cent closer to the line of equal distribution than the before-tax curve. But the movement toward equality for the tax system alone was small—2.5 per cent under variant 1c and considerably smaller

Cumulative per cent of income

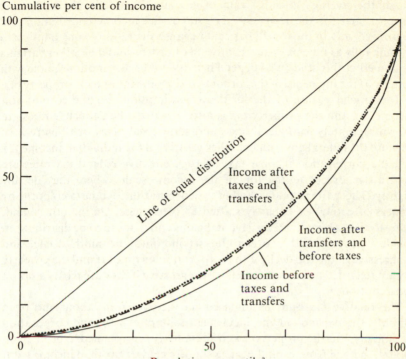

Source: Brookings MERGE file. Taxes are based on variant 1c assumptions.
a. Arrayed by size of family income.

Figure 2.2: Lorenz Curves of the Distributions of Adjusted Family Income before and after Federal, State and Local Taxes and Transfers under the Most Progressive Variant (1c), 1980

percentages under the other variants examined in this study. In the case of variant 3b—the least progressive set of assumptions—the after-tax distribution differed only slightly from the before-tax distribution (it was 0.9 per cent less equal). The change was so small that the Lorenz curves for the two distributions cannot be distinguished on the scale used in Figure 2.2.

The incidence assumptions of variant 1c were more progressive than those of 3b largely because of differences in the treatment of the corporation income tax and the property tax. Under 1c, these two taxes are assumed to be taxes on income from capital[10], while under 3b half of the corporation income tax and half of the property tax on improvements are assumed to be paid by consumers through increases in the relative prices of housing and other goods and services.[11] Since property income is heavily concentrated among families in the highest income classes, effective tax rates under the variant 1c assumptions rise as incomes rise. On the other hand, the average effective rate of tax under variant 3b is virtually proportional for the lower 90 per cent of the income distribution and regressive only in the top 10 per cent because the ratio of consumption to income falls as incomes rise. Relative tax burdens under all other variants examined in this study also depend heavily on the assumptions made with respect to the incidence of the corporation income tax and the property tax.

The crucial nature of the incidence assumptions for the corporation income tax and the property tax is also revealed when effective rates are shown separately for federal taxes and state–local taxes (see Figure 2.3). Because the federal government relies greatly on the individual income tax and the corporation income tax, average effective federal tax rates are progressive except at the top of the income scale, where they decline slightly. This pattern holds whether the corporation income tax is borne by owners of capital or is partly shifted to consumers. On the other hand, state–local tax rates are regressive at the low end of the income distribution, roughly proportional between the second and the ninth decile, and progressive in the top decile if the corporation income tax and the property tax are regarded as taxes on capital, or regressive if they are partly a tax on consumption.[12]

The relative tax burdens imposed on income from labour and from capital also depend on the incidence assumptions for the corporation income tax and the property tax. If these taxes are assumed to be taxes on capital, income from capital bears a slightly heavier tax than income from labour. For example, under variant 1c, the effective tax rate on income from capital was 21.5 per cent in 1980 compared to 19.9 per cent for income from labour. But the relative burdens are reversed if the corporation income tax and the property tax are assumed to be paid in whole or in part by consumers. Thus, under variant 3b income from capital paid an average tax rate of 14.6 per cent, while labour income paid a tax of 18.1 per cent. Labour and capital both bear a lower tax burden under variant 3b than under 1c because the burden on consumption is higher—20.5 per cent compared with 9.7 per cent in 1980.[13]

CHANGES IN THE DISTRIBUTION OF TAX BURDENS, 1966–85

The major influences on the distribution of tax burdens between 1966 and 1985 were a decline in the relative importance of the corporation income tax and the property tax a rise in payroll taxes. Since the former two are progressive tax sources and the latter is regressive, the effect of these changes was to reduce the progressivity of the tax system. The federal tax cuts in 1981 also contributed to the reduction in progressivity. Between

Effective tax rate (per cent)

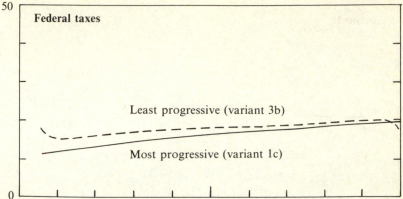

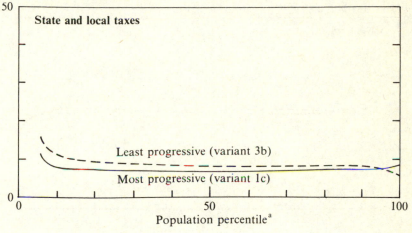

Source: Brookings MERGE file.
a. Arrayed by size of adjusted family income.

Figure 2.3: Effective Rates of Federal and of State and Local Taxes under the Most
and Least Progressive Variants, by Population Percentile, 1980

1966 and 1985 tax burdens increased in the lower part of the income scale,
declined sharply at the top, and remained roughly the same or rose slightly
in between. The effective tax rate in the highest population decile fell from
1.79 times the burden in the lowest decile in 1966 to 1.16 in 1985 under
variant 1c, and from 0.94 to 0.83 under variant 3b (Figure 2.4).

The decline in the progressivity of the tax system during this period was
caused by a decline in the progressivity of federal taxes. State and local

Effective tax rate (per cent)

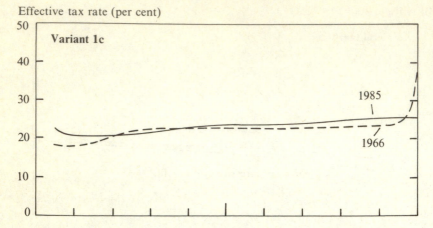

Effective tax rate (per cent)

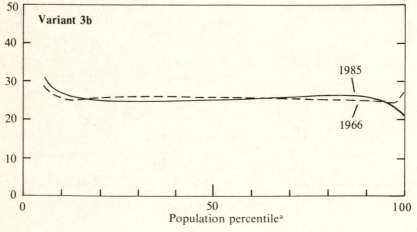

Population percentile[a]

Source: Brookings MERGE files.
a. Arrayed by size of family income.

Figure 2.4: Effective Rates of Federal, State and Local Taxes under the Most and
   Least Progressive Incidence Variants, by Population Percentile, 1966 and 1985

taxes became somewhat more progressive or retained the same degree of
progressivity, depending on the incidence assumptions. Individual income
taxes remained progressive throughout the period, but less so at the end of
the period than at the beginning because of the effect of bracket creep
resulting from the growth of real incomes as well as inflation and the
federal tax cuts enacted in 1981.

   In 1966 the tax burden on capital income was substantially higher than the burden on the labour income. This pattern was reversed by 1985 as a result of the reduced roles of the corporation income tax and the property tax and the greater role of the payroll tax.

There was virtually no change in the distribution of income as defined in this study between 1966 and 1985. However, this income concept includes transfer payments, which rose dramatically during this period. As a result, the distribution of income from market activity (wages and salaries, interest, dividends, rents and windfall profits) must have become more unequal. Because the tax system became less progressive, the distribution of income *after* taxes was more unequal in 1985 than in 1966.

SUMMARY

The US tax system is either moderately progressive or slightly regressive, depending on the incidence assumptions for the major taxes. If the corporation income tax and the property tax are assumed to be borne by capital, the very rich pay higher average effective tax than does the average family. If these taxes are assumed to be shifted to consumers to a considerable degree, the very rich pay lower effective rates than the average family.

The tax system has relatively little effect on the distribution of income. In contrast, the transfer system has a significant equalising effect.

The tax system became less progressive between 1966 and 1985, primarily because the corporation income tax and the property tax declined in importance while more emphasis was placed on the payroll tax.

NOTES

1. This ratio is lower than the commonly-cited ratio of government receipts to the national income primarily because taxes exclude receipts from nontax sources.
2. A tax is *regressive* when the ratio of tax to income falls as incomes rise: a tax is *proportional* when the ratio of tax to income is the same for all income classes; and a tax is *progressive* when the ratio of tax to income rises as incomes rise.
3. In this chapter the term 'families' refers both to individuals living alone (one-person families) and to the conventional family consisting of two or more persons, related by blood, marriage or adoption.
4. Gifts and bequests should also be included in income, but these were omitted because little is known about their distribution among families.
5. Direct taxes are automatically included in factor incomes; indirect taxes were allocated to individual family units in proportion to their shares of factor incomes.
6. The differences between actual effective rates and the effective rate of a proportional income tax are not actually shown in any of the tables or figures

in this study; they can easily be derived by subtraction.

7. Many governmental activities produce 'public goods' (e.g., national defence), the benefits of which to any specific individual cannot be evaluated. For a discussion of the problems of measuring the benefits of government expenditure, see J. Margolis and H. Guitton (eds.) *Public Economics: An Analysis of Public Production and Consumption and Their Relations to the Private Sectors* (Macmillan, 1969). For the logically correct method of distributing the benefits of public goods, see Henry Aaron and Martin McGuire, 'Public Goods and Income Distribution', *Econometrica*, Vol. 38 (November 1970). This method cannot be applied because information on consumer preferences for public goods is not available.

8. The 1980 effective rates are used here because this was the latest year for which actual tax collections were available to prepare the MERGE file. The 1985 file, to be discussed below, is based on budget projections of tax receipts.

9. A Lorenz curve shows the cumulative percentage of the aggregate income received by any given cumulative percentage of recipients arrayed by the size of their incomes. When all income recipients receive the same income, the Lorenz curve is a straight line with a slope of 45 degrees. As the distribution becomes more unequal, the Lorenz curve moves downward and to the right, away from the line of equal distribution.

10. The assumption under variant 1c is that half of the corporation income tax is borne by corporate stockholders and the other half is borne by owners of capital in general.

11. Under both variants the individual income tax is assumed to be borne by the income recipients; sales taxes and excises are assumed to be paid by consumers; and employee payroll taxes are assumed to be paid by the workers. Other differences between the two variants are that the property tax on land is assumed to be paid by owners of capital in general under variant 1c and by landowners under 3b, and that the employer payroll tax is borne by employees under 1c and shifted to the consumer under 3b. However, these differences have a relatively small effect on the distribution of tax burdens.

12. In addition to differences that arise because of differences in incidence assumptions, there are substantial variations in tax rates among various economic and demographic groups in the population that are due to the structural features of the US tax system. For example, home-owners pay lower taxes than do tenants, urban residents pay somewhat higher taxes than residents of rural farm areas, and married couples pay lower taxes than single persons. See Joseph A. Pechman and Benjamin A. Okner *Who Bears the Tax Burden?* (Brookings Institution, 1974), Ch. 5.

13. In these calculations total taxes were allocated to three categories: labour income, capital income and consumption.

Part Two
Individual Income Taxation

3. The Personal Income Tax*

The personal income tax is widely regarded as the fairest method of taxation yet devised. It is the major element of progression in modern tax systems and permits differentiation of tax burdens on the basis of family responsibilities and other personal circumstances of taxpayers. The yield of the tax expands or contracts more rapidly than personal income, thus imparting built-in flexibility to government revenue systems. The income tax is less burdensome on consumption and more burdensome on personal saving than an equal-yield expenditure tax, but the difference in aggregate terms is probably small for taxes of broad coverage. The effect of the income tax on work and investment incentives is unclear. Although personal income taxation has a long history, some of its major features still present numerous unresolved problems.

The first general personal income tax was introduced in 1799 in Great Britain, where it has been in effect continuously since 1842. Despite this early example, other countries were slow in adopting this tax. It was used for a brief period in the United States during and after the Civil War, and it was permanently enacted following the ratification in 1913 of the sixteenth amendment to the constitution. Austria adopted the income tax in 1849 and Italy in 1864; Australia, New Zealand and Japan followed in the 1880s and Germany and the Netherlands in the 1890s. Elsewhere the income tax is a twentieth-century phenomenon. It spread quickly during and after the first World War, and became a mass tax in many countries during the Second World War. Today, the personal income tax raises substantial amounts of revenue in all industrialised countries of the free world and is employed, although to a lesser extent, in most underdeveloped countries.

EQUITY CONSIDERATIONS

Analysis of tax equity has been concerned largely with the distribution of tax burdens among persons in different economic circumstances, i.e. with *vertical* equity. Questions regarding the treatment of persons in essentially the same economic circumstances—the problems of *horizontal* equity— have only received close attention since the 1930s.

*Adapted from 'Taxation: Personal Income Taxes', *International Encyclopedia of Social Sciences* (Crowell Collier and Free Press, 1968), Vol. 15, pp. 529–37.

Vertical equity

Progressive taxation appeals intuitively to most people as an equitable method of distributing the tax burden by income classes, and economists and political theorists have devoted a great deal of intellectual effort to justify it on logical grounds.

An early theory of taxation that was widely held prior to the mid-nineteenth century was that taxes should be distributed in accordance with benefits received. The benefit theorists supported a minimum of government activity, possibly including defence and police and fire protection, but not much more. The benefits of such government services were assumed to be proportionate to income and this was regarded as a major rationale for proportional income taxation. This theory of tax distribution proved to be untenable both because of its narrow view of the role of government and the arbitrary assumption it made regarding the distribution of benefits of government services.

In the latter half of the nineteenth century, progressive income taxation was justified by the sacrifice theories that emerged from discussions of 'ability to pay'. Under this doctrine, ability to pay is assumed to increase as incomes increase, and the objective is to impose taxes on a basis that would involve 'equal sacrifice' in some sense. If the marginal utility of income declines more rapidly than income increases, *equal absolute sacrifice* leads to progression, *equal proportionate sacrifice* is still more progression, and *equal marginal sacrifice* to levelling of incomes from the top down until the required revenues are obtained. The assumptions of sacrifice theories—that the relative utility of different incomes is measurable and that the relation between income and utility is approximately the same for all taxpayers—cannot be verified by actual data or experience. Nevertheless, the ability to pay idea has been a powerful force in history and has undoubtedly contributed to the widespread acceptance of progressive taxation.

The basic justification for the progressive personal income tax is now probably the socio-economic objective of reducing great disparities of welfare, opportunity and economic power arising from the unequal distribution of income. More specifically the justification is based on two propositions:*(a)* it is appropriate public policy to moderate economic inequality, and *(b)* taxation of personal incomes at progressive rates is an efficient method of promoting this objective, since it does not involve direct intervention in market activities. The acceptable degree of progression varies from time to time and place to place; it depends on the distribution of pre-tax incomes and the post-tax distribution desired by the voters. In practice the redistributive effects of the income tax have been moderate in all countries.

Horizontal equity

A personal income tax conforming strictly with the 'equal treatment' principle would apply to all income from whatever source derived, making allowances only for the taxpayer and his dependants. In accordance with the 'accretion' concept, income would be defined as consumption plus (or minus) the net increase (or decrease) in the value of an individual's assets during the taxable period, perhaps modified to exclude gifts and inheritances that are ordinarily subject to separate taxes and, for practical reasons, to include capital gains when realised or when transferred to others through gifts or bequests. In practice most of the income taxes now in existence depart from this standard by a wide margin.

Differentiation of tax liability on the basis of family responsibilities is ordinarily made through a system of personal exemptions for the taxpayer and other members of his family. The personal exemption was originally regarded as a device to avoid taxing individuals and families with incomes that were not adequate to provide minimum levels of subsistence. Today personal exemptions are not high enough to cover a socially acceptable minimum level of subsistence in most countries; they serve primarily to remove low-income recipients from the tax rolls and also contribute to progression in the lower part of the income scale. At higher income levels the purpose of the personal exemption seems to be to moderate the tax burden as family size increases, although the degree of moderation varies greatly among countries. Special exemptions are allowed in some countries for particular groups of taxpayers (e.g. the aged); these exemptions are subsidies that could probably be handled more equitably through direct government outlays.

A second type of differentiation employed in most countries is based on the *source* of income. The provisions include credits for earned income and for dividends, preferential treatment for capital gains, exemptions for transfer payments and amounts set aside for retirement, omission of the rental value of owner-occupied homes, and numerous other special benefits. The earned-income credit is regarded as a convenient method of making rough allowances for depreciation of labour skills and for expenses of earning income from personal effort which are not recognised for tax purposes. The United States abandoned the earned-income credit in 1944 for simplification reasons, but it is still in existence in the United Kingdom, Australia and other countries. Dividend credits are designed to moderate the so-called 'double taxation' of corporate profits. Preferential treatment of capital gains grew out of the English concept of income, which excluded irregular receipts from income. This treatment is now rationalised on incentive grounds and also as a procedure to avoid applying the graduated rates, in the year of realisation, to incomes accrued over a period of years.

Transfer payments are excluded because they accrue largely to low-income people. Payments by employers into pension plans are not included in employees' taxable income to promote the development of private pension plans. The rental value of owner-occupied homes is untaxed in most places because it is difficult to apply the income tax to non-money incomes.

The third type of differentiation is based on the *use* of income. Deductions are required under a 'net' income tax for expenditures that are essential to earning income. However, deductions for a wide variety of personal expenditures and for many forms of saving are also permitted. In one country or another, allowances are made for such items as medical expenses, charitable contributions, interest on personal loans and mortgages, state and local taxes, casualty losses, child care in families of working parents, deposits in saving associations, premiums for life, sickness and accident insurance, and payments into annuity, pension or other retirement plans.

Personal exemptions are an important element of a progressive income tax, but there is little justification for most of the special exclusions, deductions and credits based on the source or use of income. Such provisions narrow the tax base and require the use of higher tax rates to raise a given amount of revenue. This puts a premium on earning or spending incomes in forms receiving preferential treatment, interferes with business and investment decisions, and distorts the allocation of resources. Since the deviations from equal treatment tend to be arbitrary, they create dissatisfaction among taxpayers who are subject to discrimination and result in pressures for the enactment of additional special benefits, pressures which legislatures find it difficult to resist. This process has been called 'erosion of the tax base' in the United States, where taxable income is at least one-third lower than it would be under a comprehensive income tax. Measures to broaden the base and to use the revenues for rate reduction have been proposed by tax experts, but it is evident from the public and congressional response that progress along these lines will be slow.

ECONOMIC EFFECTS

Three major aspects of the personal income tax may be distinguished in appraising its economic effects; first, its automatic response to changes in total personal income; second, its effects on the allocation of personal income between consumption and saving; and third, its impact on work and investment incentives.

Automatic flexibility

The role of the personal income tax as a built-in stabiliser is one of its most significant features. In the United States, at the rates prevailing in the 1960s and 1970s, the personal income tax automatically offset more than 10 per cent of the reductions in personal incomes during contraction. The corresponding figure for the United Kingdom was perhaps twice as large, the difference being attributable primarily to the higher starting rate in the United Kingdom. Such changes in tax liability reduce fluctuations in disposable personal income and thus help to stabilise consumption.

Built-in flexibility operates in both the expansion and contraction phases of the business cycle, so that the personal income tax moderates the growth of incomes during a business recovery just as it cushions the fall in income during contractions. This symmetrical response of the income tax (and of other stabilisers) during a business cycle is unavoidable. It should not lead to the abandonment of the stabilisers but rather to the establishment of basic tax-expenditure relationships that would be consistent with a prompt return to high employment following periods of recession. Discretionary changes in tax rates and in expenditures may be needed to implement this objective.

The responsiveness of the income tax to changes in personal incomes is a useful characteristic for underdeveloped as well as for developed countries. An increasing proportion of the nation's resources must be devoted to public and private investment to increase the rate of economic development. Since voluntary saving is usually inadequate, the bulk of the investment funds must be provided by government. A progressive income tax automatically provides some of the financing as incomes increase. Where development is associated with rising prices, the income tax serves the dual role of moderating inflationary pressures and of increasing the rate of national saving.

Effect on consumption and saving

A personal income tax applies to the income of an individual regardless of the allocation of this income between consumption and saving. By contrast, a general consumption or expenditure tax can be postponed or avoided by delaying or eliminating consumption. It follows that an income tax is less burdensome on consumption than an equal-yielding consumption or expenditure tax which is distributed in the same proportions by income classes. In practice, where the income tax is paid by the large mass of people, much of the tax yield comes from income classes where there is little room in family budgets for reducing consumption in response to tax incentives. Under these circumstances the differential effect of the two types of taxes on total consumption and saving is likely to be relatively small.

Graduated expenditure taxes have been proposed in recent years as a method of avoiding or correcting the effects of income tax erosion, particularly in the top income brackets where exemption or preferential treatment of capital gains permits accumulation of large fortunes without tax payment. Expenditure taxation, it is felt, would discourage lavish living by people with large amounts of property and thus increase saving and risk-taking without resorting to regressive taxes. Despite its apparent advantages, the expenditure tax has not been widely used. Rates in excess of 100 per cent would be required to raise significant amounts of revenue from high-income taxpayers. The expenditure tax is more difficult to administer than the income tax in some respects and less difficult in other respects, and raises serious problems of transition (see ch. 10).

Work and investment incentives

It is difficult to evaluate the effect of personal income taxes on work and investment incentives. On the one hand, high tax rates reduce the net rewards of greater effort and risk taking and thus tend to discourage these activities; on the other hand, they may provide a positive stimulus to obtain more income because they cut down on the income left over for spending. These two effects tend to offset one another, and there is no basis for deciding which is more important.

Recent empirical studies suggest that income taxation affects the amount of labour supplied, particularly by working wives and other supplementary earners of the family. But the total reduction as compared to the amount supplied under a proportional income tax is only about five per cent. Work habits are apparently not easily changed, and there is little scope in a modern industrial society for most people to vary the hours of work or the intensity of their efforts in response to changes in tax rates.

A highly graduated income tax applying to *all* property incomes might reduce incentives to take risk somewhat, since it is impossible to reimburse taxpayers for losses at precisely the same rate at which their incomes are taxed. However, the income tax actually applies to a small fraction of property income in all countries. The opportunity to earn income in the form of capital gains—which are either not taxed at all or are taxed at relatively low rates—maybe a stimulant to risk-taking in the face of high rates on other incomes. Moreover, risk investment is to a large extent undertaken by firms operating in the corporate form; such firms are generally permitted to retain earnings after payment of more moderate tax rates than those applying to investors in the top personal income tax brackets.

STRUCTURAL PROBLEMS

The base of the personal income tax is determined by the definition of income, the allowable deductions, and the personal exemptions. Within wide limits, these elements can be combined with various tax rates to produce a given amount of revenue. Many of the difficult issues in most countries are an outgrowth of local problems and developments. Nevertheless, several structural problems in income taxation appear to be common to practically all countries, and these will be discussed briefly in this section.

Tax treatment of the family.

Throughout most of the history of the income tax, differentiation was made among taxpayers with different family responsibilities through the use of personal exemptions. Recently, there has been a trend towards the use of different tax rates to provide additional differentiation, particularly in the middle and higher tax brackets. In the United States, France and West Germany, this has been accomplished by the adoption of the principle of 'income splitting' between husband and wife, or among all family members. Other countries achieve the same objective by applying different rate schedules to taxpayers in different family situations.

In France the income of the family is divided by the number of family units, with the taxpayer and his spouse counting as one unit each and each dependent child as an additional one-half unit. The tax is then calculated as if the income of the family were divided proportionately among the family units. In West Germany and the United States, splitting is extended only to husband and wife. The United Kingdom permits separate filing by husband and wife for earned income only; investment income of both spouses is taxable to the husband. Under this system the graduated rates are applied to the separate earnings of each spouse after allowance for personal exemptions and other deductions.

Income splitting between two persons doubles the width of the taxable income brackets and thus reduces the progression in tax burdens applying to married couples. The absolute size of the benefit depends entirely on the *rate of graduation*; it bears no relationship to the level of tax rates. For example, if rates increased one percentage point for every $1000 of taxable income, income splitting would reduce the tax of a married couple with taxable income of $20,000 by $1000. This would be true whether the starting rate was 1, 10, 20 or 50 per cent.

One of the major reasons for the acceptance of income splitting may well be inadequate differentiation provided by the traditional types of personal exemptions among taxpayers in the middle and top brackets. Single people, it is felt, should be taxed more heavily than married couples because they do not bear the costs and responsibilities of raising children. But the allowance of income splitting for husband and wife clearly does not differentiate between taxpayers in this respect since the tax benefit is the same whether or not there are children. Nor does the extension of splitting to children give the correct answer, since the benefits depend on the rate of graduation as well as on family size.

Personal deductions

In principle, the use made of a given income should have no bearing on the amount of tax to be paid out of that income. In practice, some allowances are made almost everywhere for selected items of consumption or saving. These deductions may be divided into three major types: (1) those that provide a supplement to the personal exemption; (2) those that subsidise particular activities or expenditures; and (3) those that improve co-ordination of federal income taxes with state or provincial and local taxes, where they exist.

A strong case can be made for allowing some deductions for large, unusual and necessary expenditures when the personal exemptions are low. Deductions for medical expenses are the best example of this type of expenditure. They are often involuntary, unpredictable, and may exhaust a large proportion of the taxpayer's income. Expenditures for non-insured losses due to theft, fire, accident or other casualties are of a similar nature. In keeping with the purpose of this type of deduction, it should be limited to an amount in excess of some percentage of income, which would be high enough to exclude all but extraordinary expenditures for these purposes.

Subsidy-type deductions are most common for contributions to charitable, religious, educational and other non-profit organisations. In many countries heavy reliance is placed on philanthropic institutions to supplement governmental activities, and in some cases to provide services which governmental units do not perform. It may be argued that private philanthropy should not be encouraged at the expense of government funds. However, few people subscribe to this view because the activities of these organisations, with rare exceptions, are considered desirable and useful.

Subsidy-type deductions are also allowed in some countries for selected items of personal saving. Great Britain has permitted the deduction of a portion of life insurance premiums since the beginning of the income tax. West Germany allows deductions for personal insurance and for deposits in building and savings associations. A number of countries have recently enacted limited deductions for amounts set aside in annuities or retirement plans by self-employed persons and employees not eligible for company pension plans. The major motivation for these deductions appears to be to promote saving, but more particularly to encourage adequate provision for retirement and for catastrophic events that entail large outlays or loss of income. The deductions for personal contributions to retirement plans are also intended to remove the discrimination resulting from the exclusion usually granted to employer contributions to employee pension plans. The growth of allowances for particular types of saving has made substantial inroads into the philosophy of income taxation; in fact, these policies constitute a substantial movement toward the expenditure tax approach.

Suggestions have been made in recent years that the tax laws should permit a deduction for the cost of higher education. These suggestions reflect the importance of higher education for economic growth and the increased costs of a college education. On the one hand, a deduction allowed to parents would give the largest benefits to the highest income classes and would therefore be inequitable. On the other hand, some portion of expenditures for higher education is an investment which is not recognised for tax purposes as an expense of earning income. The appropriate treatment would be to regard the outlay by a parent as a gift to the child and to permit the child to write off a portion of this outlay over the earning career for, say, twenty years. However, there is no basis for estimating the proportion of educational outlays allocatable to investment, and the problems of administration and compliance would be substantial.

Deductions for income taxes paid to overlapping governmental units are required to prevent confiscation if one or more levels of government employ high rates in the upper end of the income scale. Where the rates are moderate, it is quite appropriate to levy two taxes on the same base without coordination.

A deduction for income taxes paid to state and local governments may be a practical necessity in a federal system, but the same justification does not hold for state and local sales, excise and property taxes. The latter deductions defeat the purposes of taxes levied to obtain payments from taxpayers for benefits received from state and local governments and reduce the progressivity of the combined tax system.

In the United States, where personal deductions have proliferated more than in any other country except perhaps West Germany, taxpayers are granted a 'standard' deduction, in lieu of the itemised deductions. This device was adopted in 1944 for simplification reasons, in recognition of the fact that most personal deductions are small and few taxpayers keep adequate records to support them. To an important degree, the standard deduction violates the rationale of the itemised deduction; it reduces differentiation in tax liabilities while the itemised deductions are intended to introduce such differences for the purposes selected. The existence of both a standard deduction and itemised deductions suggests that there is some ambivalence toward many of the personal deductions in the United States income tax structure.

On balance, equity would be better served by avoiding erosion of the tax base through the use of numerous costly personal deductions. This should not preclude the adoption of a restricted list of deductions for unusually large and extraordinary expenditures to prevent hardships. Subsidy-type deductions are appropriate only if they promote a significant national objective and if the deduction route is the most efficient and equitable method of achieving that objective.

Capital gains and losses

As already indicated, an economic definition of income would include capital gains in full on an accrual basis. This method is impractical for three reasons: (1) valuations of many types of property cannot be estimated with sufficient accuracy to provide a basis for taxation; (2) most people would regard it as inequitable to pay tax unless income has actually been realised; and (3) taxation of accruals might force liquidation of assets to discharge tax liabilities. Thus, where capital gains are taxable, they are included in income only when realised.

Few countries tax the capital gains of individuals, but the United States has done so since the beginning of its income tax. Realised capital gains were originally taxed as ordinary incomes, but they have been subject to preferentially low rates since 1921. The provisions applying to such gains changed frequently. Since 1984 capital gains on assets held for periods longer than six months have been subject to 40% of the tax rates on ordinary income, up to a maximum of 20%.

The treatment of capital gains is likely to be a compromise among conflicting objectives. From the standpoint of equity, it is well established that capital gains should be taken into account in determining personal tax liability. Moreover, low rates or exemption of capital gains encourage the conversion of ordinary income into capital gains by devices that distort patterns of investment and discredit income taxation. On the other hand, the bunching of capital gains in the year of realisation requires some provision to moderate the impact of graduation. On economic grounds full taxation of capital gains is resisted because it is believed that it would have a substantial 'locking-in' effect on investors and reduce the mobility of capital. It is also argued that preferential treatment of capital gains helps to stimulate a higher rate of economic growth by increasing the attractiveness of investment generally and of risky investments in particular.

Capital losses are no easier to handle than capital gains. In principle, capital losses should be deductible in full, either against capital gains or ordinary income. However, when gains and losses are recognised only upon realisation, taxpayers can easily time their sales so as to take losses promptly when they occur and to postpone the realisation of gains. There is no effective method of avoiding this asymmetry under any system of taxation applying to realised gains and losses. In the United States, capital losses of individuals may be offset against capital gains plus $3000 of ordinary income in the year of realisation and in subsequent years for an indefinite time period. This restrictive policy is perhaps most harmful to small investors, who are less likely than those in the higher brackets to have gains against which to offset their losses. The only solution to this problem is a pragmatic one which would be as liberal as possible for the small investor without opening the door to widespread abuse and large revenue losses.

Relation to the corporate income tax

Unless corporate incomes were subject to tax, individuals could avoid the personal tax by accumulating income in corporations. Short of an annual allocation of corporate incomes on a pro rata basis—a method which is excellent in theory but not in practice—the equity and revenue potential of the personal income tax can be protected only by a separate tax on corporate incomes. However, the existence of two separate taxes on the same income creates a difficult equity problem. Concern over the 'double taxation' of dividends is evident in the various devices used in different countries to alleviate its alleged discriminatory effects.

On the assumption that all or a significant portion of the corporate income tax rests on the stockholder, the effect of double taxation is to impose the heaviest burden on dividends received by stockholders with the lowest incomes. Assume a corporate income tax of 50 per cent and suppose a corporation pays out $50 in dividends. The corporate income before tax from which these dividends were paid amounted to $100. If this $100 had been subject to personal income tax rates only, the non-taxable individual would have paid no tax on it; the additional burden of the corporate income tax in this case is the full $50 corporate tax. By contrast, a stockholder subject to an 80 per cent rate pays a personal income tax of $40 on the dividend, and the total tax burden on the original $100 of corporate earnings is $90. But since he would pay $80 under the personal income tax in any case, the additional burden on him is only $10.

The simplest and most effective method of dealing with this problem would be to permit corporations to deduct all or a portion of their dividends in computing taxable income. This method would apply the regular corporate tax rate to undistributed profits and would reduce or eliminate the corporate tax on distributed earnings. It would also have two additional advantages: first, dividend and interest payments would be treated more nearly alike, thus reducing the discrimination against equity financing by corporations; second, the same proportion of the corporate income tax on distributed income would be eliminated for all taxpayers regardless of their personal income tax status.

Despite these advantages, undistributed profits taxation is not used widely. The United States experimented with it in the 1930s, but the experiment created a great deal of resentment (possibly because the differentiation between distributed and undistributed profits was made by the imposition of a penalty tax on the latter rather than by allowing a deduction for dividends). The major drawback of undistributed profits taxation is that it discourages internal financing by corporations and thus may reduce saving and investment. On the other hand, some believe it is unwise as a matter of policy to permit corporations to avoid the capital markets for financing their investment programmes.

If dividend relief is given at the individual level, there are three possibilities. The first is the 'withholding' method, under which all or a portion of the corporate tax is regarded as having been paid at the source by the stockholder. The taxpayer includes the tax paid at the source in his income and then receives a tax credit for that amount. This method was used in Great Britain from the enactment of the 1803 income tax until 1965, and was restored in 1974. Tax burdens of shareholders on distributed corporate income are the same as the burdens under the undistributed profits tax approach. The second alternative is to permit the taxpayer to exclude some or all of his dividends from his tax return; and the third is to permit him to take a credit against his final tax liability computed at a flat percentage of the amount of dividends he receives. The United States exempts the first $100 of dividends; and Canada uses the dividend-credit approach at a rate of 20 per cent.

Neither the exclusion nor the credit can be regarded as a satisfactory method of removing double taxation, since neither can remove the same proportion of the excess taxation of dividends throughout the income scale. In contrast, the undistributed profits approach and the withholding method remove the same proportion at all income levels.

The desirability of doing something about the double taxation of dividends is still in dispute. First, corporations are viable economic units with characteristics and behaviour patterns that have very little relationship to the income and other characteristics of their stockholders. Moreover, stockholders in large, publicly-held corporations have only indirect and remote influence on management policies. On these grounds, many experts believe that a modern tax system would be incomplete without a separate tax on corporate enterprises. Second, the argument for moderating or removing the double taxation of dividends assumes that the corporate tax rests on the corporation and, ultimately, the stockholder. If the corporate income tax is shifted forwards in the form of higher prices (or backwards in the form of lower wages), the case for integration collapses. My own view is that the corporation income tax is a tax on owners of capital (see ch. 2).

If integration of the corporate and personal income taxes were considered appropriate, some solution of the capital gains problem would be an essential first step. Under a system of full taxation of capital gains, including constructive realisation at death, generous provision might well be made for alleviating the double tax on distributed profits. Where capital gains are either not taxed at all or are taxed at very low rates, the case for integration is weak. No country has yet resolved all of these problems satisfactorily.

Fluctuating incomes

The use of an annual accounting period combined with progressive rates results in a heavier tax burden on fluctuating incomes than on an equal amount of income distributed evenly over the years. This type of discrimination is hard to defend on equity or economic grounds. Taxpayers do not and cannot arrange their business and personal affairs to conform with the calendar. Annual income fluctuations are frequently beyond the control of the taxpayers, yet they are taxed as if 12 months were a suitable horizon for decision-making. In addition, in the absence of averaging, there are great pressures for moderating the impact of the graduated rates on fluctuating incomes by lowering the rates applicable to them. Reduced rates on capital gains are often justified on this basis, although the reductions more than compensate for the absence of averaging.

There may also be a connection between the treatment of fluctuating incomes and incentives to take risks. Even with generous provisions for offsetting losses against gains, business incomes are taxed more heavily than other incomes under a progressive, annual income tax because (a) they fluctuate more than other incomes and (b) the losses do not come off the top of the taxpayer's income during the loss-offset period and are therefore not credited at the maximum rate. On the assumption that there is a correlation between income variability and risk, a tax system using a one-year accounting period is more burdensome on venturesome than on safe investments and thus is more discouraging to risk-taking than a tax system having a longer accounting period.

Experience with general-averaging systems has been disappointing, largely because the methods used have been based on a variant of the moving average. This requires large tax payments when incomes fall below the average and small payments when they rise above it. Taxpayers properly regard such an arrangement as highly inequitable. It is now known that the payment problem may be solved by making the averaging adjustment in the form of a refund. For example, taxpayers might be permitted to average their incomes once every five years and to receive a refund (or credit) for any amount of tax actually paid in excess of 105 or 110 per cent of the tax on the average income during the averaging period. The

United States adopted a variant of this method in 1964 and now allows individuals to average their incomes over a four-year period where the income in the current year exceeds the average of the three prior years by more than 40 per cent and this excess is more than $3000.

Many averaging systems, varying from cumulative lifetime averaging for every taxpayer to averaging over fairly short periods for specific types of volatile incomes, have been explored in the literature. All averaging proposals would create problems of compliance and administration and might involve substantial revenue losses, particularly if applied to the mass of taxpayers. With the advent of electronic machines, it will be possible to solve most of the administrative problems, but the revenue implications may remain serious.

CONCLUSION

The personal income tax is still in the process of development. Methods of differentiating tax liabilities of single persons and families of different size are unsatisfactory. There is increasing recognition that capital gains and losses should enter the tax base, but the equity, economic and administrative objectives of capital gains taxation are difficult to reconcile. The appropriate relationship between the personal and the corporate income tax continues to be disputed. Little progress has been made to alleviate the excessive burden of the income tax on fluctuating income. Finally, the concept of income subject to tax departs considerably in most countries from an economic definition of income, and too many special allowances are made for specific sources and uses of income.

Despite all these problems, the personal income tax is the best tax yet devised, and it will continue to be an indispensable and significant element of all modern tax systems for the indefinite future.

4. Comprehensive Income Tax Reform*

A modern tax system for an advanced industrial nation has a heavy load to carry. It first must raise the right amount of revenue, which depends not only on the size of the budget, but also on the state of the economy. In addition, the modern tax system should distribute the required revenues fairly among the citizens, promote economic growth and stability, and be as simple as possible to understand and to comply with. Frequently, some of these objectives conflict, and one must be sacrificed for another to be realised. Current disagreements over tax policy reflect differences of opinion regarding the impact of taxes and relative weight attached to the various objectives.

Unfortunately, the taxes we are now paying are neither sufficient to cover the legitimate costs of the federal government nor are they levied fairly and efficiently. There also is widespread agreement that the tax system has become much too complicated and that it is time to simplify it. There is considerable support for what may be called 'comprehensive tax reform', but few people understand what such reform really means and how it would affect them. The purpose of this chapter is to explain what is wrong with the income tax system and how it could be revised to meet the USA's future needs.

TAX EQUITY

Public finance experts think of the concept of fairness, or equity, in taxation in two dimensions: vertical and horizontal. *Vertical* equity is concerned with the fairness of the tax system as among people in different income classes. Most people accept *progressive* taxation as the fairest way to distribute the tax burden among income classes; that is, we believe that rich people should not only pay more than poor people but also that they should pay a larger percentage of their income. The US tax system as a whole (including federal, state and local taxes) is progressive, but only modestly so.[1]

Horizontal equity is concerned with the distribution of the tax burden

---

*Adapted from 'Comprehensive Income Tax Reform', *Tax Policy: New Directions and Possibilities,* (Center for National Policy, November 1984), pp. 13–18.

among people in similar economic circumstances. This requires equal taxation of equal incomes, except where an important national objective can be achieved most efficiently by the tax route (which is rarely the case). While the US tax system is barely consistent with the criterion of vertical equity, it violates the principle of horizontal equity to a substantial degree. Numerous special deductions, exclusions and tax credits create large differences in tax burdens among people in the same economic circumstances, and are either inefficient or detrimental to the national interest.

Few people realise how much revenue is lost through the special provisions in the tax law. Because these provisions are disguised payments to individuals, they are now officially called *tax expenditures.* The Congressional Budget Office calculates that the tax expenditures in the federal income tax system will amount to over $400 billion in fiscal year 1985, or just about as much as is now collected from individual and corporation income taxes.

It should be emphasised that these are *not* loopholes. Nor are they something that a sinister Congress slipped over on an unsuspecting public. They are not concentrated in any particular income group but run across the range of taxpayers, here favouring the high income group, there the low income groups. They give special consideration for many reasons, which at the time of enactment seemed appropriate to the Congress. But they take huge chunks out of the tax base and set precedents for still more erosion to satisfy people who believe they should be given similar favoured treatment.

How difficult would it be to patch up the income tax? Why not remove the special provisions and broaden the tax base, so that we can all have lower rates? This sounds good to most people, but when tax reformers become specific, there is considerable resistance. For example, the aged receive a double exemption; unemployment compensation is not taxed until an individual's other income is more than $12,000 if single and $18,000 if married; and half of social security benefits are taxable only to those with other income of $25,000 if single or $32,000 if married. None of these preferences is consistent with the economists' criteria for a good income tax, but there is very little support for removing them.

To take another example. Most of the personal deductions are really not needed from the standpoint of tax theory. When exemptions are modest, allowance should be made for unusual expenses, like medical costs and large casualty losses, to reach a taxpayer's real 'ability to pay'; most of the other deductions are not necessary. But such deductions as those for interest on home mortgages and other consumer debt, contributions to churches, educational institutions and research organisations, and state and local income, sales and property taxes are considered sacrosanct by Congress.

Finally, would it be desirable to eliminate the exemption for interest on state and municipal bonds? This exemption permits states, counties and cities to borrow at less cost. At the same time, it permits many wealthy people to receive large incomes without paying any tax at all. The federal government can help state and local governments in many ways, but this one is perhaps the most inefficient. Congress has rejected the idea of substituting for the income tax exemption a direct subsidy which would reduce state and local borrowing costs at less cost to the federal government.

There are, of course, many provisions in the tax law which are 'loopholes' in the sense that most people use that term. The ability to borrow money, the interest on which is deductible under the income tax, and to invest the proceeds in assets yielding non-taxable or partially taxable income is one example. Another is the financing of investments by private firms through tax-exempt revenue bonds (to pay for mortgages, pollution control equipment, airport facilities, and similar activities). Still another is the favourable treatment of profits from exports. Clearly, many revisions could be made that would fall short of comprehensive reform, yet would improve the equity of the tax system.

TAX EFFICIENCY

Every item removed from the tax base reduces revenue and probably makes the income tax less fair. Most economists also believe that special treatment of particular groups or activities is undesirable from an economic standpoint, because such treatment leads to inefficient use of resources. Many people now invest their money in ventures that do not yield a profit in the economic sense, but yield a large income after the tax saving is taken into account.

It is not easy to promote economic growth through changes in the tax structure. In the first place, the response of different individuals and businesses to particular tax incentives cannot be predicted. High personal tax rates may discourage people from earning more income through greater effort or through saving; but they also may have the opposite effect because they reduce the income left for spending. Second, to promote growth, tax changes must increase those activities that will raise the rate of growth of productivity and this, in turn, requires a greater rate of innovation and more saving and investment. This is not an easy thing to do and most of what has been done so far through the tax system has been wasteful and inefficient.[2]

Two examples of the inefficiency of tax devices illustrate the problem. First, in 1981 Congress permitted wage- and salary-earners to invest up to

$2000 a year in tax-free Individual Retirement Accounts (IRAs). Formerly, such a deduction was allowed only for individuals who were not covered by pension plans. Under the 1981 law, even individuals who are already covered by pension plans are permitted to invest in tax-free IRAs. The purpose of this provision was to increase individual saving; in fact, saving has actually *declined* somewhat as a percentage of disposable income since 1981. Most people who have invested in IRAs have simply switched funds from taxable accounts to the non-taxable IRAs without increasing their net saving. The cost to the Treasury of the expanded IRAs is now estimated to be about $9 billion a year.

A second example is the revision of depreciation allowances made in 1981. Under the old law, tax depreciation formulae had some relation to the actual wear-and-tear on plant and equipment. Under the new law, all assets are divided into four groups and the rate of depreciation allowed for each group is unrelated to actual depreciation. In addition, a 10 per cent tax credit is allowed on all purchases of equipment by business firms. Numerous calculations have been made to estimate the effect of these provisions on the taxes paid in various industries. These calculations show that the new depreciation allowances, combined with the investment credit and the deduction for interest paid on borrowed money, have introduced huge discrepancies in tax burdens.[3] Some firms and industries pay a large tax, while others are in effect subsidised on their investments. The cost of the new depreciation system and the investment credit is in excess of $35 billion a year.

Many other special provisions in the tax law erode the tax base and also produce great distortions in the economy. The effective rate of tax on the total income of corporations exceeded 40 per cent in the early 1950s, but declined almost continuously during the next 30 years until it reached 13 per cent in 1982 (see Table 4.1). The tax on many items of business equipment is either zero or negative under the corporate tax now in effect (i.e. the government is actually subsidising such investments). Economists and many other observers have concluded that the economic distortions created by the tax laws are serious and should be eliminated as quickly as possible, even if no additional revenue is obtained from the corporate tax.

TAX COMPLIANCE AND ADMINISTRATION

The most common complaint against the income tax is that it has become excessively complicated for taxpayers and administrators, as well as for tax practitioners. Millions of people now pay private business firms to prepare their tax returns. The Internal Revenue Code itself is virtually unreadable, and few tax lawyers or tax accountants are familiar with every facet of the

Table 4.1: General Corporation Income Tax Rate and Effective Rate of the
Federal Corporation Income Tax, Selected Years, 1955–82

Year	Corporation Income tax rate (per cent)	Corporation profits before tax[a] (billions of dollars)	Federal corporation taxes[b]	
			Amount (billions of dollars)	Per cent of profit before tax
1955	52.00	49.3	20.8	42.2
1960	52.00	50.2	20.5	40.8
1965	48.00	80.4	27.6	34.3
1970	49.20	78.5	26.3	33.5
1975	48.00	136.3	38.2	28.0
1980	46.00	254.8	58.6	23.0
1981	46.00	261.9	53.5	20.4
1982	46.00	238.3	31.3	13.1

Source: Joseph A. Pechman, *Federal Tax Policy* (Brookings Institute, 4th edn., 1983)
Table 5.3, p. 144.

a. Total profits before the special depreciation allowances and other tax preferences.
b. Excludes the temporary surcharge of 1968–70.

law. In recent years, the tax laws have become lengthier (the 1984 Act was
over 1000 pages long) as Congress has attempted to narrow some tax
preferences while at the same time adding new ones.

A major source of the complexity is the tendency of Congress and most
administrations to promote certain economic and social objectives through
the income tax rather than through direct appropriations. Special deductions or tax credits now are available to help reduce energy usage, increase
incentives to save and invest, encourage firms to hire disadvantaged
workers, raise private outlays for research and development, moderate the
tax burden on low-income wage-earners, and promote other objectives.
Every departure from the normal tax structure makes the income tax return
more complicated and imposes additional burdens of record-keeping on
the tax payer. The practice violates the principle of horizontal equity,
narrows the tax base, and keeps federal tax rates higher than they need to
be.

COMPREHENSIVE TAXATION

The solution to this complexity is to simplify the tax laws by repealing the special provisions and starting all over again. In the past, the forces arrayed against simplification have been too powerful to permit any progress to be made in this way. But tax simplification has become more attractive as the complications have multiplied.

The idea is to tax all incomes without any exclusions, tax credits, or personal deductions (except for those that take account of unavoidable reductions in ability to pay); the increased tax base would then be used to reduce tax rates. Individual taxpayers would add up their income from all sources, subtract their personal exemptions and unusual expenses, and calculate their tax liability from a tax table or the schedule of tax rates. Corporations would report all their receipts, deduct their actual business expenses (including economic depreciation), and pay tax on their net profits. With fully comprehensive tax bases, federal individual and corporation income tax rates would be cut by a minimum of 40 per cent across the board.

The Individual Income Tax

The base of a comprehensive individual income tax would conform as closely as possible to the concept of 'economic' income. In addition to the items now taxed, adjusted gross income would include capital gains and dividends in full, interest on life insurance savings, employer contributions to health and insurance plans, interest on newly-issued state and local government securities, workmen's compensation payments, and veterans' benefits. Under the present law, all unemployment benefits are taxed only if the taxpayer has other income of more than $12,000 if single or $32,000 if married. Under a comprehensive tax, all unemployment benefits and social security benefits in excess of the amount contributed through the employee payroll tax would be fully taxable.[4] Deductions for individual retirement plans (IRAs) would be available only to those not covered by pension plans.

Most of the personal deductions would be wiped out under a comprehensive income tax. Among all the deductions now allowed, only the deductions for unusual medical expenses and casualty losses are really needed to refine the income concept to reflect ability to pay. The law now limits casualty loss deductions to the excess over 10 per cent of income; the same limit could be applied to medical expenses without violating the ability to pay criterion. Interest payments would be deductible only up to the amount of property income reported on tax returns (with any excess carried forward to future years), on the principle that only net investment income should be taxed.

The minimum level of income subject to tax should be set high enough to exempt only individuals and families with incomes below the poverty line.

This can be done through a combination of personal exemptions and standard deductions (or 'zero bracket amounts'). Additional exemptions for the aged and blind would be unnecessary because the minimum taxable level would be high enough to exempt those who cannot pay taxes.

Tax rates under a comprehensive income tax could be set at any level and with any degree of graduation, depending on the progressivity desired. Most comprehensive income tax plans attempt to maintain the present degree of progressivity, on the ground that it best expresses the current judgement of the voters. To simplify the tax calculations, the four tax rate schedules now in the law would be replaced by one schedule. The penalty when two earners marry could be avoided by a special deduction similar to the deduction now in the law for two-earner couples.

Table 4.2 illustrates a comprehensive income tax constructed along these lines. The base for this tax is similar to the one already described, with the exceptions that only half of social security benefits and one-third of premiums paid by employers for employee health plans are included. The social security exception is made to avoid the need to compute the contributions made by taxpayers toward their retirement benefits; the health insurance exception conforms approximately with the proposals made by both the Carter and Reagan administrations. To raise the minimum taxable levels to the 1984 poverty lines for all family sizes, the personal exemption is increased from $1000 to $1750 per capita and the zero bracket amount is increased from $2300 for single people and $3400 for married couples to a flat $4000. To raise the revenue produced by the present individual income tax and to approximate present effective tax rates, a nine-bracket rate schedule ranging from 9 per cent in the bottom bracket to 28 per cent in the top bracket is substituted for the present fourteen-bracket schedule ranging from 11 per cent to 50 per cent. (The number of brackets could be reduced even more, with only a slight worsening of the approximation of present law effective rates.)

The tax liabilities under this tax and under present law may be compared by examining the first two columns of Table 4.2. Under present law, the average effective federal tax rate on total income (that is, including income that is not now taxed) rises from 0.7 per cent for those with incomes of less than $5000 to 26.4 per cent for incomes of $500,000 to $1,000,000, and then declines to 23.1 per cent for income of $1,000,000 or more. The decline at the top reflects the reduced rate on long-term capital gains, which are heavily concentrated in the top income class. The average effective rates of tax that would be paid under the comprehensive income tax are fairly close to those in present law for all income classes, except at the bottom where tax burdens would be reduced by the higher personal exemptions and zero bracket amounts.

The 'Flat' Tax

Recently new recruits have appeared in the movement for comprehensive income taxation. They are people who see the virtues of broadening the tax base from the standpoints both of horizontal equity and simplicity, but they prefer a single rate to the graduated system currently being used. The single rate would be between 15 and 20 per cent, depending on how broad the base would be.[5] Some argue that a 'flat' tax would simplify the income tax even more (which is true), but it would accomplish this by redistributing tax burdens from the highest to the low- and middle-income classes.

The third column of Table 4.2 shows the tax liabilities under a flat rate tax with the comprehensive tax base already described. To raise the revenue needed, a single rate of 17 per cent would be required. A comparison of the second and third columns illustrates the effect of substituting a flat rate for the mildly graduated system illustrated in the second column. Average tax payments would be lower under the flat tax than under present law in all income classes above $50,000 and below $10,000, while the taxes paid by those with incomes between $10,000 and $50,000 would be higher. At the top of the income scale, the flat tax would reduce average tax liabilities by 30–40 per cent. The reduction in average tax burdens at the bottom of the income scale is the result of the increase in the minimum taxable levels.

Two types of simplification would be made by the flat tax. First, a single rate would avoid 'bracket creep', that is, the higher rates experienced when inflation pushes taxpayers into higher tax brackets. Thus, it would eliminate the need to adjust the tax brackets (though not the exemptions and zero bracket amount) for inflation. Second, there would be no marital penalty under the flat tax, except for any reductions in exemptions or zero bracket amounts occurring after marriage. While these would be additional simplifications, they do not justify the wholesale redistribution of tax burdens that would be brought about by the flat tax.

Although it is arithmetically impossible to approximate the present distribution of federal tax burdens with a flat tax, this is not the case for state tax systems which stop graduation at much lower levels than under the federal tax. Such taxes can be converted to flat taxes without doing violence to the distribution of tax burdens. For example, the California income tax, which is graduated up to a rate of 11 per cent, applying to taxable income beginning at about $50,000 for joint returns, can be approximated by a flat tax of 7 per cent. A bipartisan group of state legislators has introduced a comprehensive flat tax in California and there is considerable support for this tax by conservatives and liberals alike.

The Corporation Income Tax

Like the individual income tax, the corporation income tax appears to be a very heavy tax (the nominal rate is 46 per cent for corporations with taxable

Table 4.2: Effective Tax Rates under Present Law and under a Comprehensive Income Tax Using Alternative Tax Rate Plans, by Income Class, 1984 (Income classes in thousands of dollars; rates in per cent)

Expanded adjusted gross income class[b]	Present law	Alternative plan[a]	
		Graduated rates, 9–28 per cent[c]	Flat tax rate, 17 per cent
0–5,000	0.7	0.0	0.0
5,000–10,000	4.0	1.6	3.0
10,000–15,000	6.0	4.2	7.1
15,000–20,000	7.7	6.5	9.2
20,000–25,000	9.1	8.3	10.6
25,000–35,000	10.0	10.0	11.8
35,000–50,000	11.4	12.4	13.0
50,000–100,000	15.5	16.3	14.2
100,000–500,000	23.0	22.1	15.4
500,000–1,000,000	26.4	25.4	15.9
1,000,000 and over	23.1	26.4	16.2
All classes[c]	12.0	12.0	12.0

Source: Joseph A. Pechman and John Karl Scholz, 'Comprehensive Income Taxation and Rate Reduction', *Tax Notes*, Vol. 17 (11 October, 1982), Brookings Reprint 390.

a. Assumes zero-bracket amount of $4000 and exemption of $1750 per capita plus an additional $1750 for heads of households under both plans.
b. Adjusted gross income plus sick pay, excluded capital gains and dividends, interest on life insurance and state and local bond interest, all unemployment benefits, 50 per cent of social security benefits, workmen's compensation, veteran's benefits, tax preferences reported for purposes of the minimum tax, one-third of employer-provided health insurance, employer-provided life insurance, and IRA deductions by those covered under private pension plans.
c. Rates are the same for all marital statuses: they rise from 9 per cent on taxable income of less than $5000 to 28 per cent on the amount of taxable income in excess of $150,000. Married couples with two earners would receive a deduction of 25 per cent of the earnings of the spouse with the lower earnings (for earnings up to $50,000).

profits of more than $100,000), but the actual tax paid is much lower because a considerable fraction of corporate income is not taxed (see Table 4.1). Like a comprehensive individual income tax, a comprehensive corporation income tax would tax all corporate profits, with deductions only for legitimate business expenses.

A comprehensive income tax would begin by eliminating all the special provisions now in the law for particular firms and industries. Corporate capital gains would be taxed at the same rate as other profits. Regular depreciation would be substituted for the special provisions of the oil industry (percentage depletion and the intangible drilling costs deduction).

Deferral of tax through the use of foreign subsidiaries would be eliminated and the recently enacted Foreign Sales Corporation provision, which effectively exempts from US tax about 15 per cent of the taxable income from export sales, would be repealed. All tax credits, including the investment tax credit, would be removed. The special tax rates for small corporations also would be eliminated.

The most important reform that would be made under a comprehensive corporation income tax would be to permit a deduction only for the actual wear-and-tear of plant and equipment, rather than to use an excessively generous method to calculate depreciation allowances. As already noted, the Accelerated Cost Recovery System (ACRS) enacted in 1981 subsidises many investments. It is now possible to give actual depreciation rates for various classes of assets on the basis of changes in prices of used assets, and these rates could be substituted for the arbitrary formulas used in recent years.

The average rate reduction that would be possible under a comprehensive corporation income tax is roughly the same as the rate reduction under the comprehensive individual tax. The present 46 per cent could be reduced to 28 per cent without reducing corporation tax revenues. However, tax burdens would be distributed very differently. Capital-intensive firms and industries, businesses operating abroad, and the minerals industries would pay higher taxes, while other firms and industries would pay lower taxes. The distortionary effect of the present tax would be eliminated.

CONCLUSION: HOW FAR SHOULD WE GO?

The foregoing descriptions for individual and corporation income taxes conforming to the comprehensive tax ideal is obviously a purist's dream. My own preference would be to go as far as these models suggest, because it would be difficult to justify retaining some special provisions while eliminating others. Moreover, comprehensive income taxes provide the basis for raising more revenue with minimal increases in marginal tax rates. Each percentage point increase in individual and corporation tax rates across the board would raise federal revenues by the equivalent of about 0.6 per cent of the GNP in 1989.

I recognise that few people would go as far as I would in broadening the tax base. The major competing proposals would continue some of the personal deductions, such as the deductions for charitable contributions, mortgage interest, and state and local taxes. Most also would continue some tax preferences, such as those for recipients of social security and unemployment benefits, interest on state and local government bonds, deductions for IRA contributions even for people already covered by pension plans, and so on. These are practical compromises by people who are close to the political process and are able to evaluate the trade-offs necessary to implement a more comprehensive tax approach.

Each deduction, exclusion or tax credit now in the law has a strong constituency to protect what it already has achieved. The lobbies are already working to undermine the entire tax reform effort. In view of what has happened to the tax system in recent years, it is hard to believe that these pressures can be successfully withstood. But the stakes are high and the results of this tug of war will be important for the welfare of the nation. Comprehensive income tax reform would pay handsome dividends in greater horizontal equity, less complexity, and improved economic performance.

NOTES

1. In 1980, taxes reduced the inequality of the distribution of income by less than 3 per cent, even on the most progressive assumptions regarding the incidence of the major taxes. See Joseph A. Pechman *Who Paid the Taxes, 1966–1985?* (Washington, D.C. The Brookings Institution, 1985), p. 55.
2. For a review of the evidence, see Barry P. Bosworth, *Tax Incentives and Economic Growth* (Brookings Institution, 1984).
3. See Don Fullerton and Yolanda Kodrzycki Henderson, 'Incentive Effects of Taxes on Income from Capital: Alternative Policies in the 1980s', in Charles R. Hulton and Isabel V. Sawhill (eds), *The Legacy of Reaganomics: Prospects for Long-Term Growth* (The Urban Institute, 1985).
4. Under the economic concept of income, employer contributions to public and private pension plans would be taxable to the employee and earnings on these contributions would be taxable when they accrue; the benefits would then be non-taxable when received. However, because many contributions are not set aside (vested) in an employee's account until after a number of years of service, it is not practical to estimate the contributions made on behalf of each employee or the earnings accumulated in their accounts.
5. For an illustrative list of the proposals, see Joint Committee on Taxation, *Analysis of Proposals Relating to Comprehensive Tax Reform,* (21 September 1984), pp. 39–41.

5. Erosion of the Individual Income Tax*

The US individual income tax has been eroded by numerous special provisions which remove large chunks from the tax base and reduce the revenue potential of any set of tax rates. To determine the extent of erosion of the income tax, a comprehensive definition of income must be adopted to provide the norm against which the existing tax can be assessed.[1] I use a concept which corresponds as closely as possible to an economic concept of income, i.e. consumption plus tax payments plus (or minus) the net increase (decrease) in the value of assets during the year. The modifications to this definition are dictated largely by practical administrative considerations or by historical precedents which need not (or could not) be broken for this purpose. First, capital gains are included in income when realised or when transferred to others through gift or bequest; second, gifts and inheritances are excluded from income; third, a separate corporation tax is retained, and all dividends (but not undistributed profits) are included in income; fourth, employer contributions to private pension plans are not considered current income to the employee; and fifth, imputed rent on owner-occupied homes is taxed.

The first of these modifications is made because it is probably impractical to include capital gains in income until they are realised or transferred. The second and third accept the present practice of separating estate and gift taxation and corporation income taxation from individual income taxation. The fourth is dictated by the fact that taxation of employer contributions for pensions involves difficult practical problems that would require basic revisions in the nation's private pension structure. The fifth recognises the practical difficulties of calculating imputed rent for tax purposes.

A tax base which closely approximates this modified definition of economic income would involve the following revisions of the present federal individual income tax law: treatment as ordinary income of all realised capital gains (or losses) and of gains transferred by gift or bequest;

*Adapted from 'Individual Income Tax Erosion by Income Classes', with Benjamin A. Okner, *The Economics of Federal Subsidy Programs,* a compendium of papers submitted to the Joint Economic Committee, Part 1, *General Study Papers,* 92 Cong., 2 sess. (1972), pp. 13–40; Amsterdam: and *Federal Tax Policy* (Brookings Institution, 4th edn, 1983), pp. 74–6.

elimination of the tax exemption for interest from state and local government bonds; limitation of depletion allowances to cost depletion; taxation of interest on the current-year increment in the cash surrender value of life insurance policies; taxation of transfer payments as ordinary income; elimination of the deduction for amounts in individual retirement accounts (IRAs) by those who are already covered by pension plans; elimination of most itemised deductions; elimination of the special exemptions for the aged and blind and the credit for the elderly; and elimination of the dividend exclusion. In addition, the rate advantages (but not the mechanics) of income-splitting for married couples are eliminated.

The rationale for the major revisions which are incorporated in the comprehensive income tax is as follows.

CAPITAL GAINS

Since 1978, U.S. taxpayers have been including 40 per cent of realised net long-term gains in adjusted gross income. Preferential treatment for such income has been justified on two grounds: first, full taxation of capital gains accrued over a long period of time in the year of realisation would be inequitable; and second, taxation of gains at the ordinary income tax rates would discourage sales or other transfers of assets. The problem of bunching of capital gains in the year of realisation can be handled by an averaging system, and the disincentive to transfer assets would be greatly moderated by taxing unrealised capital gains on assets transferred by gift or death, and allowing full offsets and carry-overs for capital losses against both capital gains and ordinary income. Moreover, full inclusion of capital gains in the tax base would permit a substantial reduction in the top bracket marginal rates, which would keep the tax rates on capital gains at moderate levels.[2]

STATE AND LOCAL BOND INTEREST

Complete exemption is now accorded interest received on state and local government bonds. In recent years, as their revenue needs have increased, state and local governments have had to appeal to taxpayers in lower income brackets to market their securities. In addition, state and local governments have been issuing tax-exempt revenue bonds which are used to finance purely private activities (e.g. home mortgages, airport facilities, and pollution control equipment). The response has been a sharp rise in interest rates, with the result that the benefits of the tax exemption to wealthy taxpayers have increased while the benefits of the exemption to state and local governments have been eroded. The major impediment to the taxation of interest on these securities has been the fear that the increased interest costs would be too burdensome for the states and local governments. This problem can be eliminated, however, by substituting for the tax exemption a subsidy for interest payments on state-local securities.[3]

INTEREST ON LIFE INSURANCE SAVINGS

The tax preference accorded to savings invested by individuals in life insurance results from the fact that interest accumulated on policy reserves is not taxable to the policyholder, while the insurance proceeds are not taxable to the beneficiaries after the death of the insured. The omission of this type of income from the tax base can hardly be justified when other types of property income (dividends, interest, rents) are subject to tax. The income on life insurance savings could be taxed by including in adjusted gross income the portion of the annual increases in the cash surrender value of life insurance policies that reflect interest earned on past savings.[4]

TRANSFER PAYMENTS AND FRINGE BENEFITS

Transfer payments are not taxable mainly on the grounds that most of the recipients would not be subject to tax even if such payments were included in the tax base. However, not all transfer payments are received by the poor; and some recipients are frequently much better-off than their neighbours, who cannot exclude any portion of their income in computing their tax liabilities. It would be better to include the transfer payments fully in income and to allow for ability to pay through the personal exemptions. If the exemptions are considered too low, it would be more equitable to discontinue the exclusions for transfer payments and to raise the exemptions or the low-income allowances.[5]

As tax rates rose, employee compensation received in non-taxable form grew rapidly. Non-taxable benefits now include contributions by employees to employee pension plans, employer-financed health and welfare plans, group life insurance, employee discounts, and scholarships for the children of university faculty members. Such exclusions from income are unwarranted, but Congress has not acted on these benefits for fear of alienating large employee groups and trade unions.[6]

INDIVIDUAL RETIREMENT ACCOUNTS (IRAs)

In 1981, taxpayers were permitted to accumulate tax-free amounts set aside in individual retirement accounts, even if they are already eligible for a tax-favoured pension plan. A deduction is allowed for wages and salaries up to $2000 ($2250 for a couple with only one earner). By 1983, the deduction amounted to over $30 billion, yet individual saving has not increased. The reason is that most individuals simply shifted funds from a taxable account to an untaxable IRA account without increasing their saving. Few people in the low income brackets take advantage of this provision, both because the tax advantage is negligible for them and they have no room in their budgets for saving. Such an inequitable deduction is clearly not appropriate in a comprehensive income tax.

DEDUCTIONS

There are a few strict criteria by which the personal deductions can be judged. It is clear, however, that the deductions now allowed under the federal income tax are much too generous. Our calculations allow itemised deductions only for casualty losses and medical expenses in excess of 10 per cent of income, charitable contributions in excess of 2 per cent of income, and interest up to the amount of property income reported by the individual on his tax return, and the miscellaneous itemised deductions (which consist primarily of unreimbursed expenses of employees and alimony).[7]

SPECIAL EXEMPTIONS AND CREDITS FOR THE AGED AND THE BLIND

Taxpayers over age 65 and the blind receive an additional personal exemption and the elderly and permanently disabled receive a 15 per cent tax credit on income up to a maximum of $5000 ($7500 on joint returns), less income received from public or private pension plans. The major objection to these provisions is that they give the largest tax advantage to those with the highest incomes and discriminate against those who continue to work. Again, with adequate personal exemptions, there is no need for the additional blindness or age exemptions or for the credit. The revenue gained could be used to good advantage to raise social security benefits for all aged or handicapped persons and to increase the personal exemptions, if necessary.

DIVIDEND EXCLUSION

The dividend exclusion of $100 is a vestige of the tax reform of 1954, which introduced both a 4 per cent credit and an exclusion of $50 ($100 on joint returns) for dividends to mitigate the so-called double taxation of dividends. In 1964, the credit was reduced to 2 per cent but the exclusion was increased to $100 ($200 for joint returns). In 1965 the credit was eliminated. If the additional tax on dividends resulting from the imposition of the corporation and individual income taxes is regarded as undesirable, it is widely agreed that the present exclusion does not adequately solve the problem. It would be better to eliminate the exclusion and to tackle the problem of double taxation directly; or to use whatever revenues may be available to moderate the tax burden on dividends by reductions in the general corporate tax rate.[8]

INCOME SPLITTING

Income splitting for tax purposes between husbands and wives was adopted in the United States because eight states had community property laws, which treated income as if the ownership was divided equally between husband and wife. The Congress universalised income splitting in 1948 in an effort to restore geographic tax equality and to prevent wholesale disruption of local property laws and procedures for the purpose of obtaining the benefits of income splitting. In 1951, half the advantage of income splitting was given to persons who were defined as 'heads of households'; and the Tax Reform Act 1969 reduced the tax rates of single persons in the interest of moderating the tax discrimination against them. In 1981, married couples with two earners were given a deduction of 10 per cent of the earned income of the spouse with the lower earnings up to $30,000.

The practical effect of income splitting is to reduce tax liabilities in the middle and higher income classes by very large amounts and to produce large differences in the tax burden of single persons and married couples, which are difficult to rationalise on theoretical grounds. It would be possible to differentiate among taxpayers units, if desired, by varying the personal exemptions with the size of income as well as the number of persons in units (with both a minimum and a maximum). This procedure could be used to achieve almost any degree of differentiation among families while avoiding most of the problems and anomalies produced by income splitting.[9]

The rate advantages of income splitting can be eliminated easily without restoring the old inequities between residents of community property and non-community property states. It would be necessary to have two rate schedules, one for single persons and the other for married couples with brackets half as wide as the brackets in the single person schedule.[10] Married couples would continue to have the privilege of filing either joint or separate returns, but they would be permitted to split their incomes only if they file jointly. The two-earner deduction would be retained to alleviate the so-called marital penalty on two-earner couples and to allow for the omission from the tax base of the services of the spouse who stays at home in one-earner couples.[11]

ACCELERATED DEPRECIATION

Prior to 1954, the cost of real estate and other depreciable property was usually written off using the 'straight-line method' which involves a uniform amount of depreciation each year during an assets useful life. Accelerated depreciation (i.e. depreciation write-offs which concentrate a large part of the asset cost during the early years of the assets life) was first authorised in 1954 to spur new capital investment and thereby increase the rate of economic growth. The depreciation allowances were further liberalised in 1962, 1971 and 1981, and an investment credit was enacted in 1964. In recent years, many individuals have used accelerated depreciation for great financial reward (without adding much, if anything, to capital investment), especially in connection with real estate transactions. The abuse occurs as a result of the full deduction for depreciation at ordinary tax rates and subsequent treatment of gains on sales of depreciated property at preferential capital gains rates. Largely because of this abuse, Congress has curtailed—but not fully eliminated—the conversion of accelerated depreciation into capital gains in recent years. A neutral tax base would allow a deduction for actual economic depreciation and eliminate the investment credit.

DEPLETION ALLOWANCES

The depletion allowance on oil and gas was reduced from $27\frac{1}{2}$ per cent to 22 per cent in 1969, and eliminated entirely for the major oil companies in 1976. Nevertheless, the percentage depletion allowances are still generous for small producers and persons receiving income from oil, gas and other mineral properties also benefit from immediate write-offs for exploration and development expenses. These preferences have been justified by the representatives of these industries on national defence grounds, and on the grounds that there are special risks involved in locating and developing

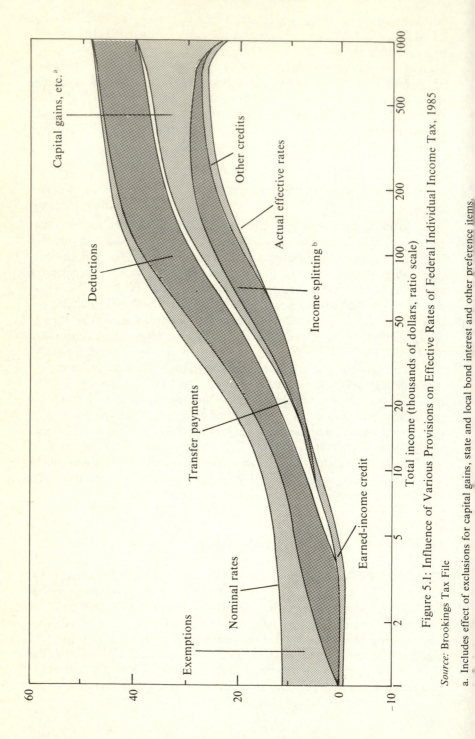

Figure 5.1: Influence of Various Provisions on Effective Rates of Federal Individual Income Tax, 1985

Source: Brookings Tax File

a. Includes effect of exclusions for capital gains, state and local bond interest and other preference items.

mineral resources. Economists have generally concluded that the generous provisions lead to over-investment in the preferred industries and hence tend to result in a serious misallocation of resources.[12]

EFFECT OF EROSION

A fully comprehensive income tax would apply to the total income of individuals less an allowance only for the personal exemptions, without any other deductions, exclusions or tax credits. As can be seen from Figure 5.1, given the US exemptions and tax rates in 1985, such an income tax would begin at a zero effective rate at the bottom end of the income scale and rise in the top levels to a maximum of close to 50 per cent, which is the top marginal rate. The effect of the various special provisions is to lower significantly effective tax rates below this theoretical line throughout the income scale, but particularly at the top. Tax liability is about 5 per cent of an average $10,000 income, 11 per cent at $35,000, and a maximum of 26 per cent at the highest income levels. Only at an income level of about $150,000 does the effective rate reach as high as 20 per cent of total income. The lowest income levels benefit the most from exemptions, while deductions have their greatest impact on the higher income classes. Income splitting is of greatest benefit to couples whose income is between $30,000 and $200,000, while the capital gains provisions are most important in the highest income classes. Because of the capital gains provisions, there is a slight amount of regressivity in the very top classes.

On the whole, therefore, the US income tax is progressive throughout most of the income scale, but the degree of progression is moderate. Moreover, as a result of the numerous tax expenditures, there are often large differences in tax liabilities among taxpayers with equal income. Clearly, horizontal equity would be better served if the same amount of tax were collected on a broader tax base with much lower rates.

NOTES

1. For an analysis of the meaning and significance of comprensive income taxation, both *pro* and *con*, see Boris I. Bittker, Charles O. Galvin, R. A. Musgrave and Joseph A. Pechman, *A Comprehensive Income Tax Base? A Debate* (Federal Tax Press, 1968). See also Richard Goode, *The Individual Income Tax* (Brookings Institution, rev. edn., 1976), chs. VI–VIII; and Joseph A. Pechman, *Federal Tax Policy*, (Brookings Institution, 4th edn, 1983), pp. 74–127.
2. For a discussion of the issues in capital gains taxation, see Martin David,

Individual Income Taxation

Alternative Approaches to Capital Gains Taxation (Brookings Institution, 1968).
3. See David J. Ott and Allan H. Meltzer, *Federal Tax Treatment of State and Local Securities* (Brookings Institution, 1963).
4. See Goode, *op. cit.*, pp. 125–33.
5. The transfer payments we include in our comprehensive tax base are: one half of social security and railworkers' retirement benefits; public assistance; workmens compensation; unemployment insurance; and veterans' disability compensation.
6. The fringe benefits included in taxable income in our tax calculations are one-third of employer-financed health insurance and all of employer-provided health insurance. As already noted, it would be difficult to value contributions by employers to pension plans for each employee because pension rights do not ordinarily vest in the employee until after a considerable number of years of service.
7. For a detailed discussion of the rationale of these revisions see Pechman, *op. cit.*, pp. 86–93.
8. The *pros* and *cons* of the controversy over double taxation of dividends have been discussed at length in the public finance literature. See, for example, Richard Goode, *The Corporation Income Tax* (New York: Wiley, 1951), and Charles E. McLure, Jr. *Must Corporate Income Be Taxed Twice?* (Washington D.C.: Brookings Institution, 1979).
9. Harold M. Groves, *Federal Tax Treatment of the Family* (Washington, D.C.: Brookings Institution 1963). See also ch. 7.
10. In practice, married couples filing joint returns would use the single person's schedule without splitting; only married couples filing separate returns would use the schedule with the split brackets. This actually would be a substantial simplification in comparison with present law which contains *four* rate schedules—one for married persons filing separate returns, a second for single persons, a third for heads-of-households, and a fourth for married persons filing joint returns. Our calculations assume that the rate reductions for single persons enacted in 1951 and 1969 would be removed along with the elimination of the rate advantages of income splitting for married couples.
11. The deduction for two-earner couples, in the calculations for the comprehensive income tax was set at 25 per cent of earnings of the spouse with lower earnings up to $50,000.
12. See Susan R. Agria, 'Special Tax Treatment of Mineral Industries', in *The Taxation of Income From Capital*, Arnold C. Harberger and Martin J. Bailey (eds.) (Washington, D.C. Brookings Institution, 1969), pp. 77–122.

6. The Comprehensive Income Tax Concept*

Professor Boris I. Bittker's long discourse on the concept of 'comprehensive income tax'[1] is a sharp attack on the large and still growing literature on broadening of the income tax base. He concludes [2] that the concept of the comprehensive income tax is vague, that its most enthusiastic supporters 'have drawn back from its implication', that 'it can make no contribution to the elimination of 'preferences' [in taxation]', and that a truly comprehensive income tax base would be a 'disaster'. He sees no easy answer to tax reform: each proposal must be considered on its merits 'in a discouragingly inconclusive process' that gives weight to economic, legal, administrative, political and other pragmatic considerations. Above all, he objects to the 'rhetoric' of the comprehensive income taxation school which has spawned such terms as 'exceptions', 'special provisions', 'preferences', 'loopholes', and 'leakages'. Professor Bittker's admonitions about terminology are useful reminders, but in the rest of his criticisms he is guilty either of setting up strawmen or of misinterpreting the state of affairs.

Professor Bittker has great difficulty understanding the particular concept of income which is used when the term 'comprehensive income' is invoked. He suggests three possibilities: (1) the difference between gross income as defined in section 61(a) of the Internal Revenue Code and expenses, losses, bad debts, and depreciation incurred in the taxpayer's business or profit-motivated transactions (as defined in ss. 162, 165, 166, 167 and 212); (2) the Department of Commerce definition of personal income; and (3) the Haig–Simons economic definition of income (consumption plus the change in value of assets over a period of time).[3]

I know of no one who has attempted to build a comprehensive income tax base beginning with the present code (although I believe that the effort to show how it would have to be changed would be very worthwhile), and Professor Bittker's reference to the code as a basis for reaching a definition of comprehensive income can only be regarded as an attempt to confuse the issue. Similarly, the personal income concept, which was created for purposes of national income accounting and not for income tax purposes,

*Reprinted from 'Comprehensive Income Taxation: A Comment', *Harvard Law Review*, Vol. 81, No. 1 (November 1967), pp. 63–7.

has been explicitly rejected as a suitable definition of income for tax purposes both by those who developed the concept and by supporters of comprehensive income taxation. Contrary to what Bittker implies, personal income has been used only to estimate the amount of under-reporting of income on tax returns and not as a 'normative model' for a comprehensive income tax.[4] Among other things, it excludes all capital gains and losses and employee contributions for social insurance, and includes receipts of non-profit organisations. The only persons who have referred to personal income as a criterion for defining taxable income are those who oppose the taxation of capital gains in full and reject the whole notion of comprehensive income taxation.[5]

Even a cursory examination of the literature discloses that the basic concept used or implied in discussions of comprehensive income taxation is the Haig–Simons definition. It is odd that Bittker has so much trouble satisfying himself that this is the case, since the Haig–Simons definition is repeated almost word for word in the passages he quotes from my article in the *Tax Revision Compendium*[6] and from statements by Brazer[7] and Sneed[8] in the accompanying *Panel Discussions*. A close reading of these basic sources clearly suggests that many other contributors (e.g. Blum, Musgrave, Steger, Surrey and White) were using the Haig–Simons definition.[9] If the literature is not explicit on this point prior to 1959, there is no reason for anybody to be confused after the publication of the *Compendium*.[10]

Professor Bittker's inability to understand what the Haig–Simons definition of income does and does not imply is explained by his failure to recall that the procedure for determining income tax liabilities involves more dimensions than the receipts to be counted as income. Since income is a flow of receipts per unit of time, the term income alone has two dimensions. A third dimension of the tax computation is the taxable unit, and a fourth the personal deductions. While there are problems in identifying the receipts to be included in income, the income concept is neutral regarding (1) the time interval over which income should be measured, (2) the proper unit of taxation, and (3) the personal deductions that might be allowed for income tax purposes. Most of Professor Bittker's discourse is concerned with these three dimensions, which are not supplied by any definition of income, comprehensive or otherwise.[11]

Bittker derives great satisfaction from taunting the proponents of comprehensive income taxation for departing from the Haig–Simons definition in one way or another. But he fails to mention that departures from comprehensiveness are permitted by the proponents, and that they have even stipulated the conditions under which departures would be tolerated.[12] These conditions are, first, that the departure must promote a major national objective and that the tax mechanism is the most efficient method of achieving it; or, second, it is impractical to tax the particular item. For example, the Haig–Simons definition of income would include capital gains as they accrue. Most tax experts believe that this is impractical, and I agree. As a substitute, capital gains are usually included in full in income when they are realised or when they are included in assets that have been transferred by gift or death. I find it hard to believe that taxing capital gains in this way supports Bittker's suggestion[13] that the supporters of comprehensive income taxation have 'drawn back' from its implications, or that this is a 'preference' in the sense that the term is ordinarily used.

The use of appropriate terminology is, however, a troublesome matter. A provision which is regarded as a loophole for one group is often justified as a major improvement in equity or as essential to promote economic growth by another. Tax reform is a serious business, and those who align themselves on one side or the other of a particular issue often use emotion-packed terms to support their positions in public and congressional statements. I have personally eschewed the use of the term 'loophole' for this reason,[14] and I agree with Bittker that it would be better to avoid emotional terms as much as possible.

But he is surely wide of the mark when he suggests that a truly comprehensive income tax base 'will, and should, remain miles away'.[15] Since he never affords himself the luxury of defining taxable income, it will be impossible to check whether his conception of a comprehensive income tax will ever be adopted. Fortunately, Bittker's doubts did not deter the Canadian Royal Commission on Taxation, whose report was published at about the same time as his article.[16] This report recommends a comprehensive income tax for Canada, complete with details for practically all the problems raised by Bittker. The base of the proposed tax would include capital gains, gifts and inheritances, property income on life insurance policy reserves, non-cash benefits provided to employees by their employers, and many other items in his long list.[17] Thus, the report not only challenges Bittker's judgement as to the desirability of comprehensive income taxation, it also suggests that his prediction may well be wide of the mark.[18]

NOTES

1. Bittker, 'A Comprehensive Tax Base as a Goal of Income Tax Reform', *Harvard Law Review*, Vol. 80, (1967).
2. Ibid, pp. 980–5.
3. Ibid., 931–3.
4. These calculations go back to the pioneering work of Dr Selma Goldsmith in bridging the gap between estimates of personal income reported on tax returns.

See Goldsmith, "Appraisal of Basic Data Available for Constructing Income Size Distribution" in *Conference on Research in Income and Wealth, Studies in Income and Wealth,* Vol. 13, no. 266 (1951). My own calculations involve 17 categories of adjustments to reconcile personal income and adjusted gross income. J. Pechman, *Federal Tax Policy* (1966), Table B-1, p. 260. They indicate that the degree of under-reporting of income with the present definition of taxable income was less than 6 per cent in 1963. (Ibid., pp. 256–7). It is amusing that Bittker implies that Richard Goode uses personal income as a normative model merely because Goode compares the amount of taxable income with personal income (Bittker, *op. cit.*, p. 933, n. 17). Although Goode favours substantial broadening of the income tax base, he does not go as far as others who support comprehensive income taxation. See R. Goode, *The Individual Income Tax* (1964), p. 314.

5. See, e.g. Wallich 'Taxation of Capital Gains in the Light of Recent Economic Developments', *National Tax Journal*, Vol. 18, no. 133 (1965), pp. 136–7.

6. Bittker *op. cit.*, p. 929 (quoting from Pechman, 'What Would a Comprehensive Individual Income Tax Yield?', in I *House Comm on Ways and Means*, 86th Cong., 1st Sess., *Tax Revision Compendium of Papers on Broadening the Tax Base* 251, 259 (Comm. Print 1959).

7. Bittker *op. cit.*, p. 930, no. 10 (quoting from Brazer, in *Panel Discussions on Income Tax Revision Before the House Committee on Ways and Means*, 86th Cong., 1st Sess. 201, 1960).

8. Bittker *op. cit.*, p. 930, no. 10 (quoting from Sneed, in *Panel Discussions* p. 12).

9. See Blum, 'Tax Policy and Preferencial Provisions in the Income Tax Base' in I *Compendium 77; Musgrave*, 'How Progressive is the Income Tax?', in 3 ibid. 2223; Steger, 'Economic Consequences of Substantial Changes in the Method of Taxing Capital Gains and Losses', in 2 ibid 1261; Surrey, 'The Federal Income Tax Base for Individuals, in I ibid. I; White, 'Consistent Treatment of Items' 'Excluded and Omitted from the Individual Income Tax Base' I ibid. 317.

10. The term 'erosion' was apparently first used by Randolph Paul in 'Erosion of the Tax Base and Rate Structure' in Joint Committee on the Economic Report, 84th Cong., 1st Sess., *Federal Tax Policy for Economic Growth and Stability 297* (Comm. Print 1955), and later in Pechman, 'Erosion of the Individual Income Tax' (1957). In response to criticism that I had not made my income concept explicit, I later included a direct reference to the Haig–Simons definition when I presented a revised version of my estimates. See Pechman, 'What Would a Comprehensive Individual Income Tax Yield?' in I *Compendium* 251, *National Tax Journal,* Vol. 10, no. 1, p. 259.

11. The question of averaging illustrates the problems associated with the time interval over which income should be measured; income splitting is a matter of the definition of the taxable income unit; and the allowances for interest, medical expenses, charitable contribution and taxes are examples of the personal deductions. Bittker has seen no analysis of the implications of the Haig–Simons definition for these and other matters because the criteria for deciding these issues cannot be derived from the income concept. It is curious, nevertheless, that in discussing these questions, Bittker raises many of the same questions raised by the proponents of comprehensive income taxation. This is particularly true of his list of questions (Bittker, *op. cit.*, pp. 950–2, 973–7) regarding personal deductions and income splitting. See e.g. 'Personal Deductions in the Individual Income Tax', C. Harry Kahn's discussion of the

personal deductions in I, *Compendium* p. 391, and my discussion of income splitting in 'Income Splitting', in I *Compendium* 473.

12. See e.g. Blum, 'Tax Policy and Preferential Provisions in the Income Tax Base' in I *Compendium*, 77, 84.
13. See Bittker *op. cit.*, p. 77, 84.
14. Pechman, 'Erosion of the Individual Income Tax' *National Tax Journal*, Vol. 10, no. 1, p. 3 n.2 (1957).
15. Bittker *op. cit.*, 983.
16. *Report of the Royal Commission on Taxation (Canada)* (1966). This report was put before the House of Commons on 24 February 1967.
17. Ibid., pp. 298–519.
18. Since this article was written, serious consideration has been given to comprehensive income taxation in the United States as well.

Part Three
Tax Issues

7. The Family*

The adoption of income splitting in the United States arose out of the historical accident that eight states had community property laws, which treated income as if divided equally between husband and wife. By virtue of several Supreme Court decisions, married couples residing in these eight states had been splitting their incomes and filing separate federal returns. Shortly after the Second World War, a number of other states enacted community property laws for the express purpose of obtaining the same advantage for their residents, and other states threatened to follow suit. In an effort to restore geographic tax equality and to prevent wholesale disruption of local property laws and procedures, Congress universalised income splitting in 1948.

The effect of income splitting is to reduce progressivity for married couples. The 1984 tax rates nominally begin at 11 and 12 per cent on the first two $1050 segments of taxable income above the zero-bracket amount and rise to 50 per cent on the portion of taxable income above $81,200. A married couple with taxable income above the zero-bracket amount of $2100 splits this income and applies the first rate to each half; without income splitting, the first two rates would apply to each $1050 segment. Thus, whereas the nominal rate brackets cover taxable incomes up to $81,200, the actual rates for married couples extend to $62,400. The tax advantage rises from $411 for married couples with taxable income of $10,000 to $9300 for couples with taxable income of $62,400 or more.

The classic argument in favour of income splitting is that husbands and wives usually share their combined income equally. The largest portion of the family budget goes for consumption, and savings are ordinarily set aside for the children or for the enjoyment of all members of the family. Two conclusions follow from this view. First, married couples with the same combined income should pay the same tax irrespective of the legal division of income between them; second, the tax liabilities of married couples should be computed as if they were two single persons with their total income divided equally between them. The first conclusion is now firmly rooted in US tax law and seems to be almost universally accepted. It is the second conclusion on which opinions still differ.

*Adapted from *Federal Tax Policy* (Washington, D.C.: Brookings Institution, 4th edn, 1983), pp. 96–101: and *Hearings on the Economic Problems of Women*, Joint Taxation Committee, US Congress, (24 July 1973).

The case for the sharing argument is most applicable to taxpayers in the lower income classes, where incomes are used almost entirely for the consumption of the family unit. At the top of the income scale, the major rationale of income taxation is to reduce the economic power of the family unit, and the use made of income at these levels for family purposes is largely irrelevant for this purpose. Obviously, these objectives cannot be reconciled if income splitting is extended to all income brackets.

The practical effect of income splitting is to produce large differences in the tax burdens of single persons and married couples, differences that depend on the *rate of graduation* and not on the level of rates. Such differences are difficult to rationalize on any theoretical grounds. It is also difficult to justify treating single persons with families more harshly than married persons in similar circumstances. As a remedy, widows and widowers are permitted to continue to split their incomes for two years after the death of the spouse, and half the advantage of joint returns is given (through a separate rate schedule) to single persons who maintain a household for children or other dependants or who maintain a separate household for their parents. This makeshift arrangement does not deal with the problem satisfactorily. For example, single taxpayers who support aunts or uncles in different households receive no income splitting benefit; if they support an aged mother, they do receive these benefits.

Pressures on Congress to treat single persons more liberally—by broadening the head of household provision, increasing their exemptions, and other devices—resulted in the adoption of a new rate schedule for single persons under the 1969 Act. In this schedule, the single person's tax never exceeds by more than 20 per cent the tax for married couples filing joint returns. In keeping with prior practice, the rate schedule for heads of households is halfway between the single person and joint return rate schedules. The result was the introduction of the so-called tax penalty on marriage: two persons with earnings split roughly 75-25, or more equally, between them paid more tax after marriage than the total tax they paid before marriage; under the pure version of income splitting, they would pay the same or less tax before and after marriage.

One problem with the income splitting approach is that differentiation among families by size is made through the rate structure rather than through personal exemptions. It would be possible to differentiate amongst taxpayer units by varying the personal exemptions with the size of income as well as the number of persons in the units with both a minimum and a maximum. This procedure could be used to achieve almost any desired degree of differentiation among families while avoiding most of the anomalies produced by income splitting. The tax rates for single persons and married couples could be equalised either by extending the rate advantages of income splitting to single persons or by requiring married couples to use the same tax rate schedule as single people. The revenue implications of this approach are large, but they can be offset by adjusting the tax rates.

Another problem with pure income splitting is that married couples pay the same tax whether there are two earners or one. The one-earner couple has more ability to pay, because the spouse who stays at home produces income (in the form of household services) that is not subject to tax. Some portion of the earnings of the two-earner couple is absorbed in providing such household services. Furthermore, the high marginal tax rate on the earnings of the second spouse may discourage some from seeking employment.

Elimination of income splitting would restore all the problems of the pre-1948 law and would not adjust correctly for the understatement of the taxable income of the one-earner couple. Another approach would have been to permit married couples to file separately on their earned income, but this would have required arbitrary rules to calculate the tax on unearned incomes and to allocate deductions between spouses, and would have greatly complicated the tax return. Instead, in 1981, Congress decided to provide a special deduction for two-earner couples: 5 per cent for 1982, and 10 per cent thereafter, of the earnings of the spouse with the lower earnings, up to earnings of $30,000. The introduction of this deduction moderated, but did not eliminate, the marriage penalty; at the same time, it gave a tax deduction to some couples who did not suffer a marriage penalty.

Since the difference in taxpaying ability of one-earner and two-earner couples is not inconsequential, the special deduction or credit should be generous. In my view, the 10 per cent deduction for two-earner couples enacted in 1981 does not deal with the problem adequately. For the rates in effect in 1985, I would increase the percentage to 25 per cent and raise the maximum earnings limit for the spouse with lower earnings up to $50,000. Of couse, the exact percentage and limit in a redesigned system for taxing the family would depend upon the rates that would ultimately be adopted under the revised income splitting technique and the desired relationship between the tax liabilities of married couples with one and two spouses working.

In brief, it is possible to retain the present advantages of income splitting and also to correct the alleged 'tax on marriage' that is now imposed on two earners. The important ingredients of the solution are, first, to keep the mechanics of income splitting for married couples but remove its rate advantages; and, second, to enact a special allowance for married couples with two earners in the form of a deduction based upon the earnings of the spouse with lower earnings. The effect of these changes would be to shift tax burdens from single persons and married couples with two earners to married couples with one earner. In my opinion, such a shift in relative tax burdens is appropriate.

8. Capital Gains and Losses*

An economic definition of income would include all capital gains in taxable income as they accrue each year. To tax them in this way would be difficult for three reasons: first, the value of many kinds of property cannot be estimated with sufficient accuracy to provide a basis for taxation: second, most people would regard as unfair the requirement to pay tax on income that had not actually been realised: and third, taxation of accruals might force liquidation of assets to pay the tax. Thus capital gains are included in taxable income only when they are realised.

The United States has taxed the capital gains of individuals since it first taxed income. But this has not been the practice elsewhere until recently, when many countries began to tax capital gains, although generally at much lower rates of taxation than those applied to ordinary income.

HISTORICAL DEVELOPMENT

In the United States, realised capital gains were originally taxed as ordinary income, but since the Revenue Act 1921 they have been subject to preferentially low rates. The provisions applying to such gains changed frequently during the 1920s and 1930s, but were stabilised beginning in 1942. In general, half of the capital gains on assets held for periods longer than six months were excluded in taxable income, and the amount of tax on such gains was limited to a maximum of 25 per cent.

The 1969 Act left all the old provisions intact, but added a new maximum rate of 35 per cent on long-term capital gains of $50,000 or more and included in the base of the tax on preference income the half of capital gains which was excluded from taxable income. Gain on the sale of an owner-occupied house was exempt if the receipts from the sale were applied to the purchase of a new home of equal or greater value within 18 months. For persons over 65, such gains were entirely exempt up to $35,000 of the sale price. The holding period separating short- from long-term capital gains was lengthened from six to nine months in 1977 and twelve months beginning in 1978 (but the holding period for gains on farm commodity and other futures contracts remained at six months).

*Adapted from *Federal Tax Policy* (Washington, D.C.: Brookings Institution, 4th edn, 1983), pp. 109–16.

The thrust toward increased taxation of capital gains under the 1969 Act was completely reversed by the 1978 Act. The portion of long-term gains excluded from taxable income was raised from 50 to 60 per cent, and the 35 per cent maximum tax rate on gains of $50,000 or more became unnecessary because the 40 per cent inclusion rate, combined with a top marginal rate of 70 per cent, reduced the maximum rate to 28 per cent. Taxpayers aged 55 or older were allowed a once-in-a-lifetime election to exclude $100,000 of gains from the sale of a permanent residence. The first $50,000 of long-term gains was excluded from the preference tax base.

The 1981 Act continued the reduction of tax on capital gains by extending the rollover period for gains on sales of residences from 18 months to two years and raising the exclusion for gains on sales of residences by elderly people from $100,000 to $125,000. The reduction in the top marginal rate on ordinary income to 50 per cent, added to the 60 per cent exclusion reduced the maximum tax rate on long-term capital gains to 20 per cent beginning in 1982. In 1984, the holding period was again reduced from twelve to six months.

THE ISSUES

From the standpoint of equity, it is well established that capital gains should be taken into account in determining personal income tax liability. Moreover, preferential treatment of capital gains encourages the conversion of ordinary income into capital gains. Business manipulation of this sort distorts patterns of investment and discredits income taxation. The low capital gains rates now apply to patent royalties, coal and iron ore royalties, income from livestock, income from the sale of unharvested crops, and real estate investments. The amount of ordinary income thus converted into capital gains is unknown, but a great deal of effort goes into this activity and it must be very substantial.

In addition to the overwhelming rate advantage, the law permits capital gains to escape income tax if they are passed from one generation to another through bequests, or if they are passed by gifts and are never realised by the recipient. The capital gain in assets transferred by gifts is taxed only if the assets are later sold. The result is that increases in the value of securities and real estate held in wealthy families may never be subject to income tax.

On the other hand, taxation on a realisation basis requires some provision to moderate the effect of progressivity when large capital gains accumulated over many years are realised in a single year. Full taxation of gains is also criticised because it might have a substantial 'locking-in' effect on investors and reduce the mobility of capital. It is also argued that preferential treatment of capital gains helps stimulate a higher rate of economic growth by increasing the attractiveness of investment generally and of risky investments in particular. In recent years, the principal argument for a reduced tax on capital gains has been that a considerable proportion of realised gains merely reflects inflation and is not real (see below for a discussion of the treatment of capital gains during inflation).

The 'bunching' problem that would arise with full taxation of capital gains could be handled either by pro-rating capital gains over the length of time the asset was held or by extending the present general averaging system to the full amount of capital gains. (It now applies only to the portion of long-term gains that is included in taxable income.) Unless the present marginal rates were reduced, however, the tax might still discourage the transfer of assets. Part of the difficulty is that adherence to the realisation principle permits capital gains to be taxed at declining effective tax rates the longer assets are held or to be transferred tax free either by gift or at death.

One solution to this problem is to treat capital gains as if they were constructively realised when given or bequeathed, with an averaging provision to allow for spreading the gains over a period of years. (This method was proposed by President Kennedy in 1963 and by President Johnson's Treasury Department in early 1969, but has not been seriously considered by Congress.) Under such a system, the remaining advantage to taxpayers from postponing the realisation of capital gains would be the accumulation of interest on the tax postponed. Unless the assets were held for many years, this advantage for long-held assets would be small compared with the advantage of the tax exemption accorded to gains transferred at death; in any event, the interest on the tax postponed would be subject to income tax when the assets were transferred. In these circumstances, the incentive to hold gains indefinitely for tax reasons alone would be reduced

ALTERNATIVE TREATMENT

In the quest to reconcile equity and economic objectives in the taxation of capital gains, tax experts differ about the best approach. Some believe that realised capital gains and those transferred by gift or bequest should be taxed in full, with a provision for averaging either over the period during which the asset was held or over an arbitrary but lengthy period. Others believe that present arrangements may be the best that can be devised, while still others insist that the capital gains rates are still too high. Most experts agree that there is little justification for granting preferential treatment to income that is not a genuine capital gain.

From 1948 to 1976 the preferential rates applied to capital gains on assets that had been held for longer than six months. This holding period was criticised as being both too long and too short. Investor groups urged that the holding period be reduced to three months, and some even recommended that it be eliminated entirely, maintaining that the resulting additional security transactions would increase capital gains tax revenues. On the other hand, if the purpose of the holding period is to differentiate between gains that are bunched and those that are not, there is no logical reason under an annual income tax to reduce the tax rate on incomes earned in less than a year. On this rationale, Congress raised the holding period from six to nine months in 1977 and to twelve months beginning in 1978. However, a proposal by representatives of the financial sector to restore the six-month holding period was enacted in 1984.

The revenue effects of various revisions in the capital gains tax are shown in Table 8.1. Since capital gains are heavily concentrated in the higher income classes, tax liabilities at the bottom of the income scale would not be much affected by changes in the capital gains tax, while those in the top classes would be substantially altered. The estimates assume that capital gains realisations would not be affected by the tax change, an assumption that may be unrealistic if present marginal tax rates remain unaltered. However, this could be moderated or completely offset if the revenue gains were used to substantially lower marginal rates in the top brackets.

CAPITAL LOSSES

In principle, capital losses should be deductible in full against either capital gains or ordinary income. However, when gains and losses are recognised only upon realisation, taxpayers can easily time their sales so as to take losses promptly when they occur and to postpone gains for as long as possible. This asymmetry can be avoided under the US system of capital gains taxation only by charging interest on the deferred tax on capital gains, a device that has never been seriously considered by Congress. The stop-gap used in the United States is to limit the deduction of losses.

From 1942 to 1963 individuals were allowed to offset their capital losses against capital gains plus $1000 of ordinary income in the year of realisation and in the five subsequent years. In 1964 the loss offset up to $1000 of ordinary income was extended to an indefinite period. The loss-offset limit was $2000 for 1977 and $3000 for 1978 and later years. In computing the offset, long-term losses were taken into account in full between 1952 and 1969; before 1952 and after 1969 only 50 per cent of the net long-term loss could be offset against ordinary income up to the limit.

The annual limit on the amount of the offset is most harmful to people

Table 8.1: Revenue Effects of Various Capital Gains Tax Revisions by Adjusted Gross Income Class, 1985 (income classes in thousands of dollars)

Revenue change and adjusted gross income class	Constructive realisation of gains at gift or death	Exclusion percentage reduced from 60 to 40 per cent	Taxation at regular rates	
			Realised gains only	Realised and constructively realised gains
Revenue change[a] (billions of dollars)	2.4	4.9	15.7	23.0
Percentage distribution of revenue change				
0–3	*	*	0.1	0.1
3–5	0.3	0.2	0.2	0.2
5–10	*	0.3	0.8	0.9
10–15	1.1	0.7	1.2	1.4
15–20	5.0	3.9	2.8	2.8
20–25	5.1	5.3	2.8	2.8
25–50	7.2	14.4	12.8	13.5
50–100	17.3	14.8	15.8	18.1
100–200	17.1	15.2	16.4	16.8
200–500	19.1	18.0	17.1	16.7
500–1,000	10.1	9.8	9.3	9.1
1,000 and over	17.7	17.3	16.4	16.0
All classes[b]	100.0	100.0	100.0	100.0
Percentage change in tax liabilities				
0–3	c	c	c	c
3–5	c	c	c	c
5–10	c	c	c	c
10–15	0.2	0.3	1.5	2.6
15–20	0.7	1.0	2.4	3.5
20–25	0.6	1.2	2.0	2.9
25–50	0.2	0.6	1.8	2.8
50–100	0.6	1.6	3.5	5.9
100–200	1.4	2.6	8.8	13.2
200–500	2.6	5.0	15.3	21.7
500–1,000	4.7	9.4	28.4	40.5
1,000 and over	8.3	16.6	50.2	71.3
All classes[b]	0.8	1.7	5.3	7.7

Source: Brookings tax file. Figures are rounded.
*Less than 0.05 percent.
a. Revenue effect for capital gains realisations estimated under the 1981 Act rates.
b. Includes negative incomes not shown separately.
c. Percentages are not shown because tax liabilities in these classes may be negative, reflecting the refundable earned-income credit.

with modest investments, since they may not have large enough gains against which to subtract the losses they may incur. The only solution to this problem would be a pragmatic one that was reasonably liberal for the modest investor without opening the door to widespread abuse of the provision and large revenue losses. One practical approach would be to adjust the $3000 limit on the loss offset for the inflation that has occurred since it was last modified in 1978.

CAPITAL GAINS AND INFLATION

Capital gains cannot be treated on a par with current income flows when measuring income during a period of rising prices. An asset does not give the owner command over additional resources until the value of the asset exceeds its purchase price at prices prevailing when the asset is sold (or during the period of accrual, if the accounting is on an accrual basis). Thus, to measure the income from appreciated assets, the portion of the capital gain that results from inflation should be deducted from the nominal capital gain. The correction can be made by multiplying the purchase price of the asset by the ratio of a general price index (usually the consumer price index) on the date of sale to the value of the same index at the time of purchase. No correction is necessary for current income flows like wages and salaries, because they give the recipient command over resources in the prices of the period during which they are earned. (The bracket effect of inflation discussed in the previous section is a separate matter. Here the concern is with the measurement of income, which can be taxable under a fixed set of rates or rates that are indexed for inflation.)

A system corrected for inflation would have a dramatic effect on the distribution of taxable income. Many apparent capital gains would be converted to real losses, and real losses and gains that are now ignored would be recognised. For example, an individual who purchases an asset for $1000 and sells it for $1200 after holding it for a period during which prices have risen 50 per cent would have a $200 nominal gain but a real loss of $300 at current prices. Assets that are fixed in money terms, such as bonds, mortgages and bank deposits, generate real losses as prices increase. On the other hand, those who borrow money on fixed-dollar contracts repay their debts in depreciated dollars and thus gain from the rise in prices. All such gains and losses would have to be taken into account to calculate inflation-corrected income correctly.

The percentage of capital gains included in taxable income under an inflation-corrected system would not be a flat percentage, as it is under present US tax law; it would vary with the rate of inflation and the length of time the asset was held. If the inflation rate were stable, the inclusion rate would actually rise with the length of time the asset was held. For example, suppose an asset purchased for $1 appreciated in real terms at the rate of 10 per cent a year in a period in which prices also rose 10 per cent a year. The real gain for a single year is just over half the nominal gain of 21 per cent $(1.21 - 1.10 = 0.11)$. After five years, the nominal value of the asset is 2.59 (1.21^5), the purchase price expressed in current prices is 1.61 (1.1^5), and the real gain measured in current prices is 0.98, or 62 per cent of the nominal gain of 1.59.

The realisation criterion would create problems if an inflation-corrected system were implemented on an equitable basis. If capital gains are taxed only when realised, the interest on the tax that is deferred during the period assets are held can be substantial. It would therefore be necessary to require taxpayers to correct nominal gains for the value of the tax deferral, as well as to permit them to adjust their gains for inflation. Such correction factors could be calculated in advance for different holding periods and provided in special tables to accompany the annual tax return.

Many proponents of the present treatment of capital gains favour an inflation adjustment for capital gains without making all the necessary refinements, including the adjustments for the real losses on assets fixed in money terms. Those who oppose the present treatment would argue against an inflation adjustment unless real capital gains were fully included in income, and some would insist on taking the value of tax deferral into account in computing tax liabilities even if real capital gains were taxed in full at realisation.

9. Adjusting for Inflation*

With prices rising at unsatisfactorily high rates, increasing attention has been given in recent years to the relation between inflation and the tax system. Inflation affects real tax burdens in two ways. First, it affects the measurement of several types of income for tax purposes, particularly capital gains, business profits and interest. These problems will be discussed in the section on inflation and accounting below. Second, the personal exemptions, the standard deduction, tax credits, tax rate bracket boundaries and other structural features of the income tax are expressed in dollar terms. If the dollar value of such features remains unchanged as prices and incomes rise, taxpayers' incomes are thrown into higher tax brackets and effective tax rates increase even if there has been no increase in real income. This increase in effective rates is known as *bracket creep*.

BRACKET CREEP

The effect of bracket creep is illustrated in the first four columns of Table 9.1, which compare the tax liabilities of a family of four at selected income levels before and after a 5 per cent inflation. Effective tax rates increase at all income levels as a result of the inflation. In percentage terms, those at the bottom of the income scale fare the worst. However, the increases in effective rates and the percentage changes in income after tax (shown in the last two columns of the table) are much more uniform throughout the income classes. The maximum effect occurs at the lower end of the income scale, where progressivity is determined primarily by the personal exemptions and the zero-bracket amount, and between $50,000 and $200,000 of income, where rate graduation increases most rapidly.

Several countries with high rates of inflation automatically index their income taxes for inflation. The technique is to raise the value of the personal exemptions, standard deductions, and rate brackets by the rate of inflation once a year on the basis of an overall price index, usually the consumer price index. As the inflation rate rose in the United States during the 1970s, proposals to index the income tax in this way received increasing support. From 1960 to 1975 discretionary changes in exemptions and tax

*Reprinted from *Federal Tax Policy* (Washington, D.C.: Brookings Institution, 4th edn, 1983), pp. 107–9, 166–72.

Table 9.1: Effect of a 5 per cent Inflation on the Tax Liabilities of a Family of Four, Selected Income Levels, 1984 (amounts in dollars; effective rates in per cent)

| Income before inflation[a] | Tax before inflation[b] | | Tax after 5 per cent inflation | | | | Effect of not indexing | | |
| | | | Without indexing[b] | | With indexing[c] | | | | |
	Amount	Effective rate	Amount	Effective rate	Amount	Effective rate	Per cent increase in tax	Percentage point increase in effective rate	Per cent reduction in income after tax
10,000	291	2.9	351	3.3	306	2.9	14.7	0.4	0.4
12,000	539	4.5	623	4.9	566	4.5	10.1	0.4	0.5
15,000	959	6.4	1,064	6.8	1,007	6.4	5.7	0.4	0.4
20,000	1,645	8.2	1,777	8.5	1,727	8.2	2.9	0.3	0.3
25,000	2,353	9.4	2,541	9.7	2,471	9.4	2.8	0.3	0.3
30,000	3,201	10.7	3,465	11.0	3,361	10.7	3.1	0.3	0.4
50,000	7,660	15.3	8,320	15.8	8,043	15.3	3.4	0.5	0.6
100,000	23,316	23.3	24,996	23.8	24,482	23.3	2.1	0.5	0.6
200,000	61,130	30.6	65,100	31.0	64,187	30.6	1.4	0.4	0.6
500,000	181,100	36.2	191,100	36.4	190,155	36.2	0.5	0.2	0.3
1,000,000	381,100	38.1	401,100	38.2	400,155	38.1	0.2	0.2	0.1

a. Assumes all income is fully subject to tax and that one spouse earns all the income.
b. Assumes tax law applying in 1984. Tax liability computed on the assumption that the family deducts the zero-bracket amount of $3400 or 20 per cent of income, whichever is greater.
c. The exemptions, the zero-bracket amount, and the rate brackets of the 1984 law are increased by 5 per cent.

rates more than compensated for inflation overall, but not evenly in all income classes. In 1981 Congress decided to index the personal exemptions and the rate brackets beginning in 1985. The adjustment is based on changes in the consumer price index for the 12 months ending with September of the preceding calendar year.

The major argument for indexing is that the increases in effective income tax rates are unintentional by products of inflation. Total tax receipts rise faster than incomes and the public sector grows more rapidly than it would in a non inflationary situation. Moreoever, the increases in the real tax burdens are not selected by Congress but depend on the rate of progressivity and the rate of inflation.

An argument against indexing is that it reduces the built-in stabilising effect of the income tax during periods of cyclical expansion and inflation. The rise in effective rates of a non-inflation-adjusted tax automatically reduces the growth of demand and thus contributes to the stability of the economy. However, indexing does contribute to stabilisation when prices rise during periods of recession.

On balance, indexing seems to be justified in periods when inflation is running at a high rate, say, at 5 per cent a year or more. At lower rates of inflation, some of the recorded increases in fixed-base price indexes may be illusory because of changes in buying patterns and quality changes of goods purchased. If indexing is to be retained, it would be more appropriate to adjust for bracket creep only for the excess of the inflation rate over some small percentage, say 2 or 3 per cent, to avoid reducing real tax burdens under the guise of an adjustment for inflation. Even in a properly indexed system, it should be noted, average and marginal tax rates would still rise as real incomes increased.

INFLATION ACCOUNTING

Business net income is calculated by subtracting from the gross receipts of a firm the expenses of generating these receipts. If all expenses were incurred. at the time sales are made, the difference between the two would provide a correct measure of net income. But there are two complications: first, business outlays are frequently made long before sales are realised; and second, the outlays and expenses are expressed in different prices. The first of these problems is handled by estimating sales and expenses on an accrual basis. If the accounting methods match expenses and sales correctly, the difference between the two will accurately represent the net income of the firm—provided the general price level is stable. If prices change, accrual accounting alone will not suffice; a further correction is required to express sales and expenses in the same prices. (The tax rates and exemption, if any, that should apply to the price-corrected net income are another matter. Under a flat rate tax without exemptions, there is no bracket creep. If the tax is graduated, bracket creep will increase the real tax burden as money income rises.)

The elements in a set of business accounting statements that are affected by inflation are depreciation allowances, costs of goods sold, and financial assets and liabilities. Separate adjustments are required for each of these elements to arrive at a measure of real income expressed in prices of the current period.

Depreciation

The purpose of the depreciation allowance is to write off the portion of the cost of a depreciable asset that is used up in producing the income of the enterprise. Even if the wear-and-tear, and obsolescence of plant and equipment could be measured, the funds accumulated in a depreciation reserve based on historical costs would not be adequate to maintain the value of the capital stock during periods of rising prices. The result would be an overstatement of profits and, thus, some tax on the capital itself. (If the general price level were stable, historical cost depreciation would be sufficient on the average, but not for particular assets because of changes in relative prices.)

Two types of adjustment are suggested by economists to correct depreciation for inflation. The first would permit firms to calculate depreciation on the basis of the replacement cost of each of its depreciable assets (or groups of like assets). The second would correct the deduction based on historical costs for the rise in the average of all prices. This could be done by multiplying the amount of historical cost depreciation by the ratio of the general price level in the current price to the level in the period when the asset was purchased. Accelerated depreciation methods based on historical costs, which are used in many countries, are often justified on inflation grounds, but they can approximate direct adjustments for inflation only accidentally. (The ACRS system enacted in the United States in 1981 is an example of an unfortunate choice of depreciation methods that was justified in part on the ground of inflation.)

An innovative idea of adjusting the system of tax depreciation for inflation is to allow an immediate deduction for the present value of the future economic depreciation that firms could claim if there were no inflation. No adjustment for inflation would ever be needed because the depreciation deduction would be taken in the same year in which the asset was purchased. If a neutral stimulus were desired, the stimulus could be provided through the initial allowance described early. The results under this approach are consistent with the results under inflation-adjusted historical cost depreciation because gains from changes in the relative prices of depreciable assets would be included in income.

Inventories

The tax law permits firms to use either the first-in first-out (FIFO) or last-in first-out (LIFO) methods of inventory valuation. Under FIFO, the deduction for the cost of materials is calculated on the basis of the earliest price paid for similar items in the closing inventory. Under LIFO, the valuation is based on the price last paid for similar items in the closing inventory. In a period of rising prices, the cost of materials is higher and net income is lower under LIFO than under FIFO and hence LIFO results in the lower tax.

As in the case of depreciation, gains and losses on items of inventory are taken into account at different times under FIFO and LIFO. Under FIFO, the change in the price of materials between date of purchase and date of use is treated as a realised gain or loss that is included in income for tax purposes. LIFO defers the date of realisation of gains and losses on inventories so long as the number of units in stock does not decline.

LIFO is in effect the analogue to replacement cost depreciation—inventory gains and losses are not included in income unless inventories are depleted or the firm is liquidated. FIFO treats the full gains and losses on inventories, including the gains and losses resulting from changes in the general price level and in relative prices, as realised on the date of use. An intermediate possibility, analogous to the use of inflated historical cost depreciation, would be to modify FIFO by raising the historical cost of materials used by the percentage increase in the general price level between the date of purchase and date of use. This would protect the firm against taxation of inventory gains caused by general inflation, but would include in net income any gains or losses caused by changes in the prices of its inventories relative to all other prices.

Financial Assets and Liabilities

A business that lends $1000 at a 10 per cent interest rate realises no real return on its investment if prices go up 10 per cent a year. At the end of the first year, for example, it receives interest of $100 but the value of the loan has declined $100. The enterprise that borrows is in the exact opposite position. It is better-off because the real value of the loan it must repay has declined by 0. Under the present tax laws, the lending firm is taxed on $100 of interest even though it has earned no income in real terms, while the borrowing firm is permitted to deduct the $100 of interest paid even though the loan cost nothing in real terms.

In an inflation-corrected accounting system, real gains and losses on net financial assets and liabilities are taken into account in calculating business profits. Enterprises with net financial liabilities gain from inflation; their profits are increased by the reduction in the real value of their liabilities. Enterprises with net financial assets find that the value of these assets erodes during an inflation and their incomes are reduced by the fall in the value of their assets. In each case, the correction is calculated by adding to, or subtracting from, profits the increase or decrease in the nominal value of the assets.

Neither of these adjustments deals with the real gains or losses of issuers and holders of bonds when interest rates rise or fall. When interest rates rise, the market value of long-term bonds declines. This decline in value is a real loss to the bondholders, which they can realise by exchanging their holdings for similar bonds. The issuers of bonds enjoy a corresponding real gain as the value of their debt obligations declines (a gain that many corporations realise by redeeming their bonds at lower prices). When interest rates decline, the gains and losses are reversed—bondholders gain and bond-issuers lose. But there is substantial disagreement about whether such gains and losses should be taken into account in calculating the real income of business enterprises.

Choice of Adjustments

It is evident that, even if it is decided to convert the tax base to a measure of real income, no single set of adjustments can be regarded as 'correct'. The choice depends on which income concept is considered appropriate for taxing business profits.

One concept that is widely regarded by economists as the best measure of income but is not embodied in current tax law is the 'accretion', or 'economic power', concept. Applied to individuals, this is the sum of consumption plus the change in the value of their assets during the taxable period, including all accrued gains and losses. Applied to business firms, it is equivalent to the change in the real market value of the firms during the taxable period before distributions to shareholders.

To correct for inflation on the basis of the economic power concept, nominal gains resulting from an increase in the general price level are eliminated from income, but all gains and losses resulting from changes in relative prices should be recognised in the period in which they accrue. Depreciation would be based on historical costs and adjusted for the increase in the general price level. Inventories would be valued on a FIFO basis and then adjusted for the increase in the general price level between the date of purchase and the date of use. Finally, real gains and losses on net financial assets and changes in the value of bonds would be recognised in the calculations of income.

An alternative concept of income, which is regarded as more appropriate for business accounting purposes by some economists, is the 'capital maintenance' concept. According to this concept, the purpose of the business entity is to produce or distribute a product or service. Changes in the value of the assets of the firm should not be taxed until the firm liquidates some of its assets or goes out of business entirely. There is thus a distinction between operating profits, which are measured on an accrual basis, and capital gains and losses, which are measured only when they are actually realised.

The capital maintenance concept would defer until liquidation recognition of gains and losses on depreciable assets and inventories resulting from changes in relative prices as well as changes in the general price level. Depreciation would be calculated on a replacement cost basis, and a strict form of LIFO, in which historical costs are disregarded even if inventories are liquidated, would be used in accounting for inventories. Real profits on net financial liabilities would be included in income, while changes in the real value of bonds would be ignored.

A major consideration in appraising real income tax accounting, under either the economic power or the capital maintenance concept of income, is that many provisions already provide generous treatment for business and property income, some of which are justified in part as an offset to the distortions caused by using historical prices during inflation. For example, the accelerated cost recovery system is not equivalent to replacement cost depreciation or to adjusted historical cost depreciation and would be hard to justify if prices were certain to remain stable. Preferential income tax treatment for capital gains would clearly be inappropriate if nominal gains from inflation were eliminated from the tax base. For these reasons, many believe that adjustment of the taxable income concept for inflation should be considered only as part of a thorough revision of the tax law that re-examined all preferences and taxed income from all sources at the same rates.

Table 9.2 compares reported corporate profits of US non-financial corporations for the years 1950 to 1979 with estimates of real profits under the two concepts of real income. The adjustments for depreciation and inventories reduce profits substantially, while the financial adjustments raise them. The net adjustments go in both directions, but the overall trend of profits is similar. In some years, the differences are substantial. Real profits are lower than reported profits in 20 years of the 30-year period under the economic power concept and in 12 years under the capital maintenance concept.

The aggregates for the 30-year period 1950–79 differ by 7 per cent or less: total profits were $1214 billion as reported, $1259 billion under the economic power concept of real income, and $1307 billion under the capital maintenance concept. However, the inflation correction would have a significant effect on the relative distribution of taxes among various

Table 9.2: Reported and Real Corporate Profits after Taxes under Two Concepts of Real Income, US Non-financial Corporations, 1950–79 (Billions of dollars)

Year	Reported profits after tax[a]	Real profits after tax[b]	
		Economic power concept	Capital maintenance concept
1950	21.6	22.0	11.1
1951	17.9	16.3	17.3
1952	16.0	14.7	13.7
1953	16.4	14.1	14.3
1954	16.4	10.7	13.8
1955	21.8	31.5	19.6
1956	21.8	32.2	19.3
1957	20.7	15.7	19.2
1958	17.5	14.3	16.1
1959	22.4	22.0	22.5
1960	20.5	7.2	17.7
1961	20.1	16.0	21.4
1962	23.5	17.9	30.7
1963	26.2	17.9	31.6
1964	31.4	24.9	36.5
1965	38.0	37.2	42.6
1966	40.8	47.2	47.3
1967	38.6	46.9	47.0
1968	39.5	31.1	48.7
1969	36.2	65.5	53.9
1970	29.8	5.3	39.3
1971	35.6	–4.6	44.2
1972	43.0	39.9	48.9
1973	56.0	106.5	57.4
1974	63.3	169.3	89.9
1975	66.1	4.9	77.8
1976	82.3	21.0	75.3
1977	96.8	95.2	91.9
1978	111.5	144.8	114.1
1979	122.5	171.6	124.0

Source: US Department of Commerce, Bureau of Economic Analysis; Jeremy I. Bulow and John B. Shoven, 'Inflation, Corporate Profits, and the Rate of Return to Capital', in Robert E. Hall (ed.), *Inflation: Causes and Effects* (University of Chicago Press, 1982).

a. As estimated in the official national income accounts.
b. Expressed in current dollars. For definitions of the income concepts, see the text.

industries. In general, those that rely heavily on equity capital and use long-lived depreciable assets would benefit, while those that rely heavily on borrowed capital and use short-lived depreciable assets would be worse-off.

10. Consumption Expenditure Tax*

The consumption expenditure tax has long been discussed in the economic literature but was not seriously considered until the Treasury Department recommended it during the Second World War. It was also recommended by a minority of the British Royal Commission on the Taxation of Profits and Income in 1955, by a British committee of experts chaired by Professor J.P. Meade in 1978, and by the US Treasury Department in 1977. Although these recommendations were not adopted, the tax has come to be regarded as a respectable possibility.

Unlike the taxes to be discussed in Chapter 11, the consumption expenditure tax is levied on the consumer rather than on the seller of goods and services. In practice, there is little difference in the methods of administering the expenditure tax and the individual income tax. Individual taxpayers submit a form at the end of the year estimating the amount of their expenditures. Personal exemptions and deductions for selected expenditures may be allowed. The rates may be proportional or graduated, although it is usually suggested that the expenditure tax be graduated.

The consumption expenditure tax is proposed either to replace or supplement the income tax. Such a shift is supported strongly by those who believe that the income tax has a large adverse effect on the incentive to save and invest, and that private saving must be increased to increase the level of output and income.

COMPARISON WITH THE INCOME TAX

The individual income tax and a graduated consumption expenditure tax are alternative methods of taxing people in accordance with ability to pay. In the case of the income tax, the measure of ability to pay is income; in the case of the expenditure tax, the measure is consumption.

Some have argued that an income tax is inequitable because it taxes income when it is saved and then again when the savings earn additional income. It is now generally agreed that double taxation is not the real issue. Both the expenditure tax and the income tax may be progressive and

---

*Adapted from *Federal Tax Policy* (Washington, D.C.: Brookings Institution, 4th edn, 1983), p. 201–4; and 'Do We Need a Consumption Tax?', *The New York Times*, 30 January, 1983.

redistributional in effect. If income is considered the better measure of ability to pay, the expenditure tax is inferior. On the other hand, some believe that it is fairer to tax individuals on what they take out of the common pool (consumption) rather than on what they contribute to it.

Some economists believe that the expenditure tax is superior to an income tax because current expenditures reflect normal or permanent income better than current income does. But it is far from obvious that current taxation should be related to income earned in the distant past or future.

Inflation would be much less of a problem under the expenditure tax than it is under the income tax. In general, there would be no need to adjust the tax base for inflation, as consumption is appropriately measured in current dollars. Under the income tax, an inflation adjustment is required to measure real income.

To avoid a reduction of progressivity, the expenditure tax rates would have to be much higher than the income tax rates. Furthermore, there is no guarantee that the expenditure tax base would not be eroded as much as, or more than, the income tax base.

DISTRIBUTION OF TAX BURDENS

On the assumption of equal yields, an expenditure tax would distribute the burden of taxation very differently from an income tax. Tax burdens would be heavier under an expenditure tax for households with high consumption ratios relative to income, such as young and large families and elderly persons, and lower for those with relatively low consumption ratios, such as families whose children have finished school and single persons in general. Tax rates on outlays for 'big-ticket' items (cars, furniture, homes) would be extremely high, and would probably be regarded as excessive by many people.

A tax that omits saving from the tax base is the same as a tax applying only to labour income and exempting all property income. For example suppose a person in the 25 per cent bracket earns and saves $4000, on which the annual return is 10 per cent. At the end of the year he withdraws his savings plus interest and consumes it all. Under a consumption tax, he pays a tax of $1100 on the $4400 he withdraws, leaving $3300 to consume. Under a wage tax that does not tax interest income, he would pay a tax of $1000 right away, deposit $3000 and earn $300 interest tax-free. At the end of the year, he would also have $3300 to consume. Most people would regard a tax that exempts property income as unfair.

Graduated expenditure taxes are often proposed as a method of avoiding or correcting the defects of the income tax base, particularly in the top brackets, where the preferential treatment of capital gains, tax-exempt interest, and depletion allowances and other favourable provisions permit the accumulation of large fortunes with little or no payment of income tax. An expenditure tax would reach such incomes when they were spent without resort to regressive taxation.

FISCAL EFFECTS

Consumption expenditures are over 60 per cent of the GNP, so that a consumption expenditure tax would have a large tax base. The base would probably be somewhat smaller than the base of a comprehensive income tax, but in practice the revenue productivity of the two taxes depends on the specific deductions and exclusions that would be allowed.

Because expenditures tend to be relatively more stable than incomes, an expenditure tax would have less built-in flexibility over a business cycle than an income tax of equal yield. On the other hand, discretionary changes in tax rates for counter-cyclical purposes would be more effective under the expenditure tax, since expenditure tax changes would directly affect the net cost of current purchases (relative to future purchases) and would therefore have a much greater effect on consumption than income tax changes of equal amount.

The expenditure tax would encourage saving more than an equal-yield income tax distributed in the same proportions by income classes. However, since the elasticity of saving with respect to the rate of return is not known, there is no way to predict how much saving would increase if the income tax was replaced by an expenditure tax.

ADMINISTRATION AND COMPLIANCE

Taxpayers cannot estimate their expenditures directly, since almost no one keeps adequate expenditure records. They must be estimated by subtracting investment outlays made during the year from total receipts. This calculation requires taxpayers to furnish information on the proceeds of dispositions of assets, the costs of newly-acquired assets, and changes in cash holdings and bank and savings accounts, as well as on the ordinary income receipts now reported on income tax returns.

Administration and compliance would be more difficult under the expenditure tax than under the income tax in some respects and easier in others. Changes in cash holdings, personal debts, and purchases and dispositions of personal assets (such as jewellery and paintings) would be hard to trace. On the other hand, the expenditure tax would avoid the

weakness of the income tax created by the use of the realisation principle
for calculating capital gains and losses; and since capital outlays would be
treated as an expense when the outlays were made, the complications of
accrual account adjustments for depreciation and depletion would be
eliminated. In distinguishing between business and personal expenditures,
both taxes are subject to somewhat similar problems, and both are subject
to tax base erosion through the proliferation of personal deductions.

On balance, the administrative and compliance problems of a consumption expenditure tax are difficult but probably not insuperable for
advanced countries that have effective income tax administration. But
most countries would find it difficult to enforce such a tax with the present
state of administrative know-how.

RELATIVE MERITS OF INCOME AND EXPENDITURE TAXES

I believe that the consumption tax does not meet the test of taxation
according to the ability to pay: it would tax the wrong people at the wrong
time; it would be as prone to erosion through loopholes as the income tax;
and it would lead to an excessive concentration of wealth.

[Income is the best measure of ability to pay taxes. If taxpayer A has
$25,000 of income and taxpayer B has $20,000 it is reasonable to say that A
has more taxpaying ability. Now, suppose A saves $5000 and B spends all
his income. A would pay more income tax than B, but the two would pay
the same consumption tax. Most people would regard the consumption tax
result as unfair.]

As already noted, substitution of a consumption tax for the income tax
would raise the taxes on the young and the old and reduce the taxes of those
in middle age who save more. Similarly, unemployed and disabled workers
who are using up their savings would find themselves paying tax even
though they had no income.

I have already explained why a tax that omits savings from the tax base is
the same as a tax applying only to labour income and exempting all
property income. Such a tax would be regarded by most people as an
outrage, yet that is what the consumption tax really is.

In theory, the progressive nature of the income tax—higher tax rates for
those with higher earnings—could be approximated by a consumption tax.
But to do so, it would be necessary to set much higher tax rates. For
example, assuming no savings, a 33 per cent income tax rate is equivalent to
a 50 per cent rate on consumption, and a 50 per cent income tax rate is
equivalent to a 100 per cent rate on consumption. Result: a 33 per cent
bracket taxpayer under the income tax would pay a $5000 consumption tax

on a car costing $10,000, and the 50 per cent taxpayer would pay $25,000 tax on a $25,000 car. Congress is hardly likely to accept such rates and the result would be a sharp decline in progressivity.

Consumption tax advocates usually compare the results of an ideal consumption tax with the imperfect income tax we have today. But most of the preferences under the income tax would probably be carried over into the consumption tax. Housing is favourably treated under the income tax and would doubtless be exempt under the consumption tax. Charitable contributions, medical expenses, state and local property and sales taxes, child care expenses, exemptions for the elderly, as well as other personal allowances would all become deductible. And with savings also deductible, the consumption tax would probably turn out to be a monstrosity not capable of raising sufficient revenues.

The transition from the income tax to a consumption tax would create great inequities. The retired elderly, who already paid tax on the income they saved, would pay tax again when they spent it. Something would have to be done to avoid taxing such accumulations under the consumption tax. Exemption of all accumulated assets at the time an expenditure tax is initiated would leave a big loophole for people with large amounts of accrued capital appreciation that had not been subject to tax, but it would be very difficult to make the necessary distinctions in order to prevent wholesale tax avoidance.

Under any consumption tax, taxpayers who save large fractions of their income would be able to accumulate large fortunes over a lifetime. Corporations, and through them their shareholders, would also amass huge aggregations of wealth without payment tax. Many, but no means all, consumption tax advocates support effective wealth and power in the hands of wealthy individuals. But there is no way to tax the income of corporations under a consumption tax and the history of taxation in this country provides no assurance that adequate death and gift taxes would be levied on individuals to supplement the consumption tax.

The present income tax is flawed, but it can be greatly improved without departing from this widely-aproved method of taxation. The solution is to tax all income alike and to eliminate all personal deductions and tax credits except for unusual medical expenses and casualty losses, which do impair ability to pay.

11. Value-Added Tax*

The value-added tax, first proposed in 1918 by a German industrial executive, was discussed sporadically for more then three decades before it was actually implemented. A modified version was adopted in 1953 by the state of Michigan and repealed in 1967; in 1954 the central government of France imposed such a tax, and most European and many other countries have since followed suit. Some people have advocated the inclusion of a value-added tax in the US federal tax system to provide a revenue source to supplement the income tax or substitute for part of it.

FORMS OF VALUE-ADDED TAXATION

For any given firm, value added is the difference between receipts from sales and amounts paid for materials, supplies and services purchased from other firms. The total of the value added by all firms in the economy is equal to total wages, salaries, interest, rents and profits, and therefore the same as the national income.

There are two types of value-added taxes, which differ only in the way outlays for investment purposes are treated. The first type permits business firms to subtract purchases of capital goods in computing the tax base. Total value added is thus equal to total retail sales of final consumer goods. With the second type, purchases of capital goods are not deducted; instead, firms are permitted to deduct an allowance for depreciation over the useful life of the asset. Thus the second type is equivalent to a tax on the national income; the first, which is now widely used in Europe, is a general consumption tax.

There are two methods of computing the allowance to be made for purchases from other firms. Under the 'tax credit' method, the tax rate is applied to the total sales of the firm, and the tax paid on goods purchased is then deducted. Where this method is used, the tax on all goods shipped must be shown separately on each invoice. Under the second, the 'calculation' method, purchases are subtracted from sales, and the tax rate is then applied to the net figure.

The two methods may be illustrated as follows. Suppose a retailer who

*Adapated from *Federal Tax Policy* (Washington, D.C.: Brookings Institution, 4th edn, 1983), pp. 179–9; and Hearings before the Committee on Ways and Means, US House of Representatives, 13 November, 1979.

pays $52.50 for an item (including a 5 per cent tax of $2.50) applies a mark-up of 100 per cent. Under the tax credit method, he charges his customers $105 ($100 plus $5 tax) and takes a credit of $2.50 in computing the amount to be paid to the government, leaving a net tax of $2.50. If the calculation method is used, the retailer deducts from the $100 the $50 paid to his supplier and then applies a tax rate of 5 per cent to the remainder to obtain the same $2.50 net tax. The customer pays the same total price of $105, which consists of the $100 price net of tax, the $250 tax paid by the supplier, and the $2.50 paid by the retailer.

Although both approaches have the same result, some administrators believe that non-compliance is easier to control under the tax credit method. In addition, the tax credit method automatically provides an accounting of the tax to be rebated on exports (the standard practice to avoid putting domestic firms at a competitive disadvantage in foreign markets) and solves some of the problems raised by the inclusion or exclusion of various items, such as charitable contributions, that are troublesome under the calculation method. In general, however, the taxation of goods and services produced in the tax-exempt and government sectors presents difficult problems under a value-added tax.

ECONOMIC EFFECTS OF THE VALUE-ADDED TAX

The value-added tax reduces or eliminates the pyramiding that would occur under the turnover tax or the manufacturers' and wholesalers' sales taxes. Since a firm receives credit for the tax paid by its suppliers, it is unlikely to apply a mark-up to its purchases in computing the price to be charged.

The base of the consumption-type value-added tax is the same as that of a retail sales tax and is confined to goods for consumption. On the other hand, the income-type value-added tax is equivalent to a proportional income tax. Whether the patterns of distribution of the burden of the two types of value-added taxes are the same is in dispute, reflecting a difference of opinion about the impact of a proportional income tax and a general tax on consumption. The income-type value-added tax is paid on capital goods at the time the purchase is made, and the tax is presumably recovered as they are depreciated. Under the consumption-type value-added tax, purchases of capital goods are free of tax. Thus, at any given time, the income-type value-added tax imposes an extra tax on net investment. Some argue that prepayment of the tax under the income-type tax reduces the return on capital; others believe that it is reflected in higher prices for final consumption goods and has no effect on the rate of return.

VALUE-ADDED TAX VERSUS RETAIL SALES TAX

The consumption-type value-added tax and the retail sales tax are similar on both economic and equity grounds. Both are taxes on general consumption. The retail sales tax involves fewer administrative problems because the determination of tax liability is somewhat less complicated and the number of taxpayers is smaller. But in practice retail sales taxes always exclude many items of consumption, while a value-added tax could probably be levied on a more general basis.

EVALUATION OF THE VALUE-ADDED TAX

The addition of a value-added tax to the tax system would be a regressive step (see Figure 11.1), and it would be highly regressive if it were used to replace a major portion of the rates in top income brackets. The US tax system is only moderately progressive, because state and local sales and excise taxes and payroll taxes offset the progressivity of the income taxes at the federal and state levels. To justify the enactment of the value-added tax, it would be necessary to argue that a shift in the tax burden from high- to low-income groups is appropriate.

It has been argued that the regressivity of the value-added tax can be offset by refundable tax credits at the lower income levels, but this argument is only partly correct. A refundable credit would make the value-added tax progressive only up to the point where the maximum credit is paid and would place the largest relative tax burden at the point where the credit phases out; beyond that point, the value-added tax would be regressive. The logic of putting the maximum burden of a new tax on people with middle incomes escapes me. Nor do I see any point in first imposing a tax on low-income recipients and then giving them a credit to offset it.

The inflationary effect of the value-added tax would not be insignificant. For example, a 10 per cent value-added tax would add as much as 5 per cent to the price level, and even more if this one-shot increase generates secondary effects through cost-of-living wage adjustments and price mark-up practices. In present and foreseeable circumstances, it is unwise to contemplate the introduction of such an inflationary tax.

In the United States the enactment of the value-added tax would bring the federal government into an area that is now one of the most important sources of state revenue and is also important in many localities. Federal use of the value-added tax would greatly complicate compliance on the part of businessmen, since the general form of consumption tax levied at the

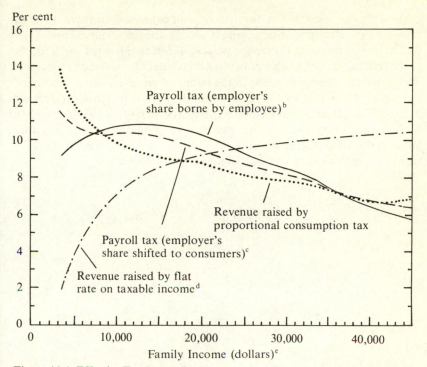

Figure 11.1: Effective Tax Rates of a Consumption Tax and Alternative Methods of Raising the Same Revenue, 1977[a]

Source: Joseph A. Pechman, *Federal Tax Policy* (Brookings Institution, 3rd edn., 1977), p. 207.
a. Tax to 11.7 per cent for wage-earners and 7.9 per cent for the self-employed. Maximum earnings subject to tax are $16,500.
b. Both the employer and the employee portions of the tax are assumed to be borne by the employee; the self-employment tax by the self-employed.
c. The employer tax is distributed in proportion to consumption by income class; the employee tax and self-employment tax by the employee and the self-employed, respectively.
d. The tax is applied to taxable income as defined in the income tax law for 1977.
e. Family income is a comprehensive definition of income, which includes estimated accrued capital gains.

state–local level is the sales tax and not the value-added tax. Thus, most businessmen would be burdened with the problem of complying with two different types of sales taxes, requiring separate sets of records and duplicate procedures for tax collection, payment and compliance. This would almost surely lead to demands for coordination between the federal and state–local governments and might ultimately lead to replacement of the state and local taxes by the federal tax.

The value-added tax is often supported on the ground that it would increase saving. Economists differ on what the effect is likely to be; my guess is that the net effect as compared to an equal-yield income tax of the type now in effect would be small. If we are serious about increasing the rate of national saving, the easiest way would be to move toward a surplus in the federal budget. Such a policy would result in federal debt repayment, which would leave more funds in the hands of private investors to finance the increases in investment so urgently needed to increase productivity growth. This effect is demonstrable and would be large, while the impact of the VAT on saving is speculative and small. Deficit reduction makes much more sense than the enactment of a whole new tax which would be regressive, inflationary and burdensome for business.

12. Estate Taxes*

Taxes on property left by individuals to their heirs are among the oldest forms of taxation. In societies in which property is privately owned, the state protects the property rights of the individual and supervises the transfer from one generation to the next. Consequently, the state has always regarded property transfers as appropriate objects of taxation.

Opinions about death taxes vary greatly in a society relying on private incentives for economic growth. Some believe that these taxes hurt economic incentives, reduce saving, and undermine the economic system. But even they would concede that death taxes have less adverse effects on incentives than do income taxes of equal yield. Income taxes reduce the return from effort and risk taking as income is earned, whereas death taxes are paid only after a lifetime of work and accumulation and are likely to be given less weight by individuals in their work, saving, and investment decisions.

Death taxes have been supported by people in all wealth classes. One of their strongest supporters was Andrew Carnegie, who had doubts about the institution of inheritance and felt that wealthy persons are morally obligated to use their fortunes for social purposes. In his *Gospel of Wealth,* Carnegie wrote that 'the parent who leaves his son enormous wealth generally deadens the talents and energies of the son and tempts him to lead a less useful and less worthy life than he otherwise would.' He applauded the growing acceptance of estate taxes and said: 'Of all forms of taxation this seems the wisest.' According to Carnegie, it is the duty of a wealthy man to live unostentatiously,

to provide moderately for the legitimate wants of those dependent upon him, and, after doing so, to consider all surplus revenues which come to him simply as trust funds . . . to administer in the manner . . . best calculated to produce the most beneficial results for the community.

Despite the appeal of estate and gift taxes on social, moral, and economic grounds, taxes on property transfers have never provided significant revenues in the United States and have been reduced to an insignificant proportion in recent years. One can only guess why heavier reliance has not been placed on these taxes. A possible explanation is that equalisation of

*Adapted from *Federal Tax Policy* (Brookings Institution, 4th edn, 1983), pp. 225–45.

the distribution of wealth by taxation is not yet accepted in the United States. In some countries, economic classes tend to be fairly stable, with little crossing-over by succeeding generations. In the American economy, membership in economic classes is fluid. The average family in the United States still aspires to improved economic and social status, and the estate and gift taxes are erroneously regarded as especially burdensome to the family that is beginning to prosper through hard work and saving.

Moreover, wealth transfer taxes are not considered equitable by many people. A surprising number resent even the relatively low taxes now imposed on estates as large as $1,000,000. This may be because the base of the wealth transfer taxes in certain respects includes more than what the public considers 'wealth' properly subject to tax. The family home, the family car, U.S. savings bonds, savings bank deposits, and similar property are not regarded as appropriate objects of taxation. The public generally is not aware that the major part of the estate tax base consists of stocks, bonds, and real estate, and that the exemption removes the wealth from the estate tax base in all but a small minority of estates.

STRUCTURAL PROBLEMS

Since wealth transfers can take many forms, estate and gift taxation is inherently complicated. Many of the structural features of the estate and gift taxes have unequal impact, depending on how and when dispositions of property are made. Such disparities are hard to justify because many people—for personal or business reasons or because of early death—cannot avail themselves of the opportunity to minimise the tax on their estates.

Transfers by Husbands and Wives

Transfers by married couples present a difficult problem because it is hard to decide whether they should be taxed as if their property is part of one estate or two.

Community and non-community property. Under the community property system, which prevails in eight of the United States, all property acquired during marriage by a husband and wife (except property acquired by gift or inheritance) belongs equally to each spouse. The community property states vary on whether the income from property owned before marriage or acquired during marriage by gift or inheritance belongs to both spouses equally or to the original owner or recipient alone. In non-community property states, each spouse retains ownership of all property acquired or accumulated out of his or her separate earnings or inheritance even after marriage.

Before 1942 federal estate and gift taxes recognised the community property system: only half the community property was taxable under the estate tax at the death of a spouse, and gifts to third parties were treated as if half were made by each spouse. In non-community property states the entire amount of property accumulated by a spouse was taxable to him or her. To equalise estate and gift taxes for residents of community and non-community property states, the Revenue Act of 1942 made transfers of community property taxable to the spouse who had earned it. In effect, the 1942 law treated community property as if it were non-community property.

The marital deduction. The Revenue Act of 1948 attempted to achieve equalisation by moving in the opposite direction. In the spirit of income splitting for income tax purposes, transfers of community property were made taxable under the pre-1942 rules, while for transfers of non-community property a deduction was allowed for the amount of the property transferred to the surviving spouse, up to half the separate property in an estate. In the case of a gift of non-community property by one spouse to another, only half of the gift was made taxable. Gifts to third persons were to be treated, if so elected, as though half were made by each spouse. The 1981 Act increased the marital deduction to 100 per cent of property transfers between spouses, and retained gift splitting between spouses for gifts to third persons.

The marital deduction greatly increases the amount of property that married persons may transfer free of tax. Beginning in 1987, when the effective transfer tax exemption will be $600,000, the total exemption for married couples will amount to $1,200,000, provided the first spouse who dies transfers half the estate to a third person. Gift splitting also in effect doubles the annual personal exclusion from $10,000 to $20,000, thus increasing the transfer tax exemption even further if gifts are made.

Transfers between spouses are subject to tax at the death of the recipient or when the recipient makes gifts, but the total tax of the couple can nevertheless be significantly reduced through the use of the marital deduction. Under progressive rates, the total tax on two estates of equal size is less than that on one large and one small estate. For example, a net estate of $5 million will be subject to a tax of $2,083,000 in 1987 and later years. If half the estate is left to a surviving spouse, the tax is reduced to $833,000. If the $2.5 million received by the spouse is later taxed in full, the subsequent tax will also be $833,000, and the total tax on the original $5 million will be $1,666,000, involving both a deferral of the tax and a tax decrease of $417,000, or 20 per cent.

Aggregation of Husband and Wife Transfers. Complete exemption of transfers between husband and wife suggests that the husband and wife are a single unit, yet the total tax paid by the couple depends on the amounts transferred by each to one another and to third parties. To achieve total equality among married couples, the combined estates would have to be cumulated for estate tax purposes. The initial instalment on the combined tax would be collected on the death of one spouse, and the remainder (figured on the basis of the cumulated estates) would be collected on the death of the second spouse. The attractive feature of this proposal is that it would equalise the taxes paid by married couples in all states regardless of the order in which they disposed of the estate.

However, estate cumulation may produce inequitable results where the wealth of the husband or wife was separately inherited or accumulated. For example, a woman married to a wealthy man for a relatively short period might be taxed at the maximum estate tax rates even though the amount of property she owned was small. This objection could be met by cumulating only as much of the property transferred by the wife (during life or at death) as was originally acquired from the husband. Tracing difficulties could be avoided by cumulating transfers of the wife only up to the dollar amount of property received from the husband. Such a compromise, however, would fail to take into account any increase in the value of the property after the interspousal transfer. Estate cumulation would also require the solution of some intricate problems involving the treatment of gifts made before marriage and the taxation of transfers by widowed or divorced persons who had married again.

Imperfect Unification of Estates and Gifts

Even though the estate and gift tax rates have been unified, wealthy people are well advised to transfer a substantial part of their property by gift during their lifetime rather than by bequest for two reasons. First, the annual exclusion of $10,000 per donee under the gift tax permits tax-free transfers in addition to the unified estate and gift tax exemption. Second, the amount paid as gift tax three years before death does not enter into the gift tax base, whereas the estate tax is computed on the basis of the decedent's entire property, including that part used to pay the tax. Furthermore, by transferring part of the estate to a spouse, a testator splits the estate into two parts, moderating the full impact of transfer tax graduation.

To minimise tax liability, a person would have to take these factors into account as well as the tax that would be due at the death of the spouse. Although there are many uncertainties, it is clear that a carefully drawn plan of wealth distribution during the life of a wealthy person can pay handsome dividends in lower tax burdens.

Use of gifts. Information on the distribution of wealth during life and at death has been collected by the US Treasury on the basis of the estate and matched gift tax returns of the wealthiest decedents for whom estate tax returns were filed in 1945, 1951, 1957, and 1959. The figures show clearly that wealthy people prefer to retain the bulk of their property until death and fail to use gifts to maximum tax-saving advantage. There are a number of reasons for the small proportion of gifts. First, most people are reluctant to contemplate death. Uncertainty regarding time of death encourages delay in making estate plans even by those with considerable wealth. Second, many wish to retain control over their businesses. Disposal of stock or real estate frequently means loss of control over substantial enterprises. Third, donors may wish to delay transfers of property until their children have had an opportunity to make their own careers. Fourth, many people—even those who are wealthy—do not know the law and often do not take the advice of their tax lawyers on such personal matters.

Whatever the reason the actual use of gifts has resulted in less erosion of the tax base than might have taken place, and the recent unification of the estate and gift tax rates has reduced further the incentive to make gifts. The major criticism of the law is that it discriminates against those who, for business or personal reasons, do not dispose of a substantial portion of their wealth during their lives. And among those who do make gifts, the law discriminates in favour of wealthier donors by rewarding them with larger tax savings than those available to less wealthy donors on gifts of the same value. This feature stems from the exclusion of the gift tax from the base of the tax.

Complete unification of estate and gift taxes. The remedy for the inequalities resulting from the separate taxation of gifts and estates is to complete the unification of the two taxes begun in 1976. A truly unified system would have a single marital deduction for lifetime transfers and bequests. In addition, any gift tax paid would be included in the base of the final transfer tax. Unification to this extent is opposed by those who believe that gifts should be encouraged. It is argued, in fact, that gifts tend to reduce the concentration of wealth by dispersing property among a relatively larger number of donees.

Trust transfers. The trust has a profound influence on the taxation of property transfers. In the United States before 1977, if the trust was properly planned, the trust property was not subject to transfer tax when one life beneficiary was succeeded by another or when the property was received by the remaindermen. An estate or gift tax was paid when the trust was created, but tax was not paid again until the remaindermen transferred the property. Given these characteristics, the trust was frequently used by wealthly people to avoid estate and gift taxes for at least one generation and sometimes more. In extreme cases, trusts were set up to last for the lives of the children and grandchildren, with the remainder going to the great-grandchildren, thereby skipping two estate and gift tax generations.

Use of trusts. The trust device has been used frequently by the wealthy to transfer property to later generations. The data from the Treasury studies of 1945, 1951, 1957, and 1959 returns indicate the following patterns:

1. In the 1940s and 1950s more than three of every five U.S. millionaires transferred at least some of their property in trust. Transfers in trust accounted for at least one-third of non-charitable transfers by millionaires in this period. The data also indicate that trusts were used primarily by wealthy people. Those with smaller estates gave much more of their property outright.

2. There was little difference in the eventual disposition of property transferred outright and property transferred in trust. Outright transfers were received in the first instance by the wife and children; these properties were in turn transferred to grandchildren and great-grandchildren. In the case of trust transfers, wives, children, and grandchildren frequently received only a life interest, so the grandchildren and great-grandchildren received the property undiminished by estate or gift taxes. About half the trust property of wealthy decedents escaped estate and gift taxes until the death of the grandchildren or great-grandchildren. Only a very small proportion of the property transferred outright escaped tax for a similar period.

The 1976 legislation. There are legitimate reasons for trusts, and it would be unwise to abolish them altogether. On the other hand, since trust transfers and outright transfers go to the same people, it seems unfair to impose lower taxes on trust transfers. Equity suggests that the two types of transfers should be treated equally. Moreover, trust property is managed more conservatively than property owned outright. Some economists have pointed out that it is unwise to encourage excessive use of the trust device because it reduces the supply of capital available for risky investments.

Several methods have been devised to remove or reduce the tax advantage of trust transfers. The 1976 legislation, which was effective for transfers in trust beginning June 12, 1976 (except transfers pursuant to a will in existence on June 11, 1976, of a decedent dying before January 1, 1983), used the direct method. Under this legislation, life estates in the United States are treated as if the property generating their income is owned by the income beneficiaries, a procedure followed in Great Britain. The capital from which the life estate is supported is taxed as if it had been included in the life beneficiary's gross estate. In effect, the trust property is taxed at the marginal transfer tax rate of the life beneficiary. The tax is paid from the assets of the trust.

The mechanism for taxing life estates in the 1976 legislation is a new tax imposed on 'generation-skipping' transfers of trust property, equivalent to the estate tax that would be imposed if the property had been actually transferred outright to each successive generation. A generation-skipping trust is one in which income or remainder interests are given to two or more generations that are younger than the generation of the grantor of the trust. The tax applies when the trust assets are distributed to a generation-skipping heir (for example, a great-grandchild of the transferror) or when an intervening interest in the trust terminates (for example, when the life interest in a trust is transferred from a child to a grandchild); but an exclusion of $250,000 is provided for transfers to each grandchild of the grantor.

The 1976 legislation was an effort to plug the former generation-skipping loophole under the estate and gift taxes. The provisions are complex and there have been difficult problems of compliance and administration. Moreover, by setting up separate trusts for children and grandchildren (as opposed to a single trust in which each has a partial right to benefit from the same property), the wealthiest individuals can escape all or a major part of the generation-skipping tax. The remedy is to apply the generation-skipping tax on trust transfers to persons more than one generation younger than the grantor's generation. But there is considerable pressure to eliminate the generation-skipping tax entirely or to further weaken it, rather than to improve its effectiveness.

Small Business and Farm Property

A perennial problem in estate taxation is its effect on small businesses and farms. Small businessmen and farmers have always felt that the estate tax is especially burdensome. Often their estates consist of little more than the business. Heavy taxation or a rule requiring payment of taxes immediately after the death of the owner-manager would necessitate liquidation of the enterprise and loss of the business by the family.

As the previous discussion indicated, a little advance estate planning would be sufficient to prevent or mitigate most of these problems. Furthermore, liberal provisions for instalment payments of estate taxes were enacted in the United States in 1976 and made even more generous in 1981. The 1976 and 1981 legislation also permitted small businesses and farms to be valued substantially below their market value for estate tax purposes if used by the decedent's family for a number of years following the death of the decedent.

First, tax payments on estates of which a small business or a farm is a large proportion may be made in instalments over a period of fourteen years. There is a special 4 per cent interest rate for the first million dollars of closely held property. Only interest is paid the first four years; thereafter the tax plus interest is payable in equal instalments over the next ten years. This option, which is exercised by the executor, is available if the value of the business exceeds 35 per cent of the gross estate. Instalment payments are limited to the portion of the estate tax accounted for by the business. A special lien is provided for payment of the deferred taxes, and when this lien procedure is followed, the executor is discharged from personal liability.

Second, redemptions of stock in closely held corporations to pay death taxes and administrative expenses are taxed as capital gains rather than dividend income. To qualify for this treatment, the value of the decedent's stock in the closely held corporation must exceed 35 per cent of the gross estate. The allowable redemption period is four years for all estates and fifteen years when an election has been made for the deferred payment of taxes. Such stock redemptions are, of course, indistinguishable from ordinary distributions of profits by private corporations, which are subject to tax.

Third, spokesmen for farm interests have alleged that farmland was often assessed for estate tax purposes at a value far in excess of its value in agricultural production. As a result, heirs to the property, who frequently wanted to keep it in family hands and continue to farm it, purportedly were forced to sell to pay the tax. Under the 1976 legislation, farmland and other closely held business real property may be assessed at its 'current-use' value rather than at its market value, but this valuation may not be used to reduce the decedent's gross estate by more than $750,000.

It is hard to estimate how far the difficulties described are attributable to an estate tax squeeze. Prices of farmland have been rising rapidly, and the increase must be due in most cases to mounting demand for the land for non-agricultural uses, particularly when it is located on the fringes of metropolitan areas. If decedents' assets are included in their estates at fair market value, it must be expected that the estate taxes will often encourage heirs to sell to people who will put the property to more profitable use. The generous liberalisation of payment provisions enacted in 1976 should have been sufficient to avoid the liquidation of farms to pay the estate tax. In fact, most estates benefiting from the special valuation have liquid assets in excess of the tax due. Current-use valuation was once in effect in the United Kingdom, but it was recently repealed because wealthy people were encouraged to shift their investments into agricultural property to reduce their death duties.

SUMMARY

In theory, estate and gift taxes are among the better taxes; in practice, their yield is disappointing, and they have little effect on the distribution of wealth. In recent years, exemptions have been increased, the top tax rate has been cut, and new ways have been provided to escape the taxes. The major avenues are the distribution of estates by gifts during lifetime and undervaluations of farms and small businesses for estate tax purposes. Generation skipping through trusts was at one time a major tax avoidance mechanism, but the 1976 legislation has closed this loophole somewhat. The revenue potential of further estate tax reform is, however, relatively modest.

Although tax theorists almost unanimously agree that taxation of wealth transfers should play a larger role in the revenue system, they have not been successful in convincing Congress. The public does not appear to accept the desirability of a vigorous estate and gift tax system. The major obstacles to the increased use of these taxes are public apathy and the difficulty of understanding their major features and how they apply in individual circumstances. The merits of wealth transfer taxes will have to be more widely understood and accepted before they can become effective revenue sources.

13. Implementing Tax-Based Incomes Policies*

The administrative and compliance problems of tax-based incomes policies (TIP) have so far been virtually ignored by its proponents. It would be impossible for me to comment on all the issues; I shall limit myself to what I regard as the most important problems.

First, there is the issue of prices. The original Wallich–Weintraub proposal increased taxes on profits of firms with excessive wage increases; prices were not involved at all. However, Arthur Okun suggested that a carrot approach might be used to provide reductions of profits taxes for firms with price increases below the average. It is clear that any kind of tax penalty or subsidy that depends on a change in average prices of particular firms is simply impractical. All the problems of constructing price indices would emerge, such as treatment of new products, quality change, and measurement of costs to be passed through, and there is no easy solution to most of them. It would be possible to substitute a limitation on gross profit margins for the penalty on price increases, but this approach has many of the earmarks of a tax on excess profits (penalty on efficiency and increased capital utilisation, encouragement of advertising and other unnecessary expenses, and lack of representativeness of the base period), which is anathema for business and Congress alike. I conclude that tax penalties or subsidies based on price changes are unworkable. I leave it to the reader to guess how labour would react to a TIP that applied only to wages and not to prices.

Second, there is the matter of the type of coverage a TIP would entail. Using data on the number of business firms in the United States for the year 1975, about 13 million firms filed tax returns in that year, including 10.9 million sole proprietorships, 1.1 million partnerships, and 2 million corporations. And there were $\frac{1}{2}$ million returns of non-profit organisations and over 78,000 government units. Most of the business firms had no employees; many report no net income; and all but a relatively small number of large businesses do not keep detailed personnel records. Yet, if a tax penalty or tax subsidy is to be designed, the law must be explicit about how every one of these units is to be treated

*Adapted from *Curing Chronic Inflation*, editors Arthur M. Okun and George Perry, (Washington, D.C.: Brookings Institution, 1978), pp. 154–8.

A penalty would be easier to administer than a subsidy because it would be possible to limit the penalty to large firms; if there are 'goodies' to be handed out, it would not be possible to limit eligibility to employees of such firms. But this does not imply that the problems of a penalty can be overlooked. As I shall indicate below, I am not persuaded that it is feasible to measure average wage changes for all economic units in a manner that would be appropriate for a tax-based wage penalty or subsidy.

If the carrot approach were adopted, I assume we would not ask the average farmer, or the average corner drugstore owner, or most self-employed professionals who have a few employees to report man-hours on a tax return. To avoid the administrative problems, the wage subsidy would probably be given to all employees in such establishments and to the owners also. This is not fatal for the wage subsidy plan on administrative grounds, but I wonder what effect the plan would have if a substantial fraction, if not a majority, of all workers received the subsidy whether or not they behaved.

A third issue is the economic unit. The unit for tax accounting purposes is a legal entity which, in our complex economy, often bears little relationship to the unit that enters into wage bargains with its employees. Large corporations generally file consolidated returns that include the operating results of many, but not necessarily all, of their subsidiaries. I assume that the wage behaviour of foreign subsidiaries is of little relevance to wage behaviour of their counterparts in the United States, so those foreign units would not be covered by the wage subsidy or penalty.

While the foreign subsidiary is the extreme case, there are numerous other instances of branches or subsidiaries located in the United States which, as far as wages are concerned, bear virtually no relationship to one another or to the parent firm. What about the oil firm that owns one of the largest retail and mail-order houses in the country? Or the textile firm that owns a Hollywood film manufacturer? Or the electronics manufacturer that owns a bread manufacturer? If the wage subsidies or penalties of one of these firms depended on the wage settlements of all the other firms included in the consolidated return, labour and management would have no way of making wage decisions in one place unless they knew what the decisions were to be elsewhere. Accordingly, the rules would have to be sufficiently flexible to permit the unit of calculation to be relevant to the wage-fixing process. Under wage controls, the business firms themselves made this decision, and I assume the control agency could modify that decision if it were necessary. But for purposes of a wage subsidy or penalty, definite rules would have to be established either in the legislation or in the regulations, so that labour and management would know exactly which wage bargains were included. If there are any usable guides on how these rules can be written, I am not aware of them.

Once such rules were prepared, it would be necessary to prescribe other rules to make inter-year wage comparisons. The range of problems include new firms, mergers, spin-offs, sales of facilities, changes in product mix, and other developments that occur in a dynamic economy. This is what is referred to in the tax jargon as 'the excess profits tax problem': that is, the problem of estimating the tax base when it depends on events and conditions in two or more adjacent years. The decisions made for the excess profits tax in the United States have been the subject of extensive and time-consuming litigation every time the tax was used, and no one in the government or the business side was ever satisfied. I can imagine a set of arbitrary rules that a group of economists or tax administrators might agree to, but that does not mean that Congress would accept such rules. For example, it has been suggested that, for new firms, a base-year wage structure might be constructed from averages for other firms in the same industry. But the only data of this type that exist are those of the Bureau of Labor Statistics, and they could not possibly be applied to a particular firm. In the end, the legislation would be complex and, like the excess profits tax, would impose unforeseen costs on business that would lead to further legislation and litigation to moderate such costs.

The problem of timing a penalty or subsidy is a fourth issue of concern. From the standpoint of administration or compliance, it would be much easier to impose a penalty or provide a subsidy after the end of the accounting period. If the proposal is for a penalty based on profits, it should be possible to rely on the business firms to take the penalty into account in its wage decisions.

The opposite is true for a subsidy to workers accepting a wage increase below the guideline percentage. To appeal to workers to accept the constraint, the subsidy must be prospective and must be incorporated in the current tax withholding tables so that the workers will have immediate tangible evidence that their disposable income will not be impaired by the policy. (Of course, this would require two sets of withholding tables, but this is only a minor complication compared with the others.)

The basic problem is that labour and management would find it extremely difficult to incorporate a prospective subsidy in their wage bargaining. Unless the bargaining unit were coterminous with the unit for determining the subsidy, no worker or group of workers would know whether the deal they made would actually trigger the subsidy until negotiations were completed with the other bargaining units in the same firm. Management would be in the same situation: how could it be sure that the construction workers would accept a wage increase that, together with the agreement with coal miners, would trigger a subsidy to both groups?

Suppose also that the firm and its workers take a chance and accept wage bargains that result in a wage subsidy effective at the beginning of the firm's taxable year. Suppose that later there is a miscalculation: after the fact, the average wage increase for the firm actually exceeds the guideline. How could the excess wage subsidy be collected? The firm would have no way of collecting from workers who had left, and the workers who remained would be up in arms to find that income already spent was really not income at all. Or the firm might be made responsible, but this could lead to excessive hardship, if not bankruptcy. Alternatively, the government might require workers to make up the excess wage subsidy by reducing their refunds or by increasing their balances of tax due when they filed their returns. To accomplish this, firms would be required to inform their workers if there were excess subsidies in time for them to fill out their tax returns, a requirement that would be highly unrealistic because most large firms take many months to complete their final tax returns. The firm could make estimates, but if these were incorrect, the workers would be even more furious.

I conclude that a penalty on profits based on wage changes is feasible, but it would have to be retrospective. For prospective subsidies to workers, there are numerous pitfalls. Frankly I do not see how the solutions can satisfy labour or management.

A fifth issue is controls versus tax-based incomes policies. I believe it is not productive to argue whether or not TIPs are another form of controls. The questions are which approach is feasible and what are the costs relative to the alternatives?

It is true that a tax-based incomes policy can be disregarded by any firm and its workers. But the rules and regulations must be written to ensure that all economic units in the country understand them and make their decisions accordingly. Even if it is agreed that some of the rules must be arbitrary, I doubt that it would be possible to arrive at such arbitrary rules through the tax legislative process as we know it today.

Under controls, Congress avoids the hard decisions and lets the controlling agency make the arbitrary rules. One reason controls seem to be acceptable is that relatively few firms are ever involved in disputes, whereas a tax penalty or a subsidy would apply to all or a large number of firms, and the perceived hardships and disputes will be numerous. Both controls and tax-based incomes policies lead to capricious results, but I am at a loss to understand why the proponents of the latter believe that their approach would be more acceptable than the other to labour management, the public and Congress.

Part Four
Financing a Federal System

14. Intergovernmental Fiscal Relations*

INTRODUCTION

Under the US federal system, state and local governments have the responsibility for providing their citizens with access to many of the most important ingredients of civilised life. Citizens of the United States depend on their state and local governments for the education of their children, the cleaning of their streets, the protection of their persons and property from fire and crime, and many other services essential to health and happiness. Improvement in the quality of these services is needed to achieve a rising standard of living.

It has been long recognised that state and local governments by themselves do not have the resources necessary to meet the demands placed on them for continually improving and expanding essential public services. The most productive and equitable source of revenue—the income tax—is intensively used by the federal government; the states and localities rely primarily on other resources—sales and property taxes. These taxes are less equitable and less responsive to economic growth than the income tax. Moreover, the resources of the states vary greatly. Even if considerably higher state–local tax rates were politically and economically feasible, the additional revenues they would yield in the poorest states would not be adequate to provide the minimum level of public services that the national interest requires for all citizens.

In the past, the nation's need for state–local services in excess of state–local resources has been met in part by federal grants in aid for particular purposes. These specific federal grants have helped to ensure minimum service levels throughout the nation with respect to specific programmes in which the national interest was particularly strong.

The states have long been pressing for a more general and far-reaching solution to their problem of meeting the needs of their citizens in all the

*Reprinted from *Strengthening State and Local Government*, Report of the Task Force on Intergovernmental Fiscal Cooperation to the President of the United States, 11 November, 1964, pp. 1–30. The task force members were Joseph A. Pechman, chairman, Samuel M. Cohn, L. Laszlo Ecker-Racz, Otto Eckstein, Robert S. Herman, Richard A. Musgrave, Alice M. Rivlin, and Jacob A. Stockfisch.

areas of traditional state–local responsibility with the financial resources available to them. They have sought some type of transfer of federal revenues which would make it possible for them to continue to perform those functions at the state–local level without transferring control of these activities or decisions on spending priorities to the federal government.

Though sympathetic to state–local fiscal problems, the federal government has found its own responsibilities too heavy to permit turning a substantial portion of its revenues over to the states. The major reason has been heavy and rising federal commitments to defence and defence-related programmes. At last, however, pressure for rapid expenditure increases in these areas of federal responsibility appears to be abating. Unless the federal government takes on substantial new responsibilities, it now seems unlikely that its expenditures will increase as rapidly as potential revenues at present tax rates. This prospect provides the long-awaited opportunity for a more general and permanent solution to the state–local fiscal problem.

The Task Force believes that the time is ripe to add a new approach to inter-governmental fiscal cooperation. We recommend the immediate creation of a National Trust Fund for the States to channel part of the growing stream of federal income tax revenues to state and local governments to meet urgent needs for public services. In this report, we discuss the reasons for setting up such a fund, and outline the details of a plan which we believe is both feasible and desirable from the viewpoint of the nation as a whole.

STATE AND LOCAL NEEDS

State and local governments account for more than two-thirds of all government spending for civilian purposes. In fiscal year 1963 federal expenditures for civilian purposes amounted to less than $30 billion, while state and local governments spent $64 billion (Table 14.1).

The amounts spent by the state and local governments have grown rapidly in recent years, and will continue to grow rapidly in the foreseeable future. These governments are being overwhelmed by the demands of an expanding population for increased public services. They must now meet the needs of a population increasingly concentrated in urban areas for water supplies, sewage disposal, sanitation and streets. On states and localities falls the obligation to provide more and better education, health care and recreational facilities. A large backlog of unmet needs exists, and new requirements are being created by economic growth and technological change.

Table 14.1: Distribution of General Government Expenditures for Civilian Purposes, by Levels of Government, Fiscal Year 1963

Level of government	Civilian government expenditures[a]	
	Amount (millions)	*Per cent*
Federal	$29,736	31.7%
State and local	64,037	68.3%
Total	$93,773	100.0%

Source: Bureau of the Census, *Summary of Government Finances in 1963* (September 1964).

a. Federal figure represents total expenditures excluding expenditures for national defence and international relations, interest on the general debt, and grants to state and local governments. State–local figure includes $8.5 billion of federal grants.

In the future, as in the recent past, the need for these services will rise faster than state–local tax revenue.

Recent Expansion of State–Local Expenditures

The burdens placed on state and local governments in the past two decades (i.e. mid-1940s to mid-1960s) have been extraordinarily heavy. Construction of public facilities virtually stopped during the Second World War and the states and localities found themselves at the war's end with a long list of deficiencies to be filled.

On top of the accumulated backlog, rapid population growth added new demands for state–local services. By the early 1950s, the post-war babies were reaching school age. In the decade 1953–63, the school-age population (those 5–19) rose 40 per cent, while the total population increased only 19 per cent. At the same time, the numbers of older people (those over 65) were rising rapidly, increasing 35 per cent between 1953 and 1963. Thus, the two age groups which require the most costly governmental services, the old and the young, were increasing much faster than the rest of the population.

The problems of population growth were compounded by mobility. People moved from state to state and from region to region; they left the countryside for the towns, and poured out of the inner cities into the suburbs.

134

Financing a Federal System

Table 14.2: State–Local General Expenditure, 1953–63[a]

Fiscal year	State–local expenditures	
	Amount (millions)	Index (1953=100)
1953	$27,910	100
1954	30,701	110
1955	33,724	121
1956	36,711	132
1957	40,375	145
1958	44,851	161
1959	48,887	175
1960	51,876	186
1961	56,201	201
1962	60,206	216
1963	64,037	229

Source: Bureau of the Census, *Summary of Governmental Finances in 1963* (September 1964); and *Historical Statistics on Governmental Finances and Employment*, Census of Governments (1962), Vol. VI, No. 4.
a. General expenditure includes current operations, capital outlays and interest on debt; excludes insurance trust, liquor stores, and public utility expenditure. Federal grants-in-aid are included.

Both the growth of population and its mobility were signs of strength for the American economy, but they imposed heavy costs on state and local governments. New schools, new roads, new sewers, new parks were urgently required in most parts of the country.

At the same time, standards of public service were rising along with incomes. People wanted not only more schools, but better schools. They sought better roads, more adequate hospitals and improved recreational facilities.

To satisfy the most urgent of these needs, state and local governments made strenuous efforts to increase their expenditures. During the decade ending in 1963, annual state and local expenditures for general governmental purposes (current operations, capital outlay, interest on debt) more than doubled, rising from $28 billion to $64 billion (Table 14.2). Over 40 per cent of the increase in state–local expenditures went to education; approximately 17 per cent, to roads (Table 14.3).

Most of the expenditure increase reflected the extraordinary rise in the dependent population (youth and aged), raising the costs of such major

Table 14.3: Distribution of Fiscal Year 1963 State–Local General Expenditure and of 1953–63 Expenditure Increases, by Major Function

Function	Expenditure in 1963, per cent of total	Expenditure increase, 1953–63	
		Amount (millions)	Per cent of total
Education	37.4	$14,549	40.3
Highways	17.3	6,075	16.8
Health and hospitals	7.2	2,306	6.4
Public welfare	8.4	2,453	6.8
All other	29.8	10,744	29.7
Total	100.0	$36,127	1.00

Source: Bureau of the Census, *Summary of Governmental Finances in 1963* (September 1964); and *Historical Statistics on Governmental Finances and Employment*, Census of Governments (1962), Vol. VI, No. 4.
Because of rounding, detail may not add to total.

functions as education, public welfare, health and hospitals. Price changes also accounted for a substantial share of the expenditure rise; construction costs rose rapidly; government employees' wages and salaries, particularly those of teachers, had to be brought closer to compensation levels in private employment. Even moderate salary increases involved large expenditure increases, since personal services constitute a substantial portion of governmental outlays. These increases in the cost of public services left little room for improvement in the quality of services.

The national figures do not disclose the differences in the growth of expenditures in the different states and communities. The improvement in services obviously has been uneven. The wide variation in expenditure levels suggests that deficiencies are far more significant in some parts of the country than in others. For example, in 1963–64, expenditures per pupil in average daily attendance in elementary and secondary schools was over $500 in four states, but less than $350 in nine states. Average payments to families with dependent children in June 1964 varied from less than $20 per recipient in six states to more than $40 in eleven states. Even when allowance is made for differing price levels among the states, these differences in expenditures are significant.

The expenditure figures cited for the decade 1953–1963 measure the amounts spent, and not the amounts that would have been spent if adequate resources had been available to finance a level of government services consistent with need. Adequate measures of the degree to which state and local expenditures fall short of need are not available, but some of the deficiencies are obvious: the overcrowded classrooms, poor housing, the lack of urban planning, the blighted areas with high levels of juvenile delinquency, air and water pollution, the need for mass transit systems in large urban areas, the inadequacy of health and hospital services and of a wide range of other public services through which a better environment could be created. These deficiencies are all the more glaring against the background of rapidly rising consumer expenditures in the private sector.

Sources of Funds

Although the annual amount of federal grants to state and local governments tripled between 1953 and 1963 (from $2.9 billion to $8.7 billion), this increase contributed only 16 per cent of the $35 billion increase in state–local general revenues. These governments obtained 84 per cent of the increase from their own resources (Table 14.4). Moreover, of the total increase in federal aid, about 45 per cent was earmarked for highways. Approximately 25 per cent of the increased aid was for public welfare (mainly public assistance payments to the aged, dependent children, the blind and disabled) and 16 per cent for education (mainly aid to schools in federally affected areas and the school lunch programme.)

Between 1953 and 1963 state and local governments increased their tax collections by $23 billion (111 per cent). Federal tax collections during the same period increased by $24 billion, but the amount in this case represented a 38 per cent increase.

Almost all of the increase in local tax collections and nearly half of the combined state–local increases came from higher property tax revenues. While increases in the tax base resulting from new construction and higher property values contributed significantly to the additional property tax revenues, tax rates were increased substantially. Although property tax rates vary widely, in some regions they are now at such high levels that further substantial increases in these rates are both unlikely and un-desirable.

Of the increases in tax collections at the state level, consumer taxes provided about 60 per cent and income taxes about 20 per cent. Although the increases in these revenues also came in large part from the higher incomes and increased spending made possible by economic growth, the introduction of new taxes and increases in the rates of old taxes were also important contributors. Since 1952, five states have entered the general sales tax field, and two-thirds of the 33 states with general sales taxes in 1952 have raised their rates (some two or three times during this period). Nineteen states now have 3 per cent sales tax rates and 8 states rates in excess of 3 per cent. In the case of the income tax, the rates of increase have

Table 14.4: Sources of Increase in State–Local General Revenues, Fiscal Years 1953–63

Source of increase	Amount of increase (millions)	Per cent of total increase	Per cent of increase in specific taxes
General revenue[a]	$35,411	100.0	
Revenue from federal government[b]	5,798	16.4	
General revenue from own sources	29,613	83.6	
Taxes	23,245	65.6	100.0
Property	10,748	30.4	46.2
Sales and gross receipts	7,508	21.2	32.3
Individual income	2,204	6.2	9.5
Corporation income	688	1.9	3.0
Other	2,098	5.9	9.0
Charges and miscellaneous	6,369	18.0	

Source: Bureau of the Census, *Summary of Governmental Finances in 1963*, (September 1964); and *Historical Statistics on Governmental Finances and Employment*, Census of Governments (1962), Vol. VI, No. 4.
Because of rounding, detail may not add to total.
a. Excludes revenue from publicly operated utilities, liquor stores, and insurance trust systems.
b. Includes in addition to direct grants-in-aid, shared revenues, amounts received from the federal government for contractual services, and payments in lieu of taxes. Excludes grants in kind (distribution of commodities, technical assistance, etc.) and net loans and repayable advances.

been greatest at the lower income levels, and the degree of progressivity has declined. Local governments in some states have moved into sales and payroll taxes.

State and local borrowing (almost exclusively to finance capital improvements) has grown even more rapidly than tax collections. Despite sizeable debt repayments ($4.5 billion in 1963) the outstanding debt of state and local governments reached $86 billion in 1963. The corresponding figure at the end of the Second World War was $16 billion. During the period 1953–1963 alone, the increase was $53 billion (Table 14.5).

Outlook for the Future

The pressure on state and local governments shows no sign of abating. Although these governments have made remarkable efforts in the past decade to meet their most urgent responsibilities, serious deficiencies remain and new needs are being created by population growth, increasing urbanisation, and rising expectations.

Table 14.5: State and Local Government Debt, Fiscal
Years 1953–63

	Debt outstanding	
	---	---
End of fiscal year	*Amount (millions)*	*Index (1953=100)*
1953	$33,782	100
1954	38,931	115
1955	44,267	131
1956	48,868	145
1957	53,039	157
1958	58,187	172
1959	64,110	190
1960	69,955	207
1961	75,023	222
1962	80,802	239
1963	86,443	256

Source: Bureau of the Census, *Summary of Governmental Finances in 1963* (September 1964); and *Historical Statistics of the United States, Colonial Times to 1957.*

This nation's great responsibilities can only be met if education outlays are substantially increased. Although total enrollments will not rise as fast in the next decade as in the recent past, there will be large increases at the secondary and post secondary levels where costs per student are much higher than they are in elementary schools. Vocational and technical training must be greatly improved and expanded both at the high school and post-high school levels if young people are to be adequately prepared for jobs in an increasingly technical world. Teachers' salaries have recently been improved, but they must continue to be raised at least as fast as other professional incomes if teaching is to attract an adequate number of well-trained persons. Classroom shortages have been partially alleviated, but crowding remains, especially in the badly deteriorated schools of our central cities. City schools must be modernised and expanded if city children are to have learning opportunities comparable with those available to children in the suburbs. But these children will need more than new classrooms if they are to have an opportunity to develop their capacities. A considerably higher per pupil outlay is needed in schools of slums and poor areas to provide remedial instruction, counselling, and other special educational services. We are just discovering the kinds of programmes needed to prepare children of disadvantaged families for working and living in our complicated society. These programmes offer hope of reducing poverty, delinquency and unemployment in the future, but the attainment of these objectives will place heavy burdens on state–local educational systems in the years ahead.

The concentration of population in urban centres will continue to create pressing needs for urban renewal and urban planning, parks and recreational facilities, better traffic control and more social services to help individuals and families adjust to the complexities of urban living. Rising incomes and increased household formation will continue to stimulate demands for rising standards of public services. Citizens will call on their governments for better schools, more adequate mental and physical health programmes, and improved recreational facilities. During the decade ending in 1963, state and local government expenditures grew more than 8 per cent per year, or more than twice as fast as GNP (see Table 14.2). There is no reason to expect a slackening of this rate of expansion unless the resources available to state and local governments prove inadequate to sustain it.

There is grave danger that, without substantial assistance from the federal government, state and local revenues will fall far short of their expenditure needs. The basic problem is that needed state and local expenditures rise faster than GNP, while state and local taxes, unlike federal taxes, are relatively unresponsive to economic growth.

The magnitude of the problem may be roughly illustrated by a projection. Suppose GNP grows at 5 per cent per annum and that state–local receipts at existing tax rates and federal grants keep pace with this growth. On these assumptions, state–local receipts would reach about $88 billion by 1970. But if needed state–local expenditures grow at 7 per cent per annum—which seems conservative in the light of past experience and the large backlog of unmet needs—they would reach $103 billion by 1970, leaving a gap of about $15 billion. Even a distribution of $6.5 billion (2 per cent of the estimated individual income tax base by 1970) from the National Trust Fund would fill less than half the gap between projected state–local revenues and expenditures. The rest would have to come from increases in state–local rates or other revenues.

In the absence of federal assistance, public service needs will not be met, or drastic increases in state–local tax rates will be required. But state and local governments are finding it increasingly difficult to raise their tax rates. In every state and municipality, fear of losing new business and of driving commerce and industry to competing jurisdictions restrains new and increased taxes. Elections in several states demonstrate the political hazards facing elected officials who support tax increases. Furthermore, from the standpoint of tax equity and economic policy, it is a matter of concern that currently these long-run requirements must be financed by the revenue sources on which state and local governments largely depend—

property and consumer taxes. If national economic objectives result in successive reduction in federal tax rates while state and local property and consumer taxes continue to increase, the overall pattern of the tax burden will become less equitable. Moreover, as the rates of rising state–local taxes reached practical limits, these governments would be forced to resort to the kind of taxes which create more problems of compliance and administration than is warranted by their yields.

The uneven geographic distribution of resources is also a basic problem in our federal system. Needs and resources do not coincide. State and local services once considered of only local interest are becoming a matter of national importance. The growing urbanisation of the country which concentrates in the cities increasingly large proportions of the less privileged and less prosperous is creating a national problem. Disproportionately heavy service loads (school-age children, unemployed, sick and aged), relatively high unit costs for governmental services; a special need for services linked to urban living; and disproportionately low taxpaying capabilities make it impossible for the cities to discharge their responsibilities as fully as the national interest requires. In some of the rural areas of the country, resources and public services are inadequate to provide a sufficient standard of education, health and welfare. The mobility of the population makes the education and health of disadvantaged individuals, regardless of where they live, a national, rather than a local problem.

Under the present division of functions, many government services critical to the attainment of national social objectives and essential for economic growth are state and local responsibilities. The inadequate revenues available to these governments to finance these services are a cause for national concern.

THE FEDERAL BUDGET OUTLOOK

By contrast with the state and local governments, the federal government has a much brighter fiscal outlook. In the next several years, it will have considerable room for increasing expenditures, for reducing taxes, for retiring the debt, or for a combination of the three. The prospects are as follows:

1. Federal tax receipts will continue to rise sharply with continued economic growth. On the assumption that unemployment will be reduced to 4 per cent of the labour force, GNP will rise from about $623 billion in calendar year 1964 to about $850 billion in 1970.[1] Administration budget receipts, currently estimated at $91.5 billion for fiscal year 1965, will grow

by about $6 billion per year during this period under present tax laws. (This estimate does not include the rise in social security and other trust fund receipts which do not enter into the administrative budget.)

2. According to the best judgement of experts whom we have consulted on the budget and on the attitudes of Congress toward additional expenditure, the rise in federal outlays is likely to be substantially smaller than the rise in receipts under the assumed economic conditions:

(a) National defence expenditures, including atomic energy, were $54.2 billion in fiscal year 1964, and are expected to decline to $52.7 billion in fiscal year 1965. There is a good chance that defence expenditures will continue to decline in the next five years by perhaps as much as $1 billion (or about 2 per cent) per year, unless international conditions seriously worsen.

(b) After rising sharply for several years, expenditures for space research and technology will reach almost $5 billion in fiscal year 1965. Annual appropriations for this programme are now at approximately this level, suggesting a levelling off of these expenditures in the years immediately ahead.

Thus, an additional $7 billion may become available each year in the administrative budget for purposes other than defence and the exploration of space. There has never been a prosperous peacetime period in our history when non-defence expenditures rose this rapidly.[2] Since the end of the Korean War, the annual average expenditure increase for purposes other than defence and space has been about $2 billion; since 1960, it has averaged $2.2 billion.

3. What is the outlook for non-defence expenditures? Clearly, there will be larger federal outlays to provide for the needs of the nation's growing population in an increasingly urbanised and complex society. More public investment will also be needed to achieve satisfactory national economic growth and well-being. But without some new or dramatic change, the growth in federal outlays will be far less than the rise of the revenue potential:

(a) The net 'built-in' increase in administrative budget expenditures is likely to average about $1 to $1.5 billion annually.[3]

(b) Expenditures on recently enacted programmes, such as the Economic Opportunity Program, will rise as they gain momentum. And some new federal activities will undoubtedly be approved by the Congress. But the amounts are likely to be relatively small in the early years. At least in part, they will be offset by cost reductions and other budgetary savings.

(c) On balance, non-defence expenditure increases in the administrative budget—'built-in' or otherwise—will probably average about as much as the increases actually experienced since 1954; perhaps as low as $2 billion per year or as high as $3 billion per year. This will be the case unless large new federal programmes capture the imagination of the people and the support of Congress.

It seems likely, therefore, that the present federal tax system will produce a substantial and growing revenue dividend in the next five years. We expect the potential revenues will grow $4 to $5 billion a year faster than prospective federal expenditures. But even if we have under-estimated the growth of expenditures by as much as $1 or $2 billion per year, there will still be a significant margin in the federal budget for tax reduction, or for debt reduction.

Experience over recent years suggests than an expansionary fiscal policy is needed to maintain an adequate rate of economic advance. For this reason, it does not seem likely that a substantial part of the annual revenue dividend could be safely alloted to debt retirement. Further tax reduction and/or expenditure increases will probably be needed to avoid slowing down the nation's economic growth. Indeed, unless the growth dividend were so used, it would probably not become available at all. Efforts to hold down expenditures while maintaining tax rates would create a 'fiscal drag', braking economic growth and making the maintenance of full employment impossible. And without continued full employment and economic growth, revenue would fall far short of the estimates cited earlier.

The effects of excessive fiscal drag in the federal budget have been amply demonstrated in history. The slow growth of the US economy beginning in the mid-1950s can be traced to the fiscal restraint imposed by a budget policy consisting of steady tax rates and little rise of expenditures, combined with a restrictive monetary policy. If expenditures had been higher, or taxes lower, and if monetary policy had been easier, the nation's income, production and employment would be higher than they are now, and unemployment lower.

The $11.5 billion tax cut enacted early in 1964 reduced the fiscal drag of the federal budget to a significant degree. As the recent figures on retail sales indicate, the cut effectively raised consumer demand, which has turned out to be the major sustaining force in the economy during 1964. But unemployment is still too high, and there is grave danger that the federal budget will begin to slow the economy down again before full employment is reached.

The remedy is to continue to maintain a fiscal policy that promotes, rather than retards, employment and incomes. This means that the government must step in to increase demand if the private economy is not strong enough. Tax reduction is one, but not the only, means available to increase demand. Higher expenditures for government services also have this effect. The difference is that the tax cut route favours private spending, while the expenditure route relies on spending in the public sector. But it is important to note that such public spending need not be at the federal level. Even though the revenue gains are federal, they may be used in part to finance state and local public services.

The Task Force believes that, in the present circumstances, there are too many pressing public needs to justify reliance on tax reduction as the sole mechanism for eliminating the fiscal drag. Since so many of the needs are within traditional state and local responsibilities, it is in the national interest to channel part of the growing stream of federal revenues to the state and local governments. The plan we propose in this report would make the states partners in the increased federal revenues that will be generated in the years ahead and would, at the same time, contribute crucially to the achievement of full employment and at a satisfactory rate of economic growth.

FOUR TAX ALTERNATIVES CONSIDERED

There are many possible ways to channel federal funds to the states. In choosing among them, the Task Force has been guided by the following criteria:

1. The amount made available to the states should be large enough to make possible a significant increase in the level of state–local services.
2. The plan should help to equalise the services available to citizens of different states.
3. The states should have wide latitude in determining the uses of the funds, since they are more familiar with the varying needs of their communities than a centralised agency could be.
4. The plan should not diminish the progressivity of the total federal, state and local tax system.

Four alternatives involving reduction of the federal tax take are frequently proposed to make revenues available to the state and local governments; (1) a general cut in federal taxes to enable the states to raise their own taxes; (2) relinquishment of specific federal taxes to the state and local governments; (3) tax credits for state and local taxes against federal taxes; and (4) tax sharing on the basis of source of collection. We have considered each of these alternatives and have found that, in varying degrees, they fail to meet our criteria.

(1) General Federal Tax Cut
One obvious approach would be to cut federal taxes in order to make room

for states and localities to raise their overall tax take (not necessarily by increases in the types of taxes to which the federal reduction applies). Such a move would increase state–local tax receipts indirectly through its effect on the national income, but by only a small fraction of the revenue released by the federal government. State legislatures and city and county councils would have to take direct action to pick up a major share of the federal revenue loss. Most of the pressures which now stand in the way of increases in state–local taxes would remain. Thus, there would be little assurance that the state and local governments would receive financial help.

Judging from the trends in state–local taxation over the last ten years, such state and local tax increases as would occur probably would be mainly in sales and property taxes. More than one-third of the United States population lives in states that rely almost entirely on property, sales and business taxes. Sales and property taxes provided 78 per cent of the increase in state–local tax revenues between 1953 and 1963. From the stand-point of tax equity and national economic policy, *there is nothing to commend the replacement of federal income taxes by state and local consumer and property taxes.*

Federal tax reduction would also fail to meet the criterion of equalising resources among the states. Poor states whose citizens pay less in federal taxes would gain less than richer states. The slow-growing, less industrial-ised states would also profit least from the indirect beneficial effects of the federal tax reduction on the economy and on their tax bases.

(2) Relinquishment of Federal Taxes to the States

Relinquishment by the federal government of certain tax sources for exclusive use of state and local governments is frequently recommended. Since the end of the Second World War discussions have related primarily to the excise area.

The administration is studying the entire excise tax system and has announced that reduction or elimination of some of them is in order. Although excise tax reduction and reforms are desirable in themselves, they are not effective ways of relinquishing tax revenues to the states and localities. The possible revenue gains to state and local governments would be small. Items subject to federal excises are already taxable under the state (and local) retail sales taxes. It is not likely that the states would either subject these commodities to a higher differential rate under their general sales taxes or impose new selective excises on them. Traditionally, the states have imposed their sales taxes at uniform rates and have made limited use of selective excises, with the exception of the excises on alchoholic beverages and tobacco and the excise on petrol which is considered a user tax. Moreover, the same pressures bought to bear on the Congress for repeal by affected industries and by consumers would be present at the state and local levels to discourage adoption of new taxes on these commodities or increases in present rates applicable to them.

Recent discussions of relinquishment of federal excise tax revenues have not been concerned with the major federal excises: liquor, tobacco, and petrol. Since 1956, the petrol tax has been earmarked for the Federal Highway Trust Fund to be expended through the state highway departments. The wide variation in the rates of state cigarette and liquor taxes seems to indicate that existence of the federal tax does not materially affect the level of state taxes. There is little basis for assuming that if the federal government gave up the $2 billion of revenue from the cigarette tax or the $3.5 billion from liquor taxes, the states would be able to increase their revenues by these amounts. Past experience indicates that reduction or elimination of a federal tax has not been followed by state and local adoptions or increases.

Tax relinquishment, like general tax reduction, would fail to channel larger shares of the released revenues to the poorer states.

(3) Tax Credits

A more effective way of increasing the chances that the states and localities would pick up the revenue released by the federal government would be to give a credit against certain federal taxes for state or local taxes paid. For example, as an alternative to a further reduction of federal income tax rates, citizens could be allowed a credit against their federal tax for state income taxes up to a certain level.

A credit would not automatically increase revenues of state and local governments, however. The credit is to the taxpayer and not to the taxing jurisdiction. The states and localities which impose income taxes would have to raise their rates. Since this could be done without raising total taxes paid by their citizens they would be encouraged to do so. The 17 states without individual income taxes would not benefit from the credit until they imposed such a tax. While encouraging states to shift to income taxes may be desirable, such a move might be regarded as federal coercion and, in some states, would run up against constitutional barriers.

The most important objection to the tax credit approach is its failure to redistribute resources to the neediest states. The maximum amount a state may pick up as new revenue is the amount released by the federal government. At best, the credit simply results in a substitution of state for federal taxation within a state.

(4) Tax Sharing on the Basis of Source of Collection

Proposals have been advanced recently that the federal government share with the states all, or a portion of, the collections originating in each state from certain federal taxes.

While sharing of tax collections is without significant precedent at the federal level, it is a common form of arrangement for transferring revenues at the state–local level. All states share one or more taxes with their local governments. The usual basis for sharing, however, is not source of collection, but some measure of local need (such as population).

A federal tax-sharing proposal being offered currently as a means of giving financial aid to states for elementary and secondary schools provides that a certain percentage of the federal individual income tax collected within each state be turned over to the state for school purposes. Such a distribution would favour the wealthier states.

Another suggestion for a possible source of funds for schools is to share with the states the revenues from the federal tax on local telephone service. The volume of telephone business tends to be concentrated in the industrial and commercial areas and, consequently, telephone tax revenue tends to be distributed in a manner which does not correspond with need for school funds.

Tax sharing on the basis of source of collection will not, therefore, meet the criterion of equalising resources of the state and local governments.

A NATIONAL TRUST FUND FOR THE STATES

The tax alternatives discussed above fail to meet our criteria for a desirable method of channelling federal funds to the states. The most important failure is that none of them makes any contribution towards equalising the public services available to residents of different states. Two of the alternatives could not even be relied on to provide substantial additional tax resources for the states.

The Task Force believes that a superior alternative is available. Specifically, we propose:

1. that a permanent *National Trust Fund for the States* be created to begin operating on 1 July 1966, or a year after congressional enactment, whichever is the later;
2. that the Secretary of the Treasury be directed to deposit in the Trust Fund each year an amount equal to 2 per cent of the federal individual income tax base (taxable income minus exemptions and deductions);
3. that the sums deposited in the Fund be distributed to the states on the basis of population (or an alternative formula which would distribute somewhat greater amounts to the lowest-income states and to those making the greatest tax effort).
4. that the states be permitted to use these funds to improve and expand public services of all types (with the exception of highways).

Operation of the Fund

The Fund would not require the creation of a new agency or administrative staff. At the beginning of each fiscal year the Secretary of the Treasury would make an estimate of 2 per cent of the individual income tax base for the current calendar year. He would then transfer one-twelfth of this amount each month from general fund receipts directly to the Trust Funds correcting for under- or overestimates of the base when more precise statistics become available.

Calculating the amounts going into the Trust Fund would impose no new burden on the Treasury. The income tax base is published annually by the Treasury Department in its official publication, *Statistics of Income.* Estimates for the current year are made as a matter of course by the Treasury in connection with its normal activities. These estimates would be corrected for the small differences that will arise when official figures become available.

Payments to the states from the Trust Fund would be made quarterly. The money would be automatically appropriated by the Congress so that the states would not be in doubt about the availability of the funds. Each state would know, by Treasury announcement in July, the exact amount it could expect to receive in September, December and March, and approximately the amount it could expect in the following June. It would even be possible for the Treasury to announce non-binding preliminary estimates further in advance to meet state legislative and planning needs. ·

The appropriation to the National Trust Fund for the States would be handled in a manner similar to the Old Age and Survivors Insurance Trust Fund or the Highway Trust Fund. The tax receipts would be simultaneously transferred to the Trust Fund and deducted from administrative budget receipts. The receipts and the expenditure transactions would be recorded by the Treasury as Trust Fund transactions. The Trust Fund technique is suggested to give recognition to the permanency of the plan and to highlight the fiduciary relationship of the federal government to the states in respect to the funds set aside from the income tax for this purpose.

Use of the individual income tax base as a basis for calculating amounts going to the Trust Fund automatically provides for increasing the size of the Trust Fund as the economy continues to grow. The income tax base rises as GNP increases, and past experience suggests that it rises by a greater percentage than income. Since 1945, the income tax base has declined only in 1948, when exemptions were increased from $500 to $600, and in 1949, a recession year. Between 1955 and 1963, when its definition remained unchanged, the tax base rose 64 per cent, as compared with a rise of 47 per cent in GNP. This responsiveness of the income tax base to increases in income will ensure that the Trust Fund receipts will grow with the size and the needs of the economy.

In 1965, the individual income tax base probably will amount to about $250 billion, permitting an allocation of $2.5 billion to the Trust Fund for each percentage point set aside for the states. By 1970, the allocation per percentage point would grow to $3 billion assuming 4 per cent annual growth in money GNP; $3.25 billion, assuming 5 per cent growth; and 5 billion assuming 6 per cent growth.

To be helpful to the state and local governments, the grants to be made from the receipts of the Trust Fund should be sizeable. We propose that the receipts set aside be 2 per cent of the income tax base. This would amount to a total of $5 billion at next year's expected income levels—or about one year's increase in state–local expenditures. It is also about 7 per cent of next year's state–local expenditures, which are expected to approach $75 billion. However, if $5 billion is too large an amount at the outset for budgetary or other reasons, the Trust Fund could be established with 1 per cent of the tax base and built up to 2 per cent in two or three years.

Although the sums proposed for the Trust Fund may seem to be large, they would actually be small relative to the increase in federal funds expected to occur in the next few years. As we have already indicated, an additional $7 billion each year may well be available to the federal government for tax reduction or additional expenditures. If this assumption proves correct, the additional funds available for these purposes five years from now would amount to at least $35 billion. Even if the amount allocated to the Trust Fund grew to say $6.5 billion in five years, this sum would be less than 20 per cent of the additional $35 billion expected to be available. Another $28.5 billion would be left for tax reduction, debt reduction, other federal expenditure increases—including specific grant programmes—which will most certainly be needed, or for the further enlargement of the Trust Fund.

We suggest that the plan be put into operation one year after the creation of the Trust Fund, but no earlier than 1 July 1966. This timing is recommended to permit the state governments to make decisions regarding the use of funds and the federal government to accommodate its fiscal policies to the new programme.

Method of Allocation to the States
Ideally, the distribution of the annual proceeds among the states should be based on their need for public services (the costs of providing given service levels in different states) as well as their fiscal capacity (their ability to provide these services from state and local resources). Neither need nor capacity, however, is easily measured.

A state's need for public services depends on many factors, including its population, the age distribution of the population, population density, the proportion of low-income individuals and families and local unit costs. A state's fiscal capacity also depends on a variety of factors, including population, personal income, and the value of taxable property and sales. An allocation formula which reflected all these factors — and possibly others, such as tax effort — would be difficult to construct and highly complex. Among simple indicators, population seems to us the most appropriate basis for allocation. *We therefore recommend that the Trust Fund be distributed to the states on a per capita basis.*

Since the cost of most public services depends on the number of people to be served, we regard population as a reasonably good indicator of general need for such services. Moreover, per capita allocation of the Trust Fund makes some allowance for capacity. Residents of high income states pay more federal income tax per capita than do residents of low income states. Hence, distribution of the Trust Fund on a per capita basis would tend to redistribute resources from high- to low-income states.

Per capita distribution, however, may not adequately reflect the special urgency of the need for fiscal assistance by the poorest states. This special urgency could be recognised by reserving a part of the Trust Fund for an additional distribution to states with particularly low per capita personal income.

It might also be desirable to include a measure of tax effort (for example, state–local tax collections as a percentage of personal income) among the factors determining a state's share in the Trust Fund. Inclusion of an effort factor would give the states an incentive to maintain and increase their own tax collections, and would allay fears that states with lower than average tax rates were 'getting a free ride'.

Table 14.6 shows how the states ranked on the basis of per capita personal income would have been affected in 1963 by five different ways of sharing $4 billion in federal revenues. The results shown in the table are discussed briefly.

1. If the funds had been distributed on the basis of federal income tax paid by the residents of each state, the high-income states would have benefited most. The ten states with the highest per capita income would have received an average of $28 per capita and the lowest only $12 per capita.
2. If the funds had been distributed on the basis of population, each state would have received about $21 per capita, regardless of its position in the income distribution. These funds would have been more important to the poorer states, however, when compared with their per capita public expenditure. An allocation of $21 per capita would have been equivalent to 5 per cent of 1963 state and local expenditure in the ten highest income states and 8 per cent in the ten lowest income states.
3. If the distribution had been made on the basis of population weighted by the ratio of average to state per capita income, the lower income states

Table 14.6: Grant Per Capita and as Percentage of State–Local Expenditure Under Five Methods of Allocating $4 Billion Among the States (based on data for fiscal year 1963)

Method of distribution	Averages for states by quintiles ranked according to per capital personal income[a]				
	10 highest	2nd 10	3rd 10	4th 10	10 lowest
Grant per capita					
Reference distribution: Federal income tax contribution	28.46	21.57	17.93	14.95	12.04
Per capita distribution—Method I	21.31	21.31	21.31	21.31	21.31
Per capita with income weight—Method II	16.70	20.11	22.04	24.98	29.48
Per capita with low-income weight—Method III	19.50	19.50	19.50	21.78	30.03
Method III with effort weight—Method IV	18.22	19.38	21.62	22.89	26.71
Grant as percentage of state–local expenditure					
Reference distribution: Federal income tax contribution	7.18	5.95	5.11	4.61	4.59
Per capita distribution—Method I	5.34	5.87	6.05	6.52	8.20
Per capita with income weight—Method II	4.19	5.54	6.24	7.64	11.38
Per capita with low-income weight—Method III	4.89	5.37	5.53	6.65	11.62
Method III with effort weight—Method IV	4.54	5.25	6.09	6.93	11.40

a. Not including District of Columbia.

would have received more and the higher income states less than under a straight per capita distribution. This method would have given the ten highest income states $17 per capita and the ten lowest $29 per capita. This is the method by which income, as a measure of capacity, is usually introduced into grant formulae, but it is often alleged that the method penalises the industrial states. These states have high incomes, but they also have particularly acute needs arising from the special problems and high costs of densely populated urban areas. Hence, we sought another formula which would help the poorest states without penalising the high income states so much.

4. To illustrate a plan for social help to the poorest states, we distributed the bulk of the fund among all the states on the basis of population, with

$8\frac{1}{2}$ per cent reserved for additional support to the 18 states with the lowest per capita income. This additional amount was divided among these states in inverse relation to per capita income in the particular state. Such a formula would have resulted in average per capita payments of $20 to the top ten states and $30 to the lowest ten.

5. If a tax effort factor had been used in addition to the low income factor, the average result for groups of states would not have been much different because effort is not closely associated with income. Nevertheless, distributions to some individual states within income groups would be substantially affected.

If the amount allocated to the Trust Fund were 2 per cent of the income tax base, the total distribution to the states would amount to $5 billion and the per capita grant would be $26.[4]

State Uses of the Funds

Some public services have special importance because they affect directly the ability of the individual to develop his own capacities. Good schools and health programmes, recreation opportunities and community services all develop human resources—they increase the ability of people to lead productive and satisfying lives.

These services are of particular national concern because Americans are such a mobile people. One out of three Americans lives in a state other than his state of birth. The harm done by poor education, poor health care and poor environment in one part of the country is carried to other parts of the country by migration.

The Task Force recommends that the states strongly be encouraged to spend the funds they receive from the National Trust Fund to expand and improve their services in the broad area of human resource development. The legislation creating the Trust Fund should have a preamble expressing national concern with the level of public services designed to develop human capacities and the intent of the federal government in establishing the Trust Fund to help the states and localities expand and improve these services.

The Task Force believes, however, that it would not be desirable to limit the expenditure of Trust Fund receipts by the states to specific types of expenditures. We would recommend a prohibition on the use of the funds for highways, since highway expenditures are already financed by the Highway Trust Fund, but no other restrictions. The purpose of the Trust Fund is to strengthen the federal system and the ability of state and local governments to respond to the needs of their citizens. The states should be free to spend the funds for programmes which seem to them to have highest priority. The Task Force believes that earmarking portions of the Fund for specific areas, or the exercising of federal controls over the specific programmes for which the states choose to spend the money, would detract from the basic purpose of providing general support for state and local government functions.[5]

The states would also be free to distribute their Trust Fund receipts to local governments in the manner most suited to their particular circumstances. The states vary greatly in the extent to which they delegate responsibilities to, and share revenues with, local governments. All states give some aid to local units and most give substantial amounts. In the aggregate, intergovernmental transfers from state to local governments account for more than half of state general expenditures and nearly one-third of local general revenues. State governments provide nearly two-fifths of the amount spent by local governments for education, although the arrangements vary greatly from state to state. The Task Force believes that the states should make allocations to local government units conforming with the relative needs of those units, but, in view of the differences among states in forms of intergovernmental cooperation, it does not seem feasible or desirable to designate a specific portion of the Trust Fund receipts for local use. The individual states are in a better position to make the allocations.

Relation to Specific Grants-in-Aid

In recommending this plan to strengthen the general resources of state and local government, the Task Force recognises that the national interest is often best served by inducing states and localities to offer specific services which they might not otherwise offer or by setting minimum service standards. These circumstances call for specific programme grants. The Trust Fund is not designed to supplant such grants, but rather to provide general support for the major functions which, under our federal system, have been the responsibility of state and local governments.

Specific grants have been the principal vehicle for federal financial assistance to state and local government in recent years. Total federal grants to states and localities tripled between fiscal years 1953 and 1963 (in large part due to grants for highways), rising from $2.8 to $8.4 billion, and are expected to exceed $10 billion in fiscal year 1965. We anticipate further substantial increases in federal grants for specific programmes of national importance.

The main advantage of the specific grant approach applies where Congress wishes to support selected activities in which there is a particularly strong national interest. It can set standards and regulate the conditions under which the funds are spent. Through matching provisions and similar devices, Congress can ensure that the federally supported programmes receive state support as well. Allocation and variable matching formulae can be used to channel funds into states where the need for the particular programme is greatest or where fiscal capacity is least.

The support of particular activities through specific grants will remain an important federal function. At the same time, there are many state–local services of national interest that can not be appropriately dealt with by specific grants. Unnecessary administrative burden on the federal government may be avoided, and varying preferences of states and localities may be allowed for more fully, if their ability to render such services is strengthened by a general grant.

We conclude that there is need in our national system of intergovernmental fiscal cooperation for general assistance to the states and to local governments, as well as for specific grants-in-aid. Both have an important job to do. The general grants to be received from the federal Trust Fund will give the states considerable latitude in allocating funds for needs that they consider most urgent. The specific grant programmes, many of which are being examined in some detail by other Task Forces, will remain an essential instrument for securing minimum service levels and encouraging those activities which warrant special attention.

CONCLUSION

The Task Force believes:

1. that high quality public facilities and services are essential to an environment in which individuals can develop their full capacities:
2. that disparities in the levels of public services provided in different sections of the country are costly to all sections:
3. that increasing the capacity of state and local governments to meet the needs of their citizens for public services is in the national interest: and
4. that allocating a portion of our growing federal revenues to the states will help to promote economic growth and stability.

We have proposed the creation of a Trust Fund that would automatically allocate a growing amount of federal revenues to the states to expand and improve public services. The plan is consistent with the spirit of our federal system of government. If our federalism is to meet the challenge of the last third of the twentieth century, we must take advantage of this excellent opportunity to strengthen the ability of the states and local governments to provide for the public services of our great and growing society.

NOTES

1. This estimate assumes that consumer prices and the GNP deflator would rise by 1.5 per cent a year, chiefly reflecting quality improvements and modest price increases for services. This assumption is consistent with stable wholesale prices.
2. An increase of $7.4 billion occurred in fiscal year 1947, but this was largely connected with post-war reconstruction outlays (e.g. there were increases of $2 billion for the Treasury loan to the United Kingdom, $1.2 billion for the United Nations Relief and Rehabilitation Administration and other foreign relief, $1.3 billion for the subscription to the International Bank and Monetary Fund, and about $3 billion for veterans' benefits). In 1959, an expenditure jump of about $6.7 billion was related to the effects of the 1957–58 recession, and to certain non-recurring factors; for example, a temporary anti-recession housing programme of $1 billion, an increase of labour and welfare expenditures—including temporary extended unemployment benefits—of $0.7 billion, an increase in agricultural expenditures of over $2 billion (due to extraordinarily large crops), and a non-recurring subscription of $1.4 billion to the International Monetary Fund.
3. Total federal payments increase by somewhat more than $3 billion each year under present laws, but most of this 'built-in' increase is in social security and other trust fund benefits, which are financed by trust fund receipts.
4. This approximates conditions for calendar year 1965.
5. Unconditional grants for general government support have had extensive and varied use in Australia and Canada. These countries have federal systems like those of the US and similar failures of the division of functions between federal and state governments to balance the division of revenues.

15. State–Local Finance Beyond Revenue Sharing*

When I was invited to give this paper, few people were predicting that the Revenue Sharing Bill would be passed by the 92nd Congress. I shall leave it to the political scientists to explain why the Bill did get through—eight years after the idea was launched by Walter Heller and worked out in detail by a Task Force which I chaired (see Chapter 14 above). But it *is* an important piece of legislation, and a significant departure from past federal grant-in-aid policies. Furthermore, it was enacted for an initial period of five years, so it cannot be regarded as a permanent feature of the federal grant structure. It is not too soon, therefore, to begin evaluating the legislation as it was finally enacted so that Congress will be able to judge the programme when the time comes to renew or abandon it.

Revenue sharing has been the subject of heated debate ever since it was proposed. It has been hailed by some as a revolutionary step in fiscal federalism, while others have warned that it would ruin state and local government in this country. I have personally never been both praised and maligned as much for any idea I have supported as I have been for this one—even though this idea has never seemed as earth-shaking to me as it has seemed to many of its zealous supporters and opponents.

In view of this rather unusual history, I thought it would be appropriate to use this opportunity—so soon after the legislation was passed—to review the rationale and original design of revenue sharing, compare the final legislation with the original proposal, and suggest criteria by which the programme should eventually be judged. Since I do not believe that revenue sharing is the solution to all the nation's intergovernmental financial problems, I should also like to suggest what additional steps need to be taken to strengthen our fiscal federalism. In particular, I feel strongly that there is an urban problem in this country which revenue sharing in its present form cannot solve and that federal and state governments will have to take strong action to prevent a national crisis.

*Reprinted from *The Economic Outlook for 1971* (University of Michigan, 1973), pp. 69–80.

RATIONALE OF REVENUE SHARING

While the states and local governments have always had their fiscal problems, their predicament reached a crisis stage during the 1960s. In the ten years ending 30 June 1970, state–local revenues from their own sources rose at an annual rate of 9.6 per cent, while GNP rose at an annual rate of 6.8 per cent. This feat was accomplished with a tax system that is much less responsive to economic growth than the federal system. To fill the gap between revenue needs—which rose faster than the GNP—and revenue growth, the states and local governments adopted new taxes and increased the rates on old taxes. Since state and local governments rely heavily on sales and property taxes, unnecessarily harsh burdens were imposed on the lowest income groups. The continued increases in tax rates met with increasing resistance from the voters, with unfortunate consequences for public services and facilities that were urgently needed almost everywhere.

The mismatch between state–local revenue needs and revenue sources was partially alleviated by unilateral action on the part of the federal government. As federal revenues continued to respond to economic growth, federal grants-in-aid increased dramatically—from $7 billion in 1959/60 to almost $33 billion in 1971/72. In addition, as the decade of the 1960s wore on, more and more attention was given to the possibility of sharing by the federal government of its growth-elastic tax receipts with the states and local governments on a more or less automatic basis and without restriction as to the use of the funds.

As soon as it was launched, the idea of revenue sharing immediately created a sharp controversy over the merits of conditional federal grants. Both sides agreed that the federal government had to increase its assistance to state and local governments. The disagreement concerned the form in which the assistance should be given. Walter Heller and I took the view that unrestricted as well as conditional grants are needed to achieve the objectives of federalism and that the system would be deficient without both types of grants.

Conditional grants are intended to encourage the states and local governments to do certain things which Congress deems to be in the national interest. They are justified on the ground that the benefits of many public services 'spill over' from the community in which they are performed to other communities. Each state or community would tend to pay only for the benefits likely to accrue to its own citizens and, as a result, expenditures for such services would be too low if financed entirely by state–local sources. Assistance by the federal government is needed to raise the level of expenditures for such programmes closer to the optimum from the national standpoint. To achieve this optimum, a conditional grant should have enough restrictions—minimum standards and matching requirements—to assure Congress that the funds will be used for assigned purposes and that states and local governments will pay for benefits that accrue to their own citizens.

Unconditional or *general purpose grants* are justified on substantially different grounds. First, the basic need for unconditional grants arises from the obvious fact that all states and local governments do not have equal capacity to pay for public services. Poorer states and communities are simply unable to match the revenue raising ability of richer ones, and cannot afford to support public services at a level that approaches adequacy. Second, federal use of the best tax sources and the fear that tax rate increase will drive citizens and businesses to neighbouring states operate to restrain needed tax increases at the state level. This justifies some federal assistance to all states, but the poorer states should receive relatively more help because of their low fiscal capacities.

Thus, conditional and general purpose grants have very different objectives and these could not be satisfied if the federal system were limited to one or the other type of grant. Conditional grants are intended to help *people* either directly through cash assistance or indirectly through the support of government programmes that will benefit them. General purpose grants are intended to help *governments* that do not have adequate fiscal capacity because too many low-income people reside within their borders. Revenue sharing cannot provide the stimulus to particular programmes obtained by the conditional grant approach. Conversely, the existence of a conditional grant programme will not provide the fiscal support needed to finance the portion of other state–local services that people at the lower end of the income scale cannot support out of their meagre incomes.

The equalisation objective is achieved in most revenue sharing plans by allocating the funds among the states and local governments mainly on the basis of population. Suppose a poor state collects $400 per capita from its residents, while another state making the same tax effort collects $800 per capita. A $50 per capita grant would increase the fiscal resources of the poor state by 12.5 per cent and the rich state by 6.25 per cent. An additional equalising effect could be obtained by weighting the population figures by the inverse of state per capita incomes or by distributing part of the funds exclusively among the bottom third or half of the states when ranked by per capita income.

It is important to stress that equalisation is the major objective of revenue sharing. While others differ with me on this point, in my view, revenue sharing would not be needed if the distribution of income and wealth was the same throughout the country. If all communities had the same average income and wealth, the same tax structure could yield the same revenues everywhere. The federal government would presumably finance programmes that provided national benefits. Each community would decide the level of expenditures, and therefore, of tax rates, to provide public services (that is, those with local or regional benefits) for the people that live within its boundaries. With the same fiscal capacity, expenditures might differ, but no community would be thwarted because of the lack of fiscal resources.

But this ideal arrangement is not possible in a national system in which the distribution of income and wealth is unequal. A simple example may help to explain the point. The average per capita income in the poorest five states is roughly $2800; it is not quite $5000 in the five richest states. Suppose one of the poor states levied a 10 per cent income tax, that is, an income tax that collected 10 per cent of the total personal income in that state, and suppose one of the richer states also levied a 10 per cent income tax. (In order to collect that much revenue, the poorer state would have to have substantially higher rates simply because the people wouldn't be in as high brackets.) The 10 per cent income tax in the poor states would yield $280 per capita; the 10 per cent income tax in the rich states would yield $500 per capita. In other words, with the same average tax rate on personal income (which would require higher nominal rates in the poor state), the rich state could afford almost twice the public services that the poor state could afford. Alternatively, to receive the same quantity of public services, a resident of the rich state would have to pay much lower taxes than a person with the same income who resides in the poor state.

But why not equalise fiscal capacity by simply giving money to people rather than to governments? The answer is that there are poor governments as well as poor people. Suppose that the federal government adopted a negative income tax that provided an adequate minimum income for all citizens in the United States. By definition, since the minimum allowance is at the poverty level, the family which receives it has no ability to pay for public services. In addition, those immediately above the minimum income level have very little capacity to pay taxes. Thus, the state and local governments with a high concentration of low income people must receive outside funds to be able to support needed public services. Some have argued that this objective could be satisfied by a set of categorical grants for the major local public services. But it is inconceivable that any such set could be devised to approximate the equalisation effect of one general grant based on per capita income or the incidence of low incomes.

THE ORIGINAL REVENUE SHARING PROPOSAL

The core of the original revenue sharing plan, with which Walter Heller and I have been identified, was the regular distribution of a specified portion of the federal individual income tax to the states primarily on the basis of population. The essential features of the plan were as follows:

1. The federal government each year would set aside and distribute to the states an eventual 2 per cent of the federal individual income tax base (the amount reported as net taxable income by all individuals). This would mean that, under the present rate schedule which begins at 14 per cent and rises to a maximum of 70 per cent, the federal government would collect 2 percentage points in each bracket for the states and 12–68 percentage points for itself.

2. The states would share the funds on the basis of population, weighted by relative tax effort. In addition, a portion of the funds could be set aside for supplements to states with low capita income or with a high incidence of poverty. The purpose of the tax effort factor was to encourage states to maintain or increase their own tax effort. The supplement to low-income states was designed to augment the automatic equalisation effect of the basic per capita distribution.

3. Whether to leave the fiscal claims of the localities to the mercies of the political process and the institutional realities of each state or to require a pass-through to them was not an easy question. Originally, we left this question open, but soon concluded that the legitimate—and pressing—claims of local government required explicit recognition in the basic formula of revenue sharing. However, the allocation among units of government cannot be determined on any scientific basis, so we did not venture to suggest any particular formula for the pass-through. In fact, this turned out to be the most difficult practical issue throughout the legislative history of the bill.

4. Constraints on the use of the funds were to be much less detailed than those applying to conditional grants. However, the funds were not to be available for highway construction, since there is a special federal trust fund with its own earmarked revenue sources for this purpose. An audit of the actual use of the funds was to be required, as well as certification by the appropriate state and local officials that all applicable federal laws, such as the Civil Rights Act, have been complied with in the activities financed by the grants.

THE FINAL LEGISLATION

Although Congress tinkered with every part of the proposal, I believe it is fair to say that the final legislation bears a marked resemblance to the original.

1. I suppose it was too much to expect that Congress would allocate funds to revenue sharing on the basis of a formula tied to the individual income

tax base. Instead, it allocated a total of $30.2 billion over the five-year period, 1972 through 1976, with the amounts rising from $5.3 billion in 1972 to $6.5 billion in 1976. These amounts will start out at somewhat more than 1 per cent of taxable income at the beginning of the period and decline to somewhat less than 1 per cent at the end. So, the Congress cut our suggested figure about in half on the average, but provided for some growth each year—which was, of course, the major objective of the formula based on taxable income.

2. The share of the revenue sharing funds going to each state includes the population, tax effort and income factors we suggested, but it also includes much more. The House Bill contained a five-factor formula under which two-thirds of the funds were to be divided among the states on the basis of total population, urbanised population, and population inversely weighted by per capita income, and one-third on the basis of state individual income tax collections and relative tax effort. The Senate preferred a formula based on population, tax effort and per capita income.

It will come as a surprise to no one that the Conference Committee decided to make the allocation on the basis of the larger amount obtained by each state from the two formulae. Since the sum of these amounts exceeded the totals allocated to the programme, they were all scaled down proportionately to yield the proper total.

The final formula gives weight to five factors: total population, urbanised population, per capita income, tax effort and individual income tax collections. Three of these factors—population, tax effort and per capita income—were included in the original revenue sharing proposal. The inclusion of an incentive for the states to collect more revenue from the individual income tax is all to the good. The urbanisation factor will help the more densely-populated states, but it may also act to neutralise the effect of the other factors.

My colleague, Robert Reischauer, has calculated that the final compromise will have a considerable equalising effect at the state level (Table 15.1). When the states are ranked on the basis of 1971 per capita incomes, the 1972 revenue sharing grants will add 3.6 per cent to the revenues raised by the richest ten states from their own sources in fiscal year 1970/71 and 7.1 per cent to the revenues raised by the poorest ten. The equalising effect is equally pronounced on the basis of personal income: the richest ten states will receive $5.30 per $1000 of 1971 personal income, and the poorest ten will receive $9.60 per $1000. Unfortunately, it is impossible to make these calculations at this time for the local units of government.

3. One-third of the revenue sharing funds going to each state was allocated to the state governments, and the remaining two-thirds to the local governments. The allocation among local governments is to be made on the basis of population, tax effort and per capita income, which were the three

Table 15.1: Relationship of Revenue Sharing Grants to State–Local Revenues from Own Sources and to State Personal Income, by States Ranked by per Capita Personal Income

	Revenue sharing grants in 1972 as per cent of:	
States ranked by 1971 per capita personal income	*State–local revenues from own sources, 1970–71*	*$1000 of personal income, 1971*
Top 10	3.6	5.3
Second 10	4.2	5.8
Third 10	4.4	6.1
Fourth 10	5.5	7.8
Lowest 10	7.1	9.6

Sources: Revenue sharing grants: *State and Local Fiscal Assistance Act of 1972*, Joint Committee on Internal Revenue Taxation (27 September 1972), p. vi; State–Local revenues and state personal incomes: *Governmental Finances in 1970–71*, Bureau of the Census, GF 71 No. 5, pp. 31–2, 52.

factors included in the original proposal. In making this decision, Congress carried through the equalisation objective down to the local government level.

4. The states will be permitted to spend the revenue sharing funds for any purpose, except that the funds cannot be used to match any other federal grant. Local governments will be permitted to spend the revenue sharing funds on a long list of items that account for perhaps a third of total state–local spending. Since money is fungible, this should give local governments much of the flexibility in spending that was sought in the original proposal. Although Congress could not bring itself to endorse the nomenclature, it gave the states and local governments virtually the same degree of latitude that was envisaged by those of us who proposed that no strings be attached.

The legislation also requires that each state and local government will report to the Secretary of the Treasury on the use of the funds and to publish a copy of the reports in a newspaper in the geographic area of the government making the report. A non-discrimination provision is also included in the Bill, as originally contemplated.

5. As an extra bonus, the Bill also gives the Internal Revenue Service the authority to collect state individual income taxes along with the federal income tax at no cost to the states. To qualify for this new 'piggybank' programme, states will be required to base their taxes on federal taxable income or collect a flat percentage of the federal tax liability. By putting the better federal collection and enforcement procedures at the disposal of the

states, this provision will increase the yield of state income taxes. Together with the bonus provided to income tax states by the basic distribution formula, the piggybank arrangement may encourage the few remaining non-income tax states to add the income tax to their tax structures.

JUDGING THE EFFECTIVENESS OF REVENUE SHARING

It would be difficult to make a complete listing of all the beneficent effects expected of revenue sharing by its proponents. The objective I have stressed most is equalisation; others have suggested that revenue sharing would promote efficiency in government, make government programmes 'more responsive to the people', and even 'revolutionise' the federal system of government in this country. I propose to list a few criteria which, while less grandiose, have the virtue that they can be applied in a meaningful way to the experience of 50 states myriads of local governments.

First, the basic test of the success or failure of revenue sharing will be whether it does in fact improve the ability of poor states and poor local governments to pay for public services. It is fortunate that the next Census of Governments will be for the fiscal year ending 30 June 1972, the last fiscal year prior to revenue sharing. This record should provide the basic data needed to determine whether differentials in fiscal capacity have in fact been narrowed by revenue sharing and whether the tremendous service disparities that exist among different localities have been reduced. On the basis of the figures I have just cited for 1970/71, it seems clear that the equalisation effect among states will be substantial. How the legislation will effect local governments is not clear.

Second, greater revenue effort on the part of the states and local governments was an objective of virtually every proponent of revenue sharing, since practically all the competing plans gave some weight to revenue effort in allocating the funds. Yet many have argued that revenue sharing would in fact reduce state–local revenue effort. This issue will be difficult to resolve, since we shall never know what expenditures might have been without revenue sharing. A number of models of state–local expenditures have already been developed, and others will doubtless appear. A cash programme may well be needed to develop an adequate model for this purpose. Five years from now, Congress will want to know whether state–local revenue effort has increased, decreased or remained unchanged as a result of revenue sharing, and economists and political scientists should be ready to answer this question.

Third, the existence of revenue sharing will give Congress an opportunity at last to decide between the categorical and non-categorical approach whenever intergovernmental financial decisions are being made. Most experts agree that the narrow categorical grants have been overworked; some revisions and even pruning of these programmes are doubtless in order. (The Nixon administration recommended consolidation of most of the grants into six major 'special revenue sharing' programmes, an approach which, I believe, goes too far in relinquishing federal control over the grant programmes.) Revenue sharing will have contributed to the rationalisation of the grant system if, after five years, there is at least a good beginning toward confining categorical grants to areas of major national interest, with enough restraints in the programme to ensure conformity of the state–local governments with the national objectives. This will be a much more difficult criterion to apply than the previous two, but qualitative judgements should not be impossible.

Fourth, just as the national government is responsible for financing public programmes that have a national interest, so the states have a responsibility to finance programmes that have a regional interest. In addition, states also have a responsibility to help equalise fiscal capacities of their own units of government. It will be necessary, therefore, to monitor the response of the state governments carefully to see that revenue sharing does not given them an opportunity to shirk their intra-state responsibilities.

Fifth, revenue sharing sailed through Congress so easily this year in part because it was seen by many of the urban representatives in the House as a device to do something quickly about the acute financial problems of the nation's major cities. The House Bill attempted to recognise this problem by giving weight to urbanisation in the distribution formula for local governments. But, in the end, the Bill omitted urbanisation from the formula. Since the total amount of money going to local governments is small relative to their total expenditures, the urbanisation factor would have had only a marginal effect in improving the financial conditions of the cities and would have also greatly benefited the rich urban suburbs. In any case, an obvious test of the success of revenue sharing is whether it will provide real financial help to the cities, but, as I shall indicate below, I doubt that general revenue sharing—in any form—can pass this test.

THE PLIGHT OF THE CITIES

During the last few years, city finances have emerged as the major fiscal problem in the nation. Many, if not most, of the largest cities have found themselves with inadequate fiscal resources to pay for their rapidly growing expenditures. The states have been of little help in most instances. New York City, Newark, Detroit, Philadelphia, are in desperate straits, yet they are located in states that have better than average fiscal capacity by any standard. In these and other cases, the states make it a practice to keep the cities on very short financial rations, instead of adopting a rational procedure for estimating the cities' expenditure needs and for helping them raise the revenues to meet these needs in a fair and equitable manner.

The fiscal plight of the cities results from two basic facts of life:

1. Throughout the entire country, the tax base is moving from the cities to the suburbs, while the expenses of operating public services for residents and commuters are rising sharply. The poor—who have no ability to pay taxes—are concentrated in the cities, while the middle- and high-income recipients are in surrounding suburbs. Few cities in the country have been able to cope with this phenomenon.

2. The state legislatures are often controlled by representatives of the suburbs who believe that it is in their interest to prevent the city from levying taxes on suburbanites to pay for the costs they impose on the city. Hence, many cities are shortchanged in state grant-in-aid programmes and others are prohibited from levying taxes on the earnings of commuters. This selfish attitude of suburbanites toward city finances helps to impoverish the city even more, and leads to further deterioration in the very places where they earn their livelihoods and satisfy most of their cultural and recreational needs.

It should be obvious to everyone that the cities of this country are a vital part of its economic and social life. They are centres of industry and commerce, education, arts and letters, theatre and sports, and other economic, cultural and recreational activities. These benefits accrue to people throughout the country, as well as to the residents of the metropolitan areas in which the cities are located. Thus the costs should not be borne by residents of the surrounding communities, and some should be borne by residents of other parts of the country. This explains why both the state and national governments should be concerned with the financing of city services.

In the absence of metropolitan government, it is the responsibility of the state government to see to it that suburbanities help pay for the cities which they use as centres of employment, intellectual activity and recreation. Where a metropolitan area is entirely within one state, the state could solve the problem in a simple way by allocating a special general or block grant to the cities out of state funds. Where the metropolitan area covers two or more states, the central city could be given the authority to levy a special income tax (piggybacked to the state tax) which would apply to the full income of its residents and to the earnings of commuters in the city. In normal practice, commuters who are residents of other states are allowed to credit such taxes on their earnings against the income tax of their state of residence, so that this arrangement should not create any serious cases of double taxation.

The federal government can discharge its responsibility by making two revisions in its grant programmes.

First, it is time that the federal government recognised that poverty is a national and not a state–local problem and that it should bear the entire cost of the welfare system. Release of state and local fiscal resources now used to pay welfare benefits would provide no-strings-attached funds, with the distribution based on the number of welfare recipients and the benefits currently paid rather than on the basis of total population and the other factors included in the Revenue Sharing Bill. The urban states and some of the large cities have been carrying the fiscal burden because the federal government has so far refused to recognise its full responsibility in this area. Correction of this inequity (as well as reform of the welfare system) is an essential step for the modernisation of the system of intergovernmental fiscal relations in this country.

Second, a special block grant to the large cities—over and above the grants provided in the Revenue Sharing Bill—is needed to recognise the special role and unique problems of the largest cities. Since the cities provide national as well as regional benefits the federal and state governments should share the cost of this new grant. The federal government could ensure the cooperation on the part of the states by matching the funds allocated by the state for block grants to the largest cities. I realise that it will be difficult to persuade the Congress to enact a programme which will benefit the constituents of only a part of its membership. But unless statesmanship overcomes provincialism, the cities will continue to lose middle- and high-income families who will neither tolerate the inadequate public services that their poor neighbours must accept, nor pay higher taxes to carry the burden for their neighbours. The result will be further decay in our largest cities and continued deterioration of city services and benefits which are so vital to the health and welfare of the nation.

CONCLUSION

Revenue sharing is not a panacea for all the fiscal problems of the state and local governments. It is a constructive piece of legislation which will provide needed revenues for public services in some places and moderate the growth of undesirable state–local taxes in others. The basic purpose of revenue sharing is equalisation of state–local resources; unless it promotes this objective to a significant degree, I shall regard the revenue sharing experiment as a failure.

I do not accept the proposition that revenue sharing will revolutionise the relationship between the federal government and the states and local governments. It may well be that, upon examination, some of the present categorical grants should be eliminated and others consolidated into broader groups; but the purpose of categorical grants is to stimulate specific governmental activities, and this cannot be done effectively without direction in some detail by the federal government. Consequently, another major test of the wisdom of this legislation is whether the Congress uses revenue sharing and categorical grants for the purposes for which they were designed. If revenue sharing is used to gut the categorical grant system, it will have been a bad bargain.

Finally, revenue sharing cannot solve the fiscal problems of the cities. The viability of the nation's largest cities is of concern to everyone—to those who live in other parts of the country as well as to those who live in close proximity to them. Those outside the cities reap substantial benefits from them, and they should be prepared to pay for the costs of running the cities. The states must give the cities enough taxing powers—including the power to tax the earnings of commuters—to pay for the extra costs imposed on them by outsiders, or provide the cities with general funds as a substitute. The federal government should in turn provide special grant funds—on a matching basis with the states—for use exclusively by the largest cities. It is still possible to save the cities, but unfortunately there seems to be little impetus anywhere to take the steps needed to prevent further decay and even bankruptcy in some places.

Part Five
Income Maintenance

16. Is a Negative Income Tax Practical?*

The war on poverty has brought emphatically to public attention the inadequacies of the nation's welfare system. The assistance given to the impoverished is pitifully inadequate in most states, and the rules under which it is given severely impair both the incentives and the potential of the recipients to help themselves. Most poor people are ineligible for public assistance, so restrictive are the eligibility requirements for the various categories of federal, state and local welfare programmes. Many eligible poor people do not accept assistance from local welfare agencies because recipients are subject to numerous indignities by the procedures employed to enforce the means test and other conditions which determine who is entitled to help and to how much. The means test is in effect a 100 per cent tax on the welfare recipient's own earnings; for every dollar he earns, his assistance is reduced by a dollar. Administration of public assistance is now largely a matter of policing the behaviour of the poor to prevent them from 'cheating' the taxpayers, rather than a programme for helping them improve their economic status through their own effforts. As a result poverty and dependence on welfare are perpetuated from one generation to the next, and the wall dividing the poor from the rest of society grows higher even as the nation becomes more affluent.

Four ideas for reform of our present system of public assistance, none of them novel, have lately received serious attention from economists, social welfare experts and public officials. One is that assistance should be available to everyone in need. Present welfare laws require not only a showing of need but also an acceptable reason for the need. Old age, physical disability, having children to feed but no husband to feed them—these are acceptable reasons. The inability or failure of the father of a normal, intact family to find a job that pays enough to support the family is not an acceptable reason. Such families cannot now receive welfare assistance in most localities. The second proposed reform is that need and entitlement to public assistance should be objectively and uniformly measured throughout the nation in terms of the size and composition of the family unit, its income and its other economic resources. There would not

*With James Tobin and Peter M. Mieszkowski. Reprint of the Yale Law Journal Company and Fred B. Rothman & Company from *The Yale Law Journal*, Vol. 77, No. 1, (1967), pp. 1–27.

be different calculations of need and entitlement from one state to another, one welfare administration to another, one case-worker to another. The third is that the public assistance to which people are entitled should be paid in cash for free disposition by the recipients, not earmarked for particular uses or distributed in kind as food, housing or medical care. The fourth reform would modify the means tests to reduce the 'tax' on earnings below 100 per cent, in order to give the recipients of assistance some incentive to improve their living standards by their own efforts.

Some or all of these objectives are embodied in specific proposals that have entered public discussion under a confusing variety of names: 'guaranteed income', 'family allowance', 'children's allowance', 'negative income tax'. These proposals can be described and compared in terms of two identifying features: the *basic allowance* which an eligible individual or family may claim from the government, and the *offsetting tax* which every recipient of the basic allowance must pay on other income. The *net benefit* to the recipient is the basic allowance less the offsetting tax. The net benefit can be considered a 'negative' income tax because it makes the income tax symmetrical. The regular or positive income tax allows the government to share in a family's earnings when those earnings exceed a minimum that depends on the number of exemptions and the size of allowable deductions. Under a negative income tax plan, the government would, by providing benefits, also share in any shortfalls of family income below a minimum similarly but not necessarily identically calculated.

The basic allowance can be regarded as the income guarantee. It is the net benefit received by a person whose other income for a year is zero and who has no offsetting tax to pay. It is therefore the minimum total disposable income (income from all sources including basic allowance less offsetting tax and other income taxes) the recipient can receive.

The basic allowance depends on the size and composition of the recipient unit. Plans differ in the schedule of basic allowances they propose, both in the adequacy of the amounts and in the variations for family size and composition. Some plans contemplate a fixed per capita allowance. Some would allow more for adults than for children. Some would add diminishing amounts to the basic allowance of a unit for successive children and perhaps impose a ceiling on the amount a family unit can receive regardless of size. Some would give no allowance for adults and would perhaps count young children more heavily than older children.

With respect to the offsetting tax, the main issue is the rate at which other income should be taxed. As already noted, current public assistance procedures generally impose, in effect, a 100 per cent tax. Some proposals for a universal 'income guarantee' retain this same tax, disguised as a federal commitment to make up any gap between a family's income and an established living standard. Other 'family allowance' plans contemplate no special offsetting tax at all; other income would simply be subject to the regular federal income tax. Some variants of this proposal would count the basic allowance as taxable income. In either case everyone in the country eligible for a basic allowance would be a net beneficiary.

So-called 'negative income tax' proposals typically subject allowance recipients to a special offsetting tax with a rate less then 100 per cent but greater than the low-bracket rates of the regular income tax. At sufficiently high incomes the offsetting tax produces a negative net benefit to the family unit as large as or larger than its liability under the regular income tax. Taxpayers in this position would exercise the option to decline the basic allowance and thereby avoid the offsetting tax.

The authors strongly support some sort of negative income tax (NIT) plan, and indeed we have some specific proposals regarding basic allowance schedules and offsetting tax rates, as will appear below. But the purpose of this chapter is not to expound the merits of the negative income tax approach in general, or of our proposal in particular. The primary purpose is the more limited one of examining some of the sticky technical problems that must be solved if any such plan is to be implemented. The larger issues of social policy are doubtless more important for the ultimate national decision, but the technical problems are neither trivial nor peripheral—nor can they be wholly divorced from the policy issues. The technical problems are in our opinion solvable. An analysis of at least one plan, with specific feasible solutions suggested for most of the problems, should advance understanding of the approach and meet some lines of criticism. A secondary purpose is to provide rough estimates of the cost of several alternative NIT plans; these are presented at the end of the chapter.

There are three major sets of problems in designing a workable plan: (1) how to define the family unit and relate basic allowances to its size and composition; (2) how to define the base for the offsetting tax and to relate NIT to the regular income tax and to existing governmental income assistance and maintenance programmes; and (3) how to determine eligible claimants, make timely payments to them, and collect offsetting taxes from them.

These questions are best discussed in the context of a specific proposal such as that described in the first section. The three sets of problems are then considered in the next three sections. The advantages and costs of the several variants of our proposal are described and evaluated in the final section.

THE PROPOSALS

Under our NIT plan every family unit would be entitled to receive a basic

Table 16.1: Basic Allowances, Breakeven Points, and Level at Which Present
Income Tax Schedule Applies Under the Proposed Negative Income Tax[a]

Family size (number of persons)[b]		*Basic allowance (received by units with no income)*	*Breakeven point (point at which no allowance is received and no taxes paid)*	*Level at which present tax rates begin to apply*[b]	*Present marginal tax rate at income in (4)*
(1)		(2)	(3)	(4)	(5)
Schedule (with a tax rate of 50%)					
1	adult	$800	$1600	$1876	15%
2	adults	1600	3200	3868	16%
3		2100	4200	4996	17%
4		2600	5200	6144	17%
5	including at	3000	6000	7003	17%
6	least 2 adults[d]	3400	6800	7857	17%
7		3600	7200	8100	17%
8		3800	7600	8359	16%
L Schedule (with a tax rate of 33⅓%)					
1	person	$400	$1200	$1420	15%
2		800	2400	3007	15%
3	persons	1200	3600	4633	16%
4		1600	4800	6279	17%
5		2000	6000	7963	19%
6	including	2400	7200	9728	19%
7	at least	2550	7650	9951	19%
8	2 adults[d]	2700	8100	10196	19%

a. The tax rates are 50 per cent for the H Schedule and 33⅓ per cent for the L Schedule.
b. Assumes one-person family is a single unattached individual with no dependants and
    that families of two or more persons are husband and wife families and file joint returns.
    Assumes also that the families are entitled to the number of exemptions shown in column 1
    (and no additional exemptions for blindness or old age) and use the standard deduction.
    Rates are those applicable to 1965 and 1966 incomes under the Revenue Act 1964.
c. A family of three or more receives basic allowances $300 less if only one of the members is
    adult.
d. A family of six or more receives basic allowance $150 less if only one of the members is
    adult.

allowance scaled to the number of persons in the family, provided it paid an
offsetting tax on its other income. Two specific schedules of basic
allowances are presented here; a High (H) Schedule which would guarantee
allowances that approach the officially-defined 'poverty lines', but would
be relatively costly to the federal budget; and a Low (L) Schedule which
would be relatively inexpensive but would guarantee only a fraction of

poverty line incomes. The schedules were chosen with some care. However, different numbers could be substituted for budgetary or other reasons.

The H Schedule would provide basic allowances ranging from $800 a year for a one-person family to $3800 for an eight-person family. Under the L Schedule the allowances would range from $400 to $2700. Two rates of offsetting tax are considered: 50 per cent and 33 per cent. Table 16.1 describes two plans: H-50 and L-33. Two other possible plans are the H Schedule with a tax rate of 33 per cent and the L Schedule with a 50 per cent tax rate.

To illustrate how the plan would operate, a four-person family under the H-50 Schedule would receive a basic allowance of $2600, and its other income would be taxed at a 50 per cent rate. However, no family would be left with a smaller net disposable income than it would enjoy under the current federal income tax without a basic allowance. For every family size there is an income at which the net tax, i.e., offsetting tax less basic allowance, under this new rule is the same as the tax under present rates. On higher incomes, the regular tax schedule would apply.

The proposal thus would not increase anyone's tax liability under the regular federal income tax (unless, of course, taxes were increased generally to finance the plan). Under the NIT proposal the government would pay net benefits to many families who now pay no taxes. Some families who now pay taxes would be relieved of these and would qualify for net benefits. Some families who now pay taxes would pay less taxes. Other families, with relatively high incomes would be unaffected.

Table 16.1 summarises the proposal for families varying in size from one to eight members. Column (2) gives the basic allowance, the amount to which the family unit is entitled if it has no other income. Column (3) which is simply Column (2) multiplied by 2 for the H-50 Schedule and by 3 for the L-33$\frac{1}{3}$ Schedule, shows the 'breakeven income'; below it the family receives a net benefit equal to $\frac{1}{2}$ or $\frac{1}{3}$ of the shortfall from breakeven income; above it the net benefit is negative, i.e., the family pays a net tax. The net tax is $\frac{1}{2}$ or $\frac{1}{3}$ of the excess of the family's income over the break-even point so long as the tax so computed does not exceed the present federal tax liability. The income at which the two calculations are equal for typical taxpayers is given in Column (4), and the marginal tax rate applicable at that income under the regular tax schedule is shown in Column (5).

The best way to understand the proposal is to consider the disposable income (DY) after tax and allowance which corresponds to every income (Y) before tax or allowance. Aside from modifications which will be mentioned below, Y is the total income of the family before exemptions and deductions. In Figure 16.1 the solid line OAB shows the relationship between DY and Y under the present tax law for a married couple with two children filing joint returns. After starting from the origin with a slope of 1, since four-person families with incomes below $3000 pay no tax, OAB then takes on successively lower slopes as income increases and progressively high tax rates apply. The total tax is the vertical distance between OAB and the 45 degree line.

The proposal under the H-50 Schedule is to substitute the relationship CDB for OAB. Below $6,144 (Column (4) Table 16.1) families will have larger disposable incomes than they do now; the dashed line CD is higher than the corresponding segment of OAB. Those with no income will get an allowance of $2600. Those with incomes below the breakeven level of $5200 will get some net benefits—and this group includes some families, those between $3000 and 5200, who now pay tax. Families with incomes between $5200 and $6144 will pay a smaller tax than they do now; and those above $6144 will not be affected.

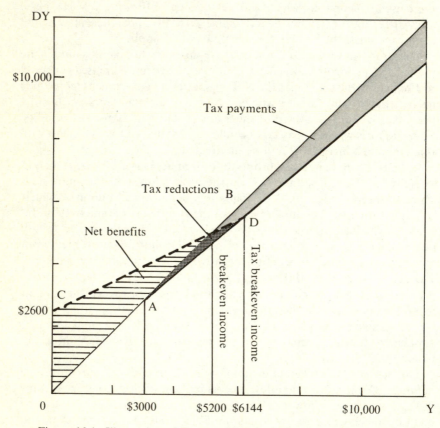

Figure 16.1: Illustration of Proposed Income Allowance Plan for four-person family under the H-50 Schedule

The plan must include units with incomes somewhat higher than the breakeven level of $5200 in order to avoid confiscatory marginal tax rates at that point. The H Schedule would wipe out all tax payments on incomes below $5200. If the regular tax schedules were applied to all income above $5200 a four-person family with an income of $5201 would pay a tax of $32, leaving it with a disposable income of $5169. In other words, the additional dollar of earned income would cost the family $32. The plan avoids this problem by giving the family the option to remain under the negative income tax system until its disposable income is exactly the same under the positive and negative income tax. For a family of four persons, this point is reached under the H Schedule at a 'tax breakeven' income of $6144.

THE FAMILY UNIT AND THE ALLOWANCE SCHEDULE

A workable and equitable definition of the family unit is crucial to the success of a negative income tax plan. The two major problems are the relative amounts to be provided as basic allowances for families of different size, and the rules governing the assignment of individuals to units.

Basic Allowances in Relation to Family Size and Composition

One consideration in setting the schedule of basic allowances is the relative cost of supporting units of different sizes at the same standard of living. By this criterion a family of five should be given just enough more than a family of four so that neither is 'better-off' than the other. In principle a schedule of basic allowances so computed would be neutral as among families of different sizes. The basic allowance should rise with family size but not proportionately, since there are economies of scale in family consumption. Beyond this qualitative indication, the criterion is not an easy tool to apply; it tends to break apart in the hands of the user. Consumption patterns vary with income, and the economies of scale will be different for different consumption mixes. Whose consumption level should be maintained as family size increases? Parents presumably get some utility, or disutility, from having children; at any rate parents' consumption patterns are not the same as if they were childless.

Another major consideration is the possible impact of the basic allowance schedule on the stability and cohesion of the family as a unit. If there are large per capita differentials between small and large families—more than are justified by economies of scale—there will be an incentive to split up large units. For example, if a family unit of two gets a basic allowance of $2000 and a family unit of four a basic allowance of $3000, a group of four people could gain $1000 by splitting into two two-person units.

In the vast majority of cases the factors governing family unit formation or splits are largely non-pecuniary in nature. Nevertheless, it would be unwise to ignore the possibility that a financial incentive might cause families to break up, or to pretend to break up. Accordingly, the objective of scaling assistance to poor families of different sizes in proportion to their needs must be balanced against the possible incentive such a standard might provide for family disintegration. The basic allowance schedules shown in Table 16.1 were designed to strike such a balance. In both schedules the per capita allowance for the first two members of the family unit is the same—$800 in the H Schedule and $400 in the L Schedule. Thus there is no incentive for a couple to define themselves as two single individuals. In the H Schedule the two $800 allowances are available only to adults; otherwise there would be an opportunity for financial gain by setting up one-adult units in which a child is listed as the second $800 member.

The allowance for children declines as the number of children increases. In the H Schedule, the allowances are $500 for each of the first two children, $400 for the third and fourth, and $200 for the fifth and sixth. In the L Schedule the allowances are $400 for each of the first four children, and $150 for the fifth and sixth. No additional allowance is provided for children after the sixth in order to give some incentive to limit family size. A corollary, in all justice, is that the government should make birth control information and supplies easily accessible.

Although the schedules provide larger per capita allowances for small than for large families, the incentive to split will normally not be great. For example, under the H Schedule a family of two adults and six children would receive $4600 if it split into four-person families, as compared with $3800 if the group remained together as one unit—a difference of only $800. Amounts of this size do not seem to be large in comparison with the other considerations that are ordinarily significant in the decision to maintain or split a family unit. For the rare cases of families with very large numbers of children, a significant financial advantage for splitting is unavoidable. For example, the H Schedule would give a family of twelve $6200 if it split in two but only $3800 if it remained together.

Membership Rules

Definition of family units for NIT purposes may be the single most difficult legal and administrative problem. The intention is clear. A single adult is a unit. A married couple and their children are a unit. A widowed or divorced mother and her children are a unit. But rules must also cover other situations—children who live with grandmothers or aunts rather than their own parents; fathers who support children but do not reside with them, married teenagers; college students; self-supporting 19-year-olds, etc. The rules should provide for genuinely split families—some children living with father, others living elsewhere with mother—without giving too much financial incentive for apparent or real splitting of intact families. The following rules have been devised with some of these complexities in mind.

A family unit consists of an adult nucleus, plus any other persons claimed as members by the adult nucleus. Government cheques are payable to the individual, or jointly to the individuals, who form the adult nucleus; and this nucleus is also responsible for payment of the offsetting tax. The following can be the adult nucleus of a family unit for the purpose of qualifying for NIT allowances:

(1) Any person 21 years of age or older.
(2) Any person 19 or 20 years of age who maintains a domicile separate from his parents or guardian and does not receive more than half his support from his parent or guardian, and is not studying full-time for his college degree. We would conclusively presume that any unmarried non-student below 19 years of age was not in fact maintaining a separate domicile.
(3) Any married couple, whatever their ages.

Individuals who are not eligible to be the adult nucleus of a unit are 'children'. The adult nucleus of a unit may claim children as other members of the unit as follows:

(1) Any child of whom he is (they are) legal parent(s) or guardian(s) provided the child is living with him (them) in the same dwelling unit, or, if not, is receiving more than half support from him (them) or is studying full time for his first college degree.
(2) Any other children residing with him (them) in the same dwelling unit and receiving more than half support from him (them). An adult claiming someone else's child without the written consent of the child's parent or guardian would have to substantiate the claim.

However, no adult can claim a child without also including in the same unit any parent or guardian of the child residing in the same dwelling unit as the child. And, no adult nucleus can claim another adult without his consent.

No person can be a member of more than one unit. No person who is take as an exemption on an regular income tax return can be claimed as a member of a family unit claiming NIT allowances. Likewise, if either husband or wife is a member of such a unit, they may not file a joint return under the regular income tax. The income of all members of a unit must be aggregated for the purposes of the offsetting tax.

In recognition of the additional expenses of college education, the adult basic allowance might be allowed for a person engaged in full-time study for his first college degree, and added to the basic allowance to which the unit would be entitled if the college student were not counted as a member. Suppose, for example, that one of the three children of a married couple goes to college. Under the H Schedule the basic allowance of the family unit would rise from $3000 to $3400 ($800 for the student plus the schedule allowance for a unit of four, $2600).

These rules leave open at least two possibilities that might be regarded as loopholes, but there are good reasons for retaining both. The first is that any adult could qualify as a separate unit and receive an allowance while remaining residentially, economically, and socially a part of a unit with adequate income. If this is deemed a loophole, it would be possible to plug it. But it seems consistent with good social policy and certainly with horizontal equity to assist adults who are incapacitated for independent living and employment by physical or psychological difficulties, even if they are attached to families of high income. The other possible 'loophole' is that married minors would be permitted to claim allowances even though they are living with a parent. Again, this is a possibility which could be eliminated. But the advantages of giving married couples of whatever age some financial independence, even if their parents are well off, seem worth the small cost involved.

DEFINITION OF INCOME

Since the basic purpose of the negative income tax is to alleviate economic need, the definition of income should not coincide with the definition used for positive income tax purposes. The latter excludes many items of income that contribute as much to the ability of the family unit to support itself at an adequate consumption level as do taxable items. To avoid paying benefits to those who are not needy, the definition of income should be comprehensive.

Receipts Included in Income

Income for NIT purposes should include many items that are specifically excluded in whole or in part from the positive income tax base. Thus, tax-exempt interest, realised capital gains, and scholarships and fellowships in excess of tuition would be included in full; income from oil and other minerals would be computed after allowance for cost depletion only; and exclusions for dividends and sick pay would not be allowed. In addition to these obvious changes from the positive income tax base, a number of other modifications seem to be necessary:

(1) The simplest procedure is not to allow any exemptions for dependants or deductions (standard or itemised) in computing income subject to the offsetting tax. The basic allowance schedule already reflects the size of unit and the standard costs of living for units of different sizes. Therefore, further refinement of the income concept seems unnecessary. The only exception might be to allow deductions for certain unusual but unavoidable expenditures, e.g., medical expenses greater than some function of the unit's basic allowance.

(2) Exclusion of the value of the services of owner-occupied homes from the offsetting tax would create the same inequities as it does under the positive income tax. Mr A does not own his home but pays rent with the $1000 of taxable income he receives from $25,000 worth of securities; Mr B, having sold his securities and bought a home with the proceeds, has no taxable income to report. To put these individuals on a par, the net value of the services provided by B.'s home should be imputed as taxable income to him. For this reason we would favour inclusion of the value of the services of owner-occupied homes under the positive as well as the negative income tax. But general reform of income taxation is not our present purpose, and it is not necessary to make the definition of taxable income the same for both the positive and negative income taxes. The reason for taxing this type of income under the negative income tax is to gear net benefits more accurately and equitably to the true economic need of the family.

The problem of calculating the imputed net rental value of owner-occupied homes is admittedly difficult. However, most persons should be able to estimate the market value of their homes by correcting their property tax assessments for the generally known rate of under-assessment in their locality. The rate of return on this market value must be imputed on an arbitrary basis. At recent interest and dividend levels, a 5 per cent rate would seem fair. As under the ordinary income tax, actual interest paid on a home mortgage would be deductible from income. Alternatively, at the taxpayer's option, the canonical 5 per cent rate of return could be applied to his equity in the home—that is, its market value less the outstanding principal of the mortgage.

(3) The value of food grown and consumed on the farm should also be imputed as income. The federal income tax law and most state tax laws omit this imputation, but it would be undesirable to extend this omission to a negative income tax. It should be possible to settle on a flat per capita amount for each state (if not for each region) to be added to the money income of farmers for this purpose. Farm families could declare a smaller amount, but the burden of proof would be on them. In addition, the value of meals and lodging provided by employers should be included in employees' incomes, at least up to the amount that the individual would normally spend for the same purposes.

(4) Whether government transfer payments should be regarded as income subject to offsetting tax will depend in large measure on how the plan is integrated with other public welfare and social insurance programmes. This problem is discussed in Section III. In general we recommend that if a transfer is intended not as a payment based on need but as deferred compensation for previous work it should be counted as income. Unemployment compensation and veterans' pensions, for example, would · thus be included in the NIT base. If on the other hand a payment is based on need and is designed to supplement the benefits of the NIT programme, it would not be counted as income. Public assistance, the benefits of the food stamp programme, and rent subsidies would accordingly be excluded from income if these programmes are continued unchanged after the negative income tax took effect.

Pensions and annuities from pension plans other than social security should be included in income to the same extent that they are included in the positive income tax base. Social security benefits are not included in the positive income tax base. But if social security beneficiaries are eligible for NIT, their benefits under Federal Old Age Survivors and Disability Insurance—but not their Medicare benefits—should be subject to the offsetting tax, at least in part. They might well be included in full, since the proportion of benefits paid for by the recipients is currently relatively low, particularly among those with very small benefits. Alternatively, a standard fraction of these social security benefits might be exluded as a return of contributions previously made from taxed income.

(5) Transfer payments from relatives, friends and private charities are as helpful in maintaining consumption as are government transfers. These gifts should not be discouraged, but neither should the government assist individuals with easy access to private sources of aid as generously as it assists others. If gifts from relatives were to be wholly excluded from the negative income tax base, adult children of very wealthy families might be elegible for negative income tax allowances. Also, inequities might arise if some individuals were more fortunate than others in the amounts of assistance they receive from private charities. We propose as a compromise that transfer income from individuals and private charities be excluded from the tax base up to an amount equal to half the basic allowance shown in Column (2), Table 16.1. Amounts in excess of half the basic allowance would be included in the tax base.

Integration with Public Assistance Programme

Current disparities among states in public assistance standards greatly exceed differences in cost-of-living; they reflect other political and economic differences among the states. They are inequitable and lead to uneconomic migrations. Although migration from agriculture and low income rural areas should be encouraged, it might well be desirable on both economic and social grounds to reverse the present tide of migration into a limited number of large northern urban areas. One of the purposes of establishing a national NIT programme is to guarantee a decent minimum standard of life to Americans wherever they reside.

Nevertheless, it is probably desirable to encourage states to maintain public assistance programmes as supplements to the national NIT system. This is particularly true if basic allowances are on the scale of the L Schedule, since these amounts would be inadequate substitutes for existing public assistance in most states (though of course much more comprehensive in coverage). Even the H Schedule falls short of welfare payments now made in some jurisdictions. State and even local supplentation is an attractive economical way to adjust for cost of living differentials. States with a greater than average sense of obligation to their less fortunate residents should be be discouraged from implementing it.

However, if the states continue to administer public assistance with a 100 per cent tax on other income, the value of the NIT as a device to maintain work incentives will be diluted. Suppose, for example, that the H Schedule is in effect nationally and a state wishes to add $400 to the $2600 basic allowance for a family of four. If the state reduces its aid dollar for dollar for other income earned up to $400, the incentive effect of the 50 per cent NIT rate would be negated unless the family could earn more that $400. To be sure, the family certainly has more incentive than under present welfare laws; with a $3000 basic allowance and 100 per cent tax the family must find a way of jumping from zero earnings to more than $3000 before there is any financial reward for self-help. But it is undesirable for even small amounts of income to be subject to 100 per cent marginal tax rates.

States should therefore be encouraged to modify their rules to avoid inconsistencies with the national plan. One possibility is to condition a federal subsidy for supplementary state allowances on adoption by the states of the federal negative income tax rules. That is, to be entitled to a federal grant-in-aid equal to, say, 50 per cent of the cost of a supplementary programme, the states would be required to use the same rate of offsetting tax as used in the federal negative income tax.

At present the federal government pays an average of 59 per cent of the cost of federally-aided categorical public assistance. The basic nationwide NIT programme would be entirely federal; thus sizeable state funds would be freed for the supplements or other purposes. The attraction of the optional state supplement plan is that it allows adequate guarantees to be offered in high cost of living states without entailing the expense of providing the same scale of allowances throughout the country. Also, individual states may find it desirable to allow for variations in the supplementary plan within the state if there are substantial cost of living differences between rural and urban areas.

Ideally, the federal NIT programme should be so generous that state supplements would be unnecessary. Although political and budgetary considerations probably make this impossible in the beginning, we believe that once an NIT programme was adopted the federal minima would eventually become adequate. The welfare-minded states would have strong financial incentives to make the federal government solely responsible for income maintenance.

Since we view the negative income tax as a superior alternative to such welfare programmes as Old Age Assistance and Aid to Dependent Children, we expect these and other categorical income maintenance programmes to be scaled down or eliminated if the negative income tax is adopted.

Whether assistance in kind should be abolished once cash assistance is increased in amount and in coverage is more doubtful. In general, we suggest that if public housing, the food stamp programme and medical programmes for the poor are to be continued, they should be justified, and modified, by considerations other than income maintenance. For example, under an adequate negative income tax the means test presently used in the determination of eligibility for public housing could be eliminated, and rent subsidies eventually could be eliminated. Eligibility for housing built under government programmes would not depend on income levels. Public funds might still be made available by the government at rates below the market rate of interest, but these loans would be related to urban renewal programmes and to the elimination of discrimination in the housing market—and not to considerations of income maintenance. On the other hand, society will not allow anyone to be without essential medical care, even if his inability to pay for it reflects improvidence rather than poverty. Therefore, it is unlikely that direct assistance in kind in the health field can be eliminated until a comprehensive, compulsory health insurance plan is adopted.

Integration with Social Security
The negative income tax might be integrated with social security in two ways. One approach would be to cover people by both social security and NIT allowances. In this case, as explained above, social security benefits would be counted partially or fully as income subject to offsetting tax.

. Alternatively, if minimum social security benefits were set at levels adequate for all groups, it would be unnecessary to include the aged and the disabled covered by OASDI in the negative income tax plan. Those who are not now eligible under the social security system could be blanketed in, and the cost of their benefits reimbursed to the social security trust fund from the general treasury. This cost would be relatively small since the vast majority of retired people are already covered by social security.

Nevertheless, to raise the benefits of social security to levels high enough to make the negative income tax unnecessary for retired people would probably be too expensive to be feasible. The present minimum social security benefits of $792 a year for a retired worker and his wife would have to be raised substantially, and it is unlikely that this could be done without increasing OASDI benefits across the board. This would be an expensive and inefficient way to meet the objectives of income assistance, because large amounts of additional social security benefits would be paid to people whose incomes are adequate.

In general, it seems advisable to separate income assistance from the other objectives of the social security system and to meet the minimal needs of retired people by NIT allowances rather than by blanketing them under social security. The two systems are based on quite different principles; they can and should be operated independently.

Application of the Offsetting Tax to Wealth

There are a number of arguments for and against taking wealth into account in computing the offsetting tax. The major argument against 'taxing' wealth is that *income* is the basic measure of ability to pay in the positive tax system. Reducing NIT benefits on the basis of wealth as well as income seems to impose a discriminatory capital levy on those with very low incomes. Moreover, the use of a comprehensive income tax base would prevent most 'tax avoidance' on the part of recipients of NIT allowances.

On the other hand, it may be argued that the analogy between positive and negative income taxation is not appropriate. Isn't a government providing financial assistance to a family on a need basis entitled to ask the family to use at least part of its wealth in its own support? Some would argue that the family should be required to exhaust its capital before becoming eligible for NIT allowances. This is an unappealing view, and not only because it is inhumane. A 100 per cent capital levy is surely a disincentive to rainy-day saving, an invitation to improvidence for anyone who thinks it likely he will be needing government help.

In practice, the use of any except the harshest capital test would have little effect on the vast majority of poor persons. It has been estimated that only 39 per cent of all family units with incomes below $3000 have a net worth of more than $5000. The average net worth of all families in these income classes was $7609, of which owner-occupied homes accounted for $3204.[1]

Nevertheless, it seems desirable to take some account of wealth, if only to avoid the charge that the programme would subsidise wealthy persons who prefer to hold their capital in forms that yield little or no current income.

Currently, an individual owning $100,000 worth of IBM stock receives cash dividends of less than $1000 per year. While it is highly unlikely that such an individual would not have enough other income to disqualify him for NIT benefits, the mere possibility that the public might be obliged to such a capitalist could discredit the programme.

One possibility is to deny to any individual or family unit a net worth of more than, say, $25,000. This solution has the merit of simplicity. However, a fixed limit would deny benefits to families with wealth just above the limit, while others just below it would be eligible. Such a 'notch' would be inequitable and would create incentives to conceal or even give away wealth in order to preserve eligibility for negative income tax.

A much more equitable approach would be to impose an offsetting tax on capital as well as on income, though not at the same rate. The offsetting tax on capital would in effect require the family to use a portion of its wealth to maintain its consumption. The offset would be a flat percentage, say 10 per cent, of the family's net worth above an exemption, most simply stated as some multiple of the basic allowance. Thus, for example, if the minimum allowance for a family of four is $3000, an exemption of eight times the allowance would be $24,000. A family with a net worth of $50,000 would have to pay 10 per cent of $26,000 or $2600 as offset against the NIT allowance to which it would otherwise be entitled.

There is room for difference of opinion on how large the exemption should be. The arguments are qualitatively the same as those for and against imposing any capital tax at all. Our own balance of these considerations leads us to suggest an exemption of 4–8 times the basic allowance.

Net worth should be comprehensively calculated, with the family's debts deducted from its total assets. Variations should be made on a current market basis; where market valuations are not available, they should be approximated by expert appraisers. As observed above, the value of owner-occupied homes may be estimated in most parts of the country by reference to the average ratio of market values to assessed values in the community.

Including the value of the equity in owner-occupied homes in net worth may be regarded as too strict. This rule might force some poor people to sell or mortgage their homes. But it would be highly inequitable to require a capital offset on the part of families with other types of assets and to exclude homes altogether. Since in any case the proposal would exempt a substantial amount of wealth for each family unit, any hardship that might be imposed on poor home-owners would be minimal. If further protection against the danger of forced sales is desired, the value of the home might be reckoned, not as market value, but as the maximum first mortgage for which it would stand as collateral.

An alternative method of dealing with wealth is to disregard property income in defining taxable income and to impose an appropriately larger offsetting tax on capital. For example, a total of 15 per cent might be imputed to the family's net worth and taxed as income. The 15 per cent equals the sum of a 5 per cent rate of return plus the 10 per cent capital offset discussed above. This procedure has the advantage of correcting for differential yields on assets; it would even impute a rate of return to cash holdings. To provide for the exemption proposed earlier, the imputation might be set at the rate of 5 per cent on a net worth up to eight times the minimum allowance and 15 per cent above this point. This method has the additional virtue that the form filed by the family would require only two items of information—total family earnings and net worth—whereas the other method would require the family to report property income as well. On balance, there is little to choose between the two.

Fluctuating Incomes

It is well known that a progressive income tax based on a one-year accounting period imposes a heavier tax burden on persons with fluctuating annual incomes than on those with stable incomes. For example, under present law, the federal incomes taxes on a single person with an income of $25,000 in each of two successive years total $17,060; if the individual receives $50,000 in one year and has no income in the second year, his two-year tax would be $22,500, or almost a third higher. To reduce this inequity, sections 1301–4 of the *Internal Revenue Code of 1954* allow a measure of 'income averaging' in federal taxation. Under these provisions, taxpayers are generally permitted to average their income for individual income tax purposes if 'averageable income' (current year income minus 133 per cent of the average of the four prior years' income) exceeds $3000.[2]

Similar inequities could arise under negative income taxation. But here the rate structure benefits rather than penalises recipients of fluctuating incomes. Fluctuations in and out of the NIT income range are advantageous. Consider an individual at the tax breakeven income level, with a regular marginal tax rate rate of 20 per cent and an NIT rate of 50 per cent. If his income exceeds that level by $1000 he is taxed $200. If his income falls short by $1000, he gains $500. Over a two-year cycle he is $300 better-off than if he had received the same total in equal instalments.

Under H-50 a family of four which earns a *total* of $10,000 spread evenly over a three-year period will receive $2800 in NIT benefits. The same family, if it earned $10,000 in one year and nothing in the two following years, would pay $1114 in positive tax and receive $5200 in net NIT benefits during the two years of zero income: its net receipts from government over the three-year period would thus be $4086.

Moreover, there will doubtless be some instances in which the use of an annual accounting period for negative income tax purposes will provide benefits to persons who are not 'poor' by most standards. Consider, for example, an individual who spends all his income when he earns it, with violently fluctuating annual income. Most people would not regard it as proper to provide negative income tax payments in one year to an individual who earned $25,000 in the year before.

In spite of these inequities and anomalies, it does not seem desirable to try to enforce income-averaging by NIT allowances recipients. Most eligible people, the real poor, gear their outlays closely to their incomes. They would suffer real hardships if their current NIT benefits were cut back because of their past income, or if in their more properous years they had to repay NIT benefits received in the past. The rich man who by design or misfortune turns up with no income in one particular year will usually be disqualified by the offsetting capital levy already discussed. If not, the best protection is simply to deny him the privilege of averaging for regular income tax purposes if he has received negative income tax benefits in any of the four preceding years. A rule of this sort would require any individual with wide income fluctuations to weigh the advantage of receiving negative income tax against the disadvantage of losing the benefits of income averaging. It has the obvious attraction that it is entirely self-administering and does not complicate the negative or positive income taxes.[3]

METHODS OF PAYMENT

Although the calendar year should be the basic accounting period, there is every reason to adopt a short payment period. Benefits should be paid weekly or twice monthly to prevent real distress among those who have little capital or credit. Such an arrangement would be analogous to the positive income tax, which is withheld weekly or twice-monthly for most wage-earners and is then subject to a final reconciliation for the entire year when the final tax return is filed.

Government welfare and other agencies have substantial experience in the payment of transfers to individuals and families, so that the mere preparation and mailing of NIT allowance checks poses no great administrative difficulties. The problem is to devise a method of payment prompt enough to prevent distress among those eligible and in great need for assistance while avoiding the paternalistic rules now imposed by the nation's welfare programmes. Among the methods we have considered, two meet the requirements: (1) automatic payments of full basic allowances to all families,[4] except those who waive payment in order to avoid withholding of the offsetting tax on other earnings; (2) payment of *net* benefits upon execution of a declaration of estimated income, patterned along the lines now used for quarterly payments of federal income tax by persons not subject to withholding.

Automatic Payments of the Full Basic Allowance

Under this system, the full basic allowance would be sent out at the beginning of each period—to all families. The cheques would be received by families who may ultimately have incomes in excess of the breakeven point, as well as those who will be eligible for net benefits. Likewise, all families would be subject to withholding at the rate of the offsetting tax on the first X dollars of their earnings, and would be required to pay the offsetting tax on other income by quarterly declaration. Final adjustment would be made by the tax return for the year filed the next 15 April.

This method may be illustrated for a family of two which, on the basis of the H-50 Schedule, has a basic allowance of $1600, a breakeven point of $3200 and an offsetting tax rate of 50 per cent, and a tax breakeven point of $3868. The basic allowance would be sent to all families in 24 instalments of $66.67. However, withholding tables would be adjusted so that 50 per cent of earnings up to $322.33 per month ($3868 a year) would be withheld. Taxpayers not subject to withholding would be expected to pay the offsetting tax quarterly

There is no reason, of course, to burden the government and the population with unnecessary exchanges of payments. Any family which does not expect to be eligible for significant net NIT benefits can always elect to withdraw. The family will not then receive the periodic basic allowance payment from the government, and its working members will not be subject to withholding (or quarterly payments) of the offsetting tax. This election could be made in writing either to the Internal Revenue Service (IRS) or to the employer. In the former case, the IRS would inform the employer not to withhold the offsetting tax. In the latter, the employer would inform the government through the IRS to stop the payments.

Declaration by Benefit Claimants

The declaration method would operate as follows. At any time families who believe they are (will be) eligible for net NIT benefits could prepare a declaration of expected income for the current year. The declaration might be a simple postcard form requiring information only on family composition, expected income for the year, income in the prior quarter, and (if the proposed offsetting tax on wealth were adopted) net worth. The federal government—whether the IRS or some other agency—would compute the estimated *net* benefit, basic allowance less offsetting tax, for the year. Taking account of payments already made to the family during the year and taxes already collected from the family, the agency could estimate the remaining net benefit due and pay it in weekly or twice-monthly instalments. Families whose incomes increased above expectation would be required to file a new declaration to stop or reduce the benefit payments. Families whose income fell short of expectation could make a new declaration at any time. Even if circumstances do not change, a renewed declaration would be required at the beginning of each year.

The withholding system would not need to be changed to collect the offsetting tax, because it would be deducted in determining net benefits to be paid.

The declaration method would not, of course, avoid the necessity of a final accounting and settlement between the family and the government for the year as a whole. This would be accomplished, as now, by the final income tax return on 15 April, which would cover obligations under both the NIT and the regular income tax. At this time the family would either claim any net benefits not previously received or pay any net amount due the government.

The major draw back of the declaration method is that it would invite many families to underestimate their income in order to obtain current payments. Claims for benefit payments would have to be compared with income information already available from prior years, from prior declarations, and employers' withholding. The computer makes prompt cross-checking of this kind feasible. Nevertheless, some families will use the NIT facility as an easy source of credit. This is not wholly undesirable, because many poor people lack credit facilities. But it would be reasonable to charge an interest penalty for underpayment of taxes or over-claiming of benefits. There will also be cases of outright fraud and these will have to be handled as severely as is fraud in the positive income tax. However, it should be remembered that the amounts potentially involved in 'negative' fraud are small fractions of the sums often at stake in 'positive' fraud.

It is difficult to choose between the two methods of payment. Both are workable. The declaration method would limit payments to families who expect to be eligible for net benefits and would not require any changes in the present withholding system. The automatic payment method, on the other hand, would be less likely to be abused by persons who are willing to take the chance of defrauding the government. The declaration method imposes the burden of initiative on those who need payments; the automatic payment method places the burden on those who do not want them. It may be argued that the latter are more likely to have the needed financial literacy and paperwork sophistication.

BUDGETARY COST OF THE PLANS

We have made a tentative and preliminary attempt to estimate the cost of the plans to the federal government. These estimates should be regarded as merely indicative and very rough. The costs are defined as the net reduction in income tax revenues which would result from superimposing the plans on the 1965 income tax code; this sum is the equivalent of the total increase in family incomes after taxes and allowances resulting from the plan. Although the tax law and rates applicable in 1965 are the reference point, the cost estimates are based on the 1962 population and the 1962 distribution of families by size and income. The reason is that 1962 was the last year for which *Statistics of Income: Individual Income Tax Returns* was published when work on these estates commenced.

We made four sets of cost estimates covering each of the two allowance schedules in turn at the rates of 50 per cent and $33\frac{1}{3}$ per cent. The costs are broken down into three parts: (A) the net benefit to family units which did not pay taxes in 1962; (B) net NIT benefits, plus reduction in income tax payments, for units which paid taxes in 1962 and which would receive net benefits under the negative income tax plan (i.e. families whose incomes are below the breakeven points): (C) the reduction in taxes for units which paid income taxes in 1962 whose net benefits would be negative under NIT but smaller than their regular income tax liability. The cost estimates for each of the four plans are given in Table 16.2.

The estimates are based on data found in Table 18 of the *Statistics of Income*; this is the basic for an estimate of the distribution of taxpaying families by size and income. In deriving these distributions we assumed that families who claim children as exemptions do not have other dependants and families who have other dependants do not have children. Secondly, it was necessary to account for the 14.1 million people who do not appear on tax returns. It was assumed that they have the same family size and income characteristics as the non-taxpaying units who filed returns in 1962. This last assumption probably leads to a downward bias in the cost estimates, as families who do not file tax returns can be expected to have very low income.

On the other hand, the costs are over-estimated to the extent that the 'adjusted gross income' concept on which they are based is narrower than the income concept proposed for NIT. Also, against the cost of the NIT programme must be set the saving on other governmental income assistance programmes which it will, at least in time, substantially replace. The federal government spends $3.2 billion for categorical public assistance, and the states and localities dispense another $2.4 billion.

On the assumption that people receiving social security also qualify for negative income tax, the single largest downward adjustment in the cost estimate would result from the inclusion of social security and veterans' pensions in the tax base. On the basis of information from the Social Security Administration,[5] it is estimated that about $4 billion of OASDI

Table 16.2: Estimates of Alternative Negative Income Tax Plans (billions of dollars)

Tax status under present law	H Schedule		L Schedule	
	33⅓% tax rate	50% tax rate	33⅓% tax rate	50% tax rate
A. Non-taxable	22.3	18.2	10.0	6.7
B. Taxable, income below breakeven point	23.2	6.7	3.3	0.2
C. Taxable, income above breakeven point	3.8	1.1	1.0	0.1
Total cost	49.3	26.0	14.3	7.0

benefits and veterans' pensions are paid to married couples whose total income (including social security) is less than $3000 and to single men and women whose income is less than $1500. Since this type of income accounts for between 50 and 60 per cent of the total income of these groups, its inclusion in the tax base under plan H-50 would increase the base by at least $4 billion and decrease the cost of the plan by at least $2 billion.

In 1962 the gross rental value of owner-occupied dwellings was estimated to be $37 billion. From the 1960 Census of Housing[6] we estimated that about 12.8 per cent of the total value of owner-occupied homes was owned by people whose income was less than $3000. We estimate that imputing a 5 per cent return on owner-occupied residences would increase the negative income tax base by about $2 billion and decrease the cost of plan H-50 by about $1 billion. Other items, part of which would be included in the broader negative income tax base include: $500 million of capital gains accruing to taxpaying units whose adjusted gross income was less than $3000, $1 billion of unemployment compensation and $2.2 billion of food consumed on farms.

Although our analysis is very imprecise, we estimate that the broadened tax base would save between $3 and $5 billion for plan H-50. It is not obvious whether the saving for plan H-33 would be higher or lower. For this plan the breakeven levels of income are higher; therefore larger amounts of income that is not now taxed would be included in the negative income tax base. On the other hand, the tax rate is lower.

Taking into account the fact that a substantial proportion of the $5.6 billion of categorical assistance would be replaced by NIT, the net cost of H-50 would be about $20 billion, while plan H-33 would cost at least twice that amount. The net cost of plan L-33 would be around $10 billion, while the cost for L-50 would be less than $5 billion.

Clearly these rough estimates do not even begin to take account of:

(1)   The growth of population and income since 1962. There are more people, but the incidence of poverty has declined. How the costs of various NIT programmes have been affected is hard to say.

(2)   Induced responses to the programme itself: Some people may work and earn more when their marginal tax rate is reduced from 100 per cent to 50 per cent or 33 per cent, while others work and earn less when the government makes them better-off and raises their marginal tax rate from zero or 14-20 per cent to 33 or 50 per cent. These responses will change the tax base, but in the absence of experience or experiment it is not possible to estimate in which direction or how much.

(3)   Savings in government expenditures other than income assistance: To an unknown degree NIT benefits may reduce the need for assistance in kind such as medical care, housing and food. We believe that a generous NIT programme would also in time diminish expenditures now devoted to controlling and suppressing the symptoms of poverty—crime, social disorder, unsanitary environments—rather than to eliminating poverty. But budgetary savings are the smallest consideration in this anticipated consequence of the programme, and they neither can be nor need to be estimated.

Although the authors believe that it is well within the fiscal capacity of this country to adopt a generous negative tax plan, there may be in the first instance a conflict between cost, the adequacy of the basic allowances, and the objective of keeping the offsetting tax rate as low as possible. The allowance levels for plan L are inadequate for many parts of the country and this plan would have to be supplemented in some way. On the other hand, if plan H were adopted for the country as a whole, the offsetting tax rate would probably have to be considerably higher than 33 per cent because of cost considerations. High tax rates unfortunately weaken one of the basic objectives of NIT, namely to improve upon the disincentive aspects of existing welfare programmes.

The course of action which we think best balances these considerations is federal enactment of plan L with a tax rate of 40 per cent. The basic allowances of this plan would then, we hope, be supplemented by individual high cost of living states along the lines outlined above. As the federal budgetary situation eases, the national basic allowance schedule could be gradually improved to approach plan H.

NOTES

1. D. Projector and G. Weiss, *Survey of Financial Characteristics of Consumers* (1966), Table A-1, p. 96, Table A-8, p. 110.
2. *Internal Revenue Code* of 1954, S. 1301, provides that the tax imposed by Section 1 for the computation year which is attributable to averagable income shall be 5 times the increase in tax under such section which would result from adding 20 per cent of such income to . . . $133\frac{1}{2}\%$ [the average income of the previous four years]'.
3. A statement of the rule might be included with the averaging form. It is doubtful that this refinement needs to be mentioned on the form filed by the negative income tax recipient.
4. This is the procedure used for 'demogrants' or family allowances in other countries. The essential characteristic of demogrants is that the payment is made to all families in the potential eligible group, regardless of income. In some cases, the allowances are subject to positive income tax, but this is not a necessary condition. Family allowances are used in many countries, including Canada, Belgium, France, West Germany, Italy, Luxembourg, Netherlands, Sweden and the United Kingdom. For data on the European countries, see Joint Economic Committee, *European Economic Systems, Economic Policies and Practices,* paper No. 7, 89th Cong., 1st Sess. (1965). It should be noted that universal payment of basic allowances under an NIT programme does not mean everyone is benefited by the programme. Most people would pay an offsetting tax large enough to repay the allowance checks. Therefore the NIT programme differs in essential respects from programmes under which everyone benefits, no matter how wealthy. There is only an apparent procedural similarity.
5. See Merriam, '*Social Welfare Expenditures, 1963–6?*' in Social Security Administration Bulletin, Table 3, pp. 3, 9 (October, 1964); Palmove, Differences in Sources and Size of Income: Findings of the 1963 Survey of the Aged, in *Social Security Administration Bulletin,* Table 1, pp. 3 (May, 1965).
6. 2 US Department of Commerce, Bureau of the Census, *Census of Housing* Part 1, Table A-3, pp. 1–5 (1963).

17. The New Jersey Negative Income Tax Experiment*

The New Jersey experiment in income maintenance was unique in several respects. First, it was the forerunner of numerous other large-scale, controlled social experiments testing the effects and feasibility of new social programmes by observing how they operate in practice. Second, it was concerned with a live policy issue that could not be resolved satisfactorily on the basis of available data: whether cash allowances, whose net benefits decline as work income increases, significantly reduce work by the recipients. Third, the data to be collected would provide an unusually rich source of information for analysis by economists and other social scientists. This information was the basis for an exhaustive report that was submitted to the US Department of Health, Education and Welfare in late 1973 and early 1974.[1]

The experiment was conducted at a time when the public and policy-makers alike increasingly were concerned about the cost of growing welfare rolls and the alleged impact of the welfare system on the incentives of the poor to lift themselves out of poverty. The traditional welfare system was designed to assist those who were not able to support themselves because of age, disability or special family circumstances. Families headed by able-bodied men generally are excluded from such programmes on the presumption that the head should support his family by working. In addition, the income of welfare recipients was taxed, often substantially, so that they were able to keep little if any of their income. Before 1967 the nominal tax rate of the federally financed assistance programme was 100 per cent of such income; thereafter, federal law allowed recipients to keep the first $30 per month plus one-third of any additional earnings, but supplementary benefit programmes enacted by some state legislatures produced considerable variation in actual tax rates.

The negative income tax idea was advanced, first, to improve the traditional welfare system by providing a minimum, non-taxable allowance to all families; and, second, to maintain the work incentives of the poor who were able to work by permitting them to keep a significant

*Reprinted from *Work Incentives and Income Guarantees: The New Jersey Negative Income Tax Experiment*, Joseph A. Pechman and P. Michael Timpane, editors (Brookings Institution, 1975), pages 1–14.

fraction of their earnings. For example, the basic allowance might be $1500 for each adult and $500 for each child, so that a family of four would receive a total of $4000. Another possibility would be $1000 for each person in the family regardless of age, which also would provide a total of $4000 for a four-person family. As well as receiving the basic allowance, the family would pay tax on each dollar of its income.[2] The rate of this tax might be 30 per cent, 50 per cent, 75 per cent, or even 100 per cent. Thus, with a basic allowance of $4000 and a tax rate of 50 per cent, a family with an income of $2000 would have a disposable income of $5000: $4000 of the basic allowance and $1000 of its own income left after the payment of taxes. With an income of $4000, the family would have a disposable income of $6000: the $4000 basic allowance plus $2000 of its own income after taxes. With an income of $8000, a family would break even—the $4000 basic allowance would exactly equal the tax of $4000—and its disposable income would be $8000.

The idea of a negative income tax met with considerable resistance, partly because of costs but primarily because many people believed that the guarantee of a minimum level of living would provide an irresistible inducement for a significant number of persons, especially able-bodied males, to reduce their hours of work or to stop working entirely. Although economists had been making econometric estimates of the effect of a negative income tax on work effort, the results had proved inconclusive.[3]

Aside from labour response, several other questions about the operation of a system of cash allowances could be answered by such an experiment. Of primary concern were the administrative problems of paying cash allowances. How should income be defined? Over what period should it be measured? Are there unusual problems of enforcement and compliance? Although these questions seem to be caught up in minor details, they are crucial to an evaluation of the workability and cost of a negative income tax.

Another set of questions concerned the effect of cash allowances on the life-style of the recipient families. Will the families use the cash allowances for such frivolities as gambling, drinking, excessive entertainment and other non-essential or harmful forms of consumption, or will they use the allowances to buy more or better qualities of such essentials as food, clothing and shelter? What effect, if any, would the allowances have on the education of the children, the physical and mental health of the family members, and leisure activity?

The conference sponsored by the Brookings Panel on Social Experimentation on 29 and 30 April, 1974, focused on these and related issues of importance to national policy. The remainder of this chapter summarises the formal papers presented at the conference, as well as portions of the discussion that followed.

PLANNING THE EXPERIMENT

The opening paper, by Robert A. Levine, who was assistant director for research, plans, programmes and evaluation of the Office of Economic Opportunity (OEO) when the experiment was funded, traces the development within the government of the idea of commissioning a negative income tax experiment. To some, the major objective was experimental—to observe the labour supply response of adult males, which they hoped would be slight—whereas to others it was mostly to demonstrate the administrative feasibility of a negative income tax. Levine's paper makes clear that the experiment was conceived by the OEO as part of a broad strategy to obtain administrative and congressional approval of a negative income tax.

The next paper, by Felicity Skidmore, describes the general design features of the experiment and the important decisions that were made in designing and carrying it out after the OEO agreed to fund the experiment and approved it in general terms. Skidmore's paper gives a detailed account of the problems that were encountered and of the administrative and analytical skill that was needed to overcome them. It was generally agreed at the conference that the experiment was carried out efficiently and that the analysis was done objectively and competently.

Skidmore's discussion reveals shortcomings as well as strengths in the experiment's design. The experiment benefited from important advances in techniques of field experimentation, notably the Conlisk–Watts design,[4] which enabled the experimenters to obtain for the same costs a significantly larger sample of relevant data than would have been possible with a simple random design. Despite problems of sample attrition and occasional disturbing influences of outside events, the basic design enabled the experimenters to collect a body of high-quality longitudinal data on the economic and social behaviour of the working poor. At the same time, it was necessary to make some hard choices that limit the analytical uses of the data. These included choices with respect to the selection of the sample, the guarantees and tax rates, the site of the experiment, and the duration of the experiment.

The experiment concentrated on poor and near poor—that is, 125 per cent or less of poverty income—male-headed families. This decision was based on a careful assessment of the policy significance of the behaviour of this group under a negative income tax, but it excluded from study another policy-significant group, poor families headed by females; it led to an under-representation of families with full-time working wives; it excluded working families slightly above the eligibility line whose labour force participation also would be discouraged by a negative income tax; and it concentrated on intact families who differed in both known (for example, more children) and unknown (for example, emotional stability) ways from fractured families.

The experiment examined eight combinations of guarantees and tax rates. This design afforded an opportunity to observe the distinct effects of these two variables, but is also increased the required sample size and costs and thus limited alternatives concerning, for example, duration and number of sites. The samples for each treatment group, however, were all quite small.

The experiment operated at three urban sites in New Jersey and one in Pennsylvania. The sample is a reasonable representation of the eligible population, with balanced social and ethnic characteristics, in the urban north-east, but it is not representative of the entire country. Clearly, any limited site experiment reflects only imperfectly the conditions that a universal programme would introduce.

The experiment was conducted for only three years in each site. A major drawback of the experiment is that the effects of a permanent negative income tax programme remain unknown.

LABOUR SUPPLY RESPONSE

The paper by Albert Rees and Harold W. Watts, who were co-directors of the experiment, summarises the labour supply findings of the experiment. The major finding is that there was only a small (5 to 6 per cent) reduction in average hours worked by the male heads of the families who received negative income tax payments. For reasons that are still not understood, this occurred entirely among white men; for black men, the response was insignificant but (surprisingly) positive, whereas for Spanish-speaking men, the response was also insignificant but negative. For white and Spanish-speaking working wives, who had a low participation rate to begin with, the negative reaction was greater—about one-third of previous work effort for whites and more than one-half for those who are Spanish-speaking. The behaviour of black working wives was not affected.

These results are evaluated in two papers by economists who had no connection with the experiment. Henry J. Aaron focuses much of his attention on the difficulties of interpretation arising from the fact that the welfare system of New Jersey was altered while the experiment was under way. He suggests that this change in the welfare system created complex and shifting incentives for individual families that are virtually impossible to quantify for purposes of analysis. Aaron also suggests other measurement problems that might lead to an underestimate of labour supply response. On the other hand, Robert E. Hall, who develops a model to evaluate the data on labour supply response obtained from the experiment, argues that the results are consistent with theoretical expectations and are statistically significant.

Nevertheless, a number of the conferees were not persuaded that the experimental data can be regarded as definitive on this score. Three major problems accounted for most of this scepticism. First, the effects noted by Aaron and others of changes in the New Jersey welfare system after the experiment was under way altered the net guarantees and tax rates in a haphazard way. Second, the limited time period covered by the experiment makes it difficult to draw conclusions about the effect of a permanent negative income tax. Third, the results for the non-white families included in the experiment, which are puzzling, may be unreliable because of high attrition rates.

Effect of the Changes in the New Jersey Welfare System

At the outset, it was considered essential to conduct the experiment in a state in which male-headed families were not eligible for any welfare assistance. Only in such a situation would the difference between the families in the experimental and control groups reflect the effect of the negative income tax alone. New Jersey was chosen as the major site partly because it had no plan under the unemployed parent part of the federally-supported Aid to Families with Dependent Children (AFDC-UP) programme, which extended aid to unemployed fathers. (Male heads were eligible for the locally-financed general assistance programme, but the benefits under this programme were extremely low). On 1 January, 1969, however, New Jersey introduced a generous AFDC-UP plan for which most of the families in the experimental sample were eligible. Such families were kept in the sample, but they were required every payment period to choose between payments from welfare or the experiment.[5]

The change in the New Jersey welfare system had two effects on the results of the experiment. First, most of the families who originally were placed in two of the least generous experimental plans—those with a minimum guarantee of 50 per cent of the poverty line income and a 50 per cent tax rate (the 50–50 plan) and a 75 per cent guarantee and a 70 per cent tax rate (75–70 plan)—either chose to receive welfare payments or had incomes that exceeded the breakeven levels (see the explanation above). The few families that chose the experimental payments under these plans were dropped from the analysis of the labour supply responses because their number was so small. In addition, relatively few of the families assigned to the somewhat more generous 100–70 plan had incomes below the breakeven level and thus most received no payments. The experiment therefore provides little basis for judging the amount of labour that might be supplied by families under a 70 per cent negative income tax plan. Moreover, the information from the remaining plans is not sufficient to measure the effects of different guarantees and tax rates.

Second, the availability of the welfare option meant that families in the experiment who were eligible for welfare faced very different guarantees and tax rates under each negative income tax plan from those faced by families ineligible for welfare. The result is that the observed differences between the experimental and control families cannot be related unambiguously to the stated guarantees and tax rates even for tax rates below 70 per cent. As Aaron explains in his paper, the net guarantees and tax rates after taking into account the welfare option are very much lower—but not in the same proportion—for each of the plans then the stated guarantees and tax rates suggest.

The implications of this point were discussed at length by the conferees. One group pointed out that, because of the existence of other government assistance programmes (in kind as well as in cash), it would have been impossible to arrange an experiment in which the net guarantees and tax rates for each experimental family were known with certainty. Under the circumstances, the experimental results should not be interpreted as providing estimates of the labour-supply response to any particular guarantee or tax rate, but rather of the response to the *difference* between the guarantees or tax rates among various plans. Such estimates still could be regarded as significant because any negative income tax plan probably will be super-imposed on other existing programmes, creating a complex environment that inevitably will alter the marginal rate that would actually apply to particular families.

Another group felt that, for the reasons mentioned by Aaron, it is virtually impossible to infer anything about the marginal effects of the different guarantee levels or tax rates on labour supply. Because the net guarantees and tax rates are lower than the stated guarantees and tax rates, the calculations from the experimental data may understate the labour supply response to the type of negative income tax plans that are offered as policy alternatives in the United States. The combination of uncertainties as to the effect of different plans also makes it impossible to estimate the costs of various national negative income tax plans on the basis of the experimental results.

Short-term vs. Long-term Effects

Although the objective of the experiment was to estimate the labour supply response of a permanent negative income tax, to simulate the effect of a permanent plan obviously was impossible in an experiment lasting only three years. Early in the experiment, the study designers urged the OEO to cover some families for a period of three years and others for a period of five years, which would have permitted them to build a duration variable into the statistical analysis. But because of budget constraints, the OEO did not provide the necessary funds for a five-year period.

The temporary nature of the experiment is important because the work behaviour of individuals may depend not only on their current needs and economic circumstances, but also on their future expectations. Whether the labour supply response in the experiment was greater or smaller than the response would be in a permanent plan is not clear. Some workers—particularly women who work to supplement their husbands' income—might be induced by the negative income tax payment to stop working temporarily or to reduce their hours of work with the expectation that they could go back to work or work longer hours after the negative income tax arrangement ceased. This factor would lead to an exaggeration of the labour supply response in an experiment of short duration. On the other hand, the enactment of a permanent negative income tax might bring on effects—for example, early retirement or less inhibition in quitting jobs—that a temporary experiment would be unable to capture.

Michael Boskin and Jacob Mincer, two of the formal discussants, as well as a number of other conferees, expressed the opinion that the temporary nature of the experiment probably led to an understatement of the labour supply response by male heads of families to a permanent negative income tax. Such workers usually are attached to a job that requires them to work a fixed number of hours a week. It is unrealistic to expect many of these workers to seek another job with shorter hours in the interest of obtaining a cash assistance payment for a three-year period, although over a longer period of time, unemployment structures might well change to make such decisions feasible. Moreover, the fact that the experimental families purchased relatively more durable goods than control families suggests that the former did not react to the additional income provided by the experiment in the same way that they would respond to a permanent change in income. Such behaviour is consistent with the hypothesis that workers consider longer time horizons than three years in making economic decisions.

Although admitting that the experiment could not reproduce the conditions that would prevail under a permanent negative income tax, other conferees took the position that the results are not necessarily biased in one direction or the other. Furthermore, it is not at all certain that the three-year duration was too brief to capture most of the labour supply effects of a permanent negative income tax. Whether the time period that controls economic behaviour is three years, ten years or a lifetime is still not known. In any event, the results of the experiment were considered to be important to a negative income tax decision. Although the long-run effects remain uncertain, the experiment suggests that there would be sufficient time to readjust the terms of any plan that is actually adopted before the full consequences of the long-run effects become evident.

The Radical and Ethnic Puzzle

A major problem mentioned by both the experimental analysts and their critics was the unexpected behaviour of the black (and, to some extent the Spanish-speaking) workers in the experiment. On the average, little change occurred in the work effort of these participants in the experiment; in fact, as compared with the control groups, the work effort of black males actually increased during the experimental period. This difference in behaviour may stem from some unobserved characteristics of the experimental and control groups, from economic differences among sites (in which racial and ethnic compositions differed), from the bias of differential attrition rates, or simply from difficulties in data collection unique for these populations. These findings need to be explained or, as Hall suggests, dismissed as unreliable.

OTHER BEHAVIOURAL RESPONSES

The income maintenance project sought information about responses other than work effort to the experimental treatments and to income changes in general. These responses, such as consumption and employment behaviour, education and health status, were useful not only as control variables to explain variations in labour supply, but also as a basis for interpreting the social significance of a negative income tax. These measures were reviewed and evaluated for the conference by Peter H. Rossi, the lone sociologist among the writers.

As already indicated, the experimental families made larger investments in housing and durable goods than the control families. There also was evidence that less job turnover occurred under the more generous plans, and that turnover which did occur was mainly among younger workers shifting to better jobs. It was reported at the conference that analysis now in progress will show significant increases in educational attainment among experimental family members. But the data for health status, family composition and individual well-being revealed few consistent and interpretable patterns among experimental families.

According to Rossi, these negative findings may reflect poor design and analysis; but to some extent, they may be the result also of the dominance of economists in the decisions on experimental design and analytical priorities. He points out, for example, that the relatively homogeneous nature of the sample population, which was considered an advantage from the economists' standpoint, made it virtually impossible to detect significant experimentally induced changes in such variables as family composition and individual well-being. He also pointed out that there has been a persistent absence of analysis that would systematically explain economic effects in social psychological and sociological terms. In particular, the small but significant reduction in hours worked and the changes in hours of job search, in job quality, and in worker satisfaction have begged for analysis, little of which has yet been done.

The conferees did not dispute Rossi's observations regarding the experimental design, nor was there disagreement that further analysis of the non-labour supply response would be useful. But several conferees challenged Rossi's contention that the experiment was dominated by economists. Other social scientists were heavily involved from the beginning and subsantial resources were devoted to the non-economic questions. On the other hand, some believed that it was right to emphasise the labour supply response as the dominant focus of the experiment—if only because the state of the experimental art was rudimentary at the time the experiment began.

In any event, given recent advances in experimentation and analysis, a much more productive combination of the disciplinary techniques ought to be possible in future experiments. Such a combination of talent could help to develop more of the richness of individual responses to experimental treatments; and the number and variety of the observations needed to obtain statistically significant results for a broad range of issues would require a much larger sample than was used in the New Jersey experiments.[6]

POLICY IMPLICATIONS

The policy implications of the New Jersey experiment doubtless will be debated for a long time. Opinions will differ, not only because of doubts about the methodological problems but also because of the changes that have occurred in US social policy since then. Many advances have been made in related areas of labour-market research since the mid-1960s, and the numerous changes in income support programmes—reforms in AFDC itself, the creation of supplemental security income for the aged, and the expansion of the food stamp programme—have created a very different environment for income maintenance policies.

Nevertheless, many of the conferees feel that the experiment will have a significant effect on attitudes toward negative income taxation. As Rees and Watts point out: 'The burden of proof would now appear to be on those who assert that income maintenance programs for intact families will have very large effects on labor supply.' Michael Barth, Larry Orr and John Palmer note that the finding that the labour supply response of male family heads usually takes the form of a reduction in hours of work rather than complete withdrawal from the labour force should moderate the pressure for a strict work test and shift more attention to distributive equity in decisions about guarantees and tax rates. They also emphasise that the experiment demonstrated the administrative feasibility of a negative income tax, including practical solutions for such problems as the definition of income and the establishment of accounting periods for determining eligibility. Various anecdotes concerning the impact already observed in executive and legislative deliberations were cited by them and others at the conference as confirming these claims of policy relevance.

Other are sceptical about these claims. Bette and Michael Mahoney argue that the experiment's design was biased toward moderate tax rates in the belief that such rates would mean greater work effort. This bias was compounded by the absence (for analysis) of several guarantees at the 70 per cent tax rate. But, the Mahoneys point out, the major effect of a moderate tax rate is to extend the work disincentive further up the income distribution. They also believe that, because the price of moderate tax rates is a lessened alleviation of poverty, the emphasis on them is unfortunate.

Other reservations were expressed. The temporary nature of the experiment, combined with the intrusions of New Jersey welfare law and some of the decisions on sample composition and on guarantees and tax rates, introduces considerable uncertainty regarding the implications of the experiment for a permanent negative income tax. Moreover, many opponents of the negative income tax did not expect widespread withdrawal of workers from the labour market. The withdrawal of only a relatively few able-bodied workers was sufficient reason for much of the opposition—and the experiment did little to remove these fears. Finally, the experiment's failure to improve the accuracy of cost estimates for alternative negative income tax plans also is unfortunate.

The conferees developed little consensus on these issues. The considerations leading to moderate tax rates were vigorously defended, as was the view that work effort is discouraged by high tax rates. It was argued that equity and politics, as well as the growth in cumulative tax rates among government cash and in-kind transfer programmes, suggested that a negative income tax was still the leading practical alternative. On the other hand, it was pointed out that the recent expansion of these same income support and in-kind transfer programmes has greatly reduced the urgency of a comprehensive negative income tax and thus the significance of the experiment's findings.

SIGNIFICANCE OF THE EXPERIMENT

What, then, is the significance of the New Jersey income maintenance experiment for policy and for the idea of social experimentation? Eight million dollars were spent, about two-thirds of it in research costs. Aside from the direct financial costs, an enormous amount of time was spent by social scientists inside and outside government in helping to design the experiment and in analysing the results. Are the benefits worth the costs?

Most of the participants at the Brookings conference felt that the answer to this question is affirmative. It was generally agreed that the New Jersey experiment was conducted with diligence and intelligence, that the insights gained in programme design have improved subsequent experiments, and that the administrative feasibility of a negative income tax has been demonstrated. In addition, the experiment corroborates and improves on other contemporary findings about the labour supply response of workers to a negative income tax. As Barth, Orr, and Palmer acknowledge, however: 'The experiment does not and should not decide for policy-makers whether to extend cash assistance to the working poor or at what levels and with what benefit reduction rates. Indeed, no empirical evidence could do so. Research, no matter how relevant and competent, cannot tell us what national policy ought to be. It can provide some hard data as one input to the process that balances competing demands for scarce public resources.' Moreover, even with all the demonstrable advances it has made, the New Jersey experiment remains vulnerable to those who distrust its scientific underpinnings or prefer to disregard its policy implications.

Hindsight suggested to the conferees that subsequent social experiments could improve on the New Jersey experience in several respects. Treatments should be sufficiently different so that statistically significant results will be more likely to be obtained. For example, the failure to detect the relative effects of different guarantees and tax rates was one of the major disappointments of the experiment. For the same reason, sample sizes and selection should not be too parsimonious, given the uncontrolled turbulence of the environment and the likelihood of unpredictable attrition. Pre- and post-experimental data collection opportunities should be explored more fully. Finally, the design and analysis of results should have an interdisciplinary character—for, as one conferee put it, 'in no other way can we hope to explain the richness of the real world.' It seems clear that any major social policy experiment will face the same types of design trade-offs and constraints that were confronted in the New Jersey trial. Yet it is impossible to say whether the state of the art in social experimentation is advancing rapidly enough—and the tempo of social change is steady enough—for the larger, more complicated experiments which were designed to improve on the performance of the New Jersey experiment.

Beyond its actual and potential contributions to research in the social sciences, the New Jersey experience doubtless will have a substantial impact on the ways in which proposals for social reform are considered. Without suggesting that social progress must wait the results of research, the experiment demonstrates that a new social idea need not be adopted before its consequences are appraised on the basis of a carefully controlled field test.

NOTES

1. Harold W. Watts and Albert Rees (eds.), *Final Report of the New Jersey Graduated Work Incentive Experiment*, vols. 1, 2, 3 and David N. Kershaw and Jerilyn Fair (eds.), vol. 4 (University of Wisconsin, Madison, Institute for Research on Poverty, and Mathematica, 1974). For a summary of the major findings by several of the authors of the report, see *Journal of Human Resources*, vol. 9 (Spring 1974), pp. 156–278.
2. Deductions might be allowed for such items as medical expenses, work clothes, union dues, and the like, but no personal exemptions would be allowed as in the positive income tax system.
3. See Glen G. Cain and Harold W. Watts (eds.), *Income Maintenance and Labor Supply: Econometric Studies* (Markham, 1973). The econometric studies generally found income and substitution effects of the predicted positive sign, but the magnitude of the effects varied considerably.
4. The full model is described in John Conlisk and Harold Watts, 'A Model for Optimizing Experimental Designs for Estimating Response Surfaces', in American Statistical Association, *Proceedings of the Social Statistics Section, 1969*, pp. 150–6. Its application is discussed further in Charles E. Metcalf, 'Sample Design and the Use of Experimental Data', *Final Report of the New Jersey Experiment*, vol. 2, Part C, Ch. 5. The design basically called for eligible families to be stratified by previous income; a predetermined number from each stratum was then assigned to the various experimental plans and the control group, with individual assignments achieved randomly.
5. The Aid to Dependent Children (ADC) programme was established by the Social Security Act 1935 to provide income-related transfer payments to families whose father had deserted or divorced the mother. Therefore, it was a programme restricted to families with females heads. The name of the programme was changed later—with no implications for the functioning of the programme itself—to Aid to Families with Dependent Children (AFDC). An amendment to the Social Security Act 1961 expanded the programme to cover certain categories of two-parent families by adding an 'unemployed parent', segment to the AFDC programme, thereafter called AFDC-UP. Because the unemployed parent invariably is a father, this programme is also referred to as AFDC-UF.

    The AFDC-UP (or AFDC-UF) programme is a state option regarding decisions as to whether it will sponsor a programme at all and as to the level of benefits and the eligibility criteria. New Jersey chose not to have such a programme until 1 January, 1969, when it instituted one of the most generous in the country. The state treasury could not support the programme at that level, however, and its generosity was cut substantially in July 1971.
6. Robert Hall contended that the labour supply results could have been replicated with a much smaller sample but he did not address himself to the question of sample size for determining other types of resources.

Part Six
Social Security

18. The Objectives of Social Security*

The social security programme aims at two related but conceptually distinct objectives.[1] One is to guarantee minimum income support for the aged, the disabled and dependent survivors. The success of the programme in attaining this welfare goal has been judged increasingly by the degree to which it keeps beneficiaries out of poverty. A second objective is to help moderate the decline in living standards when the earnings of the family head cease because of retirement disability or death. This earnings replacement objective is independent of the goal of preventing poverty; benefits go to families at all income levels. The distinction between these objectives should be kept in mind, because acceptance of the social security programme and proposals for improving it hinge on an evaluation of their comparative importance.

The case for a social security programme intended to attain these objectives depends in part on the observed inability of most people to make adequate financial provision for retirement, disability or premature death. Mainly, however, it depends on what appear to be widely shared humanitarian values: that (a) the aged, the disabled and dependent survivors of deceased family heads should not have to live in destitution; and (b) the government should help to protect individuals against catastrophic losses of income. There is also wide agreement that people should be eligible for benefits without degrading eligibility tests. Explicit acceptance of these values has important implications for social security policy, and these implications are explored in this chapter.

Widespread acceptance of the basic objectives of social security undoubtedly explains its great success, not only in the United States but also in most other economically developed countries. On the other hand, there is sharp disagreement about the proper level and structure of benefits, largely because many people think of social security as a form of insurance. In practice—as well as in principle—social security is a mechanism for transferring financial resources from the working generation to those who cannot work because of age, disability or dependency status. Evaluation of alternative means of shaping the course of the programme requires

*Reprinted from *Social Security: Perspectives for Reform*, with Henry J. Aaron and Michael K. Taussig, (Washington, D.C.: Brookings Institution, 1968), pp. 55–77.

consideration by policy-makers and the public alike of the idea that social security is a tax-transfer system and not an insurance system.

RATIONALE FOR SOCIAL SECURITY

In an economy where most economic decisions are freely made, why does society choose to override individual choice between private consumption and saving for the risks covered by social security? For simplification, the following discussion of this question is limited to the problem of providing income during retirement, but the analysis can be generalised to the other risks.

Need for a Government Programme
Each person faces daily a multitude of choices about how to spend his income or wealth—how much to spend on food, clothing, entertainment and other current wants, and how much to set aside for retirement when earned income declines sharply or ceases. In the absence of a compulsory public programme each person makes these decisions on the basis of his own tastes. He invests his savings so as to achieve what he regards as the best mix of yield, liquidity and safety. In making these decisions, the rational person balances the cost of saving (foregone consumption today) against the benefits of saving (larger income in retirement) and sets aside the amount he considers appropriate. Between his working life and his retirement years, each person should be able to achieve an allocation of consumption that better accords with his tastes than any other allocation.

In this view of the world, social security 'distorts' the allocation of consumption over time and, therefore, interferes with individual choice. Many persons may be forced to defer until retirement more of their consumption than they would desire. In the extreme case, an individual with no dependants who is certain he cannot survive to retirement age would 'prudently' defer nothing until his retirement. Yet, the government deprives him of the opportunity to dispose currently of the portion of his income claimed by social security taxes. Social security also interferes with the freedom of workers to decide how to invest this portion of their income. If they are skilled investors, they might use these funds to purchase assets with higher yields than the returns which social security implicitly provides. Such individuals would not gain from social security; actually, they may have a lower total income in retirement.[2]

Although the foregoing observations carry considerable weight with anyone who values freedom of individual choice in the making of most economic decisions, there are persuasive reasons why the principle of freedom of individual choice should be modified in the case of provision for retirement. Even the most severe critics of social security will generally concede that voluntary savings cannot yield the poor worker (that is, the worker whose income is close to the amount necessary for subsistence) an income sufficient for retirement.[3] A family which cannot feed and clothe itself adequately from current income cannot be expected to sacrifice present consumption to provide for uncertain consumption needs in retirement.

The problem of poverty does not in itself conclusively negate the argument for individual provision for retirement (even though, as will be observed, later, there is reason to presume that poor people suffer disadvantages in judging how best to allocate whatever income they may possess).[4] If some are too poor to purchase adequate amounts of any commodity, including savings, a possible solution is to supplement their incomes through transfer payments. When incomes reach whatever level is deemed socially adequate, each person could then determine the amount of retirement protection he wishes to buy. This opens up major issues concerning government policies of income supplementation for all the poor. It is sufficient for present purposes to observe that nobody has yet recommended a system of transfer payments that would provide the poor with a sufficient margin for saving, as well as for current consumption.

Furthermore, even individuals who have sufficient earnings during their working lives may have insufficient savings at retirement. Accumulated funds may be used up during prolonged periods of illness or unemployment. People may incorrectly gauge their retirement needs, or personal investments may turn out badly. Alternatively, inflation may erode the purchasing power of savings. Most people would agree that the aged poor should not be left unaided in these circumstances, and that the government bears the ultimate responsibility of providing income support for such unfortunate people. The notion that government should guarantee a minimum level of income support for all the aged on this ground has widespread acceptance.[5] But because 'subsistence' is a subjective concept, and because the costs of providing income support for the poor are large, the precise level of support to be guaranteed is a controversial issue.

Once society agrees on a minimum income guarantee, however, a further decision is required on the conditions under which the guarantee will be provided. Take two extreme possibilities: the government either can provide minimum subsistence payments to each eligible person regardless of his other income or can supplement his income to the extent that if falls below a stipulated level. The former method—the universal *demogrant*—is followed in Canada and some other countries. The latter method—the *welfare* approach—is exemplified by the public (including old-age) assistance programmes in the United States.

Old-age retirement benefits in the USA are paid on terms which fall somewhere between these extremes, although they are much closer to those of the universal demogrant than to those of the welfare method. Only persons who have worked long enough to qualify for the required status are eligible to receive benefits. Persons who meet this qualification receive payments without consideration of their income and wealth, unless disqualified by the earnings test. Further, retirement benefits are not intended solely to guarantee a subsistence income to beneficiaries.

The welfare method has one great advantage over the universal demogrant: if the proportion of the aged requiring government help is small and if the administrative costs of determining need are not excessive, the objective of preventing destitution is accomplished at minimum expense by limiting payments to those with demonstrated need.

None the less, one aspect of the welfare method severely limits its acceptability. A welfare programme separates people in two groups—those who support themselves and those who require government help.[6] The degree to which this distinction is degrading depends in large measure on the method by which eligibility for benefits is ascertained (that is, the means test). When the method involves detailed probing, and frequently degrading investigations, the number of eligible persons who will even apply for benefits is restricted; this is evident from the history of public assistance. On the other hand, eligibility for veterans' disability pensions is determined on the basis of a simple income affidavit, subject to sample audit, supplied annually by recipients. Neither a sense of alienation nor reticence to apply for benefits has been noted in this programme.

The price of rejecting the welfare method of dealing with the aged poor is much higher public expenditures to attain similar objectives. This price should be explicitly acknowledged as the cost of avoiding the means test. The historical development of the Old-Age, Survivors and Disability Insurance (OASDI) programme and old-age assistance programmes in the United States shows that society has been willing to pay this cost.

Experience with the means test under public assistance has resulted in an unfortunate emotional tendency in the community to reject indiscriminately *any* eligibility test—including the earnings test—for OASDI benefits. It should be kept in mind, however, that the savings to be derived from any device that avoids the problems traditionally associated with the means test, and yet holds down the costs of public assistance, are potentially enormous. The search for such a test, similar perhaps to the test for veterans' disability pensions, continues.

The earnings test, while unpopular, does reduce substantially the cost of social security without raising the problems outlined above. First, since only a minority of persons eligible to receive social security benefits engage in full-time employment and therefore may be subject to the earnings test, benefits are paid to the majority of the aged. Thus, the problem of segregating a minority to be singled out as the needy group does not arise. Second, because the earnings test is by design not an income test, it does not take account of the income from accumulated assets and therefore does not penalise individual savings. For this reason, however, the earnings test results in larger benefit payments to persons with investment income than to those with an equal amount of earned income.

Benefits above Poverty Levels

The argument thus far supports the establishment of a government program that guarantees a minimum of income support for the aged. But this meets only one of the objectives of social security. Many of the characteristic features of social security programmes go much further. While minimum benefits under OASDI fall well below the officially defined poverty thresholds, benefits at the upper end of the scale are above subsistence levels and bear some relationship to the individual's lifetime earnings. A number of arguments have been made in support of such a benefit structure; in combination they add up to an impressive case.

Shortcomings of individual savings decisions. The principle that individuals should bear the responsibility for the decisions that affect their own economic well-being underlies much of the intellectual opposition to social security. Individuals are deemed to be the best judges of their own preferences. That many individuals often make foolish decisions, as recognised after the fact, is not necessarily objectionable; for in learning from their mistakes, they may develop self-reliance and accumulate practical knowledge that will be to their advantage when they make later decisions. The principle of individual responsibility is the basis of the case for free choice about economic matters in general, and there is no strong objection to it in most practical applications.

Decisions about saving for retirement, however, are vastly more difficult than nearly any other economic decision which most people are called upon to make. They depend on anticipation of wants in a much later period—possibly four or five decades. They require an individual to consider his future stream of earnings and other income, and to recognise several possibilities: that he will be married and have a family; that he may be unemployed involuntarily for considerable periods of time; and that he may become disabled or die prematurely. To save intelligently, the individual must also be able to appraise the probable future purchasing power of the income from various assets. Most important of all, the individual may not be aware of his mistakes until he is close to retirement, when the consequences are irremediable.

There is widespread myopia with respect to retirement needs. Empirical evidence shows that most people fail to save enough to prevent catastrophic drops in the post-retirement income. In 1962, the median amount of investment income of all aged persons was less than $300.[7] Not only do people fail to plan ahead carefully for retirement; even in the later years of their working life, many remain unaware of impending retirement needs.[8] Unfortunately, the mistakes of youth are to a large degree irreversible, since it is generally impossible to accumulate in a short period just before retirement sufficient assets to provide adequate retirement income. In an urban, industrial society, government intervention in the saving–consumption decisions is needed to help to implement personal preferences over the life-cycle. There is nothing inconsistent in the decision to undertake through the political process a course of action which would not be undertaken individually through the market place.[9]

Even if a person plans ahead and gauges accurately his retirement needs under normal conditions, it is questionable that he has sufficient knowledge about other relevant considerations to make the necessary investment decisions. The depression of the 1930s illustrated dramatically the difficulties that even experts encounter in planning their personal investments. The information required for intelligent long-run investment planning is expensive; for small investors, the cost of hiring professional investment counselling is frequently prohibitive. Deficiencies in government economic policy that permit depressions and inflations may sweep away the carefully planned savings of even the most provident and skillful investors. The available evidence suggests that the problem of uncertainty may explain why people do not save enough. Apparently, once a private pension plan has provided a minimum base of retirement income, most people are willing to save *more* on their own, rather than less.[10]

A person who is saving for retirement generally faces the dilemma of choosing between fixed-yield assets that offer little protection against inflation and other instruments that require financial sophistication or carry considerable risk. Time deposits in commercial banks and other institutions fall into the first category. Yields on such deposits offer small returns after allowance for the steady increase in prices that has occurred since the end of The Second World War. Common stocks fall into the second category; as the *major* form of savings, they are beyond the sophistication of the majority of the population. Even if such a calamity as the stockmarket crash of 1929 is regarded as unlikely to recur, it would be dubious social policy to encourage large-scale investment by individuals in common stocks. Other savings instruments—for example, government savings bonds, cash, annuities—all suffer from one or the other of these shortcomings as vehicles for large amounts of long-term savings.[11]

It has also been pointed out that the decision to provide minimum benefits may weaken individual incentives. A government guarantee of minimum income to the aged may at the same time discourage private saving. Some people may take the opportunity to consume all income in their youth, secure in the knowledge that they can fall back on government support when they retire. In addition, the knowledge that improvident individuals may finance retirement at public expense may discourage saving by people who otherwise would prefer to provide for their own retirement needs rather than depend on government support.[12]

Private group saving. The foregoing discussion leads to the conclusion that individual saving decisions cannot be relied on to provide a socially acceptable level of income for most of the aged. This point appears to be widely recognised, and it serves as the rationale both for a government social security programme and for government subsidies to private *group* saving, principally to the numerous private pension plans. The United States, for several reasons, has adopted a mixed approach to the problem of economic security for the aged; the social security programme and private pension plans coexist with surprisingly little friction. The historical division of responsibilities between the public and private sectors is not immutable, but in this volume we shall none the less assume that social security will continue to bear the major share of the total burden. The subject of private pensions—and especially their relationship to social security—is vast and complex and requires separate treatment. It may be noted here, however, that, based on past experience in the United States, the development of private pension plans in the near future is unlikely to encroach substantially on the present dominant role of social security.[13]

The shortcomings of private pension plans persist despite incentives given by the income tax and other federal statutes for the development of adequate plans by industry. A major incentive is the provision that allows an employer to deduct from his taxable income the amounts set aside in a pension plan approved by the Internal Revenue Service. The employee is not required to pay income tax until he receives pension benefits.[14]

In 1965, only about 13–14 per cent of the total number of persons aged 65 and older received private pension benefits. By 1980, the proportion will be between one-fourth and one-third.[15] Moreover, the benefits paid are, on the whole, small. Many plans are not insured, and many are inadequately financed. Vesting is long delayed, so that workers can change jobs only if they are willing to surrender pension credits. Given the limited coverage of private pension plans, the inadequacy of their benefits for many covered workers, and their other shortcomings, they can hardly be expected to provide sufficient earnings protection in old age for more than a minority of the work force for many years to come.[16]

Social costs of inadequate provision for retirement. As pointed out earlier, it becomes difficult to hold to the principle of individual responsibility when the consequences of individual mistakes are extreme. The case for social intervention becomes overwhelming when it is recognised that one individual's mistakes affect not only his well-being but also that of his family, friends and local community. Even those believers in individual responsibility who could bear with equanimity the suffering of the individual 'responsible' for his own fate find it difficult to justify the suffering of other 'innocent' persons.

The social costs that result from inadequate provision for retirement are considerable, even if all the aged are guaranteed a subsistence income. Suppose that a person with an average income during his working years retired without any personal savings. If he were guaranteed only a minimum subsistence income, the fall in his living standard might impose substantial costs on his relatives and friends, and perhaps even his local government. Even under present social security provisions, heavy costs sometimes fall on children or others who feel obligated to support aged persons at living standards close to those which they had enjoyed earlier. To spread such costs, a government programme to provide income maintenance related to previous income standards is needed. To guarantee only a minimum, poverty line level of income is too severe a policy in a society in which maintenance of status depends so critically on the maintenance of previous levels of income.

Determining the Level of Benefits

To justify the need for some social intervention in providing for retirement is easier than to determine the proper degree of intervention. The case for overriding individual responsibility has less and less force, the higher an individual's income. Take an extreme example: It is not clear why the public should provide retirement benefits based on the full income of a high-level executive whose earnings exceeded $100,000 a year for many years. Some compromise between amounts no greater than those necessary to guarantee subsistence income levels and amounts related to incomes at the upper tail of the distribution is necessary. But the choice within this wide range is a pragmatic decision, on which analytical considerations are of little help. In reaching a decision, the desirability of making public expenditures for other purposes, or of permitting greater private expenditures by non-recipients, must be weighed against the desirability of pushing up social security benefits for those with relatively high preretirement incomes.

In practice, OASDI benefits above the minimum are determined on the basis of preretirement earnings. The ratio of benefits to such earnings is called the 'replacement rate', because benefits are supposed to replace those earnings. The benefit formula is structured so that replacement rates vary inversely with previous earnings; the higher the pre-retirement earnings, the lower the replacement rate. Thus, while high earners are entitled to larger absolute benefits, their benefits are less relative to previous earnings than are those of low earners.

This structure is roughly consistent with the two objectives discussed earlier. The high replacement rate for the low earner and the minimum benefit can be interpreted as a guarantee of minimum income support for the aged. The larger absolute benefits paid to the high earner can be viewed as an effort to meet the objective of preventing drastic declines in the incomes of the non-indigent aged. This interpretation of the OASDI benefit structure corresponds roughly to the traditional social security concepts of social adequacy and individual equity.

IMAGE OF SOCIAL SECURITY

Social security is most commonly viewed as a system of mandatory insurance, different in important respects from private insurance, but nonetheless insurance. This analogy shapes the image of social security and thereby influences the prevailing body of beliefs, conceptions and opinions that govern popular understanding of the system. It has played a major part in developing public support.[17] Many deem it necessary to continue to identify social security as social *insurance* in popular as well as legislative discussions of the system.[18] But this identification impedes progress toward achieving essential modifications of the system, since many of these modifications will move it even further from an insurance system than it is today.[19]

Sources of the Insurance Analogy

The nature of individual saving and private insurance is familiar and enjoys considerable respectability and even prestige. The flow of funds between the individual and the ultimate user of these funds is a vital part of a free-market economy. Insurance companies are an important intermediary in this process; they channel the savings of many individuals to firms that wish to add to their productive capacity. The rates of return on individual savings reflect in part the productivity of the physical capital they finance. There is, thus, a relationship among the amount an individual saves, the value of his accumulated assets at retirement, the value of the annuity he can purchase with his previous savings, and the creation of additional physical capital and productive capacity in the economy. If economic resources are fully employed, these relationships are reasonably straightforward.

The analogy between social security and private insurance is suggested in a number of ways. One way is by the very names—social insurance, old-age and survivors' insurance, and disability insurance. Payroll taxes are called 'contributions' and are paid into trust funds. Benefits to retirees, survivors and the disabled are based on pre-retirement earnings and are paid from these trust fund accounts. Since interest is credited on trust fund balances, the trust funds appear to be similar to the reserves of private insurance companies. Each annual report of the trustees of the OASDI provides a computation of 'actuarial balance' between prospective benefits and taxes over a period of 75 years.[20] Finally, statements by social security experts often tend to reinforce the parallel to private insurance. The following statement by the present Secretary of Health, Education and Welfare is representative of many similar writings:

Under Social Security the risk insured against is loss of earnings from work. When earnings stop because of disability, retirement, or death, insurance benefits are paid to partially replace the earned income that has been lost. The loss occasioned by the occurrence of the risks is actuarially evaluated, and contributions sufficient to cover these costs are provided for. Benefits are paid from those contributions on a predetermined basis when and if the risks covered eventuate. The right to these insurance benefits is a legal right enforceable in the courts. These are the characteristics that make Social Security 'insurance'.[21]

Nevertheless, when the terminology of social security is stripped away and the structure of the system is examined, it becomes clear that the insurance analogy is no longer applicable to the system as it has developed. The following statement by Barbara Wootton expresses this view:

As things are, everybody now recognizes an increasing element of fiction in current insurance schemes. As Americans have cause to realize, the coverage of income-maintenance schemes tends almost irresistibly to expand. But as these schemes become more generalized, their insurance basis becomes more and more illusory; until in cases where, as in Britain, virtually universal coverage has been attained, fiction ousts fact altogether.
   At this point, the simple facts of the situation are that benefits on a prescribed scale have been promised, and that funds must be provided to meet them; that is all. In these circumstances, the allocation of precise fractions of contributors' payments to cover particular risks becomes an academic, rather than a genuinely actuarial, exercise. The performance of this exercise in the sacred name of insurance demands, however, elaborate and expensive systems of recording the experience of millions of beneficiaries. These monumental systems are indeed a tribute to the skill and accuracy of the administrators who devise them, and to the ingenuity of the mechanical devices employed in their operation; but are they really necessary, and have they, indeed, any meaning? Is it, in fact, worth maintaining what has become no more than a façade?[22]

Simple Economics of Social Security

In practice, social security is a system of payroll taxes that are levied on current earnings of workers and of benefit payments that are based on past earnings of the insured workers. The relationship between individual contributions (that is, payroll taxes) and benefits received is extremely tenuous. Within any age group, including those persons presently retired and those still working, the values of individual benefits and taxes (appropriately discounted) vary greatly. Present beneficiaries as a group receive far larger benefits than those to which the taxes they paid, or that were paid on their behalf, would entitle them. Furthermore, this situation will continue indefinitely—though to a decreasing extent—as long as Congress maintains benefit levels in line with higher wage levels.

Some participants in private group retirement plans also receive far larger benefits than they are entitled to on the basis of their own contributions. This situation is common at the beginning of a system, since full benefits are frequently awarded to workers who have contributed to the retirement plan for only a fraction of their working lives. This practice gives rise to 'past service credits', the liability which future beneficiaries (or the employer) must bear. Past service credits are also generated when a mature retirement system is liberalised, to the extent that those near retirement age partake of liberalised benefits without having had to make commensurate contributions.

The similarities between past service credits in group insurance and OASDI make it tempting to equate the two types of programs. Despite this similarity, the analogy between group insurance and social security is nearly as tenuous as the more general analogy between individual insurance and social security. One obvious difference is that failure of a firm (or an industry) to pay premiums for a group insurance plan terminates the insurance for members of the group, whereas employees covered by OASDI carry with them quarters of coverage even if their original employers go out of business. While some private plans cover workers in one occupation or industry, no practical method has been found to broaden coverage of these plans beyond these limits.[23]

The essential difference between private insurance and social security turns on whether an individual currently in the labour force is paying for the social security benefits of current retired workers and survivors or for his own or his own or his family's future benefits. In individual insurance, each person's premiums are contractually tied to his own and his family's future benefits. No insurance company knows how many new policies it will sell and, therefore, does not know the amount of its future cash inflow from premiums. Consequently, it must charge its present customers enough to create a reserve fund sufficiently large to meet its future financial obligations. The point in question here is the basis for determining *individual* premium levels; for the economy as a whole, of course, private individual insurance is a mechanism for transferring funds from one group of individuals to another.

In social security, the level of payroll taxation is set to defray costs of benefits for the *currently* retired. The social security programme has been financed on a virtual cash, or pay-as-you-go, basis in recent years. On balance, the reserves have increased slightly to cover only approximately one year of benefit payments at present benefit levels. It is true that most Social Security Bills project surpluses in the distant future, but typically these are reduced by later legislation. Each new law contains benefits and taxes that provide a near balance in the trust funds for the first couple of years, with large surpluses projected thereafter. Before the large surpluses are realised, however, benefits are liberalised, new tax rate increases are scheduled for future dates, and the cycle is repeated. In other words, the money which workers currently pay into the funds is not stored up or invested, but is paid out concurrently as benefits to the various categories of current beneficiaries. Workers pay for benefits to eligible non-workers. The future benefits of present workers, their dependents, or their dependant survivors will be paid in similar fashion out of the contributions of the working population as of some future date.

The differences between private insurance and social security can be further illustrated by comparing the effect of increased premiums in the one system and higher taxes in the other. Typically, private insurance premiums are raised if the insured person wishes to have higher benefits (or improved coverage) in the *future;* payments by the insurer are not affected at the time the premiums are raised. On the other hand, social security taxes are determined by the level of benefits being paid currently and in the years immediately ahead. While future social security beneficiaries are generally assured benefits that are at least as large as those payable today, the current tax level would not be different if Congress decided to pay future beneficiaries larger or smaller benefits than those payable to current retirees so long as the system remains approximately on a pay-as-you-go basis.

The fact that a fund is not accumulated at some explicit interest rate does not imply that people in the OASDI programme fail to share in the growth of the economy. Economic and population growth assure to the average individual covered by the programme an implicit rate of return in a currently financed social security system, even if tax rates are fixed. If generation 1 pays t percent of its earnings, Y_1, to support retirement benefits under OASDI, its tax burden is tY_1. Generation 2 similarly pays the same t per cent of its earnings, Y_2, to support retirement benefits equal to tY_2 for generation 1. If population and the labour force grow at $100i$ per cent a year and per capita earnings grow at $100j$ per cent a year, then, after a generation of n years, $tY_n = tY_1(1+i)_n(1+j)_n$. The implicit interest rate that generation 1 receives on its OASDI taxes under the above assumptions is approximately $100(i+j)$ per cent, or the sum of the rates of growth of

population and per capita earnings. Generation 2 and all future generations will receive the same implicit return on their taxes as long as
population and per capita earnings continue to grow at the same rates.[24]

Unlike a private insurance firm, OASDI does not have to accumulate
large reserve funds to meet its future financial commitments. When
benefits promised to current workers come due, the funds will be provided
out of tax revenues as of that future date. The financial soundness of the
social security programme depends only on the government's effective
power of taxation. The government's ability to collect taxes sufficient to
provide adequate social security benefits in the future depends critically on
the maintenance of a sound federal tax system in a healthy, growing
economy. The faster the rate of economic growth, other things equal, the
lighter the burden of taxation that will be required to finance any given
absolute level of future social security benefits.

If social security taxes were increased enough to result in government
budget surpluses that were used to create a reserve fund, the 'financial
soundness' of the programme would hinge on whether the process affected
the rate of growth of the economy. If the economy were at, or below, a full
employment level of income when social security taxes were increased, and
if the government did not take some offsetting action, the result would be a
fall in the level of income and a lower rate of growth. If, on the other hand,
the government offset the surpluses by expansionary monetary policy or
by increased government capital formation, the result would be a higher
rate of growth. The point is that the creation of a social security reserve
fund is, in the first instance, only a transfer of monetary claims from the
private sector to the government. The ultimate effect of this initial
monetary transfer depends on many factors; it is certainly incorrect to
assume that there is a mechanism that automatically transforms a
government reserve fund into an increased stock of productive capital and,
therefore, increases the rate of economic growth. These are the relevant
considerations to be taken into account in planning and financing a social
security programme.[25] They raise difficult conceptual and pragmatic
problems for overall government economic policy—problems for which
the precepts of private insurance are n t relevant.

Even the basic issue of whether social security benefits can be regarded as
an earned right by recipients can be resolved without appeal to the
insurance analogy. If, in return for his own contributions to the social
security funds, an individual does not earn a *quid pro quo* in the private
insurance sense, he does earn a *quid pro quo* in a sense that is, perhaps, even
more fundamental. Since he gives up part of his earnings during his own
working life to support the aged during their retirement, he has a strong
moral claim to similar support from future working-age generations during
his own retirement. Although the benefits are earned rights, and in this

sense may be accorded protection under procedural due process, they are not accorded the property protection which funded premium rights would be given.[26] The only assurance that benefits will continue to be paid is congressional unwillingness to repeal the programme.

Implications for Financing

The practical importance of de-emphasising the insurance analogy is not to discredit the concept of social security, but rather to dispel basic misconceptions about certain aspects of the OASDI programme. Once the insurance analogy is seen to be inapplicable, the social security 'contribution' must be regarded as a tax, not an insurance premium, nor, indeed, as a 'contribution' in the generally accepted sense.[27] The financial interchange between generations does not depend on the existence of a particular tax—the payroll tax. It arises because each generation of workers undertakes to support the eligible non-working population and implictly expects similar treatment.

Social security payroll taxes are legally earmarked, but they are not *economically* earmarked. Congress and the president jointly have total discretion about which kinds of taxes (including those on payrolls) shall be used to pay for whatever expenditures they jointly conclude are worth making. If Congress should decide to end the earmarking of the payroll tax (but should allocate it to the general fund) and to earmark enough, of, say, the corporate income tax to pay for social security benefits, nothing would be changed except some accounting. Or if Congress should decide that all taxes are to be deposited in the general fund and then should appropriate sufficient funds each year to pay for social security, again nothing would be changed. In each case, the taxes paid by individuals and businesses would be unaltered, the amount of borrowing by the government from the public would be unaffected, and the expenditures of the federal government would be the same.

Labelling the payroll tax as a contribution is sometimes regarded as a crucial factor in gaining public understanding and acceptance of the programme. Presumably, this practice allows individuals to connect the lowering of income now with the promise of benefits later. But much the same effect could be achieved by devices that do not involve a payroll tax. For example, a certain percentage of the individual's income tax, or of his taxable income, could be designated as a tax to support OASDI. The tax could be withheld by the employer and labelled as the 'OASDI tax' on the individual's final tax return, very much as is done today with the payroll tax on the employee's W-2 withholding form. The psychological connection between the tax and promised benefits would remain intact under this alternative, without resort to the payroll tax.

The basic point that emerges from the foregoing observations is that payroll tax receipts are part of the total revenues of the federal government, and that the payroll tax should be evaluated on its merits as a source of taxes. This means that the desirability of changes in payroll taxes should be weighed against changes in other taxes and that social security benefits should be financed by the methods which are most equitable and most conducive to economic growth and efficiency.

In place of the insurance analogy, social security should be regarded as an institutionalised compact between the working and non-working generations, a compact that is continually renewed and strengthened by every amendment to the original Social Security Act.[28] When viewed in this light, a social security programme has the eminently desirable function of forcing upon society a decision at each point of time on the appropriate division of income and consumption between workers (the young) and non-workers (the old, survivors and disabled). Workers and non-workers alike participate in the democratic process that shapes this vital distributional decision. The social security system is the mechanism by which society settles the issue of intergenerational (worker/non-worker) income distribution throughout the political process rather than leaving its resolution to private decisions and the market.

This last point is more general than the narrow issue of preventing poverty among the aged. Consider two workers, A and B, who always earned at least the maximum taxable wage and thus quality for the maximum benefit; however, A is married to a woman aged 65 or older while B is unmarried. The benefit paid to A (and his wife) is 50 per cent greater, while they are both living, than the benefit paid to B; and a widow's benefit is payable after A's death, while only a small lump-sum payment is paid to B's survivors (as it is also to A's), despite the fact that, by assumption, each had equal earnings before retirement and the question of poverty is not at issue. The wife's benefit is an extremely important redistributional device that has no connection with the problem of poverty. In short, the benefit structure under OASDI is, like the system of personal exemptions under the personal income tax, a means by which society can adjust the distribution of income that results from the workings of the private market for nonmarket, welfare considerations, such as family size.[29]

Finally, the foregoing discussion strongly suggests that there is little basis for according autonomy to the social security system in the federal budget. This has been recognised by the changes incorporated in the budget for fiscal year 1969—following recommendations by the President's Commission on Budget Concepts[30]—which combined trust funds and other federal expenditures and revenues in a single budget. Social security today is too intimately linked on both the benefit and tax sides with the total government budget for fiscal autonomy to make sense. The integration of OASDI into government budget planning is a necessary step in rationalising the processes for attaining the objectives of social security.

SUMMARY

The case for social security rests on a solid basis. Given widely accepted humanitarian values and a few fundamental facts about economic behaviour in our culture, it follows that the government should maintain and continually strengthen the social security system to protect individuals from severe declines in living strandards in retirement and against other risks. To serve the purposes which justify its creation, the system should be financed by the best methods available to the government at any given time; it should guarantee minimum benefits sufficient to keep beneficiaries out of poverty; and it should pay benefits above the minimum level determined, at least in part, by the previous income or earnings experiences of beneficiaries.

Two basic features of the social security system which are widely approved and help to explain the public's acceptance of the system as a desirable permanent public institution can be traced to the analogy with private insurance. These features are the belief that benefits are earned rights to which no stigma attaches, and that they depend at least in part on past earnings of participants. The insurance analogy is misleading, however, in fundamental respects. On the assumption that social security will continue to be financed approximately on a current basis, the currently employed will always be taxed enough to pay for the benefits of those who are retired. The practical importance of distinguishing between social security and private insurance is that it forces the major elements of the social security system—taxes and benefits—to be considered in the appropriate perspective. Benefits of the currently retired need not, and should not, depend on their past taxes; they should be based on decisions reached by democratic political processes as to how much of the nation's total income should be allocated for retirement, disability, and survivor benefits. Similarly, the tax should not be regarded as an insurance premium, but rather as a financing mechanism—to be judged on its own merits—for a large, essential government programme. Decisions about social security taxes and benefits should be recognised as being closely interdependent with other tax and benefit decisions in the federal budget.

NOTES

1. An early version of this chapter appeared in *Old Age Income Assurance, Compendium of Papers on Problems and Policy Issues in the Public and Private Pension System*, Part III: *Public Programs*, 90 Cong. 1 Sess. (1967), pp. 5–20.
2. The views described here are expressed forcefully by Milton Friedman in *Capitalism and Freedom* (University of Chicago Press, 1962), pp. 187–9.
3. Ibid., p. 184.
4. See pp. 212–13, below.
5. See, for example, Brett Seidman, 'The Case for Higher Social Security Benefits', *AFL-CIO American Federationist*, Vol. 74, No. 1 (January 1967), pp. 1–8; and Chamber of Commerce of the United States, *Poverty: The Sick, Disabled and Aged* (1965), pp. 69–73.
6. This point is developed fully by Robert M. Ball, 'Social Insurance and the Right to Assistance', *Social Service Review*, Vol. 21, No. 3 (September 1971), pp. 331–44.
7. Lenore A. Epstein and Janet H. Murray, *The Aged Population of the United States: The 1963 Social Security Survey of the Aged*, US Department of Health, Education and Welfare, Social Security Administration, Office of Research and Statistics, Report No. 19 (1967), Table 3.18, p. 302. Estimates of the asset holdings of the aged vary greatly and the figure cited above may be understated.
8. According to a field survey taken in 1960, less than half of non-retired persons over 55 years of age were able to estimate the amount of income that they would obtain from their retirement programme and from social security. More than two-fifths were unable to estimate their income requirements during retirement. See James N. Morgan, Martin H. David, Wilbur J. Cohen and Harvey E. Brazer, *Income and Welfare in the United States* (McGraw-Hill, 1962), p. 442. See also the discussion by Derek C. Bok, 'Emerging Issues in Social Legislation: Social Security', *Harvard Law Review*, Vol. 80, No. 4 (February 1967), pp. 738–9.
9. This tendency to make economic decisions politically is reviewed by William J. Baumol, *Welfare Economics and the Theory of the State* (Harvard University Press, 2d edn; 1965). See also Stephen A. Marglin, 'The Social Rate of Discount and the Optimal Rate of Investment', *Quarterly Journal of Economics*, Vol. 77, No. 1 (February 1963), pp. 95–111.
10. See Phillip Cagan, *The Effects of Pension Plans on Aggregate Saving: Evidence from a Sample Survey*, National Bureau of Economic Research, Occasional Paper 95 (Columbia University Press, 1965); and George Katona, *The Mass Consumption Society* (McGraw-Hill, 1964), Chp. 19.
11. For a summary of a recent study of this problem, see H. J. Maidenberg, 'Personal Finance: Annuities at Age 65', *New York Times*, 22 June, 1967, p. 51, col. 5.
12. This rationale for social insurance is developed by Richard A. Musgrave 'The Role of Social Insurance in an Overall Programme for Social Welfare', in William G. Bowen and others (eds.), *The American System of Social Insurance: Its Philosophy, Impact, and Future Development* (McGraw-Hill, 1968).
13. See Roger F. Murray, 'Economic Aspects of Pensions: A Summary Report', in *Old Age Income Assurance, V: Financial Aspects of Pension Plans*, pp. 36–114.
14. Internal Revenue Code, 401–4.

15. Daniel M. Holland, *Private Pension Funds: Projected Growth,* National Bureau of Economic Research, Occasional Paper 97 (Columbia University Press, 1966), p. 49.

16. See Robert M. Ball, 'Policy Issues in Social Security', *Social Security-Bulletin,* Vol. 29, No. 6 (June 1966), p.5.

17. See Eveline M. Burns, 'Social Insurance in Evolution', *American Economic Review,* Vol. 34, No. 1, Suppl., Part 2 (March 1944), pp. 199–211.

18. See, for example, Ball, 'Policy Issues in Social Security', and Robert J. Myers, *Social Insurance and Allied Governmental Programs* (R. D. Irwin, 1965), p. 8. For the views of a representative of the insurance industry who expresses concern about the analogy between private insurance and social security, see Ray M. Peterson, 'Misconceptions and Missing Perceptions of Our Social Security System (Actuarial Anesthesia)', *Transactions of the Society of Actuaries,* Vol. 11 (November 1959), pp. 812–51. Peterson also has collected statements by various public officials which demonstrate the prevalence of the belief in the insurance analogy: see 'The Coming Din of Inequity', *Journal of the American Medical Association,* Vol. 176, No. 1 (8 April, 1961), p. 38.

19. The views in this section have been expressed many times in one form or another by numerous observers. See, for example, Eveline M. Burns, 'Private and Social Insurance and the Problem of Social Security', *Analysis of the Social Security System,* Appendix II: *Miscellaneous Documents,* Hearings before the House Committee on Ways and Means, 83 Cong. 1 Sess. (1954), pp. 1471–9; Barbara Wootton, 'The Impact of Income Security upon Individual Freedom', in James E. Russell (ed.), *National Policies for Education, Health and Social Services* (Doubleday, 1955), pp. 386–7; Peterson 'The Coming Din of Inequity'; and Paul A. Samuelson 'Social Security', *Newsweek,* 13 February, 1967, p. 88.

20. The Committee on Social Insurance Terminology of the American Risk and Insurance Association has suggested a detailed definition of social insurance which lists many of its characteristics. In presenting this definition, the Committee commented that 'in addition to possessing some characteristics that it shares with insurance written by private insurers, social insurance possesses many unique characteristics.' *Bulletin of the Commission on Insurance Terminology of the American Risk and Insurance Association,* Vol. 3, No. 1 (January 1968), p. 2.

21. Wilbur J. Cohen in a letter to the editor, *Washington Post,* 1 September 1967, p. A20.

22. In James E. Russell (ed.), *National Policies for Education, Health and Social Services,* pp. 386–7.

23. It is sometimes alleged that there is a closer similarity between private disability plans and the disability part of the social security programme, nevertheless, the differences are striking. Private disability benefits are usually computed on the same basis as retirement benefits, and rarely allow for the number of dependants—a feature which is basic to the social security program. See Bankers Trust Company, *1965 Study of Industrial Retirement Plans* (Bankers Trust Company, 1965), pp. 17–19, and US Department of Labor, Bureau of Labor Statistics, *Private Pension Plan Benefits,* Bulletin No. 1485 (1966), pp. 35–65.

24. This point has been made many times, dating back to the basic article by Paul A. Samuelson, 'An Exact Consumption—Loan Model of Interest With or Without the Social Contrivance of Money', *Journal of Political Economy,* Vol. 66, No. 6 (December 1958), pp. 467–82. See also Peter A. Diamond, 'National

Debt in a Neoclassical Growth Model', *American Economic Review*, Vol. 55, No. 5 (December 1965), pp. 1126–50; Henry J. Aaron, 'The Social Insurance Paradox', in *Old Age Income Assurance, Part V: Financial Aspects of Pension Plans*, pp. 15–18 (reprinted from *Canadian Journal of Economics and Political Science*, Vol. 32, No. 3 [August 1966], pp. 371–4): and Earl A. Thompson, 'Debt Instruments in Both Macroeconomic Theory and Capital Theory', *American Economic Review*, Vol. 57, No. 5, (December 1967), pp. 1196–210.

25. For a thoughtful discussion of the implications of social security financing see John J. Carroll, *Alternative Methods of Financing Old-Age, Survivors', and Disability Insurance* (University of Michigan, Institute of Public Administration, 1960), Chs. 1 and 3.

26. The courts have held that the 'non-contractual interest of an employee covered by the Act cannot be soundly analogised to that of the holder of an annuity, whose right to benefits are based on his contractual premium payments.' *Flemming* v. *Nester*, 363 US 603 (1960).

27. It is regarded as a tax both by the law and the courts. See Section 3101 of the Internal Revenue Code and *Flemming v. Nestor*, cited in note 26.

28. The outstanding statement of this view of social security is by Paul A. Samuelson in 'An Exact Consumption-Loan Model'. The best introduction to social security for the serious student is the entire Samuelson article and the the later exchange between Samuelson and Abba P. Lerner concerning some points raised by the article, in 'Consumption-Loan Interest and Money', 'Reply', and 'Rejoinder'. *Journal of Political Economy*, ol. 67, No. 5 (October 1959), pp. 512–25.

39. Unfortunately, these same considerations have been completely ignored on the tax side of OASDI.

30. *Report of the President's Commission on Budget Concepts* (October 1967), esp. Ch. 3.

19. Evaluation of the US Social Security System*

The social security system is the most successful social programme ever enacted by the US government. In a typical month in 1984 it provided almost $15 billion of benefits to 36 million retired and disabled people and their dependants and survivors. For most of these people, social security was the major source of income. While poverty among the aged has not been eliminated, social security has brought this goal within reach. Yet despite its success social security of late has been subject to great criticism, and radical changes are often suggested for problems that either do not exist or can easily be resolved. This chapter will explain the programme's rationale and suggest methods of improvement which will not alter its basic character.

RATIONALE OF SOCIAL SECURITY

When the social security programme was enacted in 1935 considerable emphasis was placed on its resemblance to private insurance: 'contributions' were to be paid by the worker and the employer into a trust fund: interest was credited on trust fund balances; and benefits were formally based on the worker's previous earnings. This emphasis promoted public acceptance of the system as a permanent government institution.

The insurance analogy no longer applies to the system as it has developed. Present beneficiaries as a group receive far larger benefits than the taxes they have paid plus a reasonable rate of return, and new beneficiaries will continue to get a 'good deal' as long as Congress keeps benefits in line with higher prices. Although the trust fund balances have tended to increase over the long run, they are rarely large enough to finance more than one year's benefits; payroll taxes paid by workers are not stored up or invested, but are paid out currently as benefits. When the benefits promised to people now working become due, they will be paid from the tax revenues of that future date. Social security thus is really a compact between the working and non-working generations—a compact which

---

*Adapted from *The Crisis in Social Security: Problems and Prospects*, Michael J. Boskin, editor (Institute for Contemporary Studies, 1977), pp. 31–9.

amendments to the basic programme have continually renewed and strengthened.

Under this concept, payroll taxes are not insurance premiums; rather they are a financing mechanism for a large, essential, government programme. As such, payroll taxes should be evaluated like any other major tax of the federal government. Increases in benefits and expansion of the social security programme should not be financed automatically by higher payroll taxes as they have been in the past, but by the best tax source or sources available to the federal government. On the other hand, since benefits are related to past wages, many believe that the system has sufficient insurance elements to justify taxation of payrolls to finance it. But this rationale does not, in my view, preclude the possibility of improving the payroll tax so that it is not a heavy burden on the poor and on low-income workers.

REGRESSIVITY OF THE PAYROLL TAX

Payroll taxes have a significant impact on the tax payments of the lowest income groups. In 1985 the employee and employer taxes for social security, disability and hospital care will reach 14.1 per cent of wages up to $39,600. Most economists believe that the tax on the employer as well as that on the employee is borne by the workers. Thus we extract a payroll tax of $705 from an individual with a family of four and an income of $5000, even though he is officially classified as poor by the federal government. In return, this worker will receive generous benefits, but these will be deferred for decades.

The payroll tax exceeded the 1984 federal income tax liabilities for single persons with incomes of $18,700, married persons with incomes of $29,000, and married persons (including working couples) with two children and incomes of $33,500. In 1979 the federal payroll tax for OASDHI (Old Age Survivors, Disability and Hospital Insurance) purposes was the highest tax paid by about half of those covered by social security.

To moderate the burden of the social security tax on low incomes, in 1975 Congress introduced a refundable income tax credit of 10 per cent of family earnings up to $4000 (phasing down to zero at $8000) for persons with children. (The credit is 'refundable', because cash payments are made to those whose credit exceeds their federal income tax liability or who are not subject to tax.) About 70 per cent of the payroll tax liability ($10 \div 14.1$) is eliminated for those who are eligible for the full amount of the credit, but only a minority of workers at those earnings levels are eligible.

A major share of the burden of the payroll tax at the lower end of the income scale would be eliminated if the 10 per cent tax credit were increased to the 14.1 per cent of social security tax rate, and if individuals without children were made eligible for the credit.

Another possibility would be to introduce into the payroll tax a system of personal exemptions and low-income allowances similar to those used in the individual income tax, and to eliminate the maximum taxable earnings ceiling. This would make the payroll tax a progressive tax on earnings even if there were only a single tax rate. The exemption and low-income allowance would eliminate taxes paid by earners who are below the poverty levels and, without a taxable earnings limit, an increasing proportion of earnings would be taxed as earnings rose.

Still another possibility would be to use existing receipts from the general fund of the Treasury when additional funds are required to finance benefits. Since the general fund relies primarily on progressive taxes, this would automatically improve the equity of the overall tax system.

One way to introduce general revenue financing would be to adopt the recommendation of two Quadrennial Advsiory Councils on Social Security that payroll tax receipts of the hospital insurance fund be gradually shifted to the old-age and survivors' insurance fund and that general revenue receipts be used to replace the payroll tax receipts in the hospital fund. The councils pointed out that the benefits under the hospital programme for the aged are not related to wages, and consequently there is no justification for using a payroll tax to finance these benefits.

None of the methods of moderating or eliminating the regressivity of the social security payroll tax would necessarily require a change in the method of calculating benefits. Benefits are now related to past earnings, not to taxes paid. Since the system's basic objective is to moderate the earnings decline at retirement, this relationship between benefits and past earnings can be preserved whatever the structure of the tax used to finance benefits. Under the present system, benefits are equal to a fraction of average earnings (up to the taxable ceiling). The higher the average earnings, the lower the fraction.

A ceiling on benefits is appropriate because the national retirement system should be used to guarantee benefits on the basis of earnings up to some reasonable level—beyond which private pension arrangements and personal savings can be expected to take over. Expansion of the earned income credit or use of general revenues for financing future revenue needs would not require any change in the method of calculating benefits, since the present payroll tax and the earnings ceiling would be retained. The decision to eliminate entirely the earnings ceiling would require an explicit decision on the point at which earnings replacement would terminate.

CONDITION OF THE TRUST FUNDS

The major purpose of the social security trust funds is to assure the American people that benefits will be paid at the statutory rate, without new congressional authorisation, even if payroll tax receipts do not cover current benefits for brief periods. The funds were virtually depleted in the mid 1970s and early 1980s, first, as a result of an error in the 1973 legislation which led to over-adjustment of benefits for inflation and, second, as a result of the deep recession of 1981/82. The error causing over-indexing for inflation was eliminated in 1977 and the long-run condition of the trust fund was buttressed by the enactment of bipartisan legislation in 1983 which lowered benefits (mainly by gradually raising the retirement age from 65 to 67 from the year 2000 to 2017), accelerated scheduled tax increases, and introduced partial taxation of social security benefits for the first time. Beginning in 1985, half of social security benefits will be subject to tax for married couples with other income over $32,000 and single people with other income over $25,000. The revenue from this tax will be allocated to the trust funds.

The outlook of the retirement and disability trust funds for the latter half of the 1980s and the entire decade of the 1990s is now excellent. (The Medicare funds will have problems resulting from the escalating costs of medicine, but this issue is outside the scope of this discussion.) The retirement and disability trust funds will be in surplus throughout this period, even if there are moderate recessions.

Annual surpluses are now estimated in the retirement and disability trust funds until the year 2015, assuming intermediate growth and inflation assumptions. The trust balances are not likely to be exhausted before about 2050. Thus, we still have over half a century to decide how 'the demographic changes that are now in prospect will be accommodated. If the nation prospers, there is no reason why benefits will need to be cut by substantial amounts. Modest tax increases, preferably from the general funds, will be sufficient to continue paying decent benefits.

EFFECT ON SAVING

Social security provides protection against loss of income resulting from retirement, death and disability. Before these programmes were enacted, individual savings were the only protection against such hazards. Social security may encourage individuals to set aside a smaller amount of personal saving on the ground that a major reason for saving has now been removed. On the other hand, the availability of social security provides an incentive for individuals to retire earlier, and this encourages them to save more.

Thus far these tendencies have probably offset one another. In fact, personal saving has remained between 5 and 8 per cent of disposable income in the last three decades, but many other factors have had a significant influence on the saving ratio. However, the effect of earlier retirement has been virtually exhausted (except for the trend toward early retirement at age 62), so that the incentive to save less because of the existence of social security may predominate in the future.

Some economists argue that the rate of saving is already too low in the United States, and urge that the nation should save more by raising the social security payroll tax in order to accumulate large balances in the trust funds. It is alleged that this saving, if invested in private capital, would be a 'good deal' for the worker because the rate of return would be high—as much as 12 per cent by some estimates. The data used to buttress this position are rates of return on corporate investment which are by no means indicative of the yield on all private capital. Corporate capital accounts for less than 50 per cent of the private capital stock; the remainder consists of dwelling units, farm and non-farm capital of the non-corporate sector, and land. The rate of return on the entire private capital stock has averaged substantially less than 12 per cent in recent years, even if recession years are omitted.

Furthermore, in arguing that large amounts of additional saving will yield high rates of return, these economists ignore the elementary economic point that a large increase in the private capital stock is likely to encounter diminishing returns. It would be unwise to assume that new investment can continue to earn high rates of return regardless of how much saving is pushed into the corporate sector.

There is in any case no compelling logic for assigning the responsibility for additional saving to social security, other than the pragmatic judgement that Congress will not support large government surpluses unless they are to be associated with social security. This judgement would be acceptable if increased reliance on payroll taxes were desirable and a build-up of large surpluses in the federal budget were appropriate.

An across-the-board increase in individual income tax rates of about 1.1 percentage points would raise as much revenue as a percentage point of the payroll tax. When this progressive alternative is available, advocacy of the payroll tax as a method of financing is difficult to understand.

The huge deficits of the Reagan administration have not been generated by the social security system. Most people agree that they should be gradually reduced or eliminated. The large surpluses in the social security system in the 1990s will ease the fiscal problems of the federal government. Any transition to an even higher saving rate would have to be managed carefully to maintain an adequate growth in total demand.

CONCLUSIONS

Payroll taxes paved the way for the enactment of a comprehensive system of social security that protects workers against income losses due to retirement and disability. Although the programmes were originally described as social insurance, they have substantial non-insurance components that are strongly supported by the public. Even if payroll taxes continue to be the basic method of financing the programme, the effects of these taxes on the distribution of income can no longer be ignored. Improvement of the earned income tax credit, introduction of personal exemptions and a low income allowance into the payroll tax, and removal of the maximum taxable earnings ceiling, or use of the general fund for financing increased social security benefits, would improve the equity of these taxes.

The costs of the system will rise dramatically when the people born in the baby boom following the second World War retire, but this problem has been resolved to a considerable extent by the bipartisan 1983 legislation which raised taxes and reduced benefits. Any future tax increases or benefit reductions should be delayed until the next century when the dimensions of the problem, if any, will be clearer.

Claims that the social security system has reduced national saving are exaggerated. If it turns out that more saving by the federal government will be needed in the future, the necessary revenues should be drawn from the general funds of the Treasury which come mainly from the progressive income taxes. Increased payroll taxation would be the worst possible solution.

Part Seven
Foreign Tax Systems

20. Taxation in Japan*

Japan's tax system resembles that of the United States more than those of the Western European countries. Revenues at the national level are derived primarily from individual and corporate income taxes; the prefectures and local governments rely on the property tax as well as on income taxes. The payroll tax is used to finance social security benefits and the national health insurance system. There is no general sales or value-added tax in Japan, but substantial revenues are raised from selected excise and sumptuary taxes at all levels of government. Death and gift taxes are minor sources of revenue.

Despite superficial similarities between the Japanese and US tax systems, there are striking differences not only between the structures of particular taxes in the two countries, but also between their respective attitudes and policies toward the use of taxation to promote national objectives. In the first place, the Japanese have virtually a unitary fiscal system, with limited delegation of fiscal responsibilities and powers to the local governments. Second, largely because of the high rate of economic growth, Japanese tax revenues at constant rates and exemptions have greatly exceeded the revenues needed to pay for the relatively low rate of public expenditure. This fiscal dividend has been used to augment national savings and to provide tax reductions virtually every year. Third, the Japanese income taxes are riddled with special provisions that are designed to encourage particular types of consumer and business behaviour. The Japanese tax system is probably slightly progressive on balance, but—like the US system—its effect on income distribution is not great.

OUTLINES OF THE TAX SYSTEM

In 1947, under the influence of the American occupation authorities, the schedular individual income tax was replaced by a unified tax with progressive rates, and the excess profits tax was replaced by a regular corporate income tax. Tax rates during the occupation were very high, reaching a maximum of 85 per cent on individual incomes above 5 million yen (about $14,000) and 52.5 per cent on corporate profits. In addition, a turnover tax (paid each time a commodity 'turns over' from one firm to another) was enacted to raise needed revenues.

*With Kemei Kaizuka. Adapted from *Asia's New Giant*, Hugh Patrick and Henry Rosovsky, editors (Brookings Institution, 1976), pp. 319–73.

In 1949 a commission headed by Carl S. Shoup, Professor of Economics at Columbia University, was organised to help reform the tax system and moderate the high tax rates, which had become extremely burdensome as a result of the rapid rise in prices immediately after the war. The Shoup Mission recommended a complete overhaul of the system, including repeal of the turnover tax, a comprehensive individual income tax (with full taxation of capital gains and full deduction for capital losses), a dividend credit at the individual income tax level, a surcharge on accumulated corporate earnings, a net worth tax, an accessions tax, a local government value-added tax, and a strengthened local property tax.[1]

Many of the taxes contained in major Shoup proposals were repealed or modified soon after enactment; they had proved too far-reaching for the relatively conservative and business-orientated government.[2] The turnover tax was not restored, and the supremacy of the income tax was maintained. The net worth and the accessions taxes were repealed in 1953; the enactment of the value-added tax was postponed several times, and the tax was later repealed without ever having gone into effect. In addition, most capital gains were removed from the individual income tax base, interest and dividends were made taxable at separate low rates, and the surcharge on retained corporate profits was eliminated. Comprehensive income taxation has long since been replaced by an elaborate system of tax preferences—allegedly to improve equity among taxpayer groups and to provide incentives for saving and investment. The major legacies of the Shoup proposals have been to make income taxation acceptable as the basic source of revenue in Japan, to raise the level of tax sophistication, and to improve tax administration.

The tax on individual income, which is used by the national, prefectural and municipal governments, is a hybrid of a global tax and a schedular tax. This system developed as a result of the modifications of the global income tax approach proposed by the Shoup Mission. Most incomes are aggregated and taxed at progressive rates, but some incomes either are not taxed at all or are taxed at special flat rates. Generous deductions are provided for employment incomes (currently 40 per cent for most wage-earners), and the exemptions are relatively high by US standards. The combined national and local income tax rates range from 14 to 93 per cent, but the effective rate of tax is limited to a maximum of 80 per cent.

The corporate income tax is a split-rate system similar to that used in West Germany and other European countries. Between 1970 and 1973 the combined rates for all levels of government were 48 per cent on undistributed profits and 37 per cent on distributed profits; in 1974 the rates were raised to 53 per cent and 42 per cent, respectively. The profits of small corporations are taxed at lower rates.

The tax on transfers of wealth at death is a combination of inheritance and estate taxes. The estate is divided among the heirs according to percentages prescribed by the succession law, and the tax rates are applied to each share with varying exemptions given to the spouse, children and other heirs. The total tax then is distributed among the heirs in proportion to the amounts they have received. The gift tax, which is levied on gifts cumulated for a period of three years, is also paid by the recipients. Tax rates on both bequests and gifts range from 10 per cent to 70 per cent, but exemptions are high and only a small proportion of the total wealth transferred between generations is actually subject to tax.

There is no general consumption, or sales, tax in Japan, but selective excise taxes are levied on liquor, tobacco, petrol, consumer durable goods, energy and admissions. On the whole, the tax rates are moderate: the taxes on small automobiles and household appliances, for example, are less than 10 per cent of the retailers' prices, including tax.

Payroll taxes are similar to those levied in the United States and other countries to finance social security and related programmes. Several different programmes apply to the public and private sectors, however, so the tax rates vary greatly. For employees in large enterprises the combined tax rates paid by employers and employees can reach 14.6 per cent on a substantial portion of the employees' earnings.

The property tax is used only at the local level. The prefectures levy a real estate transfer tax of 3 per cent but have no annual real estate tax. The standard real estate tax rate at the municipal level is 1.4 per cent of assessed valuation; this can be raised by the municipalities to a maximum of 2.1 per cent. As in all countries, valuations for property tax purposes represent gross understatements of true value.

SPECIAL FEATURES OF THE TAX SYSTEM

The special character of Japan's tax system cannot be conveyed by a brief description of the major taxes. Some of its particular features seem strange to a visitor from a country in which economic conditions and social attitudes are quite different. Japan's high rate of growth and moderate government expenditures (when compared with other developed countries) permit the Japanese to adopt tax policies that can well be envied elsewhere. On the other hand, there is a strong bias toward consensus and gradualism in the development of national policies. This bias does not prevent frequent changes in tax rates and personal exemptions, but it forestalls abrupt changes in the tax structure and perpetuates—and sometimes aggravates— certain tax practices that are acknowledged by experts to be less than optimal.

Those features of the system which are of particular interest to the outsider are the annual tax reductions; the tax process; the special tax measures; employee compensation and expense accounts; administrative practices; and strict control of local taxes by the national government.

Annual Tax Reductions

In an economy in which money GNP has risen by an average of 15 per cent a year or better, the annual growth in revenue is at least 15 per cent, even if the elasticity of the tax system is only 1.0 (that is, if revenues grow at the same rate as total income). Since Japan relies heavily on income taxes, the elasticity of the central government's revenues is much greater than 1.0—probably in the neighbourhood of 1.3.[5] This means that at recent rates of income growth, the growth of the government's fiscal resources without tax reductions has been in excess of 20 per cent a year.

The Japanese government has not used this tremendous revenue growth to increase the size of the public sector relative to the rest of the economy. To the contrary, it has adhered to a calculated policy of restraining the rate of growth of public expenditure relative to the rate of growth of the economy as a whole, so that the ratio of taxes to national income has crept rather than raced upward over the past two decades. Tax revenues of the national and local governments (not including social security taxes) amounted to 18.1 per cent of the national income in fiscal 1955, 19.2 per cent in 1960, 19.5 per cent in 1970, and 19.9 per cent in 1974. This policy provided the elbow-room for the unique practice of annual tax reductions that is so popular with the Japanese people and the object of envy by taxpayers and political leaders in other countries.

The Tax Bureau kept a detailed record of the annual tax reductions since 1950; its estimates are available for fiscal years 1950-53 combined and, beginning in fiscal 1954, annually. Between 1954 and 1974, individual income tax exemptions were increased in every year but three; the rates were reduced eleven times and increased but once. Corporate income tax rates were reduced six times and increased twice. The special tax measures, which apply to both individuals and corporations, were modified in some respect practically every year, more often than not bringing about a loss in revenue. Some indirect taxes were increased almost every year —because many of them are on a specific basis and do not automatically increase as the price of the product rises—but the revenue gains from indirect tax increases were small relative to the income tax reductions. Despite all the reductions in tax rates and increases in exemptions and deductions, tax collections increased at a slightly faster rate then the rate of growth of the national income.[6]

The Tax Process

To assist in the formulation of tax policy, the Japanese developed an institution that illustrates their penchant for consensus in government policy. A Tax Advisory Commission was established by the government in 1955 to assist in the formulation of long-range policy on the structure of the tax system, as well as to review and recommend year-to-year changes; it has played a significant role in the tax process ever since.[7]

The thirty or so members of the Tax Advisory Commission, appointed by the prime minister, come from different walks of life, including academic experts in public finance, journalists, former officials of the ministries of finance and home affairs, former mayors, and representatives of labour unions and of large and small business and agriculture. This diversity of membership was specified deliberately so the commission could act as arbiter among the interest groups that influence tax policy.

The secretariat of the commission consists of high-level Tax Bureau staff of the Ministry of Finance. None of the commission members is a government official, but the government has much influence on its recommendations, both because many of its members formerly were associated with the government and because the commission relies primarily on data and analyses prepared by the Tax Bureau. Outside specialists, usually academic economists and lawyers, are recruited to assist the commission, but they have a significant influence only on long-term policy.

The role of the Tax Bureau in tax policy is typical of the role of the bureaucracy in decision-making within the Japanese government. Though they have no independent political influence, the high-level staff members of the bureau (an unusually able group of career officials) are of major importance in the tax process. The interest groups concerned with tax legislation generally exercise their influence through negotiation and accommodation with the Tax Bureau as well as the Tax Advisory Commission.

In general, the Tax Advisory Commission's recommendations have been adopted virtually intact, although changes occasionally are made by the government. The government's tax proposals are usually approved by the Diet, but in recent years the influential tax committee of the Liberal Democratic party has occasionally succeeded in modifying the proposals significantly.

At the request of the government, the Tax Advisory Commission is constantly examining individual structural details of the tax system to promote efficient allocation of resources, increase built-in flexibility, and improve tax equity. In recommending tax changes to achieve these objectives, the commission diligently studies practices abroad (often by sending sub-committees to other countries) and seeks to adapt them to Japan's needs. Such major structural features as the dual-rate corporate income tax, the hybrid estate and inheritance tax, and accelerated depreciation have been devised by the commission. These policies are thoroughly discussed with the Ministry of Finance and other agencies before recommendations are actually made by the commission; but the commission is not a rubber stamp, and in some instances, the government's views have been altered as a result of discussions with its members. In the end, a consensus is reached in the commissions—which signifies that the government will accept it—thus smoothing the way for the enactment of the following year's tax changes.

Special Tax Measures

There is wide agreement in Japanese government and business circles that the tax system should be actively used to promote economic growth. Hence, numerous measures have been adopted to stimulate private investment and activities that have high national economic priority. Such measures—which include special tax-free reserves, accelerated depreciation, and the like—are contained in the Special Tax Measures Law, which is a catalogue of most, though not all, of the incentive provisions applying to the individual and corporate income taxes.[8]

A significant role in the development of the special tax measures is played by the Ministry of International Trade and Industry (MITI). The legislative process in the MITI begins in May of each year, when the director for industrial policy sends to his commodity and industry bureaus general guidelines of policy for the coming budget and, in some cases, solicits comments on specific proposals. During the summer the bureau chiefs receive suggestions from representatives of the business federations and trade associations and obtain comments on the proposals developed in the MITI and other government agencies. These views are evaluated and a set of proposals is drawn up for transmission to the Tax Bureau by the end of August. The rest of the calendar year is devoted to negotiation between the two agencies and the Tax Advisory Commission on the details of any reform proposals to be included in the budget.

Although the MITI has no seat on the Tax Advisory Commission, it maintains contact with the commission through the members who represent industry and commerce. The special tax measures proposed by the MITI are relayed to the Tax Commission by the secretariat or by the industrial members of the commission. Thus, the annual negotiations on specific proposals are at least a three-cornered affair involving the MITI, the Tax Bureau and the Tax Advisory Commission. Other government agencies also participate when their interests are involved.

The impetus for special tax measures appears to come mainly from industry and government. A majority of the Tax Advisory Commission supports this policy, but a minority—including former tax officials, experts from academic life, and representatives of labour—is either uncomfortable about this policy or openly hostile to it. As early as 1964 the Tax Advisory Commission stated officially that the special measures should be curtailed and ultimately abolished,[10] but progress toward this end has been slow. Partly as a result of the less pressing need to stimulate growth and partly in response to the pressures from the labour movement and the political left, more movement in this direction is expected in the future.

Employee Compensation and Expense Accounts

The Japanese tax system has been thoroughly adapted to the system of employee compensation that has been developed since the Second World War. Cash wages and salaries, including year-end bonuses, are taxable; other ingredients of the compensation package—for the wage-earner as well as for the executive—are either not taxable at all or are taxable only after the deduction of unusually generous allowances.

For the wage-earner, the most significant preferences are the exclusion of the value of subsidised housing from taxable income and the virtual exemption of company payments on retirement. Most of the large industrial and commercial firms provide housing to some of their employees, either rent-free or at rents that are far below market prices for comparable facilities. The subsidised portion of such rents is not taxable. No study of the value of these subsidies has been made, but they probably amount to about 10 per cent of cash wages and bonuses. About 10 per cent of all wage-earners in Japan live in subsidised housing and thus benefit from this tax preference.[11]

Most Japanese firms do not have funded pension plans; instead, they ordinarily make lump-sum payments to their employees on retirement, commonly one or two months' wages in the last year of employment (not including the semi-annual bonuses) for every year of employment with the firm. If a worker had been employed for 35 years, for example, he would be eligible for a retirement payment equal to three times his last annual wage. Partly to avoid the problem of averaging, such retirement payments (for 35 years of service) are taxable only after they exceed 10 million yen (more than $30,000 at 1974 exchange rates), thus effectively removing from the tax base the payments received by all but the highest salaried executives.

Aside from these two major preferences, wage-earners also benefit from tax-free recreational and other welfare benefits provided by Japanese firms. Many of the large firms have vacation facilities that are available to their employees and their families for long weekends without cost. In addition, the Japanese are travelling more as incomes have grown, and firms are beginning to subsidise employee tours to Taiwan, Hawaii, and even more distant places such as the continental United States and Europe. These benefits are not nearly as valuable as the housing subsidies and retirement payments, but they are growing in importance as foreign travel becomes both more attractive and more available to the average Japanese family.

For the business executive, the compensation package consists of several other tax-free elements. The corporate executive does not own large blocks of stock in his corporation, primarily because there are virtually no employee stock purchase or stock option plans in Japan. Instead, the executive is given a car and chauffeur, an expense account, and either a large, subsidised residence or a subsidised loan to purchase his own residence.

The expense account is perhaps the most distinctive of these benefits. Most executives spend several nights a week in town on business.[12] A usual procedure is to take one's guests to an expensive restaurant, geisha house or club. The cost of an evening may run to $100 or more a person, all of which is charged to the host's firm.[13] Firms, however, are permitted to deduct only 25 per cent of entertainment expenses in excess of the sum of 4 million yen plus 0.1 per cent of capital. For large firms, the amount disallowed averages about 55 per cent of the total expenditures for entertainment expenses.[14] Nevertheless, there seems to be no evidence that this restriction has reduced these expenditures. According to the official national income accounts, entertainment expenses in the private sector (which are classified as business consumption expenditures) amounted in calendar 1965 to 2.4 per cent of the GNP and 9 per cent of corporate profits plus income of unincorporated enterprises.[15]

As corporate executives move up the management scale, they tend to leave the subsidised housing provided by their firms and to purchase their own residences. To enable them to do so, many companies give their executives loans that are repayable over ten or more years at zero or very low interest. This interest subsidy is not taxable. The availability of such credit and the easy payment terms permit the exeuctive to purchase a home that, given the recent trends of land and housing prices, becomes extremely valuable by the time he retires.

The fact that he has a valuable asset does not ordinarily permit an executive to withdraw from the labour force when he retires from his lifetime career—55 or 60 for middle managers, 60 or 65 for top managers. The final payment he receives upon retirement usually is not large enough to permit him to stop working. To supplement his income, a retired executive usually moves to a subsidiary of his own enterprise or to another firm and works for another ten years or so as an adviser, inspector or active executive.

Administrative Practices

The Shoup Mission found in 1949 that Japan's system of tax administration was archaic. Because tax rates were stiff, taxpayer morale was at a low ebb, and under-reporting was more the rule than the exception. To collect necessary revenues, income tax administrators had developed a system under which each tax office was assigned a quota of collections. This quota was often met by imposing arbitrary assessments of reported tax liabilities, whether the taxpayers' reports were honest or not. In some instances such reassessments actually exceeded the total income of the taxpayer, and several of these cases received wide publicity in the press.

To improve taxpayer morale, the Shoup Mission recommended reduction of the high marginal tax rates, elimination of the goal system, simplification of tax returns for small taxpayers, public disclosure of high-income tax returns, and the elimination of anonymous accounts. Except for the anonymous accounts, the Shoup recommendations were accepted, and the quality of administration improved almost overnight. Japan's tax system is administered today at a cost only moderately higher than that of the US system.[17] Some of the more interesting practices and remaining administrative problems are discussed in the following paragraphs.

Blue returns. The Tax Administration Agency regards the 'blue return' as the cornerstone of efficient tax administration in Japan. Use of the blue return, designed to encourage small- and medium-size businesses to keep at least a minimum set of accounting records, offers certain significant advantages to individuals and corporations conforming with the accounting standards of the tax offices. The primary advantage is that the enterprise will not be subject to reassessment unless errors are found in accounting books and records. In addition, taxpayers filing a blue return are allowed to deduct reasonable amounts for wages of family members working in the same business; to accumulate reserves for bad debts, losses due to price fluctuations, and employees' retirement allowances; to carry back losses against income in the preceding year and forward against income in the following three years (five years in the case of corporations); to take advantage of special depreciation allowances, deductions for overseas transactions of technical services, and depletion allowances; and to deduct the cost of preparing the return (up to a maximum of 100,000 yen). In the early 1970s, about 80 per cent of all individual and corporation income taxpayers engaged in a business other than agriculture filed blue returns. But as in other countries, farmers seriously understate their incomes for tax purposes. Most of them do not file blue returns, and tax collection offices estimate their income on the basis of their crops.

Publicising High-Income Taxpayers. Beginning in 1947 the public was allowed access to all tax returns to encourage informers to reveal to tax authorities the names of individuals and corporations filing dishonest returns. The Shoup Mission urged that the informer system be abolished and recommended that the information contained on all but the highest tax returns be kept confidential. The recommendation to post high-income and large-inheritance tax returns was adopted in 1950, and the informer system was abolished in 1954.[19] Lists of individuals and corporations are posted on bulletin boards of district tax offices, and the top names usually are widely reported in the press and on radio and television. For calendar 1972 the posted lists included about 126,000 individuals, 14,000 corporations and 30,000 returns for estates of decedents.

Japanese tax officials seem to be lukewarm about this practice. The lists are published privately in 'who's who' types of compilation that are used for commercial and social purposes and for the solicitation of campaign contributions. Some people with incomes below the minimum required for posting deliberately inflate their income to appear on the lists, and later they file refund claims; others purposely delay filing their returns to avoid having their names posted. On the other hand, the corporate tax data are useful for research purposes by government and private agencies; and the lists of individuals may help to promote voluntary compliance on the part of the wealthy groups in the population. No serious economic or statistical analysis of the posted returns has ever been made. The major concern of the tax authorities seems to be that the posting requirement imposes heavy administrative costs on the tax offices.

Anonymous Accounts. A continuing problem in tax administration is the use of anonymous accounts to conceal investment income. This usage was banned administratively in 1950, but the ban was lifted in response to pressure by banking interests. Anonymous and fictitious accounts are commonplace in Japan and apparently are difficult to control. Business as well as individual depositors use seals rather than names and signatures for opening accounts and withdrawing deposits, and the banks make no effort to verify the identification on the seals. The government's bank examiners have attempted unsuccessfully to obtain legislation to prohibit the use of such accounts. Revenue agents may investigate anonymous and fictitious accounts when they suspect tax fraud, but these cases are unusual.

Anonymous and fictitious accounts are obviously subject to abuse by wealthy persons, who can create numerous such accounts, each with small deposits, that are not subject to tax under the Special Tax Measures Law. A study by the National Tax Administration of 105 corporate and individual income tax evasion cases in 1968 revealed that 36 per cent of total deposits were held in anonymous accounts, 31 per cent were in accounts with fictitious identification, and only 33 per cent were in accounts with correct identification.

The exemption of interest on small deposits and separate taxation of interest and dividends are justified in part on the ground that more taxpayers would use anonymous accounts if interest and dividends were taxable in full under the progressive rates. In effect, the inability to close the leakage through anonymous and fictitious accounts acts as a deterrent to evenhanded tax administration and to the improvement of the income tax structure.

Tax Treatment of Proprietors and Family Employees. Japanese tax laws reflect the broad influence of small business in the nation's politics. Throughout the post-war period tax authorities have been seeking a means of fair tax treatment for small proprietors and unpaid family members. Tax evasion by the self-employed and unincorporated businesses is known to be widespread, but the magnitude of the evasion is unknown. Since 1952 taxpayers filing blue returns have been permitted to deduct salaries of family employees as a business expense—up to a limit. This treatment was justified on the ground that blue return taxpayers keep proper books and records and therefore are able to distinguish business from household expenses. The limit was increased several times and ultimately abolished in 1968. In 1961 the privilege of deducting salaries of family employees was extended to taxpayers who did not file blue returns, but the allowable deduction remains subject to a limit (1975, 300,000 yen for each family employer). Finally, in 1973 taxpayers filing blue returns were allowed to elect to be treated as quasi-corporations for tax purposes. This permits business proprietors to deduct their own salaries as well as the salaries of family employees as expenses of doing business. In addition, the net income of the enterprise remaining after the deduction of these salaries is considered corporate income and taxed at the rate applicable to dividend distributions. Such distributions are taxed together with the imputed salary of the proprietor under the individual income tax, allowing also for the special deduction available to wage and salary income and for the tax credit that is provided for dividends at the individual level.

Valuation Of Property for Tax Purposes. The Japanese have had at least as much difficulty as other countries with keeping property tax assessments in line with the growth in market values. Officials of the Ministry of Home Affairs, which prescribes the standards to be followed by local assessors, are aware of the problem, but their hands are tied by law from raising assessment ratios too rapidly. The same problem applies to valuations for inheritance tax purposes. As might be expected, wealthy people invest heavily in real estate to obtain the benefit of low valuations: because property values have skyrocketed, the amount of property subject to inheritance taxes is only a small fraction of the true value of property that passes from one generation to the next. There is no evidence that this practice will be altered in the foreseeable future.

Taxation of Wage-Earners. An employer is in a position to discharge the full income tax liability of most of his employees through withholding, because small amounts of the employees' property income are legally disregarded for tax purposes, whereas larger amounts are subject to separate taxation. Consequently, the mass of wage and salary workers are not required to file tax returns. This arrangement is taken as an article of faith by tax policy officials and tax administrators. The advantage of the system is obvious: almost three-quarters of the individual income tax is withheld at the source and this amount is collected at little direct cost to the government. But this advantage is purchased at the cost of a system of deductions and exclusions from the income tax base that can hardly be justified on grounds of social equity. Until the tax officials are persuaded that the mass of wage earners can file tax returns, it will be impossible to replace the present fractionated system by a unified income tax.

The Local Tax System

There are two types of local government units in Japan: the prefectures, which are large regional units, and the municipalities, which consist of a variety of cities, towns, and villages. There are 47 prefectures and about 3300 municipalities. The operations of the local governments are subject to substantially more control by the national government in Japan than they are in the United States. The Shoup Mission recommended greater local autonomy than was traditional in Japan, but this advice was virtually disregarded. Practically all of the revenue sources are subject to control by the central government so that local taxes will 'not impede trade among local public entities'. The tax base and rates of most of the taxes are legislated by the Diet, on the recommendation of the Ministries of Home Affairs and Finance. Local governments are permitted to change tax rates within limits, but this discretion is rarely used for fear of an unfavourable reaction from the central government bureaucracy. Grants-in-aid are, of course, unilaterally provided by the central government. As in most countries—not including the United States—bond issues must be approved by the Ministries of Home Affairs and Finance before they are floated. Local bond issues are purchased by the Trust Fund Bureau of the national government (which buys them with postal savings and pension reserve funds), private banking organisations, and the public.

More then half of all local tax revenues comes from the individual and corporate income taxes. The structural features of these taxes, which are used by both prefectures and municipalities, are dictated by the central government; they are revised annually, concurrently with revisions in the nationwide taxes. Despite the uniformity imposed by the central government, taxpayers are required to pay income taxes directly to the prefectures and municipalities rather than combining them with payments made to the central government. A margin is available to the local governments to raise their income tax rates beyond the standard rates prescribed by the central government, but the flexibility is limited. The standard municipal individual income tax rates, for example, can be raised up to 50 per cent, and the municipal corporate tax rate can be raised up to 20 per cent.

The property tax, which is levied only by the municipal governments, accounts for a relatively small portion of local tax revenues—16 per cent in fiscal 1974. Most municipalities tax real estate at the standard rate of 1.4 per cent of assessed value, but they are permitted to go as high as 2.1 per cent.

The grants from the central government to the local governments consist of national subsidies and local allocations. The national subsidies are categorical grants for particular purposes, while the local allocations are general purpose grants which are provided on a no-strings-attached basis.

The local allocations programme is similar in many respects to—but much larger than—the general revenue sharing programme enacted in the United States. The Japanese attempt to allocate these funds on the basis of detailed estimates of need, whereas the United States allocations are based primarily on population, per capita income, and revenue effort. Notwithstanding these differences in the method of allocation, both types of grants may be used by the local governments with little or no direction by the national government. No study has yet been made of the relative merits of the two methods of allocation.

TAX BURDENS

Perhaps the most significant feature of the Japanese tax system is the relatively light load that it imposes on the taxpayer. Compared with Australia and 13 other countries in Western Europe and North America, Japan's tax burden in 1972 was the lowest. Except for the corporate income tax, all the major taxes were much lower relative to GNP in Japan than in most other countries. Individual income tax revenues were only 5.4 per cent of GNP in Japan, but they averaged 9.8 per cent in the other countries; payroll taxes, 4.1 per cent in Japan, averaged 10.2 per cent in the other countries; and taxes on goods and service, 5.1 per cent in Japan, averaged 11.8 per cent in the other countries.[22] Surprisingly, the corporate income tax appears to be much heavier in Japan than in most of the other countries—5.1 per cent of GNP compared with an average of 2.2 per cent in the others—but this is in large measure the consequence of the high ratio of corporate profits to GNP in Japan;[23] effective corporate tax rates probably are no higher in Japan than in most other countries.

Individual Income Tax

Although Japanese individual income tax rates are not low by comparison with those of other countries, the actual tax paid by taxpayers at various income levels is quite moderate by international standards. This is explained by major structural features of the tax: the relatively high exemptions, the generous deductions for employment income and family-owned businesses, and the preferential rates for property income.

A comparison of the major steps in the derivation of the individual income tax base from aggregate income is shown for Japan and the United States for 1970 in Table 20.1. Because the exemptions and deductions were so high, 32 per cent of the total income (as defined for income tax purposes) was not reported on tax returns in Japan or was reported by persons who were not taxable,[24] the corresponding figure for the United States was 10 per cent. Similarly, exemptions and deductions accounted for 35 per cent of the income on taxable returns in Japan and 31 per cent in the United States. As a result, the tax base amounted to only 33 per cent of total income in Japan, as compared with 59 per cent in the United States.

Table 20.1: Steps in the Derivation of the Individual Income Tax Base, Japan and the United States, 1970

Reconciliation item and steps	Japan		United States	
	Amount (trillions of yen)	Per cent of total	Amount (billions of dollars)	Per cent of total
Tax concept of income	50.1	100.0	677.4	100.0
Less non-reported income	12.6	25.1	45.7	6.7
Equals: income reported on individual returns	37.5[a]	74.9	631.7	93.3
Less income on non-taxable returns	3.6[b]	7.2	21.4	3.2
Equals: income on taxable returns	33.9	67.7	610.3	90.1
Less exemptions and deductions	17.4	34.7	209.6	30.9
Equals: taxable income, or tax base	16.4	32.7	400.7[c]	59.2

Sources: For Japan, estimated by Keimei Kaizuka on the basis of techniques explained in 'Tax Base of the Income Tax', in T. Hayashi and K. Kaizuka (eds.), *Nihon no zaisei* [Fiscal System in Japanese Economy] (Tokyo: Tokyo University Press, 1973). For the United States, worksheets of the Bureau of Economic Analysis, US Department of Commerce; and Joseph A. Pechman, *Federal Tax Policy* (rev. edn., Brookings Institution, 1971), table B-4, p. 275, Figures may not add to totals because of rounding.

a. Includes income of employees subject to withholding but not filing tax returns.
b. Earnings of non-taxable employees whose incomes are reported to the government.
c. Does not include $0.8 billion of taxable income of nontaxable individuals.

Table 20.2: Effective Rates of Individual Income Tax Paid by Families of Four to All Levels of Government, by Various Multiples of Average Family Income, Japan and the United States, 1974

Multiple of average family income [a]	Per cent of income paid in income taxes	
	Japan [b]	United States [c]
0.8	2.0	11.7
1.0	3.6	14.3
1.5	7.0	19.5
2.0	10.1	23.9
2.5	12.6	27.9
3.0	15.3	31.5
4.0	19.9	37.6
5.0	23.9	42.3
7.5	32.0	50.0
10.0	37.5	55.0

Source: Calculations based on exemptions and tax rates applying to incomes in calendar 1974. Taxable income for local tax purposes was assumed to be equal to taxable income for national tax purposes.

a. Average family income was assumed to be 2.4 million yen in Japan and $13,000 in the United States. All income is assumed to be earned.
b. The taxpayer is assumed to have personal deductions amounting to 5 per cent of his income, in addition to the employment income deduction.
c. The taxpayer is assumed to reside in New York State (outside of New York City) and to have deductions amounting to 15 per cent of income.

Actual tax burdens cannot be compared by income classes in the two countries because consolidated data are not available in Japan for those wage-earners who pay their tax entirely through withholding and for those who are required to file returns. But in Table 20.2, which may help to put the matter in perspective, 1974 income taxes payable to all levels of government are calculated for a family of four at various multiples of the average family income in the two countries.[25] The calculations assume that the families receive only incomes from employment, that the Japanese taxpayer is subject to the standard prefectural and local government tax rates, and that the US taxpayer pays the New York State (but not the New York City) income tax. On this basis, the average family of four paid an income tax of 3.6 per cent of its earnings in Japan and of 14.3 per cent in the

United States. The difference narrowed as incomes rose, but the Japanese family still paid about one-third less than the US family even when earnings reached ten times the average income. And in practice, because the typical family in Japan also received some property income that is either not taxable or is taxable at very low rates, the figures in Table 20.2 probably overstate the relative tax liabilities of the Japanese families.

For other reasons as well, the income tax load on the highest income classes in Japan must be significantly lower than in the United States. First capital gains on the sale of securities generally are not subject to tax in Japan, and gains on land held for more than five years are subject to a maximum rate of 20 per cent; all capital gains were subject to tax in the United States in 1974 at a top rate of 36.5 per cent. Second, Japanese taxpayers may elect to be taxed separately on their interest and dividends at a rate of 25 per cent; in the United States interest and dividends were fully taxable at marginal rates up to 70 per cent. Third, a credit of at least 5 per cent of dividends received (10 per cent for taxpayers with incomes below 10 million yen) is allowed against the final tax in Japan; in the United States, a deduction of only $100 ($200 on joint returns) is allowed. Because property income accounts for the major fraction of total income in the highest income classes, the tax burden in these classes may well be less than half as much in Japan as in the United States.[26]

Corporate Income Tax

The nominal tax rates applying to corporate profits in Japan are of the same order of magnitude as the rates in other countries, particularly when taxes paid to local governments—which are important in Japan—are taken into account. In 1974, the national corporate income tax was 40 per cent on undistributed profits and 30 per cent on distributed profits; the prefectural and local inhabitants taxes raised the total to 53 per cent and 42 per cent, respectively. In the United States, the top federal rate was 48 per cent on all corporate earnings—whether distributed or not—and the state taxes added an average of 3 percentage points, making a total of 51 per cent.[27] The United Kingdom, France and Canada levied taxes of 52, 50, and 49 per cent, respectively, on corporate profits, but they gave substantial credits for dividends received at the individual income tax level (and Canada, in addition, has provincial corporate income taxes that raise the total rate for many corporations). Germany used the split-rate system, with a rate of 51 per cent on undistributed profits and 15 per cent on distributed profits.

As is well known, however, nominal rates are not representative of relative tax burdens on business incomes, because all countries have adopted a wide variety of accelerated depreciation deductions, investment tax credits or allowances, tax-free reserves, and other devices to encourage private investment or to promote other objectives. Japan actually may have gone much farther in this direction than most other countries.[28] One measure of the effect of the special provisions on the corporate tax base is the effective rate of tax paid by corporations on gross profits: that is, profits before the deduction of depreciation allowances. A comparison of the nominal tax rates (including local taxes) with the effective tax rates on gross profits of all corporations in Japan and the United States is given in Table 20.3 for the period 1965-72.

In both countries, the effective rates are substantially lower than the nominal rates, with the US rates running over 50 per cent and the Japanese about 40 per cent of the nominal rates. In 1965 the effective rates in Japan were almost 6 percentage points lower than those in the United States; and in 1972 the effective rate was still only 20.1 per cent in Japan as compared with 27.1 per cent in the United States. However, in 1974 the nominal corporate tax rates were increased by an average of more than 4 percentage points in Japan.[29] In the future, therefore, the average effective tax rate on gross corporate profits probably will be only fractionally lower in Japan than in the United States.

Table 20.3: Effective and Nominal Rates of Corporate Income Taxes on Gross Profits, Japan and the United States, 1965-72[a] (per cent)

Year	Japan[b]		United States	
	Top nominal rate[c]	Effective rate	Top nominal rate[d]	Effective rate
1965	48	22.4	50	28.2
1966	47	19.6	50	28.5
1967	47	20.7	50	27.9
1968	47	20.1	55	30.6
1969	47	20.2	55	30.3
1970	48	22.5	52	27.8
1971	48	21.7	51	26.8
1972	48	20.1	51	27.1

Sources: For Japan, Economic Planning Agency, *Annual Report on National Income Statistics, 1974*, pp. 4–5, 144–5, 156–7. For the United States, US Department of Commerce, *Survey of Current Business* (July 1973). Table 1.14, p. 23, and prior annual July issues.

a. Based on data in the official national income accounts. Gross profits are net profits before tax plus capital consumption allowances. Taxes include central and local government taxes.
b. Data are for fiscal years ending on 31 March of year indicated in first column.
c. Rates apply to undistributed profits only and include local enterprise and inhabitants taxes.
d. Assumes state taxes add 2 percentage points to effective rates from 1959 to 1969 and 3 percentage points thereafter.

The effective tax rates are close enough in the two countries to suggest that the relative profitability of corporate investment depends on the rates of return before tax. A study by the Industrial Bank of Japan placed the income statements and balance sheets for 1070 US and 1000 Japanese industrial corporations on a comparable accounting basis and computed average annual gross rates of return before taxes for each firm on total invested capital and on stockholders' equity for the period 1967–71.[30]

The major conclusion of the study was that both the average and distributions of gross rates of return on all assets—that is, gross profits before taxes plus interest as a percent of borrowed plus equity capital— were roughly the same in Japan and in the United States. The average Japanese equity ratio, however, was roughly half of the US average: 28.7 per cent of total assets as compared with 55.5 per cent. Thus, the gross rate of return on stockholders' equity was almost twice as high in Japan as in the United States. For the period 1967-71, the average gross rate of return on equity was 46.4 per cent for the Japanese companies and 24.9 per cent for the US companies.[31] Clearly, the use of relatively large amounts of borrowed capital is a much more important factor than taxation in explaining the high rates of return on equity investment in Japan.

Inheritance and Gift Taxes

Like the other direct taxes, the inheritance and gift taxes are not onerous in Japan. Tax rates are not adjusted often, but exemptions have been increased frequently (e.g. 1966, 1971 and 1973). In 1970 only 3.4 per cent of the decedents left estates with any taxable value, and in that year the inheritance tax amounted to 19.1 per cent of the value of all taxable property transferred by bequest. For estates with taxable property of 100 million yen or more, the inheritance tax averaged 38.8 per cent of taxable value. Even these moderate percentages exaggerate the burden of the inheritance tax because land and closely held businesses are greatly undervalued for purposes of inheritance taxes. Because the gift tax is cumulative for a period of only three years, it is hardly an effective mechanism for preventing tax avoidance through gifts from one living person to another. Unfortunately, virtually nothing is known about the methods by which wealthy persons in Japan arrange to transfer their wealth to the next generation, but it is safe to assume that the transfer taxes have not been a great impediment.

Other Taxes

Half the total Japanese tax burden is accounted for by consumption, payroll, and property taxes. None of these taxes is high by international standards. Japan has been able to avoid a general tax on consumption, and the selective excise taxes it employs are not unusually burdensome. The payroll taxes can run as high as 14.6 per cent on the earnings of an industrial employee, but the entire array of payroll taxes applies to only a minority of workers. Even at 14.6 per cent, the payroll tax rates are lower than those levied in most countries of Western Europe and are only slightly higher than the combined social security and unemployment compensation taxes in the United States. As in most countries, the property tax is a weak tax for the usual reason: under-assessment of property values.

In brief, Japan's taxes are moderate or low when examined either tax by tax or in the aggregate. This fortunate circumstance can be explained in part by the absence of a defence programme in the budget, but it also reflects reluctance on the part of the Japanese government—at least in the past—to permit the public sector to expand in relation to the rest of the economy. With the rising demand for a more adequate social security system, however, and for a greater variety of public services and facilities, Japan may find it difficult to maintain the ratio of taxes to the gross national product at its recent low level.

INCOME ELASTICITY OF THE TAX STRUCTURE

The most prominent feature of Japanese tax policy during the 1960s and 1970s were the annual tax reduction. These reductions were designed to keep a roughly constant ratio of government expenditure to national income as the economy grew. Because the progressive individual income tax accounts for about a third of the central government's receipts, frequent tax reductions were needed to prevent the highly elastic individual income tax from generating too much revenue. Although rate reductions were made periodically, most of the reductions came from increases in exemptions, which helped to keep the elasticity of the tax at a high level.[32] Because revenue growth is large in any rapidly growing economy, the ability of the Japanese to reduce taxes annually without reducing the size of the government sector is not surprising. The real question is whether there are any novel features in the Japanese tax structure that make its revenues particularly responsive to income growth.

Responsiveness of the Tax System Income Growth

Although annual estimates of the tax reductions are available, the Japanese government does not publish estimates of the revenues of an unchanged tax structure over a period of years. Several analysts have made such estimates from time to time on the basis of the annual figures.[33] These estimates show a high degree of variability from year to year, because annual data reflect temporary as well as long-run factors. It is possible, however, to infer the long-run elasticities by averaging the annual figures or, as will be noted below, by computing long-run elasticities retrospectively.

Table 20.4 provides measures of year-to-year elasticities of the central government tax systems to changes in income for the period 1955–71. The responsiveness of Japanese tax revenues to income growth clearly is primarily the result of the individual income tax. Over the period 1955–71 the elasticity of the individual income tax averaged 1.8. By contrast, the yield of the corporate income tax is roughly proportional to income over the long run, while the consumption taxes rise more slowly than income. The inheritance tax is somewhat more responsive to income than the national individual income tax—its elasticity averaged 1.9 from 1955 to

Table 20.4: Year-to-Year Elasticity of the Central Government Tax System in Japan, by Type of Tax, 1955–71

Fiscal year	Elasticity[a]				
	All taxes	Individual income tax	Corporate income tax	Inheritance tax	Other taxes
1955	0.35	0.75	–0.12	2.27	0.28
1956	1.37	1.28	2.42	2.18	0.96
1957	1.49	1.28	2.84	1.19	0.94
1958	0.12	1.06	–2.48	0.50	1.33
1959	1.24	1.25	1.36	1.16	0.83
1960	1.64	2.12	2.45	1.27	0.99
1961	1.31	2.14	1.27	1.37	0.95
1962	1.06	2.97	1.02	3.48	0.09
1963	0.92	1.66	0.54	2.00	0.76
1964	1.22	1.98	1.05	1.07	0.89
1965	0.60	2.13	–0.23	2.85	0.19
1966	1.01	1.52	0.92	1.57	0.66
1967	1.28	1.56	1.53	0.89	0.91
1968	1.33	1.91	1.22	1.11	0.99
1969	1.34	1.90	1.45	1.83	0.81
1970	1.44	2.07	1.51	2.14	0.80
1971	1.01	2.43	–0.05	4.78	0.52
Average, 1955–71	1.22[b]	1.77	0.98	1.86	0.76

Source: Computed on basis of data from the annual issues of Tax Bureau, Ministry of Finance, *An Outline of Japanese Taxes,* and *Zeisei shuyō sankō shiryōshū* [Principal Reference Data for the Tax System].

a. Elasticity is the ratio of the percentage change in tax liabilities to the percentage change in GNP. The calculations are based on estimated tax receipts before the annual tax reductions.
b. Weighted average based on yields of various taxes in fiscal 1971.

1971—but it contributes very little to total revenues. Revenues from the property tax, which is levied exclusively by local governments, have risen less proportionally than incomes, even though the growth of property values greatly exceeds the growth in income.

When the erratic fluctuations of the annual data are removed, the elasticity of the individual income tax appears to have risen from about 1.5 for 1955–60 to about 2.0 beginning in 1960, and therefore fluctuated between 1.8 and 2.0. The elasticity of the inheritance tax was much higher than that of the individual income tax: 2.6 as compared to 2.0 for 1967–72. The corporate income tax continues to be erratic, reflecting largely the effect of the rate of growth of profits relative to total incomes. The elasticity of the consumption taxes seems to have declined from about 0.8 or 0.9 in the late 1950s to about 0.6 for the period 1967–72. Despite these changes, the elasticity of taxes at the beginning and end of the period was about 1.3 for the central and local governments.

These elasticities were much higher than those for the United States. The elasticity of the US federal individual income tax alone was in the neighbourhood of 1.43 in the period 1867–72, and the elasticity of the entire federal tax system (including payroll taxes) was probably about 1.10.[36] The differences between the US and Japanese elasticities was attributable entirely to the performance of the Japanese individual income tax. If the elasticity of its individual income tax were only 1.43 instead of 2.0, Japan's national government would also have had a tax system with an elasticity of about 1.10.[37]

Simulation of US Income Tax with Japanese Structural Features

To identify the reasons for the large difference in the elasticities of the two individual income taxes, the behaviour of the US tax was simulated for income growth rates similar to those experienced in Japan in recent years on the basis of a file of US individual income tax returns for 1970.[38] These simulations assumed that the relative distribution of income is not altered as incomes increase. Tax liabilities were projected, first, for the years 1970–73 on the basis of the increases in US incomes that occurred during that period and, then, to 1974 on the basis of annual income growth rates varying from 5 to 20 per cent a year.

As might be expected, the elasticity of the US income tax increases as income growth increases. The elasticity of the tax in 1974 begins at 1.52 for a 5 per cent growth in money income and rises to 1.60 for 10 per cent growth, 1.62 for 15 per cent growth, and 1.65 for 20 per cent growth (see Table 20.5). Even at the 15–20 per cent annual growth rates experienced in Japan, however, the elasticity of the US tax is significantly lower than 2.0. Using a per capita exemption that more nearly approximates the 1974 Japanese exemptions relative to their average income—$1060 instead of

Table 20.5: Elasticity of the US Federal Individual Income Tax with per Capita Exemptions of $750 and $1060, and with and without Income Splitting, at Selected Income Growth Rates, 1974

Annual income growth rate (per cent)	*Elasticity*[a]		
	Exemptions of $750 per capita, with income splitting	*Exemptions of $1,060 per capita, with income splitting*	*Exemptions of $1,060 per capita, without income splitting*
5	1.52	1.61	1.67
10	1.60	1.70	1.77
15	1.62	1.74	1.82
20	1.65	1.77	1.86

Source: Based on simulations from the 1970 US Internal Revenue Service individual income tax file.

a. Elasticity is the ratio of the percentage change in tax liabilities to the percentage change in personal income less transfer payments.

$750 per capita[39]—the same simulations give elasticities that are closer to those of the Japanese tax. The elasticity of the U.S. tax becomes 1.74 for an annual growth rate of 15 per cent and 1.77 per cent for an annual growth rate of 20 per cent. Finally, to make the rate structures more comparable, the tax rate advantages of the US income-splitting provisions were removed.[46] This raised the elasticity of the US individual income tax to 1.82 for an annual growth rate of 15 per cent and 1.86 for an annual growth rate of 20 per cent.[41] The relatively small difference between these elasticities and an elasticity of 2.0 is attributable to all other features of the Japanese income tax and the differences in the distribution of income between the two countries.

These results indicate that the Japanese have not discovered a new formula for a high-elasticity income tax. It is only necessary to combine high rates of growth of money income with relatively high exemption levels and moderately progressive rates to achieve an elasticity as high as 2.0. With an elasticity of 2.0 and annual growth of 15 per cent in money income, the yield of the tax doubles in less than three years. Such a yield offers ample room for financing increased public expenditures as well as for reducing taxes.

TAX INCENTIVES

Although most of the tax incentives under the Japanese income taxes are enumerated in the Special Tax Measures Law, a number of significant tax benefits are also contained in the ordinary income tax law. Accordingly, there is no compilation for Japan that is comparable to the comprehensive list of 'tax expenditures' that is published annually in the president's budget.[42] The Tax Bureau in Japan does, however, keep a careful record of the revenue cost of the provisions included in the Special Tax Measures Law. This discussion of tax incentives will be concerned chiefly with what the Tax Bureau calls 'special measures', but it will also cover the provisions of the ordinary income tax that may have significant economic effects.

Development of Special Measures

The special tax measures were brought together in one statute when the Temporal Tax Measures Law was enacted in 1938. During the war these measures were substantially expanded to promote tax incentives for the war effort. Just before the end of the war, the number of special measures was over 40. After the war, the Temporal Tax Measures Law was repealed and a new Special Tax Measures Law, containing about 20 provisions, was substituted. This shorter list was curtailed even further when the tax reform recommended by the Shoup Mission was carried out in 1950. The measures that survived the Shoup tax reform consisted of tax exemptions for specified types of interest income, a reduced withholding rate for dividend income, and a tax-free reserve for bad debts.

The list of special tax measures was again considerably expanded from 1951 to 1956. During this period special attention was paid to the promotion of economic growth through tax devices; as a result, the character of the Japanese tax system was changed in a distinctive way. By 1956 the total number of special tax measures exceeded 50, of which about 30 may be regarded as economically significant. These included accelerated depreciation for important industrial equipment (1951) and for newly-built rental housing (1952); additional initial depreciation for important industries (1952); a special deduction for income from exports (1953) and a tax-free reserve for losses from export transactions (1953); reduced tax rates on interest and dividends (1953 and 1954); and complete tax exemption for interest income (1955 and 1956).

The proliferation of special tax measures is a result of the process of accommodation and compromise that plays so vital a role in Japanese decision-making. Once the decision was made to use a particular incentive, people with similar needs who did not benefit from the provision demanded similar tax treatment. To avoid controversy, a new provision was adopted to placate these other groups. The new provision provoked additional demands by other groups; they were also given special treatment; and the cycle was repeated. For example, strong pressure for the reduction or elimination of the tax on interest income came initially from the banking interests. Representatives of industry supported them in the belief that the financial costs of their investments would be reduced if interest were to receive favourable treatment. Once the interest provisions were adopted, securities dealers and representatives of investment companies demanded favourable treatment for dividend income in order to maintain their competitive position relative to the banking industry. An attempt was made to distribute the tax benefits more or less equally among industries and interest groups, although the results could never be perfectly equitable, and the costs in terms of revenue forgone were relatively large.

In 1956 the Tax Advisory Commission changed its attitude toward the special tax measures and recommended that they be substantially curtailed. A few of the commission's proposals were adopted, but most of the special measures survived. In 1957 the tax exemption for interest income was abolished and the maximum amounts allowed for various tax-free reserves were lowered. At the same time accelerated depreciation for important industries was liberalised, and the special deduction for export income was increased.

Since 1957 the record has been patchy. In 1959 the tax-free reserve for losses from export transactions was abolished. In 1963 accelerated depreciation was granted to small- and medium-size enterprises, and interest income from small deposits was made tax exempt. In 1967 the initial depreciation for machinery and equipment used for the prevention of environmental pollution was increased, and tax credits were adopted for savings for housing and for increases in research and development expenditures. In 1968 interest income from small holdings of government bonds was exempted from tax. On the other hand, in 1969, capital gains on the sale of land and buildings held for less than five years was made subject to a heavy tax rate. In 1972 the accelerated depreciation provisions for export industries were abolished, the special deduction for income from exports was sharply curtailed, a new tax credit for the acquisition of a house used as a dwelling unit was adopted, and a special deduction was provided for taxpayers who file blue returns. In 1973 the increased initial depreciation for important industries was reduced and scheduled for elimination in 1976, and a heavier tax rate was applied to capital gains of corporations made from the sale of land. On the whole, the recent trend seems to have been to reduce the range of tax preferences, but there is no more reluctance now than in the past to use tax devices to promote new national objectives.

Inventory of Tax Incentives

According to the Tax Bureau, the Special Tax Measures Law contains more than a hundred provisions. About half of these provisions apply to narrow areas and involve negligible losses of revenue. This inventory will be confined to the most important provisions.

The Tax Bureau classifies the special tax measures into six different categories,[43] but this classification is ambiguous and not useful for economic analysis. As a substitute, the measures are here classified into four categories: promotion of personal saving and housing investment; promotion of business saving and investment; promotion of exports and foreign investments; and miscellaneous.

Promotion of Personal Saving and Housing Investment. The basic incentive device used to promote personal saving is the exemption of small amounts of property income from tax and the taxation of other property income at low rates. Interest income from savings deposits, government bonds, and postal savings with principal value up to 3 million yen is not subject to tax. In addition, interest from workers' saving designated as Savings for the Formation of Employees Assets are not taxable up to a principal value of 5 million yen. Beyond the actual exemption of modest amounts of interest income in these ways, the law also permits taxpayers to elect to be taxed separately on their interest and dividends at a rate of 25 per cent.

As in most countries, capital gains from the sale of securities are completely exempt, except where an individual is regarded as being engaged in continuous trading, defined as more than 50 transactions per year that involve a total of more than 200,000 shares. Capital gains from the sale of land or buildings are taxed separately at a 20 per cent rate if held for more than five years and 40 per cent if held for five years or less. An ordinary deduction of 1 million yen is allowed for all long-term capital gains, or alternative deductions varying from 2.5 million to 20 million yen are allowed for specific types of gains. The most important additional deductions are 17 million yen for capital gains on the sale of a taxpayer's house, 10 million yen for capital gains on the sale of the land under government land development or relocation programmes, and 2.5 million yen for capital gains on the sale of farmland under the government's programmes for the rationalisation of the use of farmland.

Two modest tax credits have been enacted in recent years to promote home-ownership. Taxpayers having specific contracts with financial institutions for savings for housing are given an annual credit of 4 per cent of the amount saved, up to a maximum of 20,000 yen. In addition, taxpayers who start to build or purchase a home are entitled to a tax credit amounting to 1 per cent of the standard acquisition cost of the home (100,000 yen per 3.3 square metres of floor space), up to a maximum of 30,000 yen per year.

Promotion of Business Saving and Investment. The devices to promote business saving and investment include accelerated depreciation, increased initial depreciation, tax-free reserves and credits. These devices are used freely to promote investment in particular industries or activities and in many instances two or more devices are used to promote the same objective. For example, tax-free reserves and either increased initial depreciation or accelerated depreciation are often provided simultaneously. Total depreciation is always limited to the cost of the asset.

Accelerated depreciation is allowed for plant and equipment of small- and medium-size enterprises and of firms with at least 30 per cent of their employees handicapped, for housing newly-built for rental, for facilities for storage of grain and crude petroleum, and for truck terminals and fireproof warehouses. The acceleration varies from 33 to 200 per cent of the regular depreciation allowances over a five-year period. Depreciation may be taken over a shorter period than the statutory useful lives for depreciable assets of registered hotels. Increased initial depreciation of one-tenth to one-half of acquisition cost is provided for numerous types of plant and equipment.

Taxpayers are allowed to accumulate two types of tax-free reserves. The first represents reserves that are recognised for purposes of business accounting; the second is to encourage involvement in risky activities. The size of the tax-free reserves and the amounts allowed annually are subject to specific limits, but in all cases the limits are generous in relation to the potential risks.

The tax credit device is used to encourage research and development. If a firm's outlays for research and development in any year exceed its outlays in any previous year, 25 per cent of the excess is allowed as a tax credit. The credit is raised 50 per cent for the portion of the excess above 15 per cent of the amount spent in the previous peak year. The credit is limited, however, to 10 per cent of the corporation income tax.

In addition to these measures, special treatment is given to three industries. In mining, a depletion allowance of 15 per cent of the proceeds from the sale of minerals is deductable as a current expense (up to a maximum of 50 per cent of income from mining), but this amount must be credited to a special reserve and ultimately used for mineral exploration. Timber income is taxed separately from other income, and a standard deduction of 400,000 yen is allowed for expenses. Farm income from newly-cultivated farmland also is exempt from tax.

Promotion of Exports and Foreign Investments. At one time promotion of exports was a major consideration in tax policy. From 1953 to 1965 producers of exported goods were permitted to deduct 3 per cent of their gross sales abroad, up to 80 per cent of their net operating income from exports. This provision was finally eliminated because it was in direct violation of the rules of the General Agreement on Tariffs and Trade, which prohibit export subsidies. From 1961 to 1972 firms were allowed accelerated depreciation for their equipment if they raised the proportion of their business from exports over the previous year's level.

Today, the remaining provisions for exports are minor. A special deduction is allowed for transactions involving the provision of technical services overseas. A tax-free reserve for overseas market development may be accumulated by a corporation that has capital of not more than 1 billion yen and that derives income from exports, from the processing of goods for an exporter, or from large-scale repairing of ships paid for in foreign currencies. Tax-free reserves may also be accumulated for losses from overseas investments. One-fifth of the amount credited to both types of reserves must be added back successively, after five years, to the income in five successive years.

Miscellaneous Provisions. To offset the low levels at which their fees were set under the social insurance system, physicians may deduct 72 per cent of their fees for medical care provided. Taxpayers filing a blue return may deduct 100,000 yen a year. Finally, corporations are allowed social and entertainment expenses up to 4 million yen plus 0.1 per cent of paid-in capital plus 25 per cent of any excess.

Use of the Tax Incentives

As might be expected, large corporations derive greater benefit from the special tax measures than small ones, even though they do not make as much use of the measures to which they are entitled. In fiscal 1970 small corporations—those with paid-in capital of less than 1 million yen—used almost all of the legally permitted deductions under the special tax measures, whereas the largest corporations—those with paid-in capital of 10 billion yen or more—used only about two-thirds. On the other hand, special depreciation accounted for only 3.5 per cent of the depreciation reported by the small corporations and 16.5 per cent of the depreciation reported by the largest corporations. The industries that benefited most from the special depreciation measures were construction, steel and metals, machinery and textiles. Special depreciation accounted for 29.1, 22.0, 18.8 and 16.5 per cent, respectively, of total depreciation reported in these industries.

Significance of the Tax Incentives

It is not possible to estimate the revenue loss from all of the tax incentives used by the Japanese. The only estimates that are available cover the particular provisions that are included by the Tax Bureau in its annual compilation of special tax measures. According to these estimates, the revenue loss resulting from the special tax measures varied between 11 and 13 per cent of income tax revenues in the late 1950s, declined to 8 per cent in 1961, rose to 13 per cent in 1965, and then declined to 9 per cent in 1971.

Because the special tax measures for the promotion of exports have been curtailed in recent years, revenue losses from these measures are declining relative to total income tax revenues. Special measures to promote business saving and investment declined sharply between 1956 and 1970, but they have regained importance largely as a result of the special depreciation provisions for antipollution equipment and for small- and medium-size enterprises. In 1972 the special measures to promote individual saving and investment account for 40 per cent of the revenue loss, business saving and investment for 34 per cent, exports and foreign investment for 3 per cent, and other measures (mainly the deduction for physicians' fees) for 23 per cent.

These official figures understate the significance of the whole gamut of tax incentive measures by a considerable margin. In the first place, the preferential provisions for capital gains, interest, and dividends are part of the basic income tax law and are therefore not counted as a special tax measure by the Tax Bureau. Second, the fractionation of the individual income tax into separate classified taxes[44] loses a great deal of revenue and greatly reduces the progressivity of the nominal rate structure, particularly in the top brackets. Third, a number of major business tax preferences are also not regarded as special tax measures. These include relatively short useful lives for purposes of depreciation accounting and deductions for part of social and entertainment expenses.[45] Fourth, housing subsidies provided by business firms to their employees and loans to executives at low interest rates are not regarded as special tax measures. Fifth, the official estimates are based on the economic projections included in the budget each year; these projections tend to understate economic growth and thereby the revenue significance of the special tax measures as well. The revenue loss from all the additional preferential provisions greatly exceeds the revenue loss from the official special measures, but there is little basis for making even an approximate estimate of the total. It is clear, however, that Japan sacrifices a great deal of revenue and is forced to maintain much higher nominal rates than otherwise would be needed in order to maintain its complicated set of tax incentives.

Studies of the impact of the special tax measures on Japanese economic growth are, for the most part, inconclusive. On the one hand, many of the special tax measures were used by industries that were not regarded as strategic from the standpoint of growth. For example, the textile industry received very favourable treatment under the special tax measures for the promotion of exports, yet this was an industry that grew relatively slowly. Moreover, there is virtually no relation between the special tax measures to promote household saving and the rate of private saving.[46] On the other hand, initial depreciation allowances were used widely for expansion and modernisation in such strategic industries as steel and machinery. Therefore, except for the stimulus in these industries, the special tax measures did not have a substantial effect on investment and growth.

ECONOMIC EFFECTS OF THE TAX SYSTEM

In the last two decades Japanese governments have placed great stress on taxation as an instrument of economic policy. Some part of the tax system is modified every year, often to a significant extent. Task forces of the Tax Advisory Commission are continuously studying new approaches to taxation in the interest of promoting economic growth as well as of improving tax equity; some new special tax measures are being introduced as others are being phased out. Despite all this activity, few empirical studies have been made of the impact of the tax system on economic activity, and the articles on the subject have been inconclusive.[47] The discussion in this section therefore must be largely speculative.

A tax system affects economic activity in several ways. First, it may improve or impair business and managerial incentives. Second, it may increase or decrease the stability of the economy. Third, it may encourage or discourage saving and investment and thereby raise or lower the growth potential of the economy. The effect of Japanese tax policy on each of these matters will be discussed in turn.[48]

Business and Managerial Incentives

The Japanese have opted for an individual income tax with a narrow base and relatively high marginal rates. Because exemptions and the employment income deductions are relatively high, a substantial fraction of the labour force—more than 40 per cent—is not subject to income tax. But beyond the taxable income level, the marginal rates run up rather steeply. For example, the combined national and local income tax rate for a married person with two children is 19 per cent at the 1 million yen taxable income level, 27 per cent at 2 million yen, 40 per cent at 5 million yen, and 52 per cent at 8 million yen. Thus, although the marginal rates on cash earnings are relatively moderate for the mass of wage-earners, they are fairly steep on the earnings of individuals in the managerial and professional classes and of successful self-employed persons.[49]

There is no evidence that these relatively high marginal rates have any effect on the working habits of persons who are subject to them. Anybody who observes business life in Japan cannot fail to be impressed by the tempo of hard work that seems to be characteristic of virtually all members of the economic community. As indicated earlier, corporate executives and managers do not receive large supplements to their cash salaries, except for loans to purchase a residence and lavish expense accounts that do not add to their permanent wealth; nor are their retirement benefits large by US standards. Unlike their counterparts in the United States, most corporate managers do not accumulate a personal stake, through stock purchase or stock option plans, in the firms to which they are attached throughout their working careers. The loyalty of the average Japanese worker to his organisation seems to provide the major incentive to continue to work hard even though the rate of his cash earnings after tax seems to increase only moderately as he rises in the corporate hierarchy with advancing age.[50]

Even though the typical salaried employee does not receive unusually large economic rewards for his hard work, Japan is not exactly an egalitarian society. There are many wealthy people in Japan; practically all of this wealth must have been accumulated since the end of the Second World War, and much of it is in corporate form. It seems that there are very large rewards to the business innovator and risk-taker. These rewards are scarcely touched by the tax system, which permits the tax-free accumulation of capital gains (a characteristic of all other tax systems) and requires only modest tax payments on other property incomes. Moreover, once an entrepreneur has demonstrated his capacity to operate a business successfully, he is given access to large amounts of borrowed capital through the banking system. This ability to borrow permits him to expand the scale of his operations rapidly and to enjoy a correspondingly high rate of growth in economic power as well as in business assets.

Thus, the tax system uses no unusual technique to help maintain business and management incentives in Japan. The typical middle-level executive seems to derive satisfaction from the prestige of his job, his expense account, access to a company car, and other non-cash emoluments, as well as from his cash earnings. Access to credit is much more important to the business innovator than preferential tax treatment, at least in the initial stages of his work. Later the implicit tax exemption for unrealised capital gains derived from undistributed corporate earnings permits him to accumulate a large amount of corporate wealth. This type of tax incentive—available as well in other countries—helps to explain how individuals have been able to amass large fortunes in a single lifetime. Because rates of economic growth differ widely among countries, this particular incentive cannot be regarded as a major determinant of relative economic performance.

Effects on Economic Stability

Because Japan relies heavily on income taxes, the tax system acts automatically to moderate changes in the rate of growth of private demand. As incomes rise or fall, income tax revenues rise or fall proportionately more than incomes and thus reduce fluctuations in private disposable income. Private demand becomes more stable to the extent that it depends on disposable income. And because consumer demand depends more on current disposable income than does investment demand, the individual income tax is probably a more effective economic stabilizer than the corporate income tax.[51]

The importance of the individual income tax as a built-in stabiliser may be illustrated by the following figures. The ratio of the individual income tax revenues of the central and local governments to the gross national product in 1972 was 0.054. Because the elasticity of the individual income tax is about 2, the built-in flexibility of the tax—that is, the ratio of the change in tax to a change in GNP—is 0.108 (2 × 0.054). Thus, the individual income tax alone reduces the growth of money income by about 11 per cent. For the tax system as a whole, which has an elasticity of 1.3 and is roughly 21 per cent of GNP, the same type of calculations suggest that built-in flexibility is on the order of 27 per cent. In other words, the individual income tax accounts for about 40 per cent of the built-in flexibility of the entire tax system.

The decision of the Japanese government to permit the government sector to grow only at the same rate as the rest of the economy gives it a great deal of fiscal flexibility. Without tax reduction and assuming annual growth in money incomes 20 per cent, tax revenues would grow roughly 1.0 per cent relative to GNP each year. If half this revenue increase were saved during boom times and then given away in tax reductions in periods of slow growth, the potential for counter-cyclical fiscal policy would be substantial. For example, if booms lasted three years, the build-up of tax revenues would amount to 1.5 per cent of GNP; in addition to exercising a desirable restraint during the expansion, such a backlog would provide an effective means of combating recessions.[52]

In fact, however, the Japanese rarely permit the built-in flexibility of the tax system to exercise its full stabilising effect. Tax reductions continue to be made annually regardless of the stage of the business cycle, and there is little evidence that the magnitude of the reductions is manipulated in a counter-cyclical manner.[53] Several studies of the timing of tax changes in Japan have concluded that discretionary tax policy has been, on balance, destabilising in the short run.[54] Potentially, the built-in flexibility of the Japanese tax system is a powerful tool to promote stable growth, but the government has relied primarily on monetary policy for purposes of short-run stabilisation.

Effects on Saving and Investment

The major thrust of Japanese growth policies has been to raise the rate of national saving and investment. Gross saving increased from about 25 per cent of GNP in the mid-1950s to about 40 per cent in the early 1970s. Increasing the stock of capital is important for growth because it raises productivity directly and also permits the adoption of newer and more efficient technologies. Two facets of Japanese tax policy were important in this strategy. First, the national budget was set to produce surpluses that added to national saving and helped to provide the margin of resources needed for the production of a large and growing volume of investment goods.[55] Second, numerous structural measures were introduced into the tax system to encourage private saving and investment.

Government Saving. As a practical matter it is generally difficult to maintain a budget surplus to help stabilise the economy or to promote growth. Taxpayers are always demanding tax relief, and legislatures find it hard to resist these demands when government revenues are more than sufficient to cover essential expenditures. As a consequence, government budgets are rarely allowed to generate significant surpluses, and are in balance usually only at or near high employment. With government saving close to zero or negative most of the time, reliance must be placed almost entirely on private saving to provide the margin of resources needed for public as well as for private investment. In Japan the government has been able to keep the demands for tax reduction sufficiently in check so that it was able to generate a significant amount of government saving during the 1905s and 1960s. The government succeeded in this policy by systematically underestimating tax receipts. The annual tax reductions were usually estimated to exhaust all or most of the prospective surpluses in the general accounts of the national government, yet retrospectively the budget usually turned out to be in surplus.[56]

The degree of success of this policy may be seen in the record of private and government saving since the mid-1950s. General government saving was sufficient to finance all the government's fixed investment throughout the period, with a margin averaging over 1.5 per cent of GNP. Moreover, government saving averaged about 40 per cent of private saving—a remarkable record for a country with low taxes.[57]

At the same time that government saving was kept at such a high level, total demand was allowed to grow rapidly—primarily by keeping interest rates at artificially low levels—so that the resources made available through saving would not remain idle. When the economy became overheated, the chief instrument of stabilisation policy was monetary and credit restraint and not additional fiscal restraint. Thus, although long-run strategy was to maintain a high rate of saving, short-run policy was often destabilising in the interest of maintaining a sufficiently high rate of growth of demand.[58]

Private Saving and Investment. The most striking feature of the special tax measures—aside from their complexity—is that the revenue losses are significant in relation to saving and investment aggregates. In fiscal 1970 the revenue cost of the special tax measures for property income alone equaled about 2 per cent of the saving of the entire household sector (including non-profit organisations). If the cost of all the favourable tax provisions for property income were included in the numerator and saving not directly affected by the tax laws were excluded from the denominator, the percentage would be several times larger. The increase in the balances of tax-free reserves amounted to a third or more of total corporate saving in the 1950s; in recent years, they have aggregated perhaps 10 per cent of corporate saving. The special depreciation provisions (that is, accelerated depreciation and additional initial depreciation) have accounted for about 10 per cent of total corporate capital consumption allowances in recent years.

Unfortunately, it is impossible to estimate the effects of these large tax benefits on saving and investment. What can be observed is a doubling of the rate of private saving and investment relative to GNP between 1952 and 1970. What cannot be measured, however, is how much of this spectacular increase is attributable to tax policy and how much to other factors. The high rate of household saving has been explained by the rapid growth in personal disposable income, the inadequacy of the social security system, the large share of income going to the self-employed (who are generally large savers), and the rudimentary nature of the consumer finance system.[59] As for private investment, two econometric studies suggest that the special tax measures have been fairly effective in raising the level of investment.[60] Both studies, however, use an investment function that tends to make tax incentives appear to be much more effective than do other investment functions.[61] In our view, the access of growing firms to abundant amounts of borrowed capital through the banking system is at least as important as the special tax measures. This is particularly true in Japan because the various policy instruments are coordinated to an unusual degree in the interest of promoting private investment. Komiya reports that 'Japanese bankers say that they are more willing to make loans on investment for which accelerated depreciation applies.'[62] Similarly, loans to exporters and manufacturers for export were given to the same firms that were given the special tax preferences for the export industry. Such a combination of loan assistance and tax benefits provides an extremely effective set of incentives.

Many independent Japanese fiscal experts outside the government and some members of the Tax Advisory Commission are sceptical of the effectiveness of the special tax measures.[63] They believe that any desirable effects of the special tax measures have been purchased at the price of complexity in the tax laws, substantial inequity among taxpayers, and excessive economic instability. Many of them also point out that the special tax measures greatly moderate the effect of the nominal tax rates as they apply to particular firms and individuals and wonder whether a tax structure with a broader base and lower rates would not be equally, or even more, effective. Finally, the fact that the tax burden is unusually low by the standards of other developed countries may alone be a significant factor in the explanation of the high rate of private saving and investment in Japan.

EFFECTS OF TAXATION ON DISTRIBUTION OF INCOME AND WEALTH

Data on the distribution of income in Japan suffer from the usual deficiencies of under-reporting and lack of comprehensiveness, with respect to both population coverage and the definition of income. The few analyses that have been made suggest that the distribution of income before taxes in Japan is about as even as it is in the United States and the United Kingdom and is somewhat more even than in most Western European countries. The available data also suggest that the Japanese distribution became more even from the period of the occupation to about 1953, became slightly less even between 1953 and 1961, and has become slightly more even since 1961. But on balance, the net change over the last twenty years has been small.

The information on the distribution of income after taxes is even less satisfactory than the information on a before-tax basis. Kaizuka and Niida calculated the effect of the most important direct tax payments by individuals—individual income taxes, property taxes and social security taxes—on the incomes of families of wage and salary workers for each year in the period 1953–61 On balance, this set of taxes had an equalising effect on the distribution of income, but the effect was small and declined somewhat during the period.[64]

Similar calculations have been made by Kaizuka from more comprehensive income distributions based on field surveys made by the Ministry of Welfare for the years 1962, 1967 and 1972. These surveys covered families of the self-employed and of those relying on property income, as well as those of wage and salary-earners; and the income concept included earnings from employment and self-employment and all property incomes except capital gains. According to these calculations, income before taxes tended to become more evenly distributed between 1962 and 1967 and between 1967 and 1972; but the net equalising effect of individual income, property and payroll taxes was small in all three years (3.8 per cent in 1962, 3.3 per cent in 1967, and 4.4 per cent in 1972).[65]

The taxes that were not distributed among household units in these calculations include regressive as well as progressive taxes. Consumption taxes are regressive, while corporate income and inheritance taxes are progressive.[66] Receipts from consumption taxes accounted for 24 per cent of total government tax revenues in 1972, while receipts from the corporate income and inheritance taxes accounted for 26 per cent. Thus, the effects of these taxes on progressivity tend to offset one another. Whether the offset is exact or not, it is fairly clear that the distributional effect of the entire Japanese tax system is small.

The distribution of wealth is even more of a mystery in Japan than the distribution of income. Pre-war fortunes were broken up or taxed away during and immediately after the war, and the distribution of wealth—to the extent that there was any—must have been relatively even when the occupation ended in 1951. Since then, wealth has increased rapidly as the country has prospered. Because taxes on property incomes or on the accumulation of wealth have been light, it is virtually certain that inequality in the distribution of wealth also has been increasing. Moreover, the inheritance tax is not a great deterrent to the transmission of wealth to future generations, so there is likely to be even greater concentration of wealth with the passage of time.

SUMMARY AND CONCLUSIONS

Japan began its post-war recovery with a blueprint by the Shoup Mission that would have made its tax system a model for the rest of the world. But the Shoup blueprint was quickly discarded, and a Japanese brand of taxation was substituted. Thereafter tax policy was oriented toward growth, but there is little evidence that the tax structure contributed significantly to the remarkable economic record of the 1950s and 1960s.

Like the United States, Japan places heavy reliance on the individual and corporate income taxes and eschews a general consumption tax, but the similarity between the two tax systems ends there. The major characteristic of the Japanese tax system is the low effective tax burden that results from a bewildering variety of tax preferences that makes the US tax system look like a model of tax neutrality. In addition, the Japanese are skilful tax planners: they rely heavily on annual tax reductions and reforms to balance the pressures for tax concessions and to make the tax system acceptable to the public. Little of this experience is transferable—or should be transferred—elsewhere; its viability depends on the particular character of the Japanese people and their political system.

The key to Japanese tax policy has been a determination to keep a lid on the growth of the public sector. With its spending on defence at the lowest level among the developed industrial countries, Japan is able to maintain the lowest tax rates among the developed countries. Because the income taxes are highly responsive to economic growth, and because growth was spectacular, Japan was also able to indulge in the luxury of reducing taxes ever year, thus permitting private demand to grow rapidly. At the same time, tax receipts were high enough to generate a level of public saving sufficient to finance government capital formation with a minimum of borrowing from the private sector. For reasons that are still not fully understood, private saving also has been at a high level and has grown rapidly, so that total national saving has kept pace with the extraordinarily heavy demands for investment. The productive capacity of the economy also grew rapidly because investment grew rapidly; and actual output grew rapidly because demand was permitted to rise with the growth of capacity (but not without some instability).

The structural features of the Japanese tax system that are of particular interest to outside observers are, at first, the tremendous elasticity of the individual income tax and, second, the use of special tax measures under the individual and corporate income taxes to promote national economic objectives. The elasticity feature is not unusual for a progressive income tax in a country with a high rate of economic growth. Tax preferences are not unusual in most countries, but the heavy emphasis that Japan places on special tax measures to promote national objectives is unusual.

The elasticity of the Japanese individual income tax was on the order of 2.0 during the 1960s, as compared with about 1.4 for the US individual income tax. The major reason for the difference is that the rate of growth of money incomes was much higher in Japan than in the United States. With personal exemptions at the same relative levels as those in Japan and the higher progressivity that would be achieved without income splitting for married couples, the elasticity of the US individual income tax would approach that of the Japanese individual income tax—assuming the same rates of growth of money income.

The built-in flexibility of the Japanese tax system could have been used to good advantage to promote more stable growth. But this would have required forgoing or moderating tax reductions during boom periods to build up reserves for larger tax reductions during recessions. There is little in the record to suggest that the Japanese were interested in improving the counter-cyclical effectiveness of their tax policy in this way.

The special tax measures and other tax preferences illustrate the strong orientation of the Japanese toward growth in their economic planning and their faith in tax incentives as a method of stimulating desirable business activity. In total, the erosion of the tax base through such preferences is much larger in Japan than it is in the United States and most other developed countries (even though some of the special measures have been abolished in recent years). The few studies that have been made have concluded that the tax preferences promoted modernisation of plant and equipment in the steel and machinery industries but had little influence either on savings of households or on investment in other industries. On the basis of the evidence, the Japanese would probably be better-off with a broader tax base and lower nominal tax rates.

The Japanese are skilful administrators as well as tax planners. They administer their tax system at relatively low cost, partly because they are willing to accept inequities in the interest of simplification. Withholding is applied to a much greater variety of income receipts than in most countries, and most property incomes are subject to flat rates that are not integrated with the progressive rates on earned incomes. The law exempts the property incomes of the vast majority of wage-earners, who thus are able to discharge their full liabilities through withholding and are not required to file returns. The tax preferences do complicate the tax laws and sometimes raise difficult administrative and compliance problems, but this burden is cheerfully accepted by the corporations and individual who benefit from the tax preferences.

The inequality of the distribution of income before taxes is roughly the same in Japan as it is in the United States and the United Kingdom. The tax system is only mildly progressive and therefore has little effect on the relative distribution of income. Data on wealth distribution do not exist, but the death taxes are relatively ineffective (as they are in most countries) and therefore do little to prevent an increasing concentration of wealth and economic power as the nation grows. The effect of this policy has not yet become evident to the Japanese people, but it may produce great social and political strains if continued for long.

NOTES

1. General Headquarters, Supreme Commander for the Allied Powers, *Power on Japanese Taxation by the Shoup Mission*, vols. 1–4 (Tokyo, 1949).
2. The official explanation is that 'their intentions seemed somewhat too idealistic to fit in with the reality of the Japanese economy and standard of living of the Japanese people.' Tax Bureau, Ministry of Finance, *An Outline of Japanese Taxes, 1974* (Tokyo, 1974), pp. 7–8.
5. Estimates of the elasticity of the major taxes and of the tax system as a whole are given below, under *Income Elasticity of the Tax Structure*.
6. The annual tax reductions were suspended after the international oil crisis in 1973.
7. The official description of the tax system by the Tax Bureau states that 'since then [1955], the succeeding tax reforms of each year have been mainly based on the reports submitted by this Tax Commission.' *An Outline of Japanese Taxes (1974)*, p. 9.
8. The distinction between those tax provisions which are regarded as special and those which are not is unclear to an outside observer, since the ordinary income tax laws contain numerous provisions that are preferential in nature. Special tax measures are usually—but not always—adopted with a termination date.

Hereafter, the term 'special tax measure' is used to refer to the provisions of the Special Tax Measures Law, and 'tax preferences' to refer to the preferential provisions in the ordinary income tax laws as well as in the Special Tax Measure Law.

9. The Industrial Structure Council was established in 1964 to advise the MITI on short- and long-range economic policy. The council is made up of 130 individuals from all walks of life who are named by the prime minister for two-year terms.

10. *An Outline of Japanese Taxes, 1974*, p. 11.

11. This figure is based on interviews with a number of Japanese government officials. Nine per cent of Tokyo households occupied company housing in 1968.

12. Executives in government agencies and academic and non-profit institutions also have entertainment expense accounts, but they are more limited than those provided by private companies.

13. Usually, the host leaves his calling card and the cost is charged directly to the firm. A sizeable portion of these accounts is never paid, and unpaid accounts receivable in restaurants are large.

14. Tax Bureau, Ministry of France, *Zeisei shuyo sanko shiryoshu* [Principal Reference to Data for the Tax System, 1973] (Tokyo, 1973), p. 131.

15. Economic Planning Agency, *Annual Report on National Income Statistics, 1974* (Tokyo, 1974), pp. 32, 34, 142. Total business consumption expenditures, which include welfare and travel expenses and other employee outlays, amounted to 6 per cent of GNP. Data for later years have not been published in Japan, nor are similar estimates available for other countries.

17. In fiscal 1972 administrative costs amounted to 1.4 per cent of national revenues in Japan, compared with 0.7 per cent for the cost of administering the federal revenue system in the United States. (National Tax Administration Agency, *An Outline of Japanese Tax Administration, 1972* (Tokyo, 1972) pp. 6, 22; and *The Budget of the United States Government, Fiscal Year 1974* (1973), pp. 268, 341.) Much of the difference in cost is probably attributable to differences in scale.

19. The minimum amount to be posted has increased over time: it started at 500,000 yen for individual returns and 1 million yen for returns of corporations and of decedents. Since 1971 the minimum amounts have been 10 million yen for individuals, 40 million yen for corporations, and 40 million yen of taxable value (100 million yen total value) for decedents.

22. The averages for the other countries are based on the median.

23. Comparable figures are not available for all countries, but the following are the calender year 1969 ratios of corporate profits to GNP product for the five that are available: Japan, 11.9 per cent; United States, 9.1 per cent: Switzerland, 9.2 per cent; France, 7.4 per cent; and Belgium, 6,6 per cent. *National Accounts of OECD Countries, 1953–69* (Paris: OECD, 1971).

24. For purposes of this calculation, wages subject to withholding are considered to be reported on tax returns whether a tax return is actually filed by the wage-earner or not.

25. Average family incomes in 1974 were assumed to be 2.4 million yen in Japan and $13,000 in the United States. These assumptions were based on projections of average incomes reported for 1972 in the annual *Household Survey* of Japan and the annual *Consumer Population Survey* of the United States.

26. For example, suppose a married taxpayer with four exemptions receives

$100,000 of interest, $100,000 for dividends, and $200,000 of capital gains on the sale of securities held for more than six months, and reports deductions amounting to 20 per cent of his adjusted gross income. The US tax on this $400,000 of income would be $133,492, whereas the Japanese tax would be no more than $50,000. (The latter figure is calculated on the assumption that the taxpayer is allowed no deductions or exemptions in computing his tax liability, since he would elect to be taxed at the maximum rate of 25 per cent on his interest and dividends.)

27. Forty-five of the 50 states levy corporate income taxes at rates ranging from 2 to 12 per cent; the median rate is 6 per cent. (Advisory Commission on Inter-governmental Relations, *Federal–State–Local Finances: Significant Features of Fiscal Federalism* [1973–74], Table 148, pp. 286–9.) Because the state taxes are deductible in computing the federal tax, the net burden is roughly half the nominal rates.

28. See the discussion of the special tax measures, under *Tax Incentives*, below.

29. The central government rates were increased by 3.25 percentage points on undistributed profits and 4 percentage points on distributed profits; and the municipal inhabitants surtax was increased from 9.1 to 12.1 per cent.

30. Industrial Bank of Japan, *Differences in Accounting Practices and Returns on Investment between the United States and Japan: 1,000 Industrial Companies, 1967–1971* (Tokyo: IBJ, 1973; available from Standard and Poor's Corporation). The companies were selected from the listings on the major stock exchanges in the two countries; some large unlisted Japanese companies were also included. The major adjustments were to correct gross returns and assets of Japanese firms to account for additions to special tax-free reserves.

31. These conclusions held for most industry groups, except that chemical firms reported a higher gross rate of return on total assets in the United States, and iron and steel companies reported a higher rate of return in Japan.

32. By maintaining the tax rates for relatively long periods, the Japanese in effect safeguarded the additional revenues generated by rate graduation as incomes grew rapidly.

33. See, for example, Wayne Snyder and Tsutomu Tanaka, 'Budget-Policy and Economic Stability in Post-war Japan', *International Economic Review*, vol. 13 (February 1972), pp. 85–110. The same type of estimates were made independently by Sei Fujita in *Nihon zaiseiron* [Fiscal Policy in Japan] (Keiso Press, 1972).

34. Elasticity is the ratio of the percentage change in tax receipts to the percentage change in an income aggregate, such as national income, personal income, or gross national product. The calculations in Tables 20.4 are based on estimated tax receipts before the annual reductions.

35. Joseph A. Pechman, 'Responsiveness of the Federal Individual Income Tax to Changes in Income', *Brookings Papers on Economic Activity* Vol. 2 (1973), p. 393.

36. This assumes that the elasticity of the corporate income tax was 1.0 and that of all other federal taxes 0.8. The weights for each tax were assumed to be in proportion to receipts in fiscal 1972. It should be emphasised that the elasticity of the US federal tax system has grown tremendously since 1967–72 as a result of the unusually large growth in money incomes.

37. Based on weights for fiscal 1972, assuming the elasticities of the period 1967–72.

38. For a description of the file and the other assumptions used in the simulations,

see Pechman, 'Responsiveness of the Federal Individual Income Tax to Changes in Income'.

39. In 1974 the minimum taxable level for a family of four in Japan was 1.02 million yen (including the minimum deduction of 160,000 for wage-earners yen), or 42.5 per cent of estimated family income of 2.4 million yen. The minimum taxable level in the United States was $4300 (including the low-income allowance of $1300), or 33.1 per cent of estimated family income of $13,000. Thus, the Japanese minimum taxable level was 28.5 per cent higher relative to the average income for a family of four. The $3400 US minimum taxable level becomes $5526 when increased by 28.5 per cent; deducting the low-income allowance of $1300 gives a total exemption for the family of four of $4226, or $1060 per capita (rounding from $1056). It was not necessary to change tax rates because the range of rates in Japan is roughly similar to the range in the United States.

40. This means that single persons, heads of households and married couple filing separate returns would all use the rate schedule now applying to married couples filing separate returns.

41. Higher exemptions reduce the average rate of tax on personal income but do not change the marginal rate significantly. Because elasticity is the ratio of the marginal to the average tax rate, it rises if the average rate falls more than the marginal rate.

42. According to the official definition, tax expenditures are exceptions to the 'normal' structure of the individual and corporate income tax. To emphasise the close relation between tax benefits and outright subsidies, the estimates are broken down by the functional categories used in the federal budget. These estimates are required by the Congressional Budget and Impoundment Control Act 1974. For the most recent list of tax expenditures, see 'Tax Expenditures', *Special Analysis, Budget of the United States Government, Fiscal Year 1976*, pp. 101–17.

43. Until 1974 the official classification had the following categories: promotion of savings; promotion of environmental quality and regional development; promotion of development of natural resources; promotion of technological development and modernisation of industrial equipment; strengthening the financial position of firms; and miscellaneous. Beginning in 1974, the special taxation measures were rearranged and the number of categories increased to eight.

44. For employment income, business income, interest dividends, capital gains, real estate income, retirement income, timber income, occasional income and miscellaneous income.

45. In fact, because standard accounting practice permits deductions for such expenses, the revenue gain from the portion of social and entertainment expenses that is disallowed for tax purposes is entered by the Tax Bureau as an offset against the revenue losses from the other special tax measures.

46. Fujita, *Fiscal Policy in Japan*, and Ryutaro Komiya, 'Japan', in *Foreign Tax Policies and Economic Growth* (Columbia University Press, 1966), pp. 39–96.

47. See, for example, Sei Fujita, 'Tax Policy', in Ryutaro Komiya (ed.), *Post-war Economic Growth in Japan* (University of California Press, 1966), pp. 32–59; and Komiya, 'Japan'. The references in these articles suggest that the literature in Japanese is equally inconclusive.

48. Revenues from the tax system also provide the financing for social overhead capital, which may be as important as, or more important than, private

investment. Some knowledgeable Japanese believe that public investment in facilities to improve the quality of life has been unnecessarily neglected in years. Whether this neglect will show up in a reduced rate of measured growth as an attempt is made to remedy the deficiency is unclear; the question is beyond the scope of this study.

49. A salaried person who is married and has two children and a taxable income of 8 million yen probably has earnings of about 12 million yen. At current exchange rates (300 yen to the dollar), this is equivalent to roughly $40,000. Such incomes are earned in Japan only by corporate executives and the most successful doctors, lawyers and other professional people.

50. For an analysis of the vertical nature of Japanese society and its effect on employees' attitudes toward their own business organisations, see Chie Nakane, *Japanese Society* (University of California Press, 1972).

51. Corporate taxes absorb a major share of declining corporate earnings during a downswing and of rising earnings during an upswing. This permits corporations to maintain dividends at a stable rate during a business cycle. But because dividends are a relatively small proportion of after-tax corporate incomes in Japan, the effect of more stable dividends on consumer incomes must be relatively small. Investment demand depends only to a limited extent on current incomes, so the moderating effect on private investment of the type of corporate income tax used in Japan and other countries must be small.

52. Translated into US figures, a 1.5 per cent reserve would amount to over $20 billion at the 1974 GNP level of about $1400 billion.

53. Gardner Ackely and Hiromitsu Ishi conclude that, in the last 20 years, the variations in the annual amounts of tax reduction have been in the wrong direction about half the time in relation to the business cycle (see *Asia's New Giant*, Ch. 3). The 1974 tax reductions, the largest in history in absolute amount (though not relative to national income), came at a time when Japan was suffering the largest inflation since the one immediately after the war.

51. See, for example, Keimei Kaizuka, 'The Stabilization Effect of Fiscal Policy', in *Postwar Economic Growth in Japan*, p. 224; and Snyder and Tanaka, 'Budget Policy and Economic Stability in Postwar Japan'. On the other hand, Hiromitsu Ishi finds that the government surplus and deficit correspond rather well to the peaks and troughs of the Japanese business cycles; see his 'Cyclical Behaviour of Government Receipts and Expenditures: A Case Study of Postwar Japan', *Hitotsubashi Journal of Economics*, Vol. 14 (June 1973), pp. 56–83. Ishi notes, however, that most of the counter-cyclical movement of the tax system is attributable to the corporate tax, which is much less effective as an automatic stabiliser than the individual income tax.

55. National saving is the difference between national output and consumption; investment is the portion of the national output that is not consumed. Thus, saving is equal to investment for the economy as a whole. By saving, a nation in effect sets aside resources that are used for investment purposes; otherwise, the resources would be used for consumption purposes.

56. Ishi, 'Cyclical Behavior of Government Receipts and Expenditures', pp. 60–1.

57. In the United States, government saving has contributed little to national saving in the last 45 years. It is difficult to compare Japan with the United States because public investment expenditures are not segregated from other current outlays in the US national income accounts. If government saving in the United States were equal to the Japanese figure of about 17 per cent of GNP, it would amount to over $95 billion at current levels. This is more than

three times public construction outlays and probably is about that much higher than total net capital formation in the public sector.

58. See Komiya, 'Japan', in *Foreign Tax Policies and Economic Growth*, p. 49; and Snyder and Tanaka, 'Budget Policy and Economic Stability in Postwar Japan', pp. 102–4.

59. Ryutaro Komiya, 'The Supply of Personal Savings', in *Postwar Economic Growth in Japan*, pp. 157–81; Miyohei Shinohara, *Structural Changes in Japan's Economic Development* (Tokyo: Kinokuniya, 1970), pp. 40–97; and Toshiyuki Mizoguchi, *Personal Savings and Consumption in Postwar Japan* (Tokyo: Kinokuniya).

60. Ratcliffe estimated that for the period 1956–67 gross investment in manufacturing was raised about 5 per cent by the special depreciation provision and about 1 per cent by the special tax-free reserves and other special deductions. See C. T. Ratcliffe, 'Tax Policy and Investment Behavior in Postwar Japan' (PhD thesis, University of California, Berkeley, n.d.). Kinoshita estimated that accelerated depreciation increased net investment in 1955–57 by from 10 to 20 per cent in four major industries (iron and steel, general machinery, electrical machinery, and transport equipment), but the effect tapered off to from 3 to 8 per cent in 1959–61. He also estimated that the reduction in useful lives for depreciation purposes increased net investment by from 1 to 8 per cent in 1961 and 1963, and that the 1958 corporate tax cut increased net investment by from 3 to 9 per cent in 1958–60. The latter calculations included food, textiles and pulp, as well as the four industry groups covered by the accelerated depreciation calculations. See Soshichi Kinoshita, 'Investment Behavior and Postwar Tax Policy', *General keizai* [Contemporary Economics], Vol. 5 (June 1972), pp. 180–98.

61. The functions used are similar to those originated by Dale Jorgenson of Harvard University. For a comparison of results based on these and other approaches to the measurement of the impact of tax incentives on investment in the United States, see Gary Fromm (ed.), *Tax Incentives for Capital Spending* (Brookings Institution, 1971).

62. The reason given is that 'they can recover the loans within a shorter period and with more certainty', Komiya, 'Japan', in *Foreign Tax Policies and Economic Growth*, p. 83.

63. See, for example, Fujita, 'Tax Policy', in *Postwar Economic Growth in Japan*, pp. 56–59: and Komiya, 'Japan', pp. 89–90.

64. As measured by the Gini coefficient, disposable income was distributed more evenly before-tax income by 8.1 per cent in 1953 and by 5.5 per cent in 1961 The Gini coefficient is the ratio of the area between the Lorenz curve and the line of equal distribution to the entire area below the line of equal distribution.

65. The before-tax and after-tax distributions are so close that they can barely be distinguished on a Lorenz curve diagram. The Gini coefficient are as follows:

	1962	1967	1972
Distribution before taxes	0.3894	0.3743	0.3538
Distribution after taxes	0.3747	0.3618	0.2284

These estimates were based on data in Ministry of Welfare, *Income Redistribution Survey* (1964, 1969 and 1974).

66. The corporate income tax is progressive on the assumption that the tax is borne by corporate stockholders or by owners of capital in general. Some economists believe that part of the corporate income tax is shifted forward to consumers in the form of higher prices. If this is the case, part of the corporate tax is distributed in the same way as a consumption tax.

21. Taxation in Great Britain*

Taxation is one of the most controversial issues of public policy in the United Kingdom. The tax philosophies of the two major political parties differ markedly, and each party makes adjustments in the tax system when it is in power; as a result, the tax structure has changed frequently in the post-war period. It is widely held that the tax system distorts economic behaviour, though the degree of distortion is hard to quantify. How Britain deals with its tax problem may have a significant effect on its future economic performance and on the stability of its social and political system.

TAX BURDENS

The aggregate tax burden in the United Kingdom, when compared with that in other developed countries, does not seem excessive. In 1976 UK tax revenues (including social security contributions) amounted to 36.7 per cent GDP (at market prices), which was 2 percentage points lower than the median level for 12 other advanced industrial countries in Europe, North America and Asia. Germany, Italy, Canada, the United States, and Japan had lower tax ratios—in the case of Japan, substantially lower. The ratios for Austria and France were slightly higher than that of the United Kingdom, and the ratios for the Scandinavian and Benelux countries were much higher.

Among the various revenue sources, only the individual income tax seems to be relatively high in the United Kingdom. Its individual income tax accounted for 14 per cent of GDP in 1976, which was higher than in all other countries except Sweden, Denmark and Norway. Its consumption and payroll tax ratios were below average. Taxes on corporations and on wealth are relatively small sources almost everywhere, and the United Kingdom is no exception. Following Anglo-Saxon tradition, the United Kingdom relies more heavily on the property tax (for local tax purposes) than other European countries do.

Individual Income Tax
The individual income tax in the United Kingdom starts at a lower income

*Adapted from *Britain's Economic Performance*, Richard E. Caves and Lawrence B. Krause, editors (Brookings Institution, 1980), pp. 199–240.

level and has higher initial starting rates than in most other countries. The 1978–9 top-bracket rate of 83 per cent on earned income was close to the highest in the world; the top rate of 98 per cent on investment income was surpassed only in Algeria (which had a top rate of 100 per cent). Beginning in 1979–80, the top rate was reduced to 60 per cent.

For the average UK production worker, the *average* rate of income tax paid on 1976 earnings was 20 per cent; if employee payroll tax rates are included, the average tax rate was 26 per cent. The *marginal* rates were 35

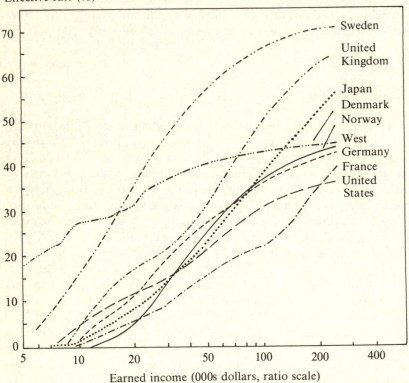

Figure 21.1: Effective Personal Income Tax Rates on Earned Income for Married Couples with Two children, by Earned Income Level, Selected Countries, 1978[a]

a. Income has been converted to US equivalents on the basis of the estimated ratios of relative earnings of production workers in 1978. Standard deductions and average employment deductions were allowed where applicable. Assumes there is only one earner in the family.

per cent for the income tax alone and 41 per cent for income and payroll taxes. These rates were very high when compared with the rates in such countries as France, Germany, Italy and the United States, but low when compared with the rates in Sweden and Denmark. The 1979 reduction in the basic rate to 30 per cent will still leave the marginal rates on earned income of the average production worker at a higher level in the United Kingdom than in most European countries, Canada and the United States.

At higher income levels, the UK income tax in 1978–9 was clearly among the highest in the world. For income that is entirely earned, the UK tax was not as high as the taxes in Sweden and (in most brackets) Denmark, but higher than in other European countries, Japan and the United States (Figure 21.1). For investment income, international comparisons are difficult because some countries (such as Sweden, Denmark and West Germany) have wealth taxes, while the United Kingdom has the investment income surcharge. Nevertheless, the taxes paid by the wealthy on investment income were at least as high in the United Kingdom as in the Scandinavian countries and were certainly higher than in the other European countries.[1]

A major element in the public debate on taxation in the United Kingdom was the rise in real individual income tax burdens as inflation pushed people into higher tax brackets. The personal exemptions did not keep pace with inflation from 1973/74 to 1976/77, and tax rates were raised significantly in 1974/75 and 1975/76. From 1977 on, personal exemptions have been indexed; tax rates were reduced moderately in 1977/78 and 1978/79 and sharply in the top brackets in 1979/80. As a result, between 1973/74 and 1978/79 effective tax rates rose in real terms for practically all taxpayers. Thus a married person with two children paid a tax of 10.9 per cent on an earned income of £2000 in 1973/74.[2] In 1975/76, when the tax rates reached a peak, the tax on the same real income was 16.3 per cent. Even though the rates were reduced, the tax in 1978/79 still amounted to 12.2 per cent at the same real income level (Figure 21.2).[3] For real earnings of £5000 in 1973/74, there was a net increase in the tax burden of 3 per cent of income over the five-year period; and for earnings of £8000 and over, the increase amounted to 10 per cent or more. The 1979/80 tax reductions reduced real tax burdens substantially below the 1973/74 levels for taxpayers with 1973/74 real earnings above £20,000, but those with real earnings between £5000 and £20,000 still paid higher taxes in 1979/80 than in 1973/74, and those below £5000 paid about the same taxes as in 1973/74.

To give some idea of the combined burden of all the elements of the UK individual income tax (income tax plus investment income surcharge plus capital gains tax), the effective income tax rates in the United Kingdom are compared with those in the United States in Table 21.1. To make the comparison, the rates in both countries were applied to an estimate of the

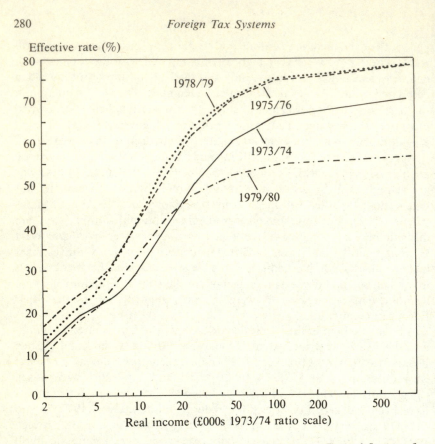

Effective rate (%)

Real income (£000s 1973/74 ratio scale)

Figure 21.2: Effective UK Personal Income Tax Rates on Earned Income for Married Couples with Two Children, by Real Income Level, 1973/74, 1975/76, 1978/79, 1979/80

distribution of income in the United States in 1978.[4] Because a two-earner married couple in the United Kingdom may elect separate taxation of the wife's earnings, separate calculations were made for households with one earner and two or more earners. For purposes of these calculations, UK incomes were translated to an equivalent US basis by using a 2.81:1 ratio, which in 1978 was approximately the ratio of average production worker earnings in the United States to those in the United Kingdom.[5]

Table 21.1 shows that in 1978, for the great majority of household units, the UK income tax was clearly much heavier than the US tax—particularly in so-called middle-income brackets. In the $10,000–$12,500 income class (which is close to the median household income in the United States), the average effective tax rate for a one-earner household was 20.3 per cent at the U.K. tax rates and only 11.5 per cent at the US rates. For households at this income level with two or more earners, the UK effective rate was 12 per cent and the US rate 5.8 per cent. Above the median, the UK rate for two-earner married couples flattened out because of the option to be taxed on their earnings separately;[6] as a result, the UK effective rate was lower than the US rate for such couples with incomes between $30,000 and $60,000.

Table 21.1: Effective Rates of Personal Income Taxes for One-Earner and Two-or-more-Earner Households, by Income Class, United Kingdom and United States, 1978

Income class[a] ($000s)	Cumulative per cent of household units in United States	Effective rate (%)			
		One-earner households		Two-or-more earner households	
		United Kingdom	United States	United Kingdom	United States
0–3	20.8	0.6	–1.6[b]	3.8	–3.2[b]
3–4	23.6	4.9	–1.7[b]	6.4	–3.7[b]
4–5	25.9	10.7	1.6	4.5	–3.0[b]
5–7.5	33.0	12.1	5.4	5.4	–0.3[b]
7.5–10	41.0	17.1	9.1	9.1	3.2
10–12.5	49.3	20.3	11.5	12.0	5.8
12.5–15	57.6	21.8	13.2	14.8	7.6
15–17.5	65.7	23.6	14.9	16.7	9.2
17.5–20	72.6	24.0	16.7	16.7	10.6
20–25	82.6	25.1	18.0	16.7	12.0
25–30	89.3	26.0	20.0	17.2	14.0
30–40	95.2	29.0	22.3	15.6	15.5
40–50	97.4	31.6	27.0	16.4	17.9
50–60	98.3	35.3	26.9	17.6	19.3
60–75	99.0	41.2	35.3	22.2	21.7
75–100	99.5	49.5	29.3	30.9	25.5
100–500	100.0	52.2	36.4	48.9	35.0
500–1,000	100.0	45.3	45.9	59.9	47.3
1000 and over	100.0	46.1	47.2	54.6	51.0
Total[c]	100.0	22.1	14.2	18.4	14.1

Source: Calculations based on Brookings 1970 MERGE file projected to 1978. UK incomes are translated to an equivalent US basis by using a 2.86:1 ratio. Figures are rounded.

a. Money factor incomes plus realised capital gains. Income does not include tax imputed to dividends, but tax is net of the dividend credit.
b. Effective tax rates are negative, reflecting cash benefits for children in the United Kingdom and the earned income credit in the United States.
c. Includes household units with negative incomes not shown separately.

Thereafter, the UK tax increased more rapidly and again exceeded the US tax. In total, when applied to the US income distribution in 1978, the UK income taxes were 56 per cent higher than the US income taxes for one-earner households (22.1 per cent vs. 14.2 per cent) and 30 per cent higher for households with two or more earners (18.4 per cent vs. 14.1 per cent).

Taxes on Corporate Earnings

In contrast to the UK individual income tax, the UK corporation income tax before 1985 was modest by international standards. The general tax rate of 52 per cent was close to the rates usually adopted by the developed countries.[7] The capital consumption allowances and investment grants available in the United Kingdom were as generous as those in most other countries. In addition, full write-offs were allowed for plant and equipment; these write-offs and the stock relief provisions virtually eliminated the corporate tax for industrial and commercial companies.[8]

Under the imputation system that was adopted in 1973, the portion of the corporate tax on distributed earnings that is equal to the basic individual income tax rate (33 per cent in 1978/79, 30 per cent in 1979/80) is regarded as an advance payment of tax by the corporation on behalf of the stockholder. The advance corporate tax is added to the dividend of the shareholder and included in his taxable income, but he is allowed to deduct it as a credit against his tax liability.[9] For example, a person who received a dividend of £48 in 1978/79 included £23.64 (33/67×48) of advance corporation tax in his taxable income and then received a credit of £23.64 against his final tax liability. Taxpayers with marginal tax rates of less than 33 per cent (23.64÷71.64) received a credit or refund for the difference, while those with marginal rates of more than 33 per cent paid additional tax to make up the difference. For 1979/80 the advance corporation tax and credit on a £48 dividend was £20.57 (30/70×48), and the breakeven point at which no refund or additional tax was due was at a marginal income tax rate of 30 per cent.

However, as a result of the 98 per cent maximum rate in 1978/79, the top rate on *distributed* corporate earnings was higher in the United Kingdom than in any other country—higher even than in those countries where the classical system has been retained.[10] For example, in Sweden the corporate rate was 55 per cent and the highest individual income tax rate (including local tax) was 83.8 per cent. Together, the maximum combined tax on distributed earnings was 92.71 per cent (55+0.838×45). In the United States, where the corporate rate was 48 per cent and the top individual income tax rate was 70 per cent, the maximum combined tax on distributed corporate earnings was 84.4 per cent (48+0.7×52). The reduction of the top UK marginal rate to 75 per cent in 1979/80 reduced the maximum rate on distributed earnings to 82.8 per cent, which is slightly lower than the corresponding top Swedish and US rates.

The actual combined tax paid on corporate profits depends on the degree to which profits are taxed at the corporate level and the percentage of after-tax corporate profits paid out in dividends. In the United Kingdom the effective rate of tax on corporate profits is very low because of the generous allowances for capital consumption and the adjustment that has been made in recent years to eliminate inventory profits from the tax base.[11] Dividend pay-out ratios seem to be 50 or 60 per cent of the net profits of corporations as calculated for tax purposes, but only about 10 per cent of profits before capital consumption and inventory allowances.[12] Thus, even though the theoretical maximum rate on distributed profits remains above 80 per cent, the total tax burden on corporate earnings is in practice relatively low in the United Kingdom.

Table 21.2 compares the tax burdens on corporate earnings in the United Kingdom with those in the United States, by income class, for the year 1978. To make this comparison, retained profits and the taxes paid at the corporate level were allocated to shareholders, the marginal personal tax rates on the dividends (after the dividend credit, in the case of the United Kingdom) were calculated, and the sum of the taxes paid at the corporate and personal levels was then expressed as a percentage of the total corporate earnings in each income class.[13] Again, UK incomes were translated to an equivalent US basis by using a 2.86:1 ratio.

As expected, at all income levels the total tax burden on corporate earnings is much higher in the United States than in the United Kingdom. In the lower-income classes the combined corporate and individual income tax (net of the dividend credit) in 1978 was about 40 per cent of corporate earnings under the US tax rates and 15 per cent under the UK rates. The burden increased in both countries as incomes rose above this level; the rise in the United Kingdom was somewhat more rapid because of the faster rate of individual income tax progression. Nevertheless, the UK tax rate remained below the US rate even at the highest levels. At the top of the income scale (incomes of $1,000,000 or more), the total tax burden on corporate earnings was 35.8 per cent in the United Kingdom and 52.6 per cent in the United States.[14] The combined personal and corporate taxes on all corporate earnings was 83 per cent higher in the United States than in the United Kingdom (48.6 per cent vs. 26.5 per cent).

TOTAL TAX BURDEN

The aggregate burdens of all taxes in the United Kingdom and the United States at 1978 tax rates are compared by income levels in Figure 21.3.[15]

Table 21.2: Effective Rates of Combined Personal and Corporate Income Taxes on Corporate Source Income, by Income Class, United Kingdom and United States, 1978[a] (Income classes in $000s; rates in per cent)

Income class[b]	United Kingdom	United States
0–1	9.7	39.0
1–2	14.5	40.2
2–3	12.6	40.3
3–4	15.2	40.6
4–5	15.9	40.8
5–7.5	16.7	41.8
7.5–10	17.0	42.2
10–12.5	18.2	42.7
12.5–15	17.9	43.0
15–17.5	18.2	44.0
17.5–20	17.7	44.6
20–25	19.1	45.5
25–30	20.4	45.9
30–40	20.6	46.9
40–50	23.4	48.4
50–60	26.7	49.5
60–75	25.3	50.2
75–100	31.2	50.2
100–500	35.8	52.9
500–1,000	36.1	53.2
1,000 and over	35.8	52.6
Total[c]	26.5	48.6

Source: Calculations based on Brookings 1970 MERGE file projected to 1978. UK incomes are translated to an equivalent US basis by using a 2.86:1 ratio. Figures are rounded.

a. Includes only household units with income from dividends.
b. Households are classified by their total money factor incomes plus realised capital gains plus retained corporate earnings and corporate tax allocated to shareholders.
c. Includes household units with negative incomes not shown separately.

Because payroll and consumption taxes were higher in the United Kingdom than in the United States, the total tax burden was much heavier in the United Kingdom at all levels except in the top 5 per cent of the income distribution. For example, in the $10,000–$12,500 class, the total tax burden was 27.9 per cent of income at the UK tax rates and only 15.8 per cent at the US rates. Beyond this point, the differences narrowed, with the

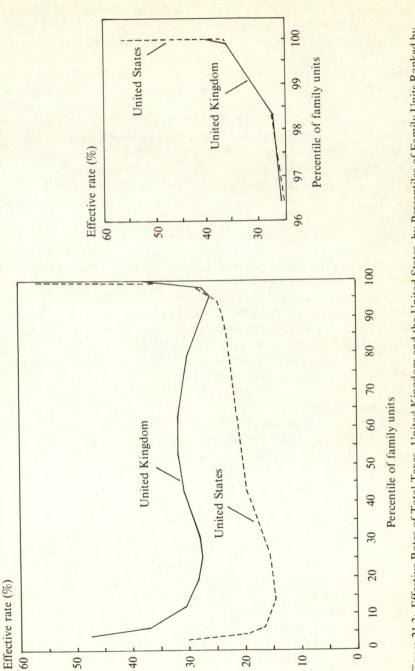

Figure 21.3: Effective Rates of Total Taxes, United Kingdom and the United States, by Percentiles of Family Units Ranked by Adjusted Family Income, 1978

Source: Brookings 1970 MERGE file projected to 1978.

rates converging between $60,000 and $75,000; above $75,000 the UK tax rates were lower than the US rates. For the entire income distribution, taxes averaged 29.9 per cent of income under the UK tax system and 23.8 per cent under the US system.

In 1978 the UK tax system was regressive for about the bottom quarter of the income distribution, became slightly progressive up to the median income, turned regressive again from the median to the 96th percentile, and was progressive in the top 4 percentiles. The US tax system was regressive for the bottom quintile of the income distribution, mildly regressive up to the 98th percentile, and steeply progressive in the top 2 percentiles.[16] The large reduction in the high-bracket rates in 1979 undoubtedly increased the regressivity of the UK tax system in the top part of the income distribution.

ECONOMIC EFFECTS OF TAX POLICY

It is extremely difficult to evaluate the effects of tax policy on the economic behaviour of individuals and business in any country. Many other policies besides tax policy have had a significant influence on Britain's economic performance. Moreover, the debate over tax policy reflects fundamental disagreements over equity and distributional objectives, although such views are often disguised as economic arguments. It is worthwhile, nevertheless, to review the principal areas of concern and to summarise the evidence to see whether a clear picture emerges.[17]

The Labour Market
The effect of the tax structure on labour supply and productivity is a major issue in British tax policy. The high marginal tax rates on earnings are alleged to reduce work incentives, encourage the development of methods of nontaxable compensation (through the so-called perks), and promote widespread tax avoidance and evasion.

Work Incentives. With marginal tax rates exceeding 40 per cent for the average production worker and 40 per cent or higher for professional or managerial employees, the incentive to substitute leisure or non-market activity for paid employment in the United Kingdom is substantial.[18] Whether this incentive has been translated into reduced hours of work or lower work effort is difficult to establish. In the first place, the desire to maintain a given standard of living in the face of high tax rates (the income effect) offsets the negative influence of such rates on work and effort (the substitution effect), and it is impossible to predict which effect will predominate. Second, it is difficult to vary working hours and the quality of work in modern, industrial society. English economists have been trying to determine the substitution effects on the supply of labour by empirical means, but without any more success than economists in other countries have had.[19]

Oddly enough, the studies most frequently cited are by American economists. The earliest study, by George Break of the University of California, was based on intensive interviews of 306 English solicitors and accountants in 1956.[20] Some 40 per cent of the respondents reported that taxation had, or would have, some influence on their work, but the positive and negative effects almost cancelled out one another. On the basis of this evidence, Break concluded that the net effect of taxation was small. In 1969 Donald Fields and W. T. Stanbury repeated the Break study, this time for a sample of 285 English solicitors and accountants.[21] The percentage of respondents reporting negative effects on their work rose, but the net effect after allowing for those reporting definite positive effects remained small.[22] Studies by other Americans, based on US data, generally confirmed these results.[23]

Another set of American estimates of the effect of tax policy on labour supply is based on the results of several negative income tax experiments conducted in the United States in the late 1960s and the 1970s. Under the negative income tax plans, the experimental group received a minimum income, but their earnings were taxed at 50 per cent rates or higher. The conclusion reached in these studies is that a negative income tax would reduce the supply of labour, but the reduction would be substantial only for supplementary family earners (spouses and children) and relatively small for family heads. Unfortunately, these studies shed little light on the effect of the positive tax system on work incentive because the experimental samples were confined to the poor and the near-poor and also because it was impossible to separate the substitution effect from the income effect in the empirical analysis.[24]

The only large-scale study of the impact of taxation on work effort in England was conducted by C. V. Brown and E. Levin, who interviewed 2068 weekly-paid workers to find out whether taxation affected the number of hours of overtime worked. The vast majority of workers reported that taxation had no effect on overtime hours. Among those who reported some effect, males who claimed they worked more overtime because of taxation slightly outnumbered those who claimed they worked fewer hours; females were much less affected by taxation, but more of them reported working fewer hours than those who reported working more hours.[25]

The Royal Commission on the Distribution of Income and Wealth (the Diamond Commission) established that since 1969 there has been a large decline in the relative earnings of high-paid employees, both before and after tax.[26] The commission also concluded that UK managerial salaries before tax were above those in Sweden, about the same as in Australia and the Netherlands, and lower than in other countries of the European

Community.[27] These trends have been exacerbated by the recent incomes policies, which have narrowed differentials between high-paid and low-paid workers. But there is no evidence that a decline in the work effort of business managers has occurred.[28] Nor do the data show any significant effect on migration of professional and managerial workers, despite the gap between top salaries in the United Kingdom and those in other countries.[29]

Several studies have attempted through the interview technique to find out how professional and managerial employees react to the high tax rates, but here again the results are inconclusive. As might be expected, the surveys do indicate that high-paid employees are unhappy about the decline in their real earnings and feel that the tax system treats them unfairly. But repeated studies have found that, despite the high tax rates and reduced differentials, the work performance of business executives has not been noticeably affected. According to their own responses, top managers have not changed their hours of work or work effort, their propensity to move on to other jobs, or their attitudes toward working overseas.[30]

Non-Taxable Fringe Benefits. It is not surprising that the high marginal tax rates have encouraged the development of methods of compensation that remove a large part of employee compensation from the tax base. Information submitted to the Diamond Commission indicates that the non-taxable or lightly taxed portion of total remuneration of high-paid employees is two or three times as large in the United Kingdom as it is declared to be in France and West Germany.[31]

The largest and most widespread non-taxable fringe benefits are the pension arrangements. Contributions to approved pension plans by employees as well as employers are not taxable when they are made. An approved plan may provide a pension of as much as two-thirds of the employee's last year of salary, but an amount equal to $1\frac{1}{2}$ times that salary may be withdrawn in a lump-sum free of tax.[32] This feature is especially valuable for high-paid employees and is apparently widely used.

In addition to pensions, business managers and directors have a number of highly visible, special perquisites, which receive considerable attention in Great Britain. Business firms pay the dues of their executives for private dining, health and recreational clubs, serve expensive meals in executive dining rooms at little or no cost to the employee, reimburse the outlays of their top managers for admissions to theatres and sports events and for other entertainment expenses, and provided private medical insurance and low-interest mortgages for their higher-paid employees. Tax may be due on some of these benefits, but the amount taxed is much less than the cash value.[33]

The most obvious 'perk' for the business manager is the company car, which is available to him for personal as well as business use. Until recently, the firm's expenditure on the car was taxable to the employee in the proportion of private to total mileage used. In practice, the proportion allocated to private mileage was small and, in any case, understated the value of the car to the employee. To reduce the tax advantage, new regulations adopted in 1976 require those who have company cars at their disposal to count as taxable income specific imputed amounts for the benefits they receive. But since the amount included may represent a small percentage of the use value of the car to the employee, the personal use of company cars is hardly being discouraged.[34]

The rank and file (in tax terms, those with salaries of less than £10,000 a year in 1979/80) also receive a variety of non-taxable fringe benefits, though such benefits are not as valuable to taxpayers in the lower tax brackets as they are to top-bracket taxpayers. Business firms often subsidise canteen meals for their employees and provide discounts on purchases by employees of goods produced or distributed by the firm. British Rail and airlines allow their employees and their families to travel free of charge. Subsidised loans were provided tax free to employees before 1976, when the cash equivalent of the subsidy above a certain level was made subject to tax.[35] Until recently, many business firms paid the school fees of the children of their high-paid employees, but this practice may stop as a result of a ruling adopted in 1978 requiring that such awards be made available to the children of all employees on a non-discriminatory basis.

Tax Avoidance and Evasion. The most serious development that has occurred in response to the high tax rates has been the growth of what has been called the 'hidden economy', which may now represent as much as 7.5 per cent of GDP.[36] Many workers engage in moon-lighting on jobs for which they insist on payment in cash. Plumbers, carpenters, painters and other self-employed craftsmen routinely quote higher prices for their services if payment is to be made by cheque rather than in cash. (In such cases, the incentive to evade tax is the saving not only in income and payroll taxes but also in VAT.)

Besides outright evasion, tax avoidance is widespread in the United Kingdom. There are many tax consultants whose speciality is to devise wholly artificial transactions that exploit loopholes in the tax laws in order to reduce or eliminate tax liability. As fast as the Inland Revenue discovers a loophole and blocks it, others are found.

The amount of revenue lost through the various arrangements used to minimise taxes is not known, nor can the impact on economic efficiency be estimated.[37] It is clear, however, that such practices do have an effect on economic behaviour and reduce taxpayer morale.

Saving and Investment

Many special provisions and preferences have been introduced into the tax law to promote particular types of saving and investment, including income tax deductions for specified personal saving items, preferential rates for capital gains and dividend relief, and generous investment and employment subsidies. These provisions have greatly moderated the effect of the nominally higher tax rates on unearned incomes and have also had the effect of channelling saving and investment into the preferred areas.

Personal Saving. Table 21.3 provides a list of the preferences under the UK income tax law for personal saving and an estimate of the revenue loss from each item in 1975/76. The largest item is the deduction for payment of interest on mortgage loans, which amounted to £865 million in that year.[38] This is followed by the deduction for life insurance premiums and the exemption for employee pension contributions, each of which amounts to one-quarter of the cost of the mortgage interest deduction. There are also deductions for a wide variety of savings, but the amounts are relatively small. In total, however, the value of all the saving preferences was not small: they reduced the income tax yield in 1975/76 by a minimum of 12 per cent.[39]

Partly because of the preferential tax treatment, investment in owner-occupied housing, pension funds and life insurance account for almost all net personal saving in the United Kingdom.[40] The result of this kind of saving structure is alleged to be a reduction in the savings that are available for risky investment and particularly for small business. Evidence exists that small business is much less important in the United Kingdom than in other industrialised countries, and that it has lost a great deal of ground in the last 40 years.[41] But there is no way of knowing how much these trends have been affected either by the higher tax rates on earned income in the United Kingdom or by the special provisions for savings that are not available to small business. Furthermore, the United Kingdom, like other countries, provides tax relief to small business in many ways, but this policy has not been much success.[42]

Another trend that has been associated with the incentives in the tax system has been the institutionalisation of stock ownership. According to Kay and King, stock ownership by individuals in the United Kingdom declined from 56.1 per cent of the total in 1963 to 39.8 per cent in 1975; the proportion owned by financial companies and institutions increased from 30.4 to 48.1 per cent in the same period.[43] This trend, which is almost universal in the industrialised world, raises the cost of equity capital and probably reduces the supply of capital that would otherwise be available for risky investments. Again, there is no way of disentangling the effect of the tax factor from all the other factors that have contributed to this trend.

Table 21.3: Income Tax Reliefs for Personal Saving in the United Kingdom, 1975/76 (£ millions)

Item	Tax treatment	Revenue loss
Home mortgages	Interest deductible on mortgages up to £25,000	865
Life insurance premiums	Relief provided for one-half the basic tax on premiums, up to one-sixth of total income.	235
Pension contributions	Contributions by employees are fully deductible	289[a]
Pension fund accumulations	Income and capital gains not taxable	333[b]
Contribution by self-employed for retirement annuity	Contributions up to 15 per cent of earnings are deductible, with maximum of £3,000.	50
National savings certificates (maximum holding £1,500)	Interest untaxed.	55
National and Trustee Savings Bank	First £70 of interest untaxed.	35
SAYE (contractual saving of up to £20 a month)	Interest untaxed.	c
Premium bonds[d]	Winnings untaxed.	c
Building society accounts	Interest taxed at the estimated composite rate of depositors.	c
Government securities	Capital gains exempt if held for a year.	c

Source: J. R. M. Willis and P. J. W. Hardwick, *Tax Expenditures in the United Kingdom* (London: Heinemann Educational Books, 1978).

a. Does not include exclusion of employer's contribution from employee's income, which amounted to £1000 million in 1975–76.
b. Extrapolated from Willis–Hardwick estimate for 1973/74.
c. Revenue loss is unknown, but amount is small.
d. No interest is paid on premium bonds; the interest equivalent on each issue is used to pay for winnings on the annual drawings.

The Corporate Sector. As already noted, the tax on corporation earnings is very low and must, therefore, have little effect on the economy as a whole (though not necessarily on such features of the corporation sector as debt–equity ratios and dividend pay-outs). The imputation system, which provides relief for almost one-half of the corporate tax at the individual level, greatly reduces the burden of the corporate tax for low- and middle-income shareholders. Even for those in the higher income levels, the combined effective tax rate on corporate earnings is moderate because the corporate tax on industrial and commercial earnings has been virtually wiped out by the first-year depreciation allowances of 100 per cent for plant and equipment and 50 per cent for industrial buildings and the adjustment for inventory profits, while only a small percentage of profits is paid out in dividends.[44] The low rates of tax on capital gains (a maximum of 30 per cent, with reduced rates on gains of less than £9500 in 1979/80) also make corporate investment attractive.

As King has pointed out, the 1965–72 tax structure encouraged UK corporations to rely heavily on retained earnings for their major source of finance, discouraged the issue of new shares, and increased the attractiveness of borrowing.[45] The adoption of the imputation system in 1973 encouraged dividend distributions and increased the attractiveness of equity financing. There does seem to have been an increase in corporate equity issues more recently, but the dividend pay-out ratio has not changed significantly. Thus retained earnings have remained the main source of equity finance in the corporate sector.

Despite the low rate of tax on corporate earnings, during the mid 1970s the rate of return on UK corporate investment was at the lowest level since the end of the War. On a replacement-cost basis, the pre-tax return of industrial and commercial companies declined from over 10 per cent in 1966–69 to less 5 per cent in 1974–78.[46] The after-tax return declined from 6 per cent to less than 4 per cent in the same period (Figure 21.4). The share of profits of industrial and commercial companies in gross corporate product also declined in this period.[47] But even though profitability declined, private capital formation seems to have held up fairly well. Gross investment of industrial and commercial companies, which averaged 13.5 per cent of GDP in 1966–68, averaged 16.3 per cent in 1976–77. The sustained rate of investment in the face of declining profitability may well have been due to the generous tax treatment accorded to private investment.

Subsidies. The United Kingdom has experimented with a large variety of direct and indirect subsidies to promote investment or regional development, or both. In contrast to the United States, which uses a modest investment credit (currently at its peak rate of 10 per cent for equipment purchases only) and the asset depreciation range (ADR) system, the United Kingdom has used, at one time or another, accelerated depreciation, high initial depreciation allowances, investment allowances (up to 40 per cent of the amount of the investment), and investment grants (which, in the case of investment in development areas, have been as high as 45 per cent of the amount of the investment) and, in most instances, has applied these allowances and grants to plant as well as equipment expenditures in manufacturing and construction.[48] Employment subsidies have also been

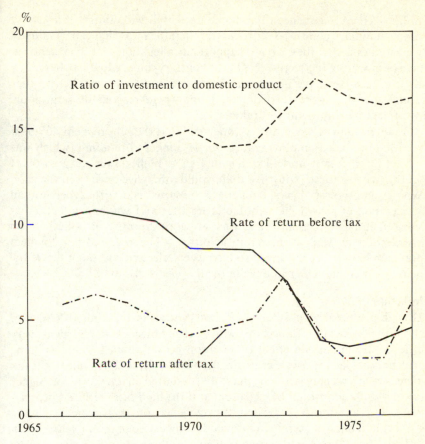

Figure 21.4: Real Rates of Return before and after Tax and Ratio of Gross Private Domestic Investment, Industrial and Commercial Companies in the United Kingdom, 1966–77

Source: Bank of England

paid to industrial firms generally (under the Selective Employment Act 1966, which expired in 1977) and to those located in designated development areas (under the regional employment premium from 1967 to 1971). Prest estimates that the cost of all subsidies amounted to at least £3000 million in 1972 (almost 25 per cent of total UK tax revenues in that year) and was rising sharply.[49] Mellis and Richardson estimated that a firm investing in plant and machinery can, in present value terms, recover between 41 and 63 per cent of the cost of the investment.[50]

The effectiveness of these subsidies has been the subject of a great deal of research using interview as well as econometric techniques.[51] The numerous studies of investment incentives come up with a wide range of answers; Lund's summary concludes with the view that the most that can be said for these studies is that they 'do not support any allegation that the incentives have been wholly ineffective.'[52] On the contrary, most experts believe that the tax incentives have increased investment, and some even believe that capital subsidies were carried to a point where reasonable returns on investment were difficult to obtain.[53]

Brian Reddaway's committee concluded that the selective employment tax (SET) reduced employment in wholesaling and retailing (which was subject to the tax) and also resulted in a higher rate of growth of productivity in these industries than would otherwise have been the case. Whitley and Worswick have challenged this view, arguing that there was an acceleration of growth in manufacturing after SET was enacted and that some factor other than SET was at work to raise productivity in distribution as well as in manufacturing.[54] The regional employment premium has also been judged to have been effective, although the actual increase in employment in development areas is disputed.[55]

Inflation

Though a great deal has been said and written in the United Kingdom about the impact of inflation on individual and business tax burdens, very little is said about the effect of taxation on inflation.[56] There is some evidence that labour bargains on an after-tax basis, so that some of the tax increases in recent years may have been shifted in the form of higher prices.[57] Inflation would be exacerbated if the high rates reduced productivity, but as already indicated the evidence on this is unclear. The corporation tax has been increasingly deemphasised in recent years, when inflation has skyrocketed, which indicates nothing about the effect of the corporate tax on prices except that other factors have been much more important.

The substitution of VAT for purchase tax in 1973 was not intended, on balance, to raise revenues. In fact, the ratio of taxes on goods and services in the United Kingdom to GDP actually declined slightly from 1973 to 1976[58], which suggests that the authorities were aware that a rise in consumption taxes would be unwise in a period of inflation.[59] But in June 1979 the new Conservative government accepted the inflationary consequences of a higher VAT in order to provide replacement revenues for cuts in the individual income tax. This was expected to raise the retail price index by 3.5 percentage points.

Increases in employment taxes have also contributed to inflation. The tax paid by employers was raised in two successive budgets—by 2 percentage points in April 1977 and 1.5 percentage points in October 1978—to offset the revenue loss from tax cuts made elsewhere. These actions raised employment costs by about 3 per cent, and it may be presumed that the increases were fully reflected in higher prices. The increase in October 1978 was forced on the government because the opposition parties insisted on a reduction in the basic income tax rate (from 34 to 33 per cent) even at the expense of raising a tax that directly increased business cost.[60]

Distribution of Income and Wealth

Much effort has been devoted in Great Britain to the measurement of the inequality in the distribution of income and wealth and to the identification of the determinants of these distributions. The Diamond Commission, which was appointed in 1974 to undertake an analysis of current and past trends, stimulated a great deal of research and issued several reports and background memoranda on various aspects of its work.

The estimates of the Diamond Commission reveal that the shares of total personal income received by the top 1 per cent and top 5 per cent dropped between 1959 and 1974/75 both before and after income tax. Before tax, the share of the top 1 per cent declined from 8.4 to 6.2 per cent, and the share of the next 4 per cent declined from 11.5 to 10.6 per cent. After tax, the decline was from 5.3 to 4.0 per cent for the top 1 per cent and from 10.5 per cent to 9.7 per cent for the next 4 per cent. The average income tax burden increased 75 per cent in the period (from 10.5 to 18.3 per cent). But the increase in the top 5 per cent was small (because they were already paying high taxes), while the increased burdens on the lower- and middle-income groups were very large.[61] The movement of the income distribution toward equality cannot therefore be attributed directly to changes in the income tax, and there is simply no way of determining how much, if any, of the declining share of income at the top is attributable to reduced work and saving incentives.

Wealth is much more concentrated than income in the United Kingdom (as it is elsewhere), but the inequality in the distribution of wealth has also been declining in the last two decades.[62] Between 1960 and 1975 the share of personal wealth owned by the top 1 per cent of persons with recorded wealth (about half the adult population) declined from 28.4 per cent to 17.2 per cent and the share of the next 4 per cent declined from 22.5 to 17.8. Inclusion of the value of occupational and state pension rights reduces the overall level of inequality, as might be expected.

According to the Diamond Commission, the main influences at work on the distribution of wealth have been, first, the large and sustained rise in real incomes, which allowed many people to buy their own homes and to accumulate other assets, and, second, the impact of the estate duty, which reduced wealth inequality directly and also encouraged wealthy people to distribute their wealth before death.[63] According to Harbury and McMahon, however, the role of inheritance in the creation of the largest wealth holdings remains large, even if these holdings are accounting for a smaller proportion of total wealth.[64]

It is still too early to evaluate the effect of the capital transfer tax, which replaced estate duty in March 1975. Technically, the capital transfer tax is much superior to the estate tax because it taxes all gifts (not just those made before death) as well as bequests, and the tax base for any one person is cumulative for all taxable transfers made during his or her entire life.[65] But the original legislation provided lower tax rates for life-time gifts up to £300,000, and in 1976, 30 per cent of small business property and 50 per cent of agricultural property were excluded from the tax base. In 1977 the 30 per cent exclusion for business property was raised to 50 per cent and a new exclusion of 20 per cent for minority shareholdings in unquoted companies was introduced. Further, while the top-bracket rate of 75 per cent was carried over from the estate tax, the rate of graduation is less steep under the capital transfer tax—presumably in the expectation that gifts would make up the revenue loss. Thus far the effect of the exemption of inter-spousal transfers and of the lower tax rates has predominated: the estate tax produced £459 million in 1972/73, £412 million in 1973/74, and £339 million in 1974/75; in 1977/78 the capital transfer tax yielded £331 million and £87 million was collected from the estate tax for previous years.

OPTIONS FOR CHANGE

The picture that emerges from the foregoing discussion of the burdens of the UK tax system and of its effects on economic behaviour is one of sharp contrasts. On the one hand, the nominal tax rates on both earned and unearned incomes were pushed to inordinately high levels. On the other hand, the tax system contains all sorts of preferences and subsidies that are clearly designed to take the curse off the high rates and to promote particular kinds of activity. For an outsider, it is difficult to understand how a country that imposed a maximum nominal tax rate of 98 per cent on investment income also adopted capital consumption allowances that virtually wiped out the corporate tax on industrial and commercial companies, provided relief for almost half the remaining corporate tax on any dividends that are paid, taxed realised capital gains at a maximum rate of 30 per cent while providing reduced rates for the first £9500 of gains, and exempted capital gains transferred at death. And it is not easy to understand why the marginal tax rates on earned incomes of the middle-income class were allowed to creep up above 50 per cent, when at the same time a wealth tax was being considered, to cut down the wealth of the super-rich.

How much economic damage the country did to itself by adopting such a policy cannot be quantified. Clearly, however, the tax system generated distortions in labour and capital markets and produced highly inequitable results for people and businesses in essentially the same economic circumstances. In addition, the system produced the inevitable tug-of-war between taxpayers who seek methods of getting out from under the high tax rates (through better fringe benefits, improved perks, conversion of income into capital gains, and other devices) and the tax administrators who try valiantly to stem the tide—but with indifferent results. The growth of the hidden economy, in which taxpayers of modest means are now participating, is particularly disturbing.

Whether the economic limits of taxation had been reached or not, it is clear that the political limits were reached long before the sharp reduction in income tax rates made by the new Conservative government in June 1979. Every budget in recent years contained tax proposals that mitigated the effects of the high tax rates on particular groups. Many of these provisions were second-best solutions to problems that should have been dealt with by rate reductions or by nontax methods.[66] The newspapers kept up a steady barrage of stories illustrating new loopholes, providing further evidence of cash dealings to avoid taxes, or reporting an Inland Revenue ruling that upset still another tax avoidance scheme. Social conversation frequently turned to discussions of the tax system, and the major political parties put tax reform at or near the top of their legislative agenda.

Now that the top-bracket rates have been cut, the next step in tax reform should be to reduce substantially the marginal tax rates for the large mass of wage and salary works. The investment income surcharge, which remained at 15 per cent but with a threshold that was raised to £5000 in 1979, was later repealed outright.[67]

To maintain fiscal responsibility, large rate reductions for the lower and middle income classes would require substantial cuts in public expenditure or offsetting increases in taxes or both. Analysis of the UK budget is outside the scope of this paper, but most of the offsetting revenue will probably have to come from the tax side of the budget.[68] It should be emphasised that the question of offsetting tax increases is neutral with regard to the overall progressivity of the tax system: it should be possible to maintain progressivity where it is or to raise or lower it. The various tax options range from repairing the base of the present income tax to introducing new taxes to make up the revenue loss.

Broad-based Income Taxes
It is probably too much to expect the United Kingdom (or any other country, for that matter) to adopt fully comprehensive personal and corporate income taxes,[69] but there is plenty of room for movement

between the present tax system in the United Kingdom and the theoretical comprehensive tax. The exclusions for savings could be curtailed, the highly favourable treatment of pension contributions and benefits could be modified, the preferences for home-owners could be reduced or eliminated, economic depreciation could be substituted for the generous depreciation allowances now allowed, dividend relief could be repealed, and capital gains could be treated as ordinary income. Along the same lines, the capital transfer tax might be strengthened by reducing or eliminating the generous exclusions for small business and farm property from the tax base.[71]

Such changes, combined with the rate cuts, would increase tax equity and improve tax morale. But every one of the provisions has staunch defenders and change in any one of them will be strongly resisted. Furthermore, while it would be difficult to broaden the tax base at any time, it may be particularly difficult when inflation is still at an unsatisfactory level. The alternatives are to index the tax base so that only real rather than normal incomes are subject to tax or to wait until the inflation has subsided. Fiscal officials are cautious about indexation because it might be seen as an official acknowledgement that inflation would be tolerated by the government; and tax administrators worry that indexation would introduce significant complications for tax compliance and administration.[72]

Wealth Tax

If, as might be expected, the effort to broaden the income tax base is only partially successful, consideration might be given to the adoption of a low-rate, annual, personal net wealth tax. Because such a tax would reach wealth that has been lightly taxed or not taxed at all under the individual income tax, horizontal equity would be improved. Furthermore, a net wealth tax could encourage people to shift from safe, low-yield investments to riskier, high-yield investments. The receipts from a wealth tax, which would be confined only to the top wealth owners, could be used to finance a further reduction in the top marginal income tax rates. An annual net wealth tax with a top rate of 2 per cent combined with an income tax with a top rate of 50 per cent would be a substantial improvement over the income tax with a top rate of 98 per cent or even the reduced 75 per cent in 1979.

It would be virtually impossible to administer a wealth tax that applied to the mass of taxpayers, but the problems would not be insuperable if the tax were confined to the top 5 per cent of wealth owners. Low-rate wealth taxes are already a standard element of many tax systems, though the revenues collected are generally small.[73]

Value-added Tax

The 1979 reductions in income tax rates were financed in large part by an increase in the value-added tax from the dual-rate structure of 8 and 12 per cent to a flat rate of 15 per cent. Additional revenue could be obtained from further increases in the new 15 per cent rate. Such a large shift from income taxation to value-added taxation would increase the regressivity of the tax system. This could be avoided if the income tax base were broadened to include incomes in the higher income classes which are not now taxed. Aside from adding to the regressivity of the tax system and making it hard to prevent under-reporting of sales by small service and retail establishments, heavier reliance on value-added taxation has the disadvantage of raising the price level and thus contributing to inflation. Most observers believe that the 1979 VAT increase exacerbated inflation.

Expenditure Tax

Taxation of personal consumption expenditures instead of personal incomes is an old idea that has recently been revived by Nicholas Kaldor, the US Treasury, the Meade Committee, a Swedish legislative committee, and many tax experts in Britain and the United States. Expenditure taxation is strongly supported by those who believe that the income tax excessively discourages saving. It is also supported as a method of taxing incomes not reached by the income tax. The tax would be levied at graduated rates, and could be used as a replacement for, or as a supplement to, the income tax.

There is sharp disagreement among tax experts over the equity of expenditure taxation and its practical feasibility. Proponents of expenditure taxation regard expenditures as the preferred base for taxation because it does not reduce the reward for saving and therefore makes future consumption relatively as attractive as present consumption. Proponents of income taxation believe that personal taxation should be based on the ability to pay of an individual, as measured by his total income, that is, by the amount accumulated as well as the amount consumed. Administration and compliance would be more difficult under the expenditure tax than under the income tax in some respects and easier in others. Taxation of large personal outlays, such as those on homes and consumer durables, would raise particularly difficult problems under the expenditure tax. On the other hand, the fact that receipts and expenditures would be counted on a cash flow basis under the expenditure tax would greatly simplify tax accounting for business and property incomes. Moreover, correction of the tax base for inflation would not be needed under an expenditure tax.

Expenditure taxation would be a radical departure in taxation for the United Kingdom (or for any other country). It is hard to believe that it would be easier to tax expenditures on a comprehensive basis than it is to tax incomes on such a basis or that the political forces that make income tax reform so difficult would accept a shift to an expenditure tax.

CONCLUSION

The highest priority for tax revision in the United Kingdom should be to reform and simplify the income tax. The tax base should be broadened by removing the special provisions that erode the tax base and the revenue should be used to reduce the tax rates, particularly for wage and salary workers who are still subject to very high marginal rates. If the replacement revenues cannot be obtained through income tax reforms, other sources must be found. All the non-inflationary alternatives seem impractical, but they are clearly better than the present state of affairs.

NOTES

1. Sweden had a maximum effective rate of 85 per cent of the sum of income and wealth taxes. But because the wealth tax cannot be reduced by more than 50 per cent, taxpayers with low income could pay a tax of more than 85 per cent of their income. The United Kingdom has no maximum effective rate.
2. The £2000 level was slightly below the average 1973 earnings of manual workers in the United Kingdom. The tax calculations assumed that the tax-payer had deductions (in addition to the personal exemptions) of 5 per cent of his income and the children were under 11 years of age. The cash benefits for children introduced in April 1976 are treated as tax credits in these calculations, and the family's exemption is reduced by the 'clawback' for the family allowance given to the second child.
3. The consumer price index rose 48 per cent from 1973/74 to 1975/76 and 78 per cent from 1975/76 to 1978/79 (calculated between the midpoints of the fiscal years). Thus an income of £5000 was equivalent in real terms to £7400 in 1975/76 and to £13,170 in 1978/79.
4. Because of the lack of data for the top brackets in the United Kingdom, it is impossible to calculate the effective tax rates when the US and UK tax rates are applied to the UK distribution.
5. Average production worker earnings are assumed to represent relative incomes in the two countries. The classification in table 1 is by total money factor incomes plus realized capital gains. Income excludes the tax imputed to dividends, but the tax is net of the dividend credit. The income data were obtained by projecting the Brookings 1970 MERGE file to 1978. The file contains earnings figures for both spouses in a two-earner couple; the tax on such couples is on a separate and combined basis, whichever is lower. The U.S. figures include state and local income taxes.
6. The flattening of the UK rate above the median is also the result of the wide basic rate band, which extends up to a taxable income of $27,000 for a married person.
7. The rates for 1978 were 56 per cent in West Germany, 55 per cent in Sweden, 50 per cent in France, and 48 per cent in Belgium, the Netherlands and the United States. Only Japan had a substantially lower rate—40 per cent. These are the rates for undistributed earnings. Some of these countries tax distributed earnings at lower rates or provide credits for dividends received at the

individual income tax level, so that total effective tax rates on company earnings cannot be inferred from the corporate rates alone.

8. According to John Kay and Mervyn King, corporate tax liabilities of industrial and commercial companies declined from £1.5 billion in 1969 to £0.2 billion in 1976, while those of financial companies increased from £0.3 billion to £1.1 billion. The 1976 figures do not include £1.0 billion of advance corporation tax paid. See J. A. Kay and M. A. King, *The British Tax System* (Oxford University Press, 1978), p. 177; and Central Statistical Office, *Economic Trends, Annual Supplement*, 1979 edn (London: HMSO, 1979), p. 150.

9. When originally introduced, the 52 per cent corporate tax rate for the imputation system was chosen to give the same average yield as the 40 per cent rate for the previous 'classical' system.

10. The imputation system greatly reduces the taxes paid by shareholders on distributed corporate earnings in the lower income classes, but does very little for those subject to very high individual income tax rates. For example, under the classical system, the combined effect of the corporate tax of 52 per cent and the 1978/79 individual income tax rates up to 98 per cent ranged from 52 per cent to 99.04 per cent. The imputation system reduced the marginal rates on distributed corporate earnings from a range of 52–99 per cent to 28.36–98.57 per cent. The reason is that a shareholder who was not otherwise subject to tax benefited from the full reduction of 23.64 percentage points in the corporate tax; but at the top of the income scale, the 23.64 percentage point credit was taxed at 98 per cent and thus, on the balance, provided virtually no relief.

11. According to R. W. R. Price, the effective rate of tax on corporate profits net of interest payments but before capital consumption allowances varied between 14 and 23 per cent in the period from 1960 to 1973. Since 1973 the effective rate has been less than 10 per cent. See Price, 'Budgetary Policy', in F. T. Blackaby, (ed.), *British Economic Policy, 1960–74* (Cambridge University Press, 1978), p. 164, for the figures from 1960 to 1973. Estimates for later years were kindly supplied to me by Mr Price.

12. Mervyn King, *Public Policy and the Corporation* (London: Chapman &Hall, 1977), p. 168; and Central Statistical Office, *Economic Trends, Annual Supplement* edn 1979, pp. 150, 155.

13. The definition of corporate earnings follows the official definition of corporate profits in the US national income accounts. The effective US corporate tax rate was estimated by applying the UK depreciation allowances to US capital stock figures and adding the net additional payment for advance corporation tax. It was assumed that the adjustments of inventories for inflation are, in the aggregate, roughly the same under the UK method of adjustment and the US last-in first-out (LIFO) method. The UK calculations assumed that the dividend credit would not affect the US dividend payout ratio. If pay-outs increased, the combined tax under the UK calculations would be lowered.

14. These figures do not allow for any capital gains tax that might be paid on the sale of corporate stock. In 1978 the maximum capital gains rate was higher in the United States than in the United Kingdom (40 per cent vs. 30 per cent), so that the tax on corporate earnings including the capital gains tax was also higher at the top income levels in the United States. (In a few cases the maximum US capital gains rate was as high as 49.25 per cent.) In 1979 the US capital gains rates were lowered to a maximum of 28 per cent; this narrowed the differences in the taxes on corporate earnings between the two countries.

15. The income concept in these calculations is a comprehensive concept of

economic income that includes money factor incomes, cash transfer payments, the value of fringe benefits, imputed income of owner-occupied homes, and corporate earnings allocated to shareholders, but excludes transfers in kind (such as Medicare and Medicaid). To avoid duplication, realised capital gains on corporate stock, which reflect undistributed corporate earnings, are omitted. Customs receipts and death and gift taxes are excluded. The assumptions used in allocating taxes are the progressive incidence assumptions generally associated with Arnold C. Harberger. For the methodology used in this analysis, see Joseph A. Pechman and Benjamin A. Okner, *Who Bears the Tax Burden?* (Brookings Institution, 1974). The assumptions in Figure 21.2 are the same as variant 1c in that book (see Table 3–1, p. 38). UK incomes are translated to an equivalent US basis by using a 2.86:1 ratio.

16. If the less-progressive incidence assumptions associated with Richard A. Musgrave are used (that is, half the corporate tax is borne by consumers and the property tax on improvements are taxes on shelter or passed on to consumers), both the UK tax systems are roughly proportional in most of the distribution except at the bottom. The US average effective rates turn up at the very top of the distribution, but the UK rates remain flat as a result of the low corporate tax and the low capital gains rate.

    The high degree of regressivity in the lowest income classes for both tax systems reflects the fact that consumption exceeds income at this end of the distribution. If income were measured over periods longer than a year, this regressivity would be greatly reduced or eliminated. See Pechman and Okner, *Who Bears the Tax Burden?* pp. 52–4.

17. The evidence is anecdotal as well as quantitative. My impressions about the effects of tax policy in Britain have been obtained from conversation with tax experts during frequent visits over the last 15 years, from numerous interviews with political, business and labour leaders and tax experts in the spring of 1978, and from the extensive literature on taxation (which is of very high quality).

18. Those who are beneficiaries of the welfare system or receive social security or unemployment benefits are subject to the highest marginal tax rates, creating a 'poverty trap', which is the subject of great concern in the United Kingdom. However, reform of the welfare, social security and unemployment systems is outside the scope of this chapter.

19. Summaries of the results of the major studies undertaken in England and the United States over the past 25 years are provided in Organisation for Economic Co-operation and Development, *Theoretical and Empirical Aspects of the Effects on the Supply of Labour* (Paris: OECD, 1975); N. Stern, 'Taxation and Labour Supply—A Partial Survey', in *Taxation and Incentives* (London: Institute for Fiscal Studies, 1970); and an unpublished paper by the Confederation of British Industry, 'Managers' Pay—A Survey' (London, June 1978).

20. George F. Break, 'Income Taxes and Incentives to Work: An Empirical Study', *American Economic Review*, vol. 47 (September 1957), pp. 529–49.

21. D. B. Fields and W. T. Stanbury, 'Income Taxes and Incentives to Work: Some Additional Empirical Evidence', *American Economic Review*, Vol. 61 (June 1971), pp. 435–43.

22. The percentage of respondents reporting some tax effect on their work in the two studies were as follows:

Study	Disincentive	Incentives
Break	13	10
Fields and Stanley	19	11

23. See, for example, Robin Barlow, Harvey F. Brazer and James N. Morgan, *Economic Behavior of the Affluent* (Brookings Institution, 1966); and Daniel M. Holland, 'The Effect of Taxation on Effort: Some Results for Business Executives', in National Tax Association—Tax Institute of America, *Proceedings of the Sixty-second Annual Conference on Taxation, 1969* (Columbus, Ohio: NTA-TIA, 1970), pp. 428–517. More recent work by Jerry Hausman of the Massachussets Institute of Technology suggests that the earlier studies underestimated the labour supply response to high tax rates.

24. For a summary and evaluation of these studies, see Joseph A. Pechman and P. Michael Timpane (eds.), *Work Incentives and Income Guarantees: The New Jersey Negative Income Tax Experiment* (Brookings Institution, 1975); and John L. Palmer and Joseph A. Pechman, *Welfare in Rural Areas: The North Carolina–Iowa Income Maintenance Experiment* (Brookings Institution, 1978).

25. The percentage of respondents showing no effect and either a positive or negative effect on overtime hours were as follows:

Sex	No effect	Positive effect	Negative effect
Male	74	15	11
Female	93	2	6

C. V. Brown and E. Levin, 'The Effects of Income Taxation on Overtime: The Results of a National Survey', *Economic Journal*, vol. 84 (December 1974), pp. 833–48.

26. Royal Commission on the Distribution of Income and Wealth, *Higher Incomes from Employment*, Report 3, Cmnd. 6383 (HMSO, 1976), pp. 5–43.

27. Ibid., pp. 44–85.

28. In a study published by the Institute for Fiscal Studies, Brian Reddaway and associates were not able to detect any significant effect of the tax system on the mobility and performance of senior executives in 94 manufacturing firms. The interviews took place between February and October 1978.

29. Royal Commission on the Distribution of Income and Wealth, *Higher Incomes from Employment*, pp. 81–3, 185–207. Data from the Department of Employment indicate that net migration of managers and administrators increased from about 1000 a year in the period 1965–73 to 4500 in 1975 and 3000 in 1976.

30. See, for example, Opinion Research Centre, *The Motivation of Top British Management* (OPR, 1977).

31. Kay and King, *British Tax System*, p. 41, citing evidence submitted to the commission by Hay-M. S. L. Ltd. in 1976.

32. There is no limit on the amount of the lump-sum payment or on the annual pension benefits, and it is possible to inflate an employee's last year's salary without increasing his responsibilities.

33. In the United States, outlays by business for the maintenance and operation of facilities such as yachts and hunting lodges were made non-deductible under the Revenue Act 1978. Restrictions on the deductibility of other benefits of high-paid employees—such as country club dues, admissions to theatres and sports events, and first-class air travel—were proposed by the administration but were rejected by Congress.

34. For 1978/79 an employee who received a company car originally valued at more than £12,000 was required to include in his taxable income £880 if the car was under four years old. Such a car probably provided services of £3600 a year (for insurance, operation and maintenance costs, and depreciation); even if only half the mileage of the car was for personal use, the understatement of £920 was equivalent to an annual gross salary of £5412 at the top-bracket rate of 83 per cent in 1978/9.

35. The interest subsidy on mortgage loans continues to be non-taxable, though the interest payment would, in any case, be allowed as a deduction (on mortgages up to £25,000).
36. Statement of Sir William Pile, chairman of the Bank of England, as reported in the *Financial Times*, 27 March, 1979.
37. Estimates of the revenue effects of special provisions in the personal and corporation income taxes—called 'expenditures'—have recently been prepared in the United Kingdom in a study sponsored by the Institute for Fiscal Studies: J. R. M. Willis and P. J. W. Hardwick, *Tax Expenditures in the United Kingdom* (London: Heinemann Educational Books, 1978). Most of the data used in these estimates are from the national income and product accounts and other official sources that do not provide any information on the type of non-taxable fringe benefits and tax avoidance and evasion schemes discussed in this section.
38. This does not include the revenues from the exclusion of imputed net rent on owner-occupied homes (that is, rental income after the deduction of interest paid), which is at least as large as the revenue lost from the interest deduction alone.
39. The tax value of the preferences for which estimates are available in Table 21.3 was £1862 million, while total income tax, surtax and capital gains tax collections amounted to £15,536 million in 1975/76.
40. According to calculations by Kay and King, these three forms of saving accounted for about 90 per cent of total UK saving in the period 1972–76, as compared with 56 per cent for the United States in 1974. See *British Tax System*, p. 60.
41. A few years ago the proportion of manufacturing employment in establishments with less than 200 employees was the lowest in the United Kingdom among a group of 13 countries. The number of small firms in the United Kingdom has been cut in half in 40 years, while the number has doubled in the United States.
42. Special rates are provided under the corporation tax for firms with profits of less than £85,000; gains on the sale or gift of a family business are exempt up to £50,000 if the person is 65 or over; gains realised in the replacement of certain business assets are not taxed until disposal without replacement; and the value of small business firms can be reduced by 50 per cent for capital transfer tax purposes. Many of the limits in these provisions were revised in the 1978 budget, at a cost of £204 million in a full year.
43. Kay and King, *British Tax System*, p. 67.
44. It should be noted that the immediate write-off for plant and equipment automatically eliminates the problem of under depreciation in a period of inflation.
45. King, *Public Policy and the Corporation*, pp. 204–27.
46. 'Profitability and Company Finance, A Supplementary Note', *Bank of England Quarterly Bulletin*, Vol. 19 (June 1979), p. 183. These calculations take into account the gains resulting from the reduced value of debt during the recent inflation.
47. 'Measures of Real Profitability', *Bank of England Quarterly Bulletin*, Vol. 18 (December 1978), p. 514.
48. Initial allowances and accelerated depreciation cannot raise total depreciation taken over the life of an asset above its cost; investment grants are given on top of the depreciation allowances.
49. A. R. Prest, 'The Economic Rationale of Subsidies to Industry', in Department

of Industry, *The Economics of Industrial Subsidies* (HMSO, 1976), p. 66.

50. C. L. Mellis and D. W. Richardson, 'Value of Investment Incentives for Manufacturing Industry 1946 to 1974', in ibid., p. 34.
51. For an excellent summary of this research, see Department of Industry, *Economics of Industrial Subsidies*.
52. Ibid., p. 261.
53. Geoffrey Maynard is a notable proponent of the view that taxation has helped to increase labour costs relative to capital costs, with the result that capital has been substituted for labour and the rate of profit on capital has declined in line with the fall in the real cost of capital. Unpublished memorandum, 'A Non-Keynesian Model of Inflation, Unemployment and Balance of Payments Deficits as Applied to the UK'.
54. The dispute has not been resolved. See W. B. Reddaway and others, *Effects of the Selective Employment Tax, Final Report* (Cambridge University Press, 1973); J. D. Whitley and G. D. N. Worswick, 'The Productivity Effects of Selective Employment Tax', *National Institute Economic Review*, No. 56 (May 1971), pp. 36–40; W. B. Reddaway, 'Reply', ibid., No. 57 (August 1971), pp. 67–8; Whitley and Worswick, 'Rejoinder', ibid., No. 58 (November 1971), pp. 72–5.
55. See B. C. Moore and J. Rhodes, 'A Quantitative Analysis of the Effects of the Regional Employment Premium and Other Regional Policy Instruments', and R. R. MacKay, 'The Impact of the Regional Employment Premium', and their comments on each other's papers in Department of Industry, *Economics of Industrial Subsidies*, pp. 191–244.
56. See, for example, Sandilands Commission, *Report of the Inflation Accounting Committee,* Cmnd. 225 (HMSO, 1975); Institute for Fiscal Studies, *The Structure and Reform of Direct Taxation*, Report of a Committee chaired by Professor J. E. Meade (London: Allen & Unwin, 1978); and Kay and King, *British Tax System*.
57. See J. Johnson and M. Tinbrell, 'Empirical Tests of a Bargaining Theory of Wage Determination', *Manchester School of Economic and Social Studies*, Vol. 41 (June 1973), pp. 141–69; Organisation for Economic Cooperation and Development, *Public Expenditure Trends* (Paris: OECD, 1978), pp. 51–8, 81–7; and S. G. B. Henry and P. A. Ormerod, 'Income Policy and Wage Inflation: Empirical Evidence for the UK 1961–1977', *National Institute Economic Review*, 85 (August 1978), pp. 31–9.
58. The ratio was 10.1 per cent in 1972 and 9.7 per cent in 1976.
59. Specific duties on such items as tobacco and alcoholic beverages have not been raised for the same reason, even though their value has been eroded in real terms because of inflation.
60. This neglect of the inflationary consequences of payroll taxes is by no means confined to the United Kingdom. For example, the United States enacted a multi-stage payroll tax increase that will raise payroll tax receipts by $26 billion, or 20 per cent, by fiscal 1983.
61. From 1959 to 1974/75 the average income tax burden of the top 1 per cent increased 9 per cent, while the burden of the middle quintile of the distribution tripled. Royal Commission on the Distribution of Income and Wealth, *Third Report on the Standing Reference*, Report 5, Cmnd. 6999 (HMSO, 1977), pp. 13–66, 199–204.
62. In fact, the movement toward equality in the wealth distribution goes back as far as 1911. See Royal commission on the Distribution of Income and Wealth,

Initial Report of the Standing Reference, Report 1, Cmnd, 6171 (HMSO, 1975), p. 97.

63. Royal Commission on the Distribution of Income and Wealth, *Third Report on the Standing Reference*, p. 76, and *Initial Report on the Standing Reference*, p. 12.
64. C. D. Harbury and P. C. McMahon, 'Inheritance and the Characteristics of Top Wealth Leavers in Britain', *Economic Journal*, Vol. 83 (September 1973), pp. 810–33.
65. Moreover, the gift tax is included in the cumulative tax base gross of tax rather than net of tax.
66. In the 1978 budget, full-year costs of over £200 million were for 'tax proposals helpful to small business', and £65 million for relief for capital gains recipients.
67. In my view, the classical arguments in favour of taxing property income more heavily than earned income do not justify a large differential. The appropriate method of differentiation would be to provide a deduction or tax credit for the additional costs of earning income, but such an allowance would be modest compared with the 15 per cent UK investment income surcharge. See Richard Goode, *The Individual Income Tax*, rev. edn (Brookings Institution, 1976), pp. 238–42.
68. Reductions have already been made in public expenditure in recent years, and the new Conservative government made additional reductions of about 3 per cent in the June 1979 budget. Public expenditure was 46.5 per cent of GDP at market prices in 1975/76, and 42 per cent in 1978/79.
69. In the United States, President Carter campaigned for the adoption of a comprehensive income tax, but he gradually watered down his own proposals within a year after being elected and even these proposals were, for the most part, rejected by Congress. In the end, he signed a bill for a tax that was even further removed from a comprehensive income tax than the tax he had campaigned against.
70. For a detailed discussion of the major elements of a comprehensive income tax, see US Department of the Treasury, *Blueprints for Basic Tax Reform* (Government Printing Office, 1977); Joseph A. Pechman (ed.), *Comprehensive Income Taxation* (Brookings Institution, 1977); and Institute for Fiscal Studies, *Structure and Reform of Direct Taxation*, esp. pp. 127–49.
71. Even if the exclusions under the capital transfer tax were removed, small business would be better off if the savings preferences that channel personal savings into institutions were eliminated.
72. For methods of adjusting the tax system for inflation, see Thelma Liesner and Mervyn A. King (eds.), *Indexing for Inflation* (London: Heinemann Educational Books, 1975); Henry J. Aaron (ed.) *Inflation and the Income Tax* (Brookings Institution, 1976); and Institute for Fiscal Studies, *Structure and Reform of Direct Taxation*, pp. 99–126.
73. The tax is now used in all the Scandinavian countries (Sweden, Norway, Finland, Denmark and Iceland), Austria, West Germany, the Netherlands, the Swiss cantons, the Indian subcontinent (India, Pakistan and Sri Lanka), and in a few countries in Central and South America. Ireland recently introduced an annual net wealth tax but then repealed it. For a discussion of annual wealth taxation, see Alan A. Tait, *The Taxation of Personal Wealth* (University of Illinois Press, 1967); C. T. Sandford, J. R. M. Willis and D. J. Ironside, *An Annual Wealth Tax* (London: Heinemann Educational Books, 1975); and Institute for Fiscal Studies, *Structure and Reform of Direct Taxation*, pp. 350–66.

22. Implications of International Tax Trends*

Although the Brookings tax project relates only to the United States (see Chapter 2 in this volume), I draw inferences in this chapter from the results of that project about trends in the distribution of tax burdens in other countries and then examine the implications of these trends for tax policy.

MAJOR FINDINGS

The differential burdens imposed by the various taxes used in the United States are not surprising. The individual income tax is progressive over virtually the entire income scale, but it becomes regressive at the very top, where a substantial proportion of total income is not subject to tax. Sales and excises are unambiguously regressive throughout the entire income scale. Whether they are borne by labour alone or shared with the consumer, payroll taxes are proportional up to the maximum taxable earnings level, but regressive beyond this level. For the corporation income tax and the property tax, the relative tax burdens depend on the assumptions used. On the assumption that these are taxes on owners of property, they are highly progressive. If it is assumed that half the corporation income tax is a tax on consumption and that the property tax on improvements is a tax on shelter and consumption, the progressivity of these taxes disappears: the burden of the corporation income tax becomes U-shaped (because of the ratio of property income to total income is U-shaped) and the property tax becomes regressive throughout the income scale (because the ratio of total consumption and housing expenditures to annual incomes falls as incomes rise).

When the effective rates of all these taxes are combined, the progressive taxes are more or less offset by the regressive taxes—and this occurs regardless of the incidence assumptions used. As a result, the tax system turns out to be virtually proportional or only slightly progressive for the vast majority of families in the United States. On the average, US taxes in 1980 amounted to a little over 25 per cent of income. There is very little deviation from this average for the broad range of incomes between the

*Adapted from *International Trends in the Distribution of Tax Burdens: Implications for Policy* (Institute for Fiscal Studies, 1973).

third and ninth deciles of family units. Thus, under the most progressive set of assumptions examined in the study, taxes in 1980 reduced inequality (as measured by the Gini coefficient) by 2 per cent; under the most regressive assumptions, inequality increased by one-quarter of 1 per cent.

The only exceptions to the flatness of the effective rate curve appear at the very bottom and at the very top of the income scale, where the rates rise sharply. The high rates for those in the lowest income classes are probably not representative of the tax burdens they pay over longer periods of time than a year, because in these classes there is a heavy concentration of retired persons and others with temporarily low incomes. If income were measured over a longer period, the regressivity at the bottom of the income distribution would be greatly moderated or might even disappear.

The very rich pay high taxes because a substantial proportion of their income comes from property income. But the total tax burden at these levels depends crucially on the assumed incidence of the corporation income and property taxes. If these taxes are regarded as taxes on income from capital, the tax burden of those with incomes of $1,000,000 or more was 30 per cent in 1980, or roughly 20 per cent higher than the rates paid by most families. If these taxes are assumed to be shifted in whole or in part to consumers, the tax burdens at the highest income level was about 20 per cent, or about 20 per cent lower than the effective rates paid by most families.

In addition to differences that arise because of differences in incidence assumptions, there are substantial variations in tax rates among various economic and demographic groups in the population that are due to the structural features of the US tax system. For example, home owners pay lower taxes than tenants, urban residents pay lower taxes than residents of rural farm areas, and married couples pay lower taxes than single people.

Perhaps the most interesting calculation we were able to make was to estimate the relative tax burdens imposed on income from labour and capital. In 1966, when we first started making these calculations, income from capital bore a much heavier tax burden than income from labour. By 1985, the situation was reversed: the average tax burden on labour exceeded the tax burden on income from capital. On the most progressive assumptions, the average tax rate on income from capital in 1985 was 18 per cent compared with about 21 per cent for income from labour. On the least progressive assumptions, income from capital paid an average tax rate of only 11 per cent, while labour income paid 19 per cent.

TAX BURDENS IN OTHER COUNTRIES

Although we have not made similar tax burden calculations for other countries, it is not difficult to infer what the situation is on the basis of the distribution of revenue sources. Throughout the last three decades, there has been a trend away from the use of income taxes toward greater reliance on consumption taxes. Payroll taxes have always been a much more important source of revenue in European countries than in the United States, because European social security and related programmes—which are financed mainly through payroll taxes—are more elaborate than the US system, and therefore require more revenue. Furthermore, in practically every country, allowances and tax credits for investment have been greatly liberalised in the interest of promoting private investment, but they have not been financed by raising income tax rates. This practice has reduced the revenue productivity of the corporation income tax almost everywhere.

The result of these trends is that progressive tax sources now account for much less than half of total tax revenues in most developed countries. According to recent estimates prepared by the OECD, Japan, Canada and most European countries rely about as heavily as the United States on the individual and corporation income taxes (when measured as a ratio to GDP. But consumption taxes and payroll taxes play a much larger role in Western Europe than in the United States. In the United Kingdom, consumption taxes and payroll taxes accounted for 46 per cent of total revenue in 1982 as compared with only 34 per cent in the United States. In France and Italy, where it is apparently impractical to levy an effective personal income tax, consumption taxes and payroll taxes account for more than 60 per cent of total tax revenues. Even in Scandinavia, where income taxes are relatively high, consumption taxes and payroll taxes account for over 40 per cent of total revenues.

Given these facts, it does not require knowledge of higher mathematics to visualise the approximate shape of the distribution of tax burdens in other countries by extrapolating from the US data. In Western Europe, the two major sources of revenue—consumption taxes and payroll taxes—are clearly regressive. Even in the United States, where the income taxes are more important, they are just barely sufficiently progressive to offset the regressivity of the consumption taxes and payroll taxes. It follows that, on the whole, tax systems are not very progressive anywhere in the world. In Canada, Australia and Japan, taxes are probably distributed roughly in proportion to income. But, with the possible exception of Denmark and Sweden, taxes are regressive in Western Europe and, in some of these countries, they must be very regressive indeed.

AGENDA FOR REFORM

The preceding discussion leads me to the conclusion that the objectives of progressive taxation are honoured only in the breach throughout the world. Politicians find it useful to support progression in principle, but then turn to regressive sources when new revenue needs arise. There is no evidence of a concerted effort anywhere except the United States to improve the personal income tax so that it will be an effective instrument of progressive taxation. Furthermore, in the search for methods of promoting economic growth, governments inevitably turn to tax devices that reduce revenues from the progressive sources, but have uncertain, if not downright perverse, economic effects. I suggest that the time has come for the public finance fraternity to make an effort to help restore progressive taxation to its proper place in the hierarchy of national objectives. The following are among the major revisions that might be considered for any reform agenda.

1. The first order of business should be to make the personal income tax a progressive tax in fact as well as in name. My use of the term 'progressive' should not be interpreted as a synonym for 'punitive'. Excessively high tax rates on incomes do have undesirable effects on work, saving and investment incentives. They also encourage taxpayers to use legal and sometimes extra-legal means of avoiding them. But there are two sides to this coin. Proliferation of special tax favours to particular groups—for whatever reason—narrows the income tax base, which in turn requires the use of higher rates to raise needed revenues. Taxpayers who cannot take advantage of these special provisions find that they are paying much higher taxes than others with equal incomes, and they demand and frequently get equal treatment. This leads to further erosion of the income tax base, which leads to the use of regressive tax sources when revenue needs become urgent. The way out of this dilemma is to reverse the cycle of erosion of the income tax base. With a comprehensive definition of income for tax purposes, it should be possible to raise needed revenues from the income tax with reasonably moderate rates.

I am not familiar enough with other tax systems to be able to make the calculations but it is evident from a cursory examination of present practices that income tax erosion is not confined to the United States. Most countries still do not tax capital gains, allow deductions of selected items of personal saving and of personal expenditures, permit income splitting or the equivalent, exclude transfer payments from the tax base, and so on. If a determined effort were made to use a comprehensive definition of income as the basis for personal income taxation, marginal tax rates could be lowered everywhere without affecting the revenue potential of the tax. The advantage of this approach is that it would greatly improve horizontal equity and economic efficiency, without increasing rates to such levels that they might impair incentives. It would also improve taxpayer morale, which is so vital to the success of a modern tax system.

2. The corporation income tax should not be regarded as an ugly

appendage to the tax system, as most businessmen and some finance ministers view it. Data for the United States indicate that, without the corporation income tax, the tax system would lose the tax that contributes most to progression in the top brackets. (Even if half the corporation tax is assumed to be shifted, the other half—which is borne mainly by middle- and high-income shareholders or owners of capital in general—is still significant.) The corporation income tax is needed, therefore, to safeguard much of the progression the system possesses.

It follows that any structural change that reduces the corporation income tax substantially also reduces progression substantially, and this is exactly what has happened in most countries. For example, the US corporation income tax rate was reduced only by 6 percentage points between 1964 and 1982, from 52 to 46 per cent. In the interim, depreciation has been liberalised several times and a 10 per cent investment credit has been adopted. The result has been that the corporation income tax has dropped from 43 per cent of economic profits (i.e. profits after economic depreciation) earned by corporations to 13 per cent in 1982.

The US experience is not an isolated one. The corporation income tax has been whittled away in most developed countries during the past two decades; it is now a secondary source of income almost everywhere. I am not aware that this trend has been moderated to any significant degree by offsetting increases in the tax burdens of those who benefited from these significant tax reductions. In view of these developments, I suggest that any additional inroads into the corporation income tax—by straight rate reductions, further liberalisation of investment allowances, structural changes to provide relief for distributed earnings, or any other such devices—should be resisted unless they are accompanied by structural revisions or rate increases that will raise offsetting revenues from the income classes where the tax reductions are concentrated.

3. Perhaps the most puzzling feature of modern tax systems is the continued acceptance of regressive payroll taxation as a major source of revenue. The payroll tax was originally used in Europe as the basic method of financing old-age benefits on the principle that the workers were buying their own annuities. This idea is doubtless responsible for the widespread acceptance of social security; but the insurance analogy is no longer applicable—if it ever was—as social security systems have developed. In growing economies, present beneficiaries receive far larger benefits than the taxes they paid would entitle them to—a situation that will continue indefinitely, so long as benefits keep pace with the rise of wages. Even if the device of a trust fund or a special account is used, the payroll taxes paid by the worker are not stored up or invested; they are used to finance current benefits and sometimes even other government outlays. When benefits provided to people now working come due, the funds for their payment will

be provided out of tax revenues as of that future date and not out of taxes they paid earlier.

Another reason why payroll taxation is tolerated is that the tax is usually levied on both employers and employees. Even the portion that the worker pays is withheld from his pay cheque, and few countries require that a statement of the total tax withheld during the year be furnished to the worker. Most economists believe that the burden of the employer tax, as well as the employee tax, falls eventually on the worker (either by substituting for larger wage increases or raising prices). Most workers are not aware that, in one form or another, they pay the employer share of the tax as well as their own.

At this late stage, I doubt that the payroll tax can be dislodged from its pre-eminent position in social security financing. But there is no reason why it cannot be transformed into a much more respectable tax. A first step would be to carry over the income tax concept of a minimum taxable level. Individuals and families who are considered too poor to pay income taxes have no more ability to pay a payroll tax. A second step would be to lift the maximum taxable earnings level for payroll tax purposes. The additional taxes that would be paid by middle- and high-income earners would be more than enough to pay for the tax now paid by the poor.

4. The value-added tax has become the largest single source of revenue in Europe. In many countries, VAT substituted for turnover taxes or other types of consumption taxes that placed unjustifiably heavy burdens on some producers and treated others very lightly. In such cases, enactment of VAT was a great improvement. Moreover, VAT is unquestionably an easy tax to coordinate among countries that are associated in a common market or customs union.

Despite these advantages, I am not persuaded that VAT deserves its present popularity. The burden of a value-added tax is distributed roughly in the same proportions as a general retail sales tax. Even if food is exempt, the burden of such general consumption taxes is regressive. At the high rates that are used in some countries, VAT is oppressive on families in the bottom third of the income distribution. Granted that VAT is sometimes useful for reasons of international economic policy, steps should be taken to lift this burden from those who should not be asked to bear it.

There is no general consumption tax in the United States at the federal level, but 46 out of the 50 states have various forms of retail sales taxes. To take the sting out of the regressivity of these taxes, several states have adopted tax credits against their individual taxes for the imputed amount of VAT paid on the first $1000 or so of consumption for a family of four. Refunds are given to those who do not pay income taxes. Although such credits cannot eliminate the regressivity of a general consumption tax, they do help to alleviate the burden of the tax on the poor and near poor. The tax credit device is more urgently needed in Europe than in the United States because European VAT rates are much higher than US sales tax rates.

5. Death taxes are regarded by many economists as a much better instrument of redistribution policy than income taxes because they have less adverse effects on incentives. Nevertheless, the revenue from death taxes is pitifully low in every country. Although rates are progressive and usually reach very high percentages for large amounts of taxable wealth, rich people manage to escape paying death taxes on most of their estates through one device or another. Gift taxes are either weak or non-existent; land and other property is undervalued; and, in Anglo-Saxon countries, wealth put in trust can escape taxation for several generations. Even if the aditional revenue were used entirely for income tax rate reduction, death and gift tax reform would be well worth the effort.

SUMMARY

In the United States, taxes are essentially proportional for the vast majority of families and therefore have little effect on the distribution of income. Since the United States relies most heavily on progressive tax sources (perhaps with the exception of Sweden), taxes are probably regressive on balance in most other countries. The major culprits are the consumption and payroll taxes, which are almost universally the major sources of revenue. If there is a will, there are methods of improving the progressivity of tax systems without adopting prohibitive tax rates. The time has come to pay attention to progression in the development of tax policy throught the world.

Acknowledgements

The author and publishers would like to thank the following for permission to reprint the essays in this volume: The Brookings Institution for chapters 2, 5, 7, 8, 9, 10, 11, 12, 13, 17, 18, 20, 21; Center for National Policy for chapter 4; *Havard Law Review* for chapter 6; Institute for Contemporary Studies for chapter 19; Institute for Fiscal Studies for chapter 22; Macmillan Press for chapter 3; *New York Times* for chapter 10; *The Public Interest* for chapter 1; University of Michigan for chapter 15; *Yale Law Journal* for chapter 16.

Index